In Miserable Slavery
Thomas Thistlewood in Jamaica, 1750–86

Douglas Hall

The University of the West Indies Press
Barbados • Jamaica • Trinidad and Tobago

The University of the West Indies Press
1A Aqueduct Flats   Mona
Kingston 7   Jamaica

Printed in the United States of America
ISBN 976-640-066-0

06   6

CATALOGUING IN PUBLICATION DATA

Hall, Douglas G.
   In miserable slavery: Thomas Thistlewood in Jamaica,
1750-86/Douglas G. Hall

   p. cm
   Previously published: London : Macmillan Press, 1989
   Includes bibliographical references and index
   ISBN: 978-976-640-066-8
   1. Jamaica – History. 2. Thistlewood, Thomas,
   1721-1786 – Diaries.
   3. Plantation life – Jamaica – History.
   4. Slavery – Jamaica. I. Title

F1874.H35 1999   972.92'033 – dc20

The author and publisher wish to thank Lord and Lady Monson for kindly
giving their permission for the use of the Thistlewood papers for this book,
and the Lincolnshire Archives Office as custodian of the papers.

The author and publisher acknowledge with thanks the use of the
following illustrations: Fig. 1, courtesy of the British Library,
London; Figs 2, 3a, 3b, 4 and 6, courtesy of the National Library of
Jamaica; Fig. 5, courtesy of the Lincolnshire Archive Office,
England and the National Library of Jamaica.

Cover design by Adlib Studio, Kingston, Jamaica

Contents

Foreword

Douglas Gordon Hall needs no introduction. He is the doyen of
Caribbean historians, a scholar of widely acknowledged international stature. In a scholarly life which has spanned half a century, his
achievements are many and outstanding by any yardstick. Most of
his professional career was spent at the University of the West Indies
(UWI) which he joined in 1954. While there he, along with Elsa
Goveia and Roy Augier primarily, pioneered the research and shaped
the teaching of Caribbean history for both the secondary and tertiary
levels. His *The Making of the West Indies*[1] (along with Roy Augier,
Shirley Gordon and Mary Reckord) served to introduce generations
of West Indian students to Caribbean history, and most of the post-
colonial Caribbean historians were actually taught by him at UWI.

Douglas Hall was appointed Professor of History in 1964 and
was the first West Indian to chair the Department of History. He also
served as Dean of the Faculty of Arts at Mona. Always keen to pro-
mote research in Caribbean history, it was under his leadership that
the postgraduate programme in history at UWI was started; and as
editor of both the *Jamaica Historical Review* and the *Journal of
Caribbean History,* and as adviser to the Caribbean Universities
Press, he constantly sought to open doors for Caribbean scholars to
publish their research. A founding member of the Association of
Caribbean Historians, he was elected president in 1980. The following year he retired from university life and became the first historian
to be honoured with the title of Professor Emeritus at UWI.[2]

Although he is best known as a specialist in the economic history of the postemancipation Caribbean, the research interests and
publications of Douglas Hall are considerably more diverse. His best
known publications are *Free Jamaica* and *Five of the Leewards;*[3] but
he has also published several papers which examine a number of
issues related to the economies and technology of the Caribbean
slave system. No less important have been his explorations into the-
oretical issues in economic history as reflected in his *Ideas and
Illustrations in Economic History.*[4]

If his withdrawal from active university life permitted him to
put into practice some of the farming techniques he had discovered

as a researcher and thus to embark on a new successful career as a small farmer in deep rural Jamaica, it did not put an end to his academic life. Since 1981 Douglas Hall has published four fine books, and as Professor Emeritus can still be seen on the Mona campus engaged in one form of research or other; and he is the editor of a new biography series published by The Press UWI. This, therefore, has been no less productive a period of his life than before. *In Miserable Slavery,* first published in 1989,[5] is one of the great products of Hall's prolific post-retirement.

It is the diary of a small penkeeper, Thomas Thistlewood, who resided during the mid-eighteenth century in the same parish of Westmoreland, Jamaica as Douglas Hall now lives and farms. Indeed, Hall cultivates some of the same vegetables and herbs that Thistlewood once grew. Thistlewood lived in Jamaica in the heyday of the plantation sugar economy and the slave labour system that built it. It was also a period of intense international conflict, much of which was played out in the Caribbean, and of considerable internal instability characterized by the ever-present threat of slave rebellion, of which Tacky's (1760) was the most dangerous during Thistlewood's time. His diary, therefore, naturally excites enormous interest among researchers of that period for whatever insights it might shed on the Jamaican economy and society, and on social relations at the individual and group levels, during those trying times.

Diaries can be exceedingly valuable historical sources, but they do present certain problems for researchers. Why were they kept in the first place? How informed, thorough and objective was the diarist in record keeping? Apart from these considerations, Hall was challenged by the ambitious task of capturing the essence of what Thistlewood recorded in 10,000 pages of close written manuscript over a thirty-six year period, for presentation in readable form as a book. This naturally involved a high degree of selectivity: what should be included and what omitted? Would the end result accurately reflect the reality of daily life that concerned Thomas Thistlewood?

Hall was conscious of these problems, and he tells the reader in the "Introduction" the reasons why he gives weight to some issues over others: the health and mortality of Thistlewood's slaves, their punishment when excessive, sexual and other relationships among individuals of all classes, contact with the Maroons, leisure activities, etc. In order to remain as faithful as possible to what Thistlewood recorded, he deliberately keeps his intrusions to a minimum. Casting himself in the role of narrator and commentator rather than historical analyst, he concentrates on explaining and making informative linkages in the data in order to make the text coherent for the nonspecialist reader. Very importantly, he allows maximum space for Thistlewood's own words, which serves to give the reader a firsthand feel for the diarist's mind. What emerges from this long and tedious process is a highly successful presentation of Thistlewood's diary, organized chronologically into eleven chapters. Douglas Hall uses his well-known flair as a raconteur and superb skills as a writer of distinction to excellent effect in his narration and commentary, and manages to transform the raw jottings of a diarist into a literary and historical account that is both exceedingly easy to read and very informative. Among other things, his recapturing of Thistlewood's concern about making profits from his pen, of his obsession with diseases and cures, his periodically shocking brutality towards slaves under his control, and his long-term relationship with his 'slave-wife' Phibbah, sheds new light on the complexity of Jamaican slave society. His voracious libido which manifested itself in countless sexual encounters with other dependent female slaves (and several adventures with gonorrhea) is so well recounted by Hall that it raises new questions about sex and power in master-slave relations. Did Thistlewood rape these women or were they consenting, if unequal, partners within the restricted parameters of a patriarchal slave system? And was Thomas Thistlewood typical among men of his class? These are some of the tantalizing questions raised by *In Miserable Slavery,* which make it one of the more fascinating books yet written on Caribbean slavery.

Brian L. Moore
Department of History
University of the West Indies, Mona
July 1998

Notes

1. F. R. Augier, S. C. Gordon, D. G. Hall, and M. Reckord, *The Making of the West Indies* (London: Longmans, 1960), 310 pp.
2. Douglas Hall was appointed Professor Emeritus in December 1981.
3. *Free Jamaica 1838-1865: An Economic History* (New Haven: Yale University Press, 1959), 290 pp; *Five of the Leewards 1834-1870: The Major Problem of the Postemancipation Period in Antigua, Barbuda, Montserrat, Nevis and St Kitts* (Barbados: Caribbean Universities Press, 1971), 205 pp.

4. *Ideas and Illustrations in Economic History* (New York: Holt, Reinhart and Winston, 1964), 164 pp.
5. *In Miserable Slavery: Thomas Thistlewood in Jamaica 1750-86* (London: The Macmillan Press Ltd. 1989), 322 pp.

Acknowledgments

I owe my introduction to the Thistlewood diaries to my long-standing friend Kenneth E. Ingram, one-time Librarian in the University of the West Indies, in his *Sources of Jamaican History, 1655–1838, a bibliographical survey with particular reference to manuscript sources,* Inter Documentation (Switzerland and London) 1976, Vol. 2, pp. 694–5. Excited by the existence of such a body of papers dealing with life in Westmoreland (my home parish) in the eighteenth century, I went on my next study leave in England to the Lincolnshire Country Archives where they are kept.

There, the Archivist and staff warmed the chill of the Castle rooms with the kindness with which they facilitated my first, very cursory, look at the diaries which I was told were the property of Lord Monson, whose permission I would have to obtain if I proposed to publish work based on them.

Back at the University of the West Indies, Kenneth Ingram was requested by the Vice-Chancellor to seek permission of Lord Monson to have a copy made of the Thistlewood papers. Lord Monson kindly gave his assent and that copy is now lodged in the University Library on the Mona campus. In this the very necessary cooperation of the Lincolnshire County Archivist was readily given.

Later, Miss M. E. Finch, then Acting County Archivist, very helpfully acted as intermediary between Lord Monson and myself when I requested his permission to publish, and I am most grateful to Lord Monson, and to Miss Finch, for the granting and the receipt of that permission.

Throughout my struggles with the manuscript I became increasingly indebted to the work of Professors Frederick Cassidy and Robert Le Page whose books on Jamaican language and expression were constantly at my elbow (Cassidy, *Jamaica Talk,* Institute of Jamaica, Macmillan, 1971; Cassidy and Le Page, *Dictionary of Jamaican English,* C.U.P., 1980); and Philip Wright's compilation of "Monumental Inscriptions of Jamaica", Society of Genealogists, London, 1966, helped me to move with Mr Thistlewood among the Westmoreland plantocracy.

As the work proceeded many friends and colleagues in the

Department of History at the University of the West Indies read and commented on particular chapters or part of chapters, and I thank them all. My greatest indebtedness in this respect is to the late Dr Neville Hall, who read the first five chapters of a first draft, and to Professors Barry Higman and Keith Laurence who read all of the second draft. Their helpful criticisms have enabled me to improve the work and I alone am responsible for its remaining faults.

My thanks are also due to Mr Tony Clarke and Mr Igol Williams of Westmoreland, who kindly allowed me to roam at will through their respective properties – Mr Clarke's Paradise (incorporating Salt River); and Mr Williams' Rock Dondo and Altavelta (the present names of Thistlewood's Breadnut Island Pen and Hugh Wilson's adjacent property beside the Cabaritta).

Darliston, Westmoreland   Douglas Hall
Jamaica   November 1987

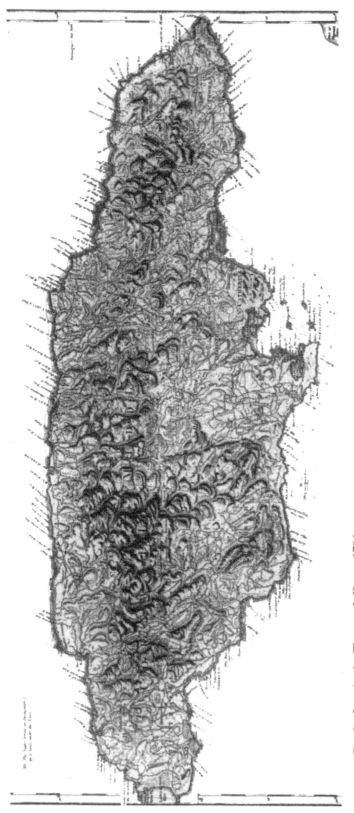

Fig. 1   Jamaica by Thomas Jefferys, 1794.

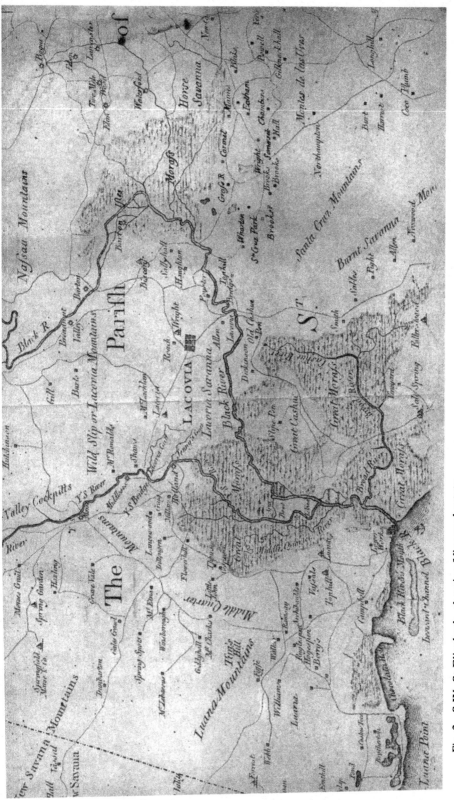

Fig. 2 S.W. St Elizabeth, showing Vineyard estate.

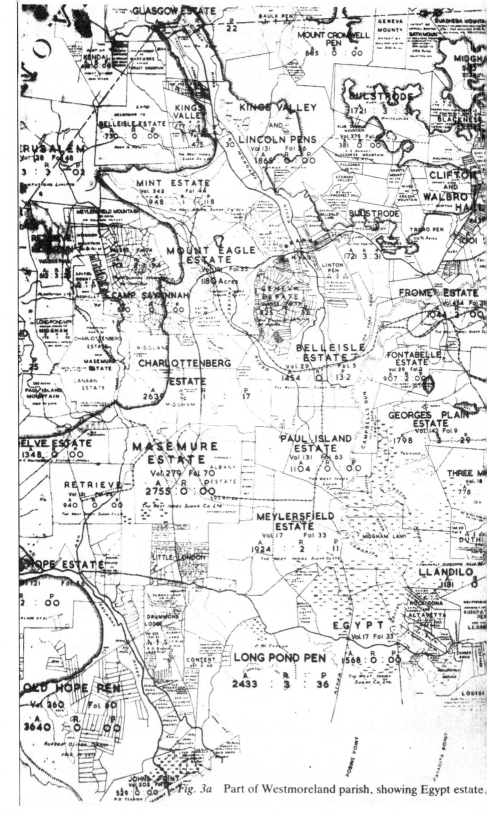

Fig. 3a Part of Westmoreland parish, showing Egypt estate

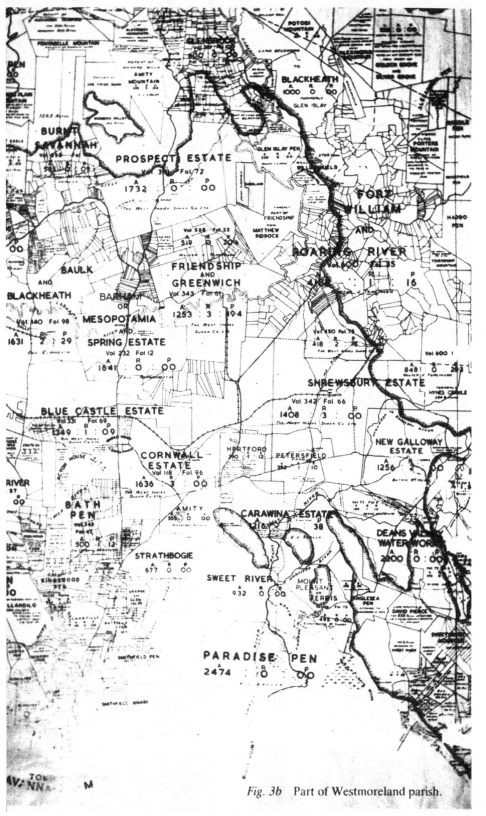

Fig. 3b Part of Westmoreland parish.

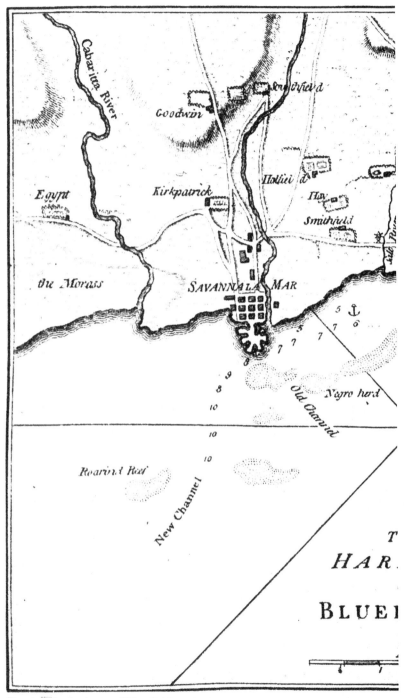

Fig. 4 The harbour of Bluefields.

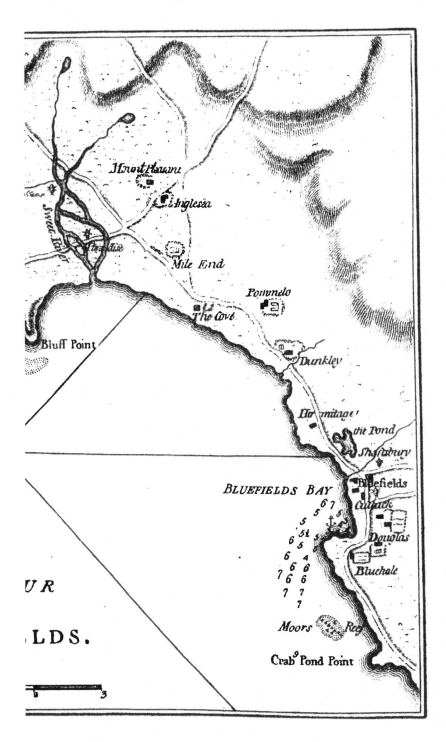

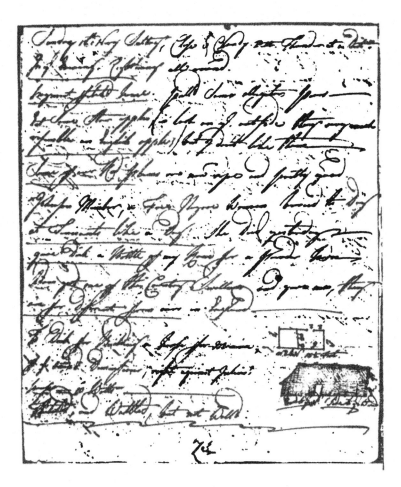

Fig. 5 A page from Mr Thistlewood's diary with his sketch of the house he had built for Marina.

Fig. 6 A bridge scene in Jamaica, given to Mr Thistlewood by Mr Beckford.

General introduction

Thomas Thistlewood came to Jamaica in 1750. He was 29 years old. He lived here until he died at the end of 1786. He had come, like many others, to try his fortune but in that he was only moderately successful.

His first job of any importance was as Penkeeper on the Vineyard Pen, a cattle property in the southwest of the parish of St Elizabeth. In the latter part of 1751 he left that employment and accepted the Overseership of Egypt, a sugar-estate west of the town of Savanna la Mar in the adjacent parish of Westmoreland. Until 1767 he remained, almost constantly, a sugar-estate Overseer; and for most of that time in the employment of William Dorrill and then his son-in-law, John Cope, whose wife owned properties in that parish.

In 1767 he acquired his own property (160 acres, of which more than half was swamp land) on which he grew livestock, vegetables, and flowers, and shot wildfowl. He had also by then become the owner of some thirty slaves whose labour he sometimes hired out to neighbouring sugar-planters. He died on that property, which he called Breadnut Island Pen, at the end of November and was buried in the Parish Church, Savanna la Mar, on the 1st December 1786.

Beginning before he came to Jamaica and throughout his life, he made a record of his daily activities – his work, his dealings with other people, including his sex life, and his observations of things and actions which he found interesting. Those diaries, fortunately, have survived.*

The **interest** of such documents is beyond question. Here are the daily observations of a man (who happened to be intelligent, inquisitive, and reasonably well educated) living and working in Jamaica at the height of its slave-sugar prosperity in the eighteenth century.

The **value** of such documents, as reliable sources of information, depends on the answers to two questions: first, why did Thistlewood

---

* He also kept two other sets of records which have not been consulted in the writing of this book; one in which he listed and commented on books and papers he read, and the other a set of weather books.

write his diaries; and second, to what extent can we come to general conclusions about Jamaican society on the basis of the evidence provided by a single diarist?

Thistlewood does not say why he kept a record. He was well read and, without doubt, was familiar with the works of earlier diarists such as John Evelyn. He was a very self-assured young man, and though we get no abrasive rub of conceit in his writing, he clearly must have possessed that degree of egocentricity necessary to support the labour of recording his daily deeds. The nature of the diaries themselves suggests that they were intended simply as private, personal, *aides-mémoire*. Thistlewood tells 'what', but seldom 'why'; he very seldom reveals the content of a letter or of a conversation – he simply notes that it happened. He very rarely explains his, or anybody else's reason for doing – he merely notes the deed. The record contains very little that can be dubbed 'explanation' or 'opinion' – most of it is 'occurrence'. There is, therefore, little reason to think that Thistlewood was writing in order to persuade or to deceive, and we may reasonably accept the account as trustworthy.

On the point of generalization the assessment becomes more difficult. There can be little question that Thomas Thistlewood was better educated and more intellectually alive than most of his fellow overseers and book-keepers. He, certainly, had no doubt on that score; and the fact of his diaries, and their contents, support the view of his superior competence and attainment. In that sense, he was not one of the crowd. At the same time, his accounts of his own activities and of the activities of others display no great disparities of behaviour; and it is clear that although there were a few with whom he was not on good terms he was well liked. In summary, generalizations based on the Thistlewood diaries, if made with care, should be reliable rather than not. The lack of comparative information must weaken our willingness to accept without questions; but, on the other hand, it should not be allowed to strengthen disbelief.

The diaries contain about 10,000 pages of closely written manuscript. Obviously, I have had to be very selective in putting this account together, and the question must therefore arise of my own bias in presentation. I have, indeed, tended to quote Mr Thistlewood more heavily, in proportion, on some matters rather than others. I have, for instance included more of his references to yaws and venereal infections than to other ailments because their very common and chronic incidence emphasizes the putrescence with which all classes of the slave society were affected; I have quoted heavily from his comments on relationships (sexual and other) between individuals of all social strata, free and slave, because I found these relationships more human, and therefore far more complicated, than our generally stereotyped views have allowed us to observe; I have omitted many instances of the flogging of slaves but I have reproduced every account of punishments that seemed to go beyond even the understood excesses of the time; I have mentioned most instances of births, deaths, and miscarriages among Thistlewood's slaves; I have given emphasis to his accounts of his and other people's engagements in activities we do not normally associate with the very mercenary West Indian plantation society, such as reading and discussing books, and indulging in a friendly rivalry in the horticulture of exotics; and I have included, I think, every mention made of the Maroons because of the uniqueness of these brief references by a planter who dealt with them and knew some of them personally. In these and other instances of disproportionate quotation I have intended to illuminate and have tried to avoid distortion in so doing.

There is another way in which I have interfered with Mr Thistlewood's accounts. I have generally tended to 'modernize' his spelling and I have increased the number of punctuation marks (which he used very sparingly) again with the object of clearer presentation; but I have wittingly done nothing to alter the sense of his remarks.

There have, however, been difficulties in reading Mr Thistlewood's handwriting. He normally wrote a clear script, but there were pages on which the paper, the quill, or his own temper at the time failed him; moreover, some of the original sheets have been slightly torn or discoloured, and I have been working from a copy of them. But even with the handwriting at its clearest there remained some sources of confusion. His vowels were not always clearly made, so it was not always possible to distinguish between words such as 'come' and 'came', 'find' and 'fend' or even 'fund', unless by an obvious meaning of the sentence. The names of persons and places presented another difficulty. His spelling was inconsistent for example, Cudjue/Cudjoe, Cubbah/Coobah, Mordenner/Mordiner; and evidence of that remains in the present work.

The diaries of Thomas Thistlewood hold much more than these pages can possibly display and, hopefully, they will more and more attract academic research and interpretation. This account is intended as much for the enjoyment of the curious layman as for the introduction of scholars and students of history to a source of enormous variety and wealth. It offers no explanation or analysis of slavery, or of production, or of Jamaican society. It does however, tell much about life in Westmoreland as Thistlewood saw it in the second half of the eighteenth century.

In preparing a single volume of limited size I had to make one general and basic decision. I had to choose between presenting less of Mr Thistlewood's own account and more of my own remarks on it; or giving space to Mr Thistlewood and keeping my own verbiage well trimmed. I chose the latter. I have interposed only that explanatory detail and linking commentary which I have judged necessary or found impossible to withhold. In short, I have used whatever understanding I may have of the mid-eighteenth century as a guide to the **selection** of more material from the diaries rather than as a qualification for the discussion of less of it.

The Jamaica to which Thomas Thistlewood came in 1750 was the most productive of the British slave-plantation, sugar-producing colonies in the West Indies. Of a total of about 45,775 tons of sugar imported into Britain in that year just over 20,400 came from Jamaica. The annual average price of muscovado sugar in London, after a brief decline, increased by nearly 3s a cwt in 1751 to reach 30s 6d. It never again in the mid-eighteenth century fell below 30s. Indeed it tended to move between 35s and 40s. Encouraged towards sugar monoculture, landholdings had been increased in size to accommodate that production. A survey in Jamaica in 1670 had shown only 47 proprietors holding estates of 1,000 acres or more. In 1754 there were 467. To support this export-oriented, estate-centred cultivation a net supply of 177,600 slaves were brought into the island between 1751 and 1775. The net import into the other British West Indian colonies combined in the same period, was 259,800*. The population structure reflected this large importation of African slave-labour.

By the late 1760s, on rough approximations or estimates made about that time, about 18,000 whites and a much smaller number, perhaps about 7,000, Free Black and Coloured people, were the possessors of about 170,000 slaves, most of whom were African born. But throughout the period of Thistlewood's sojourn, the numbers of Free Blacks and Coloureds, originally the offspring of white masters and black slaves, were growing. As the numbers and the wealth of the class of Free Blacks and Coloureds increased, the whites in control of the Legislature passed laws restricting their right to hold large landed property and to participate in the political and administrative affairs of the colony.

*The above statistics are all based on figures given by Richard Sheridan in *Sugar and Slavery. An Economic History of the British West Indies, 1623–1775* (Barbados: Caribbean Universities Press, 1974).

Though the largest of the British Caribbean islands, Jamaica is only about 145 miles long with a maximum width of about 50 miles, containing just over 4,400 square miles, much of which is in high rugged mountain and cockpit country. The areas most suitable for cane cultivation are the larger inland valleys and the alluvial coastal plains and river deltas. One such large area lies in the parish of Westmoreland through the low-lying, extensive George's plain and adjacent Savannas and the final stretches of the Cabaritta river.

After its capture from the Spaniards in 1655, English settlement in the island had radiated from the plains of Liguanea, but movement westward and north-eastward had been restricted by the opposition of the Maroons, who were originally the escaped slaves of the Spaniards. Protracted fighting between British settlers and forces and Maroon guerrilla fighters did not end until 1739 when, in mutual exhaustion, the colonists offered, and the Maroons accepted, overtures of peace. By a treaty signed in that year the Maroons were assured of their independence on areas of land granted to them. In return, among other clauses, the Treaty stipulated that they should keep roads open from their two western townships into the parishes of St Elizabeth and St James; that they should, for reward, apprehend and return any slaves runaway from their owners; and that they should, if called upon, assist the British and Colonial authorities in the suppression of local riot or foreign attack. In the west, the two leaders of the Maroons (both parties to the Treaty) were Colonel Cudjoe and his brother Captain Accompong. In 1750, that Treaty was only eleven years old, and the whites, still remembering previous danger, regarded the 'Wild Negroes' with thinly concealed apprehension.

The parish of Westmoreland had been established, carved out of St Elizabeth, in 1703. Except for Hanover, separated from Westmoreland in 1723, Portland (in the north-east) created in the same year, and Trelawny, to be separated from St James in 1770, Westmoreland was the most recently formed parish in Thistlewood's day. Like the other parishes, Westmoreland sent two members, elected by freeholders, to the Colonial Assembly. The parochial administrative body was the Vestry which consisted of the *Custos Rotulorum,* who was the Governor's representative and chief Magistrate, as chairman, two local magistrates, the rector, two elected churchwardens and other elected members to bring the total strength, excluding the *Custos,* to ten; but this number was frequently exceeded by the inclusion of more magistrates ex-officio.

The *Custodes* of Westmoreland during Thistlewood's time were his neighbour James Barclay, and, after Barclay's death, his employer, John Cope. Both were men of large property, though John Cope was to lose most of his, which he had come to by marriage through his wife Mary, née Dorrill. There were more than forty proprietors owning estates of more than 1,000 acres in that parish in the 1750s*. The names of some – Beckford, Storer, Dorrill, Senior, Vassall, Williams, Goodwin, Lewis, Ricketts, Dunbar, Campbell, Blake, Witter, Woollery – will become increasingly familiar as we follow in the path of Thomas Thistlewood.

And so too with some of the largely silent majority – the slaves on whose labours the landed proprietors depended. There is no other document known to us which by daily record over thirty-six years, allows us to find **people,** rather than names, among the work force of the time.

*'List of landholders in the Island of Jamaica in 1754'. Institute of Jamaica. Ms. West India Reference Library.

CHAPTER 1   The road to Egypt

Introduction

In this chapter we meet the remarkably active, inquisitive, and intelligent, young Thomas Thistlewood in search of employment and good fortune; and we follow him from London to Egypt, a slave-worked sugar estate in western Jamaica. From his home in Tupholme, Lincolnshire, the road to Egypt was long, and with two major diversions − first, a voyage of about two years in the service of the East India Company (1746−1748), and then a trading expedition of two months in western Europe. Six months later, on 1st February 1750, he boarded ship for the West Indies to try his fortune in the sugar colonies.

We shall simply note Thistlewood's travels to Europe and the Far East. Much more is recorded of his doings in London and in Tupholme by way of introduction to him, for we learn something of his character and his interests by his accounts of his activities. We also meet a youngster whom we shall encounter again in Jamaica, his brother's son, John, who, years later, would die by drowning in the Cabaritta river in Westmoreland.

In the Lincolnshire countryside were the seats of the landed gentry and their gardeners, several of whom had West Indian connections. Thistlewood's visits to them may have sparked off the idea of going out to Jamaica; on the other hand, it is possible that he visited them because he had already considered such an adventure. Perhaps his uncle, John Longstaff at Stainfield Hall, had something to do with the final decision. Perhaps it was in conversation in the Jamaica Coffee house, one of the best-known of those popular London resorts of the time, that the idea had been born. Thistlewood does not say.

With him on the long trans-Atlantic voyage were several others going to Jamaica, but whereas they all seemed to be going to previously arranged employment, Thistlewood was travelling with letters of recommendation, great expectations and self-confidence, but no certainty. The recruitment in Britain of estate overseers and other white employees in the sugar colonies was done largely by family connection, by word-of-mouth recommendation, and, in the case of skilled tradesmen, by indenture. Once in the colony, new arrivals would face competition for supervisory positions from numbers of Creole (West Indian born) whites in search of similar employment, and, as skilled workers from other Creoles and, indeed, from skilled slaves sent out on hire.

As in the other West Indian colonies, nearly all the chief towns of Jamaica were on the coastline. This reflected the dependence of European settlers on the arrival and departure of ships, the only means by which their links with their European antecedents could be maintained. In Jamaica, following the nearly total destruction of the notorious pirate-city of Port Royal by an earthquake in 1692, Kingston had developed as the chief port and commercial and business centre, although the island's capital and seat of government was at inland Spanish Town, served by wharves and jetties on the nearby coast.

Like Spanish Town, originally called Santiago de la Vega, many places in Jamaica carried (and still do) names reflecting the early Spanish occupation (1494–1655) of the island. Bluefields, in the west, was originally Oristan, a fortified Spanish settlement as was Savanna la Mar, the capital of the parish of Westmoreland, where Thistlewood disembarked on Friday, 4th May 1750, unknowingly on his way to Egypt, but still with a diversion or two ahead.

His Jamaican employers would soon experience his readiness to confront them if he thought they treated him unfairly or incommensurately with his competence. He would soon experience the devastations of a tropical hurricane, such as would, towards the end, wreck his fortune. But now, in the beginning, the road to Egypt.

In 1727, Robert Thistlewood, a farmer in the county of Lincolnshire, England, died leaving two sons – John, born in 1716, and Thomas, born in 1721. To the latter he bequeathed £200 sterling.

In 1729, the boy Thomas was sent to school in Yorkshire. He boarded with Mr Robert Calverly, a relative by marriage, and until 1735 attended three successive schools where he learned reading, writing and arithmetic, and began the study of Latin and Greek. In that year he returned home to Tupholme, in Lincolnshire, and was put to learn agriculture for the next three years. In 1738 he went to stay at Hatton, in the same county, with Mr John Webster who taught him mathematics. In the following year he went to Wadingworth to live with Mr William Robson, his uncle. He would pay £5 a year for his keep and he would live on the farm and learn about agriculture.

Having come to the end of this semi-formal apprentic
Thomas Thistlewood spent a few years buying and selling livesw—
until, in 1746, having gone to London, he signed on for a voyage to
the Far East as purser of supercargo on a ship belonging to the East
India Company.

> 'I got on bd. the Ship *Portfield*, Capn Francis D'Abbadie, 30th
> May 1746, about 4 o'clock in the morning in ye Thames at
> Gravesend.'

The voyage to India and back, around the Cape of Good Hope and
touching at Bahia in Brazil on the return journey, ended on Saturday,
27th August 1748 when '[we] came to our moorings at Blackwall.'
On the following day Thomas Thistlewood disembarked. On Friday,
16th September:

> 'Received at the India House £24 2s 0d wages, for 24 months 9
> days my purserage, and 2 months pay, received in my absence
> making the sum of £30 7s 3d nearly.'

In addition, he would have been expected to make some profit by
trading on his own account; and so he did, for he returned to
England laden with various eastern and Brazilian products.

The next couple of days were passed settling his affairs with
Captain D'Abbadie and the East India Company. All that done, in
the afternoon of Friday 16th he paid 2d to go into the Artillery
ground where:

> 'Long Robin, and Wagmark, got 27 at Crickett, against Falkner,
> and Harris who got but 15.'

Also, having now got his money, he began to purchase clothing:
some fine cloth at 11s 6d a yard, and shoe and knee buckles of silver
for 17s.

Sunday 18th he paid 6d to hear orator Henley in Lincoln's Inn
Field; and on Monday 19th he bought a half-share in a fighting cock
for 5s 3d; paid 1s to fight it in the Red Lyon Cockpit; and lost 6s
betting on it. He consoled himself in the next few days by buying
more cloth, buckles, and a pennyworth of oysters.

> 'Thursday 22nd: was at Mr Hewitt's, gave him some Brasil
> tobacco, and to Mrs Hewitt some persian dates, and ½ a pound
> of Brasil snuff.'

The Hewitts, who lived near Kensington, were close friends and
when, later, Thistlewood was in Jamaica Mr Hewitt was to be his
chief correspondent and agent in London.

On Friday and Saturday there were more purchases: a cut wig

for £1 2*s* 0*d*, 2 pairs of worsted stockings for 8*s* 4*d*, and a ticket for 1*s*.

'. . . for to see acted at Drury Lane, playhouse, Hamlet, and an Entertainment called the Anotomix [?]. The part of Ophelia, by Mrs Clive.'

Early in the next week he walked with friends in the countryside, stopping at pubs to quench their thirst; he bought 'for reading, Hamilton's *Account of East India*'; he went to Covent Garden playhouse to see 'The Beggars' Opera' with the part of Macheath played by Mr Lowe; and he noted 'Sturgeon spawn, a great provocative?' And then, on Wednesday 28th: 'In the Evening, to *Mulier* 2*s*. Spent 2*s* 6*d* in D [rury] L [ane].' This was his manner of recording sexual intercourse. He used the latin word *mulier* to indicate a prostitute. The 'g' above her title marked her as the seventh woman [an alphabetical notation] with whom he had indulged; but we have no evidence to show where or when he had enjoyed the previous 'a' to 'f'.

On the morning of Thursday, 6th October 1748 Thistlewood set off by stage-coach from 'the 3 Cups' Inn in London to Lincolnshire. The route lay through Hatfield, Stevenage, Biggleswade, Huntington, Stilton, Stamford, Grantham, and Ancaster into the city of Lincoln below the hill. Thence, on Sunday 9th to short-ferry by the River Witham, then:

'Met my brother, and his son John, at Greatwell, and got to Tupholme about Noon.'

Thomas Thistlewood had come home. He remained there until Sunday, 2nd April 1749.

'Tuesday, 18th October 1748:   The woods, and hedges, as yet are all green, but today is a cold stormy day.
Gave my sister Nanny 2 handkerchiefs and some muslin, fan, shells, etc. and Dryden's *State of Innocence*.
Tuesday, 26th October 1748:   *Cum E. B. in nostro domo, apud noctem*. Tup. [*Bis*].'[1]

E. B. was probably Easter Boston who seems to have worked for his brother. There were three women whose company he obviously enjoyed while in Lincolnshire. The closest was Bett Mitchell who lived with her parents at Fulsby but was apparently staying in Thomas Toyne's house. Thomas Toyne, married on 20th January 1749, had left Thistlewood to fodder and care for his cattle. Soon after their return Bett Mitchell would return to Fulsby.

'Thursday, 2nd March 1749: Sat up till almost morning, with Bett Mitchell, at Thomas Toyne's. She is going away.

Saturday, 4th March: Sat up at Thomas Toyne's with Bett Mitchell part of the night. Gave her a Cazimbazar Silk handkerchief, &c.

Sunday, 5th March: Lent to Thomas Toyne a guinea. *Cum* B. ᴷM. in T [homas] T [oyne's] *domo apud Noctem.* Tup.

Thomas Toyne gave me a pair of white gloves for looking after his cattle when he was married.

Gave Bett Mitchell a Cornelian Stone, and a toothpick case with a spring. She gave me an ivory fish. I gave Mrs Toyne some *farinha de pan* [cassava flour]. I sat up with Bett Mitchell most part of the night ...

Monday 6th: About noon accompanied Bett Mitchell towards Bucknall, She is going home, and took my leave of her in the bottom SE corner between Mr Fowler's moor and the old house.

Tuesday, 7th March 1749: Went [in the forenoon] to Stainfield-hall to see my uncle John Longstaff: walked in the park, &c. with Mr Ellison, who has bought Sir John's timber, and Mr Blades his steward. Stayed all night at Stainfield-hall.

Friday 10th: Betimes in the morning I went to Gandby-hall, and Mr Tagg and I, accompanied by Mr Norfolk walked to Carr Brakenberg Esqr's at Pandon to see Mr Thomas Harrison Butler, and Mr Treddaway Butler, gardeners. We went through Hatton Churchyard. We were greatly made of at Pandon-hall. I was over the gardens, groves, &c. (Saw Harry Fielding) [Henry Fielding, the novelist, 1701–1754?].

Wednesday, 22nd March 1749: In the evening took a walk into William Robson's turnalds, went 3 running leaps, 20 hops, &c. with John Robson.'

A few days later Thistlewood went to Fulsby:

'Monday 27th: ... To Mr George Mitchell's, to see his daughter Bett Mitchell. I got there about 6 o'clock p.m. or before. I asked her father and mother leave to sit awhile with her.'

It turned out that he spent the night at the Mitchell's and left between 3 and 4 o'clock the next afternoon. Thistlewood gives no explanation of his visit, and no indication of what passed between himself and Bett Mitchell or her parents. He recorded only that he was 'entertained with great civility'. It is a guess that he went to propose marriage and was politely rejected by her parents.

The other two ladies of interest were Jenny Cook, whose husband was at sea, and Mrs Thomas Toyne, the former Elizabeth Browne; but for the time being, and perhaps because of his very close involvement with Bett Mitchell, those relationships were no more than friendly.

And, as a final example of his Tupholme activities, there was Thistlewood's constant predilection for recording information which amused or interested him:

'Tuesday, 24th [January 1749]:   2*d* of bitter apples, steeped in Beer and took at twice, it is said will cause abortion certainly. J. Cook.

Thursday, 23rd [February 1749]:   For a simple clap − take every other day a dose of any purging pills, and continue that course (if your strength will allow it) until the running change both its colour and consistence and appears the same as the semen. After that to stop the gleet, take every other day (morning) 20 or 30 drops of Balm Capive, dropt on a piece of loaf sugar and if it does not stop the gleet, with taking physick twice a week take Syderham's Common purging draught twice a week.'[2]

At the beginning of April, 1749, Thomas Thistlewood prepared for a return to London. He distributed farewell gifts, said his goodbyes to friends, received £3 9*s* 0*d* 'in full of all accounts' from Thomas Toyne, enjoyed a farewell breakfast at his brother's house, gave Easter Boston a final 2*s* 6*d*, and 'about 1 o'clock set out from Tupholme'. He arrived in London on 5th April.

There were signs that Thistlewood was not entirely at ease. He was, and had for sometime been unemployed, and was occasionally dependent on loans from his landlady, Mrs Gresham. He seems to have written to his brother asking for a sum that would enable him to take some of his goods out of the King's warehouse and to engage in trade. Also, he bemoaned his lack of the company of a good woman.

'Monday, May 1st 1749:   Took a walk in the long fields. Borrowed off Mrs Gresham 5*s*. *Ecclesiastes* Chap. 7th. Verse 28th: which yet my soul seeketh but I find not: one man among a thousand have I found, but a woman among all these have I not found.'

Two days later he received a letter from his brother dated 1st May, and containing an order to receive sixty pounds.

He proceeded to take his Mocha coffee from the customs house; he took over from Mr Alexius Emerson, an acquaintance in trade,

'34 fish-skin rasor cases full and complete at 16s'; he
sundry other items, and he began to prepare for a tradir
into western Europe. On 17th May he booked his pɛ
Middleburg in the Netherlands, and arrived there on 1st J

During June and July he visited Ghent, Antwerp, Brussels,
Bruges, Ostend, Dunkirk and Calais. He went sightseeing, recorded
a variety of observations on agriculture, architecture, social behaviour, church music, and the trading fair at Antwerp which fell below
his expectations. At Bruges he arranged to send some of his goods
to the Frankfurt fair and to receive in return wares from Dresden.
At the beginning of August he set out from Calais and was landed at
Dover in the evening of 3rd August.

Next day he was on the coach to London passing through
Canterbury, Sittingbourne, Chatham, Rochester, Gravesend and
Dartford. He arrived in London at about 7 p.m. on Sunday 6th. Just
outside London, on the road, he had approached '. . . a poor but
honest M[ulier]'. Later he found what he was looking for: '*Cum
Mulier* in Alley West of Fleet Market 1s spent 8d.'

On Monday, 2nd October Thistlewood visited, as he often did,
the Royal Exchange and then the Bank Coffee House where he
drank coffee for 2d. Then for the first time, as far as his notes
inform us, he went to the Jamaica Coffee House and sat there
drinking coffee.

There is no clear indication of when or why he began to consider
trying his fortunes in Jamaica, but it would seem that the decision
had been made before he went to the Jamaica Coffee House, for
three days later he set off for Tupholme to pay a farewell visit to his
family and to collect letters of recommendation.

His acquaintance with so many of the gardeners, wardens,
game-keepers, and other employees of the landed gentry, and his
own apparently engaging personality and obvious intelligence put
him in good stead with those who had connections with the West
India plantocracy; and it is not impossible that the idea had been
born during his visits in the Lincolnshire countryside earlier in the
year. Indeed, as we shall see, Mr Robert Vyner, Esquire, of Gandby
and of Conduit Street, near Hanover Square, London, seems to
have had something to do with it. Thistlewood arrived at Tupholme
at dusk on Sunday 8th.

'Monday 9th: In the afternoon I waited upon Mr Vyner at
Gotby [Gandby] to return him thanks for his letters. He was
well pleased. From thence I went to Wragby to wait upon Mr
Collgrave, who received me well (he is ill of the gout).'

Mr Collgrave had been in Jamaica and had connections there. On Thursday 19th Thistlewood set off to Wragby to see Mr Collgrave again; but he was out, and they met the next day at Mr Parnell's grounds at Pandon. Thistlewood was suitably impressed:

> 'Mr Peter Collgrave . . . is not yet 35 but is an excellent orator, and of a sound judgment – a very clever man.'

Collgrave promised to send him letters 'from Workshop in Nottinghamshire where he lives'. About three weeks later he received, as he had been promised, a letter of recommendation from Mr Vyner at Gandby 'to a gentleman of great interest in Jamaica', namely, William Beckford Esquire.[3]

Business had been attended to before pleasure. Having received Mr Collgrave's promise of letters of recommendation of 20th October, Thistlewood felt free to engage in other matters. On the 21st he began a torrid affair with Elizabeth Toyne.

> 'In the evening called at Mr T[oyne]. *Cum* Mrs T[oyne] in the parlour *sup. lect.* Stayed all night, lay with her and J[enn]y C[oo]k. *Cum* Mrs T[oyne] in the night 4 *tempora* in ditto parlour *sup. lect.*'

Where Mr Toyne was at the time remains a mystery. From then on until he left Tupholme in mid-November Thistlewood visited Mrs Toyne almost daily, at noon or at nights. It was not that Thomas Toyne was away from home.

> 'Friday 27th: In the afternoon went to see Thomas Toyne dress out a pond in the hill close. He expected fish, but there was none. I went from thence to Wadingwood, played at cards, won 6d. Stayed all night at William Robsons.'

Next day, at noon, he was with Mrs Toyne, and so until 1st November when they shared the height of their abandon:

> 'In the evening was at Mr Thomas Toyne's. Stayed all night, lay in the parlour bed, *Cum* E. T. – *Cum Illa in nocte quinque tempora.*'

Having received the letter of introduction from Robert Vyner to William Beckford, Thistlewood made ready to depart from Tupholme. On that day, 10th November he visited Mrs Toyne at mid-day for the last time. He spent the evening with them all and gave Mrs Toyne and Jenny Cook each 'some Myrh and frankincense.' On Sunday 12th:

> 'In the morning was at Thomas Toyne's, *Cum* Jane Cook *Sup. Lect. in Chamb. in Aurora.*'

And so to London to prepare.

There, in the week beginning 19th November, he bought maps of Jamaica; and took his letter of introduction from Mr Vyner to Little Grosvenor Street and Brook Street, near Grosvenor Square:

'... to enquire for Mr Beckford Esqr, Member of Parliament for Shaftesbury in Dorsetshire, but was informed he is now in Jamaica.'

He acknowledged letters of introduction received from Peter Collgrave, and collected another from Mr Scott, a gardener at Turnham Green. He resumed his walking with Patty Hatcher a young friend with whom, extraordinarily, he had a platonic friendship; and his excursions into the lanes and fields in search of '*Mulier*'. By the night of 31st January, immediately preceding his departure, he had exhausted the first round of the alphabet.

'In the evening, *Cum Mulier*, up an alley to the west of Fleetmarket in a Chamb. *Sup. Lect. 6d.* Spent *3d.*'

That month had been spent, very largely, in equipping himself for the adventure; making arrangements with Mr Hewitt at Brompton to look after merchandise still in Europe; collecting recipes and cures for illnesses he might encounter; and, in between visits to the Jamaica Coffee House, where he eventually arranged his passage, buying more cloth, and refusing an offer to go back to trade in Flanders, he remembered to leave his measurements with Peter Greenough, his friend and tailor. Thistlewood was something of a dandy in his dress and he did not propose to go to seed in the plantations.

At five o'clock on the morning of Thursday, 1st February 1750 Thistlewood set out for Jamaica.

'... set out in the Gravesend tiltboat, got there about ½ past 9. For myself, and hammock, &c, boating, 1s. For boating aboard the *Flamborough*, 6d. ... Found my case broke open, my Arrack, Brazil rum and Lisbon wine gone. The looking-glass Mrs Gresham gave me, broke. Note, we are moored. Ready money 4 guineas, one ½ ditto, 3 shillings, sixpence and 5d of half pence = £14 18s 5d. The *Flamborough* is said to be a prime sailor. At night, Capt. Bonnell come on board.'

The following morning brought an interesting event. These were days in which people were still being kidnapped on the streets of the port towns in England and hustled on board vessels bound for the plantation colonies where they would be sold into indentured labour.

'Today, officers come on board, mustered the passengers, and examined them, lest any should go against their will.'

For the next two days the *Flamborough* remained at anchor and then, through rolling seas, made a sickening start, especially for the six young women on board. They were among those going out into service on the plantations and, except for one or two who had been taken into the company of the Captain or one or other of the 'gentleman' passengers on the Quarter Deck, they were, like Thistlewood, accommodated below. On the evening of Friday 2nd March they passed the Isle of Wight. Gradually, the weather improved. The *Flying Flamborough* had fallen from prouder days. She had been *The Flamborough* one of His Majesty's frigates of 20 guns, but was now a merchant vessel, of 350 tons burthen, 116 feet from stem to stern and 28 feet in the beam, and she was to protest against bad handling on the voyage. She was bound for Antigua and Kingston, Old Harbour, Black River and Savanna la Mar, in Jamaica.

Among the passengers there were the six unnamed girls about whom Thistlewood had little to say except when they were in trouble. This happened on a couple of occasions, the most notable being when the Yorkshire girl was found to have stolen some butter and some of Miss Jones' clothes. Miss Jones was the Captain's companion, and the cause of much strife, especially between a merchant, Mr Duprie, and the Captain.

Mr Duprie was not one of Thistlewood's companions at sea. Perhaps one of the reasons for his recurring disputes with the Captain was his rather lonely intermediate social position amongst the passengers. As a merchant he would not have considered Thistlewood and the majority of the others as social equals. As a merchant, he would not have been accepted as an equal by the few 'gentlemen' passengers to whom Thistlewood made reference on arrival at Antigua.

'In the afternoon, when the gentlemen went ashore, (I also went in the barge) one of these gentleman is a clergyman, one a captain of a ship, and the other a very old gentleman, who is chief owner of the island of Barbuda.'

He does not even mention their names, and probably did not know them although he had noted, during the voyage, the presence of a Captain Spellman. There is no knowing who the clergyman might have been, or if there were other unacknowledged 'gentlemen' on board; but of one there is no doubt: 'the very old gentleman who is chief owner of the island of Barbuda', as Thistlewood described him, was Christopher Codrington, to whose family that island had been leased in 1685 by King Charles II.

Thomas Ashlin and Thomas Bottomley were Thistlewood's messmates. Ashlin was going to Mr Joseph Wetherby, overseer to Mr Beckford at Old Harbour, Jamaica. Bottomley was going to be at Mr Long's in Clarendon, Jamaica. Mr Eleanah Edwards was Thistlewood's companion ashore in St John's Town, Antigua.

'Mr Edwards and I walked about the Town to see it (St John's Town). Here is a pretty piece of modern architecture, not yet finished, built of their own stone which they are vastly proud of. It is for a sort of Stadt House, and may serve to have Assemblies in, &c. Spent at the great tavern or punch house, which is a sort of Change, in punch, 6d which here is 9d. For 8 yams 6d, for 56 limes 6d Many wood houses, some of a kind of brick or stone, some glass windows. But an indifferent sort of place; streets rugged and stony, and everything dear. Saw in the Negro market, some yams, limes, cashoo apples, guinea corn, plantains, &c. Some black girls laid hold of us and would gladly have had us gone in with them.' [13/4/1750]

Mr Burgess, who came from Glastonbury in Somerset, was going to his brother Thomas in Annotto Bay, Jamaica. Sadly, on arrival in Kingston, he had news that his brother had died. Mr Fowler, who with Burgess had one evening had supper with Thistlewood on board the *Flying Flamborough*, was going to Mr Fuller's at Spanish Town. Fowler and Burgess, it appears, had joined company on board before they came to know Thistlewood. The three and another, a Mr Lightenhouse, became friends and went ashore together in Kingston.

It had been a long and troublesome voyage. There had been times of games and merriment, but there had been fights and quarrels and expressed dissatisfaction with the manner and performance of the Captain and Chief Mate. It was with some relief, therefore, that those Jamaica-bound watched the ship's approach to Morant Bay on the south-east coast. There, at 4 p.m. on Monday, 23rd April, '. . . a Negro pilot came on board us'. At 7 p.m., they were at Port Royal. On the 24th, at about noon they came alongside in Kingston and so, with his friends, ashore, where they got lost. At about 8 p.m. they turned up at a guest-house, Mrs Davenport's in Temple Lane, and there they lodged.

In the evening of Friday 27th, probably in the company of Mr Fowler and Mr Burgess (who on that day received news of his brother's death), he

'. . . walked to Captain Cornishe's, about 1½ miles to the eastward by the seaside. He says he is 81 years old, has mostly drank water alone this 37 years, and a great deal of chocolate.

He is fresh and nimble, walked out in the country with me, &c. He keeps a genteel mulatto girl, though some say she is from white parents of both sides, which I can scarce believe.'

Two days later:

'In the evening, Mr Fowler, and I walked to Spring Path, to the westward of the Town, to see Negro Diversions – odd Music, Motions, &c. The Negroes of each Nation by themselves.'

The next day, after breakfast at the White Cross, Thistlewood and Fowler walked to the Wherry Wharf, from whence the latter set out for Spanish Town and Thistlewood boated to Port Royal. Port Royal, he was to decide, had '. . . somewhat a grander look in the streets than Kingston' where 'much old glass, and old iron about the streets, &c'.

Although the *Flying Flamborough* was bound for southern ports on the way to Savanna la Mar, Thistlewood did not rejoin her. Perhaps because of previous unpleasantness, perhaps, also, because the desertion of some of her crew had delayed her departure. Indeed, some of them had, like Thistlewood, decided to go to Savanna la Mar by a different vessel.

'About sunrise went aboard the *John and James* (an open boat) James Rogers Commander, for Savanna la Mar. We weighed, were standing out, when the *Queensborough's* boat came on board [the *Queensborough* was one of several English warships then in the roadstead] took out McGradh, Alexander Burt, William Denny, and another man who was concealed, took them on board per force. Note they fire 2 guns to alarm the shipping and fort not to let us pass although Captain Rogers had already cleared out.'

On Thursday, 3rd May, just as the morning gun was fired, Captain Rogers weighed anchor and, having once again been searched, began the 30 leagues to Savanna la Mar. After a stop at Bluefields at about one o'clock in the morning they arrived at Savanna la Mar at noon on Friday, 4th May 1750.

'Went ashore, took my things with me, put them in McHogan's store house. To Captain Rogers for passage a pound currency, i.e. 32 bitts. For dinner 4 bitts. Spent 2 ditto. Shaving 1 ditto. Walked to William Dorrill's Esqr. Gave him Mr Collgrave's letter, was well received.'[4]

Next day Mr Dorrill lent him a horse and he rode to Mr Storer's.[5]

'. . . gave him Mr Collgrave's letter, was well received, dined with him. He offered me to go to his plantation next week, and stay there, ready to succeed his overseer who leaves him in about 2 months.'

Mr Thistlewood had now met the Jamaican plantocracy. The brothers, William and Thomas Dorrill, were landowners and merchants. Thomas Dorrill lived in Savanna la Mar. William Dorrill with whom Thistlewood was directly concerned, was the owner of Salt River, Bowen's (renamed Paradise) and Egypt estates, the two first named lying east of the town and the other to the west. William Dorrill lived at Salt River.

'Mr Dorrill's house is pleasantly situated about ¼ of a mile from the sea and about 2½ or 3 miles from Savanna la Mar, to the eastward. Faced with wood, backed with stone, or more properly lined. Has port holes for defence. Wood columns on each side. Near Salt River.' [11/5/1750]

With him lived his daughter, Mary (nicknamed 'Molly'), then about 14 years old, who was later to marry John Cope of Strathbogie. Also permanently resident in the Salt River house was 'Mrs Elizabeth Anderson', whose relationship with the Dorrills was not explicitly stated by Thistlewood. She was, in fact, 'Elizabeth Anderson of the parish of Westmoreland aforesaid single woman ...' and the mother of William Dorrill's 'natural son Thomas commonly called Thomas Dorrill' and his 'natural daughter Mary commonly called Mary Dorrill begotten by me on the body of the said Elizabeth Anderson ...' Nonetheless, as the clauses of his last will and testament to be made in 1754 would also indicate, Mr Dorrill seems to have been a little unsure of his exclusive enjoyment of her favours.[6] Even before his death Thistlewood indicated that Mrs Anderson was entertaining Mr Forrester, the Salt River overseer, and shortly after Mr Dorrill died she married William ('Billy') Mould, his store-clerk. Though Thistlewood nowhere describes her, it would seem that Mrs Anderson was a 'free coloured' woman for she subsequently bore a daughter whom Mould said was 'a Mulatto'.

By Wednesday, 9th June, Thistlewood was to let Mr Storer know if the offer made to him on his arrival was acceptable. He had decided that it was not. He 'had better views which prevented me'.

On Sunday, 20th May, he set down for the first time his 'better Views' about possible employment.

'Oft overhear gentlemen whom Mr Dorrill mentions my intent to be a surveyor to, say that it will be a very good thing for me, if I understand but enough figures for it. Which gives me great hopes.'

vas not a completely new interest. He had learned some mathematics at school, and in London, shortly before embarking for the West Indies, he had purchased *The Practical Surveyor*, by Samuel Wild. Monday 21st, he stayed at home at Salt River writing letters which he was able to send off by the *William*, Captain Glendenning (one of Dorrill's vessels), addressed to his brother in Tupholme, Mr Hewitt, and Mr Collgrave. His news must have been optimistic. He was now employed, but this was to be only briefly.

He would later be called upon, from time to time, to put his surveying skills to use, but now, following the death by drowning of Mr Crawford, his associate assistant surveyor, and differences of opinion with Mr Wallace, the surveyor, he gave up. He had, however, noted one memorable meeting during his travels. On Thursday, 29th May, on the road to St James:

'Between 8 and 9 miles from Dean's Valley, met Colonel Cudjoe, one of his wives, one of his sons, a Lieutenant and other attendants. He shook me by the hand, and begged a dram of us, which we gave him. He had on a feathered hat, sword by his side, gun upon his shoulder, &c. Barefoot and barelegged, somewhat a majestic look. He brought to my memory the picture of Robinson Crusoe.' [1/6/1750][7]

And, disappointingly for us, not a word more about the meeting with the Maroon leader. Soon after, Crawford and Thistlewood reached the Great River, about 1 ½ miles from Dean's Valley, 30—40 yards wide, inviting, cool water, and 'I bathed in it'. That afternoon they arrived at the soldiers' barracks where they dined; and Thistlewood, happy and energetic, 'cat leap up to catch swallows' — but apparently without success.

By nightfall the survey was over and they were back at their hut in a plantain-walk, where

'Eat some Clucking hen broth, and pepper pot, and also Tum Tum of plantain and fish beat together, with old Sharper who is a sensible Negro.'

His brief employment as a surveyor was followed by a period of idleness. Then, on the 29th June, Thistlewood made up his mind.

'In the morning rode to Sweet River plantation, and agreed with Florentius Vassall, Esqr. to be his pen-keeper at 50 pounds per annum.'

For that sum, a weekly allowance of 2 bottles of rum and 2 lb of sugar and a quarterly allowance of a barrel of beef, he was to supervise the pen and provide Mr Vassall with regular accounts of his stewardship. Obviously, Vassall had made the offer before. On Sunday, 1st July, Thistlewood rode past Strathbogie Castle to Mr Vassall, who was at his other Westmoreland estate, Friendship. There he received 2 pistoles to cover his expenses on the journey to Vassall's St Elizabeth property 'Vineyard Pen', an order to the Sweet River overseer, Mr Walker, to provide a mule and the boy Sampson as Thistlewood's guide, and letters confirming his appointment.

Thus armed, and having bid his farewells at Salt River and Savanna la Mar he stored his belongings once more, this time with Mr Bowen at Mr Dorrill's barcadier store. Having divided five shillings among the domestic slaves at Dorrill's house, Thomas Thistlewood set out for the Vineyard. He had '. . . not one farthing of money left, but what is laid by.' He carefully noted the values of the current coins:

'1 Ryal [Real] or bitt was 7½d Jamaica currency. Ten Ryals made 1 Dollar sometimes called Cobb, the equivalent of 6s 3d. Thirty-eight Ryals equalled 1 pistole which was £1 3s 9d. Sixty-two Ryals made 1 moidore or £1 18s 9d currency. And £140 currency was the equivalent of £100, sterling.'

The Vineyard Pen was a property of about 1,170 acres in south-west St Elizabeth in the plains between Burnt Savanna Mountain and the sea.

'This Penn and some small part of the land adjoining it is accounted very hot, the reason may be the abundance of flat rock reflects the heat of the sun very strong: and Burnt Savanna Mountain stretches along from NE to SE, probably keeps off the winds very much: to the eastward the mountain is very high . . .' [3/7/1751]

To a man coming from Westmoreland the change of climate was remarkable, the more so because the Vineyard area in particular had been suffering a prolonged drought since December 1749.

'Altho' we have had some abundance of rain in Westmoreland before I left it, and now we have vast falls daily within 3 or 4 miles of us, yet we can get none; has been excessive dry many months, vegetables all scorch'd up . . .' [11/7/1750]

Indeed, as we shall see, much of Thistlewood's concern during his first weeks of management was in providing foodstuffs for the slaves and feed for the animals.

Of the Pen's more than 1,000 acres much was in swamp. Of the balance, most was in common pasture, but the fattening pasture of about 23 acres was planted in guinea grass and scotch grass. The pastures were enclosed by railed wooden fences, or *palisadoes* as they were called, with prickly penguin planted alongside. Protected in this way from the livestock were the provision grounds of the slaves and of the Pen itself.

The Pen carried a variety of livestock, large and small: cattle, horses, mules, asses, sheep, goats, pigs, ducks, turkeys, and fowls. It produced timber, mostly mahogany, and dye-wood (logwood). In the estate's garden and grounds, and in the slaves' provision grounds, there grew a variety of trees, and vegetable crops. Income accrued from the sales of livestock (mainly cattle), mahogany, and logwood chips, but probably because of the unkind climate, it was not a very profitable enterprise.

The costs of management were small. Thistlewood was the only supervisory white and he was a quick learner and efficient, but the maintenance of the tools and equipment of the property, and the cost of feeding the slaves and the livestock in time of drought were obviously burdensome. Vineyard was surrounded by sugar estates and the Vineyard cattle were often tempted.

The buildings on Vineyard were, it seems, adequate and unpretentious. The great house, as one would expect, provided the most spacious accommodation, but it was not a structure in the grand manner. In June 1751 Thistlewood had 'two hands employed making mortar' to repair the walls and they followed common custom:

> 'When mud walls are sufficiently dry, and very much cracked (in this country) they mix water, soft cow dung, and wood ashes with a small quantity of fire mould, till it be pretty thick so as scarce to run out of the hand. With this, they rub the walls once or twice over, and it will fill and cover all the cracks, &c.' [9/6/1751]

The house he lived in was modest indeed. It was walled by wattles plastered as described above, and roofed with thatch, in which from time to time he found interesting inhabitants. The overall outer dimensions were 28 feet by 15¼ feet, divided across into three rooms, the two at the ends being of equal size 8½ feet by 15¼ feet and the largest in the centre 11 feet. This central room had four doors, two connecting with the other rooms, and two others facing and leading out of the house on each long side.

Near to the great house lay the garden and a 'new private pasture' brought into use during Thistlewood's time. In the garden there were about half-a-dozen sweet, and a great number of seville, or sour, orange trees. There was also a grape arbor and a variety of other fruit trees, shrubs, and flowers in which Thistlewood took great interest. Apart from his own horticultural inclinations, he was intrigued by the variety of tropical flora and fauna, and as we shall see by his frequent parenthetic 'as is done in this country', he was constantly comparing with his knowledge of England and other places he had visited.

Through the pastures, and by pathways through the morass, a way led to the Vineyard barcadier, or jetty. Every estate that had access to a waterway had its barcadier, however small, where supplies to and from the property might be loaded on to canoes or larger craft to save heavy carriage on the rutted roadways. And since the barcadier led by the morass and Thistlewood was both alligator-hunter and amateur naturalist, he went there more often than business demanded.

'Went to the barcadier this forenoon, got some wild cinnamon bark from a tree about as thick as my leg, one just by 7 or 8 inches square very thick blossoms, purplish close shaped flower, smell like crows foot in our meadows in England.' [1/6/1751]

Lacovia, then the parish capital, was the centre at which the quarterly returns of slaves and livestock populations had to be made for purposes of taxation. Thistlewood went three times: in October 1750, January 1751, and in April 1751.

On the second occasion 8th January, 1751, he gave in one white, 39 Negroes, 232 cattle, and recorded:

'Today first saw a white person since December 19th that I was at Black River.'

And, in his usual non-commital style, but with great detail:

'Capt. Compoon [Accompong] here, about my size, in a ruffled shirt, blue broad cloth coat, scarlet cuff to his sleeves, gold buttons, & he had with [that] white cap, and black hat, white linen breeches puffed at the rims, no stockings or shoes on. Many of his wives, and his son there.'

Thomas Thistlewood worked on the Vineyard Pen, between Lacovia and Black River, for almost exactly one year until he quarrelled with Mr Vassall and left of his own accord. During that time, as the only white employee on the property he mixed much with the slaves and was introduced by them to the local fauna and flora. There were only about 40 slaves on Vineyard: 24 males and 18 females, on his arrival. Of the latter, Phibbah, the chief domestic servant, introduced him to Jamaican fruit, foodstuffs and local culinary practice. Marina, a field slave became his 'wife' and lived with him, occasionally protesting his sexual pursuit of many of the other women. On leaving the Vineyard he had a cottage built for her and entrusted her to the care of Julius whom he seems to have regarded as the most responsible of the Vineyard men.

'On the 23rd June 1751: Put up my hanging bookshelf in Marina's parlour for a bed for her, fitted it up with the mat which I bought from Caesar.

On Saturday, 6th July: At night gave Marina some sugar, 4 bottles of rum, some beef and pepper-pot, with 18 pints of corn made into fungi, to treat the Negroes, and especially her shipmates withal at her housewarming. They was very merry all night. Mr Markman's Caesar sang and drummed, Guy and Charles, Phibbah and Wanicker danced Congo, &c. Some top performances was had. Marina herself got very drunk as well as many others. I sat up good part of the night seeing their tricks.

Charles ate fire – struck his naked arm many times with the edge of a bill, very hard, yet received no harm, &c.'

Then, on Sunday 7th, his last day at Vineyard: 'Spoke to Julius about Marina, he assented to speak.' And for Marina, more gifts: some thread, old caps, 2 old handkerchiefs, a white shirt, 2 pairs of old trousers, a long cuttakan,[8] a basket, a cassava roaster, wild cinnamon, wax light, a bench, a little stool, a cupboard which he hung for her, and a chest 'to put her chattels in' which also he put in her house, a barrel for corn, a barrel of beef brine with a piece of beef, potatoes, 3 bottles of rum, sugar, butter, &c.

'As to the little pot I had in my house, left it with the girl who lived with me, else she has nothing to boil her victuals in.'

Then '*Pro. temp. a nocte. Sup. lect. cum* Marina,' and in the morning.

'Got up just by moon rise, gave Marina a bottle of rum, water pail, &c., and took leave of her in my parlour.'

Almost exactly one year later they would meet again, briefly, in Westmoreland. From the Vineyard, through Black River and along the coast for most of the way, the road led to Mr Dorrill's at Salt River.

As the epitaph on his tombstone at Salt River tells us, there seemed always to be company at Mr Dorrill's table. Sometimes they were frivolous:

'After dinner they oft all round take hold of the table cloth, lift it up, and shake all the crumbs upon a plate in the middle, a ready way Jamaica fashion.' [6/9/1751]

And sometimes bawdy:

'Old Tom Williams says he pleases his mistress yet
night; first by putting his thigh over her, which pleases her by
putting her in expectation − next, he pleases her by taking it
off, when she is weary of the weight.' [17/7/1751]

Life at Salt River was very different from life at Vineyard. At
Vineyard he had been the only white in residence; here, he was
continuously in the company of whites. There, when he sought
conversation of an evening he had found it with the slaves; here he
found it at a planter-merchant's house and table. There he had
recorded what slaves had told and shown him, learning from them,
more than from any other, the names and uses of unfamiliar things.
Here, in the smarter set, under the candelabra, he also heard the
gossip of the whites.

There is no suggestion that on leaving Mr Vassall's employment
Thistlewood had any other prospect of a job. Indeed, during the
following weeks at Salt River, where again he was a guest at Mr
Dorrill's house and table, the review of possibilities was resumed.

Captain La Bruce, the swash-buckling sailor and slave-trader
whom he found there, told him that he had made three voyages
from Brazil to Guinea, about twenty five days sail from coast to
coast, and that a common price for a slave at Pernambuco was a
pound of gold, and that four pieces of eight (Spanish dollars each
worth 6s 3d Jamaica currency) invested in Brazilian tobacco would
fetch about fifteen times that much in Guinea. [10/7/1751]

Thomas Dorrill, the merchant, advised that cargoes of books
brought in yearly:

'... Chiefly history, poetry, &c. all books of entertainment,
The History of the Devil goes off well, &c. He had about 50
pounds worth, which were soon all gone.'

Saddles, boots, and greatcoats, too, he said would do very well, but
'Not to trust a Bitt of the money.' [15/7/1751]

Samuel Mordenner, who did not really understand Thomas
Thistlewood's ambition, or who was simply commenting without
suggestion remarked that shoe-blacks and razor-grinders were much
needed and might make money.

Mr William Dorrill suggested that great profit might be made
selling 'Flanders laces, Hollands, Soaps, &c.', if the person lived in
or near Savanna la Mar. [30/7/1751]

The possibilities of trade might have interested Thistlewood,
who had some experience in that, but he does not say so. He spent
his days walking, fishing, listening, writing his journal and writing
letters: to his brother, to Henry Hewitt, and to Alexius Emerson.

These had all in some way been involved in his European trading enterprise, but, in customary style, Thistlewood gives no hint about the content of his correspondence. On the same day on which he sent letters off, the 24th August:

> 'Mr William Wallace the surveyor being at our house proffered me 50 pounds per annum for the first year to assist him, and live as he lives, and 100 pounds for the 2nd.'

No other comment! But we know that he refused.

On Sunday 8th he walked down to the barcadier with Mr Thomas Tomlinson Jnr and 'run & leaped with [him]: beat him.' He does not say so, but perhaps he was trying to emulate an Irishman in Hispaniola who, according to Captain de la Bruce, had leapt '22 feet at a single running leap upon a level.' [24/8/1751]

Nor were his other, often athletic, proclivities entirely neglected:

> '[Tuesday, 10th September] about ½ past 10 a.m. *Cum* Flora, a congo, *Super Terram* among the canes, above the wall head, right hand of the river, toward the Negro ground. She been for water cress. Gave her 4 bitts.'

And, next morning, in the very small hours:

> 'About 2 a.m. *Cum* Negroe* girl, *super* floor, at north bed foot, in the east parlour. *unknown.'

On the same day he was to experience a less manageable aspect of life on the plantations.

At about 6 a.m. the wind freshened. At noon it was at gale force with the hard gusts spraying the seawater like a mist. From 3 p.m. to sunset the hurricane passed over.

> 'Blew the shingles off the Stables and boiling house, and all the thatch off the cooperage and trash house; burst open the great house windows that were secured by strong bars; blew the weather boards and ridge boards off the great house &c. every room full of water. The jasmine tree by the Tombs blown down and many of the orange trees out of the rows before the great house. All the pomegranates in the garden blown down, and everything tore to pieces almost. Plantain trees all presently down.
>
> About sunset all the white people, viz, Mr Dorrill, Capt. Riviere de la Bruce, Mr Peter Fookes, Mr Samuel Mordenner, & myself — all leave the great house and shelter in the storehouse and hurricane house. About 11 p.m. returned to the great house, went to bed, that is laid down …'

except Mr Fookes who was 'so timorous that he sat up all night the wind, though now much abated, blew hard all night with rₑ and lightning

At noon next day Thistlewood went down to the barcadier. 'Strange havoc there ...' Mr Mordenner's house 'quite down' (he was in charge of Mr Dorrill's barcadier's store), the new store house walls severely damaged, two-thirds of the stored timbers strewn along the shore and floating out at sea.

> 'The boards, staves and shingles blown about as if they were feathers. Most of the new wharf washed away, vast wrecks of sea weeds drove along way upon the land, a heavy iron roller case carried a long way from where it lay, and half buried in the sand.'

In Mr Dorrill's recollection, the sea had not raged so furiously in the hurricanes of 1722 and 1744.

Thistlewood was amazed, excited, full of detail in recording this new terrifying experience. He walked along the seaside, a long way each side of the barcadier:

> 'No birds stirring ... many fish thrown up dead upon the shore. Broke my penknife cutting a mangrove.'

And, breaking the quiet of the birds, he shot two snipe.

Mr Beckford's barcadier was also in a state of 'strange havoc', and, looking landwards

> '... all the woods and mountains look open and bare, and very ragged, the woods appear like our woods in England in the fall of the leaf, when about half down.' [13/9/1751]

The news from Black River told of equal devastation there. Stores damaged, and Mr Bennett's place at Rowe's barcadier 'quite floated, and his sloop lately purchased supposed to be lost.' [14/9/1751]

At Mr Dorrill's Egypt plantation the overseer there, John Filton, and 'his Negro wife' had taken shelter in the curing house cistern. Perhaps that was considered a negligence. On Monday, 16th September:

> 'A little before dinner, walking in the Plantation [at Salt River], Mr Dorrill offered me if I would accept to be overseer of Egypt Estate (he would give me 60 pounds per annum). I willingly accepted of it.'

No time was lost. On the same day:

> 'About 2 p.m. I set out for Egypt, on the horse Billy, guided by Salt River Quaco. [Mrs Anderson had given him some biscuits

and a roll of chocolate, and had seen him fitted out with saddle and bridle]. Got there about 4 ditto. Went into the field, found 42 Negroes at work clearing the ground at Top Hill of trash, Quaco & Morris mending the garden fence. John Filton did not come home till past 8 at night. Gave him his discharge wrote thus: Westmoreland 16th September. I have this day discharged Mr John Filton from my service. Wm. Dorrill.'

And another order, wrote thus:

'Mr John Filton, Deliver up all the Keys, as also the Estate, and everything belonging to me, to the bearer Mr Thomas Thistlewood, who I hope will take better care of the Estate than you have done. Yrs. Wm. Dorrill. Salt River. 16th September 1751. Received the boiling house, curing house & corn house keys.'

And that was that. Not a word of John Filton's reactions, nor of his own feelings at so sudden a move, but we can sense a note of triumph in the account. Thomas Thistlewood might well have felt some compassion for John Filton, but, even more likely, he was probably full of approval of a move which seemed clearly to recognise in him a superior competence. In his own mind there was no doubt at all that he had it. But Egypt was a sugar estate, not a cattlepen, and Mr Dorrill, friend and companion to the bright, engaging young adventurer from England, might take a rather different view of a bright, self-confident, and independently-minded overseer.

On Wednesday, 18th September 1751, Thomas Thistlewood put himself in charge of Egypt. On that day 'In the afternoon, I rode all over the plantation.' And, had he not come to Egypt, he would not have worked for Mr Wallace the surveyor, nor would he have tried to set up as a merchant in Savanna la Mar, for, at last, he put down what he'd had in mind:

'Had I not come here, I should have gone to Hispaniola with Captain Riviere de la Bruce, to have learnt make Indico.'

Here, at Egypt, he was to make his name as a sugar estate overseer; lay the foundations of his own proprietorship by the purchase of land and slaves; quarrel with his various employers, none of whom, however, seemed to wish to lose his service; harden in his attitude towards his slave labourers; and, his many casual interferences apart, he would go from a passionate affair with one slave woman into a lasting match with another who would bear him a son and live with him until he died.

Notes

1 Thistlewood noted his sexual occasions in such Latin as he remembered. Thus, to translate, 'With E.B. in our house, towards night. Tup[holme]. (Twice).' Other much used expressions which we shall encounter are *Sup. Lect.* (on the bed), and, more often in Jamaica, *Sup. Terr.* (on the ground), with an occasional *In Silva* (in the woods), *In Mag.* [or] *Parv. Dom.* (in the Great [or] small house); and, on less satisfactory occasions, *Sed non bene* (but not well).

2 Gonorrhoea, or 'the Clap', and syphilis were, in the eighteenth century subjects of much discussion and advertisement, but little understanding. Of 'the venereal poison' it was admitted 'We know nothing of the poison itself, but only its effects on the human body' (John Hunter, *The Venereal Disease*, London 1788, p.11.) In England the newspapers carried remedial suggestions, such as that recorded by Thistlewood. In the West Indies, as in Europe, medical men published their treatises, but here with special reference to the incidence and cure of venereal diseases among the slave population. See, for instance, Thomas Dancer's *The Medical Assistant or Jamaica Practice of Physic: designed chiefly for the use of Families and Plantations* (1801), and James Thompson's *A Treatise on the Diseases of Negroes as they occur in the island Jamaica* (1820); both published by Alex Aikman, Kingston, Jamaica. Dancer and Thompson both discuss the efficacy of medically prescribed and of local herbal remedies, but without much confidence. For the most recent, thorough discussion, see Richard Sheridan's *Doctors and Slaves: A medical and demographic history of slaves in the B.W.I., 1680–1834*, Cambridge University Press, 1985.

3 The Beckford family owned Shrewsbury (Roaring River) and other estates in Westmoreland where the village of Petersfield is named after Peter Beckford whose grandson, William Beckford was twice Lord Mayor of London. The William Beckford to whom Thistlewood refers was the Lord Mayor's nephew. By 1780, however, the estates were to become heavily indebted.

4 The 'bitt' was 7½d Jamaica currency.

5 Mr Storer was the owner of Belle Isle estate, where the family mausoleum now lies in broken ruin, and others.

6 I am grateful to the Jamaican Government Archivist, Mr Clinton Black, for this reference:

William Dorrill had his doubts of Elizabeth Anderson's constancy. In his last will and testament made on 5 March 1754 he left Salt River Estate with slaves and livestock 'unto my nephew Christopher Senior . . . and his three sons, Gilbert Senior, William Dorrill Senior, and Thomas Keith Yeeles Senior and my niece Mary Williams wife of Joseph Williams'; to Elizabeth Anderson he had bequeathed Egypt estate house, outbuildings and garden, 10 acres of land on Egypt, one Negro woman named Phibbah and her child, another Negro woman named Frank [house slaves at Egypt and Salt River] and £60, Jamaica currency, per annum for life 'provided nevertheless that if the said Elizabeth Anderson shall at anytime after my decease Intermarry or behave immodestly then my will is that the said aformentioned bequests . . . shall be null and void to all intents and purposes . . .' In such event, the bequests to her would go to his natural children, Thomas and Mary 'begotten by me on the body of the said Elizabeth Anderson.' To them and their lawful heirs, he directly bequeathed all else of his property, namely, Paradise Estate, Egypt estate, and 'right of access to and use of the Salt River barquadier and the Crane Stores wharf and all other appurtenances thereto belonging . . . .' (Records Office, Jamaica, Wills No. 30, p.13, 1754.)

7 By the Peace Treaty with the Maroons Captain Cudjoe was recognised as 'chief commander' of the Maroons settled in Trelawny Town. Next, in order of succession were his brother Captain Accompong (whom he had established at a second Maroon township, Accompong), then his other brother, Captain Johnny followed by Captain Cuffee and Captain Quaco. In each Township, a white man appointed by the Governor would reside as a kind of liaison officer.

8 Culákan, Culácoo. A woven field bag carried by a strap over the shoulder. In Thistlewood's day probably woven of palm thatch.

CHAPTER 2   Thistlewood's first crop

Introduction

Attempts to develop Egypt as a sugar estate illustrated the magnetic pull towards sugar production in a time of good prices. In fact, and as even William Dorrill seemed to realise, Egypt was far more suited to the kind of diversified production in which Thistlewood later became involved on the property he would acquire just across the Cabaritta river. As most of the sugar planters of the time understood, and as Bryan Edwards, the eighteenth century planter-historian so clearly set forth in his *History of the West Indies*, the ideal sugar estate should contain '... three parts: the Lands, the Buildings, and the Stock.' Of the lands (and Egypt contained a quite sufficient acreage), about one-third should be canefields, about one-third provision grounds, and the remainder in woodlands. The aims were sugar, food supplies for the slaves, and timber for fuel and for construction. As we shall see, Egypt could come nowhere near such divisions. Most of it was under water. Thus, sugar production was at best too small to be profitable, provisions were often very scarce and there was much recourse to purchasing in the markets or from better favoured properties, and the advantages of fishing and duck shooting were by no means compensatory. Thus, William Dorrill seemed always to be in uncertainty about cane planting on Egypt, and later, his daughter and her husband would be forced to sell for indebtedness. Nonetheless, Thistlewood's account of his first crop allows us a close view of the routine of cane cultivation, harvesting and the manufacture of raw (muscovado) sugar, even though on an inferior estate.

We also begin to learn a little more about human relationships in the slave society. Master-slave, man-woman, owner-overseer, and other relationships begin to appear less stereotyped than we have tended to picture them. Thistlewood lashes his slaves, abuses the women, but clearly becomes fascinated by Nago Jenny's physical charms, and sometimes seems moved by more than concern for the well-being of a piece of property when he has to deal with an ailing or injured slave. And, as his diary unfolds, we shall see more and more of this.

Other, less personal, matters are also in some degree elucidated. We can more clearly understand one of the ways in which information, as much as goods, could be moved around. As far as possible estate owners and managers avoided the transportation of heavy goods over the rutted tracks and roadways on which draught animals stumbled and fell, and wains and waggons were often damaged. The way to go was by water, along the trenches, canals and rivers, and along the coastline, from one estate's barcadier or jetty to another, in all manner of small craft, manned by slaves who heard and carried news. And as we shall learn, the slaves moved about, by river and by road, on their owners' business and on their own, with far more freedom than we have supposed.

The name 'Egypt' is today recognized only by local residents, who more affectionately call it 'Capture Land', that is, ruinate property settled by squatters long undisturbed in their possession. It was never a great sugar producing property, though it lies on the southern coastal margin of one of Jamaica's main cane growing areas. Rising in the higher lands of northern Westmoreland, the Cabaritta river, fed by several tributary streams, winds down to the sea just westward of Savanna la Mar. In the last few miles of its course the river enters into a maze of morasses and man-made drains and canals – some of which date back to Mr Thistlewood's time – and it is there that Egypt lies. Bounded on the north by part of Meylersfield, Midgham and Kirkpatrick (now know as Llandilo); on the east by Paradise Pen (now known as Rockdondo and Altavelta) and the morasses west of Savanna la Mar; on the south by the sea, from about Cabaritta Point westwards, past the river's mouth, to the River Styx; and on the west by Long Pond and part of Meylersfield, Egypt contained just over 1,500 acres of which about 1,200 acres consisted of water and morass. The areas of dry land were, in fact 'islands' in the swamps, which explains Thistlewood's frequent references to runaway Negroes 'marooned' on hidden patches of habitable land, and ·his constant concern with drains, paths and bridges on the estate. And he distinguished the last named. 'Such bridges as that of ours going to the hogstyes are called Barbecue Bridges; as that going to Hill, Congo Bridges; those in the canepieces are Common Bridges.' The canepieces, many of them named by Thistlewood, have disappeared, taking their names with them. In the mid-1750s, of Egypt's total acreage, only about 150 acres were in cane, and that was distributed about 33 canepieces of which 14 were more than five but less than ten acres each, and 19 were under five acres with the four smallest being under two acres each. There were 65 acres of pasture; and scattered through the canes and commons were over six acres of ponds ranging in size from the Egypt great pond, covering over two acres, to the quarter acre pond in the Old Scotchgrass canepiece. The Negro provision ground at Hill, near the coast west of the mouth of the Cabaritta, was perhaps situated at a place now called 'Cookell', a name maybe derived from Hill, which became Cook's Hill (there was later a Mr Cook in that area), and so to Cookell. Egypt today is occupied by small settlers engaged mainly in swamp and river fishing, small livestock raising, rice farming, or labouring at the inland (pond) fisheries, the rice mill, or the stone quarry, all of which now operate where Thistlewood drove Mr Dorrill's slaves to make sugar, rum and molasses.

In that labour they faced great difficulty in transporting things within the boundaries of the estate, from canefields to factory or from provision grounds to kitchens. Transportation of the estate's produce outwards to market was easier. Large canoes carried heavy freight along trenches and up and down the slow-moving Cabaritta, while the King's Highway passed through the property cutting it into almost equal parts, north and south of the road. Egypt great house, which was by no means 'great', standing on a slight elevation in the 'Home Pasture', near the roadway, was a frequent resort, not only of its owner's friends, but also of tired, hungry, and weather-beaten travellers seeking food and shelter.

Unlike that of the Vineyard, the slave population of Egypt was highly unstable. There were frequent transfers of people between Egypt and Mr Dorrill's other properties at Salt River and Bowen's, or Paradise as it was re-named. There were more runaways, though few remained long in the tentative and uneasy freedom of the escapee in an area much frequented by Cudjoe and his lieutenants and Maroon parties. There were the comings and goings of individuals and groups of slaves hired from other properties as need arose, and there were purchases of newly arrived slaves to fill out the ranks of the Egypt working force.

Nonetheless, there was a nucleus of Egypt people who remained on the property during most or all of Thistlewood's regime and, as the diary unfolds, we take a closer interest in the fortunes of those few whose names and activities were most often recorded. For a start, as did Thistlewood himself who listed them on Friday, 1st November 1751, we know only their names. The men of Egypt were:

Achilles	Hazat	Port Royal	Adam
Hector	Quacoo	Ambo	Jimmy

	Cruddon	London	Roger
	Morris	Sam	Cyrus
Nero	Sancho	Daniel	Old Sharper
Tony	Dickson	Old Tom	Will
Dover	Plato	Abraham	Glasgow
Plymouth	Hannibal	Titus	
			(Total 31)

The women of Egypt were:[1]

Abigail (Ebo)	Hannah	Old Sarah (?)	Agnes
Jenny (Nago	(Nago)	Basheba	Little Mimber
or Bastard	Phibbah	Lucy	(Creole)
Papah)	(Creole)	Teresa	Sibyl
Quasheba	Belinda (Ebo)	Betty	Beneba
Bella (Congo)	Margie (Ebo)	Yabba	(Creole)
Mirtilla (Ebo)	Violet (Ebo)	Prue	Old Catalina
Old Moll	Mary		Big Mimber
Celia (?)	Old Phibbah		(Creole)
Hagar			Chrishea
(Mandingo)			(Ebo)
			(Total 29)

The boys were:

Davie	Joe	Humphrey	Sampson
George	Frank		Total (6)

The girls were:

Clara (?)	Rose (Ebo)	Cynthia (Ebo)	Yara
Dinah	Silvia (Ebo)	Dido (Creole)	Sibbe
Ellin (Ebo)			(Total 9)

The children:

Male:

Coffee	Nague	Fortune	Nimine
Jasper	Robin	Jumper	Tom
			(Total 8)

Female:

Accubah	Quasheba	Jenny	Susanah
Franke	Dido		(Congo)

(Total 6)

On Friday 20th, Thistlewood 'gave the Negroes today', and himself went on a tour of inspection:

> 'a.m. Went in the fishing dory down the river to Hill, walked over the plantain walk, Negroes ground, etc.'

On Saturday 21st he continued:

> 'Walked to the young plantain walk at the Sandy Ground, was weary enough, such bad road & mosquitoes so thick. The Negroes employed cutting down the plantain trees and hoeing the cassava and potatoes at Hill.
> Quaco and Adam cutting down the other plantains in the little plantain walk.
> a.m. About eleven o'clock, *Cum* Ellin, an Ebo, by the morass side, *Sup. Terr.* toward the little plantain walk.'

And, on the same day, he dealt with the first accident to occur since his arrival. The boy Frank, tending cattle, was gored by a bull and had to be sent to Salt River for attention by Dr Horlock who was employed to attend to all Mr Dorrill's slaves. He remained there for three weeks.

On Monday 23rd, Thistlewood turned his attention to the cane-pieces. Next day he issued new hoes to Hector, Plymouth, Jimmy, Plato, George, Hazat, Teresa, Agnes, Margie, Yara, Big Mimber, Old Moll, Chrishea, Quasheba, Cynthia, Yabba, Mirtilla and Abigail. He also reported, but did not name, 'many sick'. That night Abigail ran off for a second time since the beginning of September and on the afternoon of the 25th, 'Little Mimber and Beneba wanting: They hide'. Perhaps he didn't know, but Little Mimber was then in the first months of pregnancy. At any rate, neither of them seems to have been punished. The work now being done was perhaps the hardest, though not the nastiest, of canefield work. The hoe was the tool used in preparing the land for planting – caneholes, to be dug row by row, acre by acre, in the blazing sun. Later, the bills would be distributed for the nastier task of stripping and cutting through the dust and the knife-edged blades on the matured cane stalks. The land now being holed and dunged was being planted with new canes for the 1753 crop. Until they began to reap the present crop in

January 1752 the work continued as before: hoeing, planting, and weeding canes, hoeing and planting provisions. Then as crop time drew nearer and the provision grounds came into bearing, efforts were turned to preparing estate roads and factory buildings for the tansporting of cane and the making of sugar. Additionally, there was hurricane damage to be mended. Some roofs needed to be re-thatched and, in the field, some canes and provision crops had to be replanted. Between Egypt and Salt River the Egypt messengers, Clara, Joe and Susanah, went back and forth carrying letters and small produce for the Salt River household and bringing back small items sent by Mrs Anderson or William (Billy) Mould, who was Mr Dorrill's store clerk. For the movement of heavier goods, the canoes were brought into use down river and along the coast eastwards to the Salt River barcadier.

On Thursday, 26th September, Abigail was brought home by Quacoo, who had been sent in search. On the 30th she was again away, as were Will and Jimmy. All three returned during the course of the following day. On the 5th October, Abigail, again, and Margie and Glasgow were 'wanting'. Plato and Quacoo were sent to find Abigail. They didn't, but she came back a month later, on 4th November. Thereafter, she settled down until early February.

On Friday 27th Chrishea took off, and Sam brought home his 'wife', Bella, who had gone off the day before. These, it would seem, were testing times; but the new overseer seems to have taken it all very calmly. No punishments were recorded. At Salt River, however, it was soon thought necessary to take action, and on 9th October Thistlewood recorded, as so often without comment, a vicious retaliatory act of warning:

'Received a letter from Mr Peter Fookes, and the boys Humphrey and Sampson; also Robin's head, who was hanged yesterday for running away with those two boys. Put it upon a pole and stuck it up just at the angle of the road in the home pasture.'

Presumably, they had been apprehended at, or near, Salt River, and Salt River Robin had been adjudged ringleader. Nonetheless, exactly a month later Humphrey again ran off, but he returned next day of his own accord.

The fact that Thistlewood recorded no punishments meted out by him to runaways is not evidence that he took no action against them. He was to prove himself a hard slave-master, but from the beginning he also showed a willingness, not uncommon among the Westmoreland planters, to protect 'his' slaves against any outsiders. On Friday, 27th September, he had noted:

'Messrs Jemmison and Mason call here a little before n Quarrel! They pretend to bring an order from John Filton the fishing dory, old canoe, he gave the Negro driver (Quashe), old seine he gave Phibbah [in charge of the great house kitchen], &c. I desired them get out of the plantation.'

At about the same time there arrived at Egypt a new employee.

'In the forenoon received a note from Billy Mould by Robert Robertson, who Mr Dorrill has hired as driver for here, the first Quarter at the rate of 20 pounds per annum. Wrote by him to Mr Dorrill. He brought bed, pillowcase and mosquito net or pavilion.'

Next afternoon, though Robert was apparently not well, for Thistlewood had received that morning 'by Clara' from Mrs Anderson, 'a vomit for Robert', he was taken down river to Hill 'to show [him] the place, and get plantain trash for his bed.'

Sundays, free of the more onerous plantation labours, were days of comparative relaxation and opportunity for visiting and passing the news. On Sunday, September 29th, there was news of a local uprising, apparently unsuccessful:

'Heard of a white man and the Negroes rising upon Capt. Leister. He afterwards told me the story himself.'

And, internationally, Mr Hudson a local planter, taking an account of all the whites and free people, by order of the Governor, explained that there was 'Said to be a great force both Marine & Land at Martinico, an invasion expected.'

At Egypt,

'In the morning, Doctor Gorse (usually called the little Dr) came here and dined at the Negro house with Phibbah.'

Phibbah, as we shall see, was a remarkable person. As manager of the Egypt cookhouse she was in frequent communication with Mrs Anderson at Salt River and with others in the surrounding countryside. In mid-November, for instance Thistlewood 'wrote to Mr John Jones, overseer at Quacoo Hill, for Phibbah.'

But Sunday, 29th September, was to become a memorable date for Mr Thistlewood for other more personal and painful reasons. Following his assault, al fresco, upon Ellin eight days before, he had taken Dido on several occasions and, on Sunday 29th, she stayed with him all night. Next day he:

'Perceived a small redness, but did not regard it
Tuesday, 1st October: Last night *Cum* Dido.

A greater redness, with soreness, and scalding water. About 9
a.m., a running begin, of a yellowish greenish matter.
Thursday 3rd: In the night painful erections, and sharp pricking,
great torment, forced to get up and walk about.
Tuesday 8th: Symptoms increase. Kernels swell on each side;
flying pains, &c. Breaking out on the thighs, etc. Loathsome
linens, &c. &c.
Wednesday 9th: Spoke to Dr Joseph Horlock. A rank
infection.'

His initiation into Jamaican eighteenth century plantation society
was now complete. On the next night Dr Horlock stayed at Egypt
and examined Dido, but there was 'Little perceptible.'
There followed weeks of painful treatment. On Tuesday, 26th
November he summed it up. On that day:

'. . . To Mr Joseph Horlock, for curing me of the Clap. £2 7s 6d
(yet am in some doubts if perfect). Was 44 days curing, from
11th of October to 23rd November in which time was blooded,
and took 24 mercurial pills (purging pills), 4 at a dose; 3 single
mercurial pills, and one dose öf 5 ditto. Also took many papers
of salts and cooling powders, a large gollypot of electuary, a
bottle of balsam drops, etc.; besides bathing the penis a long
time in new milk night and morning, rubbing with probes, and
syringing away above 2 phials of injection water.
Tuesday, 3rd December 1751: Last night *Cum* Jenny 111 in
me. lect. Wednesday 4th. Jenny continue with me *ad noctibus.*'

Having been taken three times on his bed on the Monday night, she
subsequently spent the nights with him. Then, Jenny and others
notwithstanding, another series of meetings with Dido.
Meantime, he had abandoned a sentimental reminder of an
English attachment:

'Sunday, 19th January 1752. Threw away the ivory fish given
me by E[lizabeth] M[itchell].'

Now, with an obviously increasing infatuation, he turned to Jenny
and there developed an affair which, with many quarrelsome inter-
ruptions, lasted until December 1753. He certainly did not confine
his attentions to her, but he took her as he had taken Marina on the
Vineyard Pen. Very early he had begun to shower her with gifts. On
15th December, 'some beads, &c.', on the 17th:

'For 2 yards of Brown Oznabrig, 4 bitts; 4 yards of striped
Holland, 8 bitts; and an handkerchief, 3 bitts. Give them all to
Jenny.

Friday, 8th May: Have within these few days given Jenn blue bordered coat, a plain blue d°, and a bordered zacca.'

Next day, John Filton, Thistlewood's predecessor on Egypt, and his Negro man, visited Egypt.

'Sunday 10th: Differ with Jenny for being concerned with John Filton's Negro man at the Negro house, &c. Also took away from her, her necklace, bordered coat, &c. – At night she in the cookroom with London.'

But on that night 'Jenny come again to me', and on the 16th he gave her back her beads and coat, etc. And so it continued, Jenny with him at nights, and, in the days, frequent side-steppings in different directions: Susanah, Big Mimber, Dido, and Belinda. But none of these was ever reprimanded for 'being concerned' with any other man, and none of them got gifts as Jenny did.

Thistlewood must have been one of Dr Horlock's last patients. In early February 1752, the doctor died after having over exerted himself when out shooting in the morass. Thistlewood had not abstained throughout the entire period of treatment. On Sunday, 10th November he had, for the first time, taken Nago Jenny. Then he returned to Dido until the end of that month, when again he turned to Jenny.

None of all that, however, kept him from overseeing the estate. On 1st November, he had ridden to Salt River in the forenoon, dined there, and then gone into the fields to see them plant – presumably for his own information as cane planting was in progress at Egypt.

On 3rd October, he had been able to unpack:

'Received a note from Wm Mould, by Quacoo, betimes in the morning, with a canoe in which came chest, case, &c. – also a barrel of pork, tierce of rice, barrel of rye flour, and 19 pound weight of biscuit.'

The rice was being served out to some of the slaves, certainly to some of the young. In mid-April 1752, he recorded: 'Gave over serving rice to Davie, Humphery, Sampson and Cynthia', and a few weeks later, on 1st June, he noted that Silvia and Nimine, two of 'the poorest Negroes' now got mackerel daily, as the rice was finished. Meantime, there had been supplies of provisions arriving, from time to time, from Salt River. On 11th October 1751, Salt River Caesar had arrived at Egypt with a bag of corn, but this was probably for planting, for three days later the slaves were planting corn in the Cow Pen piece. On the 16th, more corn arrived, 'about 70 weight ... shelled, bag included'. On the 24th:

> 'Received by the canoe, a dozen of bills, 3 barrels of mackerel, and one of flour – and a letter from Mr Fookes. Wrote to Mr Fookes, sent back in the canoe, stones, old gun, 3 new iron staples, 36 pieces of old iron, under the care of Pompey who came in the canoe.'

In November there arrived more corn, shelled, and rice in the ear.

The return cargoes were not always made up of stones and old iron. Clara, Joe and, less frequently, Susanah, were almost daily on the road to Salt River with crabs, fish, eggs, ducks and other wild fowl, fruit, and other Egypt produce for Mr Dorrill's table. The most important return cargo, however, was from the crop. On the 27th November 1751, for instance:

> 'Sent home the canoe to Salt River and by her 2 tierces of sugar & cask of rum, an empty butt, some lignum vitae wood[2], her load made up with stones. Wrote to Mr Dorrill.'

The sugar and rum were from the Egypt stores. The 1751/52 crop taking had not yet begun.

On 18th October, they began planting canes in land they had dunged at Top-hill on the 10th. On Monday 21st, they finished. Next day they were hoeing canes in the Old Scotch Grass piece. Hoeing and weeding continued until the end of the month, and more land was brought into use at Top-hill.

> 'Wednesday, 30th October: Planted corn at Top-hill, also cleared a place and planted peas, by some called clay-coloured peas, by others Spanish mulattoes, some few black eyes among them. Also planted my brother's samples of Charltons and Ormirots, but they never come up.'

On Friday, 1st November the slaves were given the day and Thistlewood and Robert:

> 'Went to Hill ... in the canoe, was all over the Negro grounds, canes over the bridge, &c. &c.'

On Monday, 11th November most hands were in the canefields:

> 'Employed hoeing canes. Finished them in a very slight manner, not half as they should be.'

And, at work in the coffee ground canepiece:

> 'Old Sybil, bit with a spider ... which makes her delirious, singing her country, &c. &c.'

Morris, Will, Plato, Dover and Roger were collecting mahoe bark, as they had been for some days, for rope-making. In the evening some were employed carrying trash into the cattle pen; at suppertime Thistlewood killed a black snake in his house, and, as he had been doing, 'continued taking the Electuary, &c.'

The stripping of bark for rope-making was a clear sign of the advent of crop taking. Now came another. On Wednesday, 13th November new bills were issued to Ambo, Plato, Nero, Adam, Cyrus, Jimmy, Port Royal, Humphrey, Sampson, Frank, George, Davie, Basheba, Yabba, Old Moll, Chrishea, Hannah, Lucy, Mirtilla, Margie, Bella, Jenny, Yara, and Cynthia. The day was spent in beginning to make a road to Hill and mending the road to the Sand Ground plantain walk.

Meantime, preparations were being made for the repair of estate buildings.

> 'Tuesday, 12th November: In the morning I borrowed Quashe's canoe off him, took Robert with me, and Quacoo and London to row.
>
> Went to the land between the river mouth and Savanna la Mar to look for thatch ... was at Hill, coming home saw a huge alligator swimming across the river. Got home just before noon.'

Of those at work on the 18th, Cudjoe was cutting withes and a large gang were cutting 'scotch grass such as sold at Savanna la Mar', tying it in one bitt' bundles, and loading it on to the canoe. By ten o'clock at night they had loaded 83 bundles.

> 'Tuesday 19th: Before day in the morning sent away the canoes. Cudjoe steers her, Morris, Dover, London, and Adam are the oarsmen. Sent a letter to Mr Dorrill of yesterday's date.
>
> Sent Nero, Will, 'Hector and George to the seaside to load the canoe back with thatch.
>
> Received canoe-load of thatch soon after noon. Sent the canoe away again loaded with 86 bundles.'

The next few days were similarly spent, sending out loads of grass (by Wednesday evening 340 bundles had been dispatched) and bringing in thatch which was immediately put to use.

> 'Friday 22nd [continued] thatching in the Millhouse. Some thatching, others getting withes to tie on the wattles, and others getting long thatch, vizt. the palmetto royal, for ridging, &c. &c. &c.'

Old Tom, the rope-maker, was also busy. Put to this work on Monday 25th he disappeared and was found by Thistlewood next day when he went by the hogstyes. On the 27th he began delivering rope, 30 feet per day 'as I ordered him.' On the 25th:

'Finished thatching the Mill-house. Put a shelter over the oven, and built a shelter for the horses. Repaired the thatch of the buttery, fowl-house, &c. &c. &c. Ground the Negroes axes and bills, &c. &c. Betty and Hagar wanting.'

The women were found and brought home next day by Quacoo. Prue, who had 'marched off' after breakfasttime on the 22nd was still out.

On the 27th came another indication of the near approach of the crop taking. They began 'cutting copper wood' which would be stored and used to fire the boiling house ovens. This labour continued almost daily and with increasing intensity. By mid-December carts and canoe were being used. Quacoo, London, Dover and Adam in the canoe, Cyrus, Roger, Davie and George leading the carts.

On Tuesday, 10th December Colonel Barclay called at Egypt.[3] He had come to tell Thistlewood that he:

'... was appointed surveyor of the highway, from the River Styx to his gate, equal to himself, and that I might take this for sufficient warning.'

On Thursday, 12th December penkeeper Cyrus brought in from Salt River, '6 draught steers, vizt. one spell of cattle.' A week later 3 more arrived. On the evening of the 12th the canoe was sent to Salt River for shingles and other materials for repair of the works. Two white carpenters and their 3 slave assistants sent from Salt River were soon joined by Cruddon and Frank, detailed by Thistlewood to work with them. A few days later Davie replaced Frank who seems to have been sent off to work with Cyrus the penkeeper.

As we shall see, Salt River where sugar was also produced, provided much technical assistance to Egypt. The establishment there as listed in August 1752, was much larger. A total slave force of over 200 included 3 coopers (Pompey, Moreland, Flanders); 3 carpenters (Sharper, Robin, Dorset); 2 masons (Isaac, Sampson); 2 blacksmiths (Charles, Hercules); 3 penkeepers (Cyrus and 2 boys); 3 fishermen (Dubbo, Jack and Quaw); and 3 drivers (Caesar, Oliver, and Peter). Of the whole force 62 were men, 37 were 'great boys', 15 were 'small boys', 71 were women, 10 were 'girls', and 16 were 'small girls'. Additionally, there was a considerable number of white supervisors and tradesmen, free and indentured, who were involved in the Dorrill brothers' various enterprises in the field, sugarworks, shipping and trade.

By Saturday evening, 21st December, 116 cartloads c perwood had been delivered by the boiling house. Thistlewoo that evening, inspected the sugar works:

'Saturday 21st: In the evening, *Cum* Susanah (a Congo Negro) Stans, in curing-house.'

On the 23rd, Joe was sent to Salt River with 100 oranges and a letter to Mrs Anderson who sent back '2 gollypots of salve for the Negroes.' In the evening, the canoe arrived with more boards, shingles, nails and other cargo. And, one way or another, Thistlewood received news that Mr Dorrill, just that day returned from a visit to Kingston, had bought another sloop.

Christmas Eve, Christmas Day, and Boxing Day, 1751:

'Tuesday ?4th: Received home 5 canoe loads of copperwood. Shot a diver in the great pond. A very hard shower this afternoon.

Employed raising the trash and weeding the plant-cane sprouts in the Stoop See piece. Also weeded our peas.

Had Yule cake tonight. Brought home at 4 cart loads about 8 bundles of scotch grass for to serve the cattle in the holidays.

Two draughts heading wood from the trench side to the stokehole.

Cruddon and Frank assisting the carpenters. Ambo and Cudjoe lopping fences. Old Tom brought home his five fathoms of rope as usual.

Lent Robert two pistoles, and gave him leave to go to Mr Williams's Savannah and see his wife.

Wednesday 25th: In the morning a pretty strong north, and coolish pleasant day at times cloudy with some drizzling rain.

Served a barrel of mackerel (384) amongst the Negroes. Also gave a pint of rum and some sugar to each Negro (the children excepted).

Thursday 26th: The Negroes drumming and dancing all night along.

A very fine morning. Went and dined at Salt River. In the evening came home. Mr Richard Pirot and his wife there, who are going to set up a school at Savanna la Mar, to be opened the 16th of January next.

At dinner had gooseberry tart. Today one of Mr Dorrill's sloops came in with 42 mules.

In the news is a long account of the flying engine, in shape of a bird, performed by quicksilver and wheels, managed by a person with a large tail fastened to his thighs, by a Jesuit 20 years in India.'

Following Christmas, hard labour was not resumed until Monday 30th. Then everyone was back at work: cutting the road to the Negro ground at Hill, previously begun but more recently given up for more pressing business and now to be completed on 2nd January; working on the fences; bringing in copperwood; making rope; and repairing the sugar works.

On the 31st, 'Came a white youth named Will to assist the carpenters' who, with their Salt River assistants, had not been allowed off work on the 27th and 28th. And:

'In the forenoon Morris cut himself badly with an axe in the leg. Sent him to Salt River.'

He returned on January 2nd, but it seems that he might not yet have fully mended for, a fortnight later, he was laid up with 'a swelled leg and foot.' He is next heard of on the 24th when he is employed steering the canoe.

The ceiba cotton trees were now in full bearing, and as 1752 opened Mirtilla and Beneba were sent around to gather it. From Hill they moved to Mulatto ground and Sand ground, gathering two baskets full each working day until mid-January.

'Saturday, 4th January 1752: Beneba and Mirtilla gathering cotton at Hill; in the evening received by them two baskets which they had gathered. Rest of the Negroes billing the home pastùre.
The white carpenters here, but would not work because Salt River Negroes have today.'

On Monday 6th, work on the high road maintenance began. Thistlewood, Robert and about 40 slaves from Egypt with two carts were involved daily until the evening of the 8th, when the work was done. Colonel Barclay had also been required to supply labour and had, it seems, spent some time supervising their work himself. This brought him into conversation with Thistlewood, and they seemed to get on quite well:

'Colonel Barclay says, put hog-plum tree bark in a pot to boil with water till strong; then place it over a gentle fire, & keep the feet in it as hot as can be bore for nine days and nights, and it will effectually cure the crab-yaws that he cures all his Negroes so.'

Thistlewood appears to have adopted the remedy for we are later told of 'crab-yawsy' Negroes being sent off to stay at Hill and 'steeping' their feet for several days.

On the 9th the slaves returned to complete billing the pasture. The carpenters who had received more nails and from Salt River, were at work in the still house. The bridges over the trenches in the canefield were mended. Old Tom, given his supply of mahoe bark in the morning, made no rope, he 'being out of order' on this day. Quacoo who had been put to watch the canes by the roadside when the roadwork began was still on that job. Thistlewood and Robert, before dinner, walked over the Congo ground; and, after dinner:

'... went to Hill in a canoe. Looking for the best place to build a lime-kiln.'

They located it, and next morning a gang of slaves was sent there to begin gathering stones for the building.

On 13th January Mr Dorrill sent one of his white tradesmen, Joseph Peter, with nine men to help with the work. On the 16th the job was done, the kiln was fired, and Peter and the men went back to Salt River.

On Thursday 16th, Old Tom brought in rope, as usual; but it was the last lot for the time being for the bark was finished. He now turned to making trash baskets. The rope was given out in preparation for the crop. The Egypt sugar mill was animal-driven.

'Saturday 18th: Delivered out to Quacoo, who is Boatswain of the mill 16 Trace ropes, 12 foot long each equals 32 fathoms. 4 Swingle Tree ropes, 10 foot long each, equals 6 fathoms, 4 feet [They were larger ropes, of 2 8/10 inches circumference] 16 Head or Casting ropes, 18 feet long each equals 46 fathoms, 4 feet 12 Cattle ropes (to the Cartmen) 15 feet each equals 28 fathoms, 2 feet [These were smaller, of 2 ½ inches circumference] ... Also examined the carts, chains, yokes, bows, collars, harness, coppanses, steps, ladles, skimmers, &c. &c.'

In addition, the cisterns in the still house, the boiling house and the curing house were tested and washed out.

For Thistlewood it had not been all work. On the 8th, 9th, 10th and 11th he had dined in company. On the first two occasions he had entertained Thomas Tomlinson, Jnr and Mr Deeble. On the 10th they had again sat at his table together with Mr Dorrill, his daughter Molly and Mrs Anderson from Salt River, Mr Pirot, the new schoolmaster and his wife, and Mr Lee, another Savanna la Mar merchant. On the 11th it was Tomlinson and Deeble again, with Mr Donaldson and his brother and a Captain Oswell. Thistlewood found them 'very good company.'

Mr Deeble had been to India. He knew Captain D'Abbadie, with whom Thistlewood had sailed a few years before, and he:

'. . . says he never was so elevated as he has been in India, with chewing crude opium, betel nut, &c. &c. Seemingly in paradise.'

He had also been in playful mood, to the annoyance of Mr Pirot. On the 10th:

'. . . Mr Tomlinson, Mr Deeble, Mr Lee, Miss Dorrill, Mrs Pirot and myself all in the Curing house, I showing them where Filton lay in the cistern during the hurricane. Mr Deeble took the opportunity to lock us up and throw the key out at the windows. At last, Mr Pirot came and opened the door for us, and swore he had good mind to blow out Mrs Pirot's brains for being with us. Silly mortal.'

Mr Pirot's school did not last long. In mid-April 1752, he and his wife left Jamaica for England. He came to Egypt to bid farewell, and Thistlewood showed him around and gave him parting gifts of cinnamon bark, cinnamon berries, and an alligator's egg shell.

On Monday 20th 'An old Negro man from Salt River, named Oliver' came to help with the sugar boiling, and Joe was sent there, from Egypt with 'a ladle, a skimmer, and a chain to mend.' Cruddon and Jimmy were dispatched to Hill to dig potatoes, and others gathered green peas and planted 'scratch toyer' in the garden. Quacoo was busy making collars for the draught mules, repairing the shingling on the cookroom of the great house, and doing sundry other 'needful jobs.' Salt River Quashe arrived with a canoe for lime. It was taken to Hill and loaded there; then with additional cargo of all the old lime taken out of storage in the boiling house and some pieces of still house equipment for repair, it was sent back to Salt River. The Egypt slaves who had helped load lime at Hill now each brought down 'a basket for temper' in the Egypt boiling house.

On Saturday 25th, Quacoo and Port Royal were sent to Salt River for mules. They brought some, '. . . but not half enough.' Most of the others were:

'Employed cutting canes towards Dunbar ground. Cut a little piece we call the corner piece, and began another we called the Dogwood tree piece, from dogwood tree growing on it. *(Both plants, though very poor). I say called, because none of their cane pieces here have names, so that it is hard to distinguish one from another in discourse therefore gave them names. Received home 7 loads of cane, and 6 loads of tops for the cattle and mules.'

Crop taking had begun:

> 'Monday, 27th January.   Came a Negro man from Salt River (named Caesar) to be Boatswain of the Mill. Received some more mules, which with those brought on Saturday make the number 36, and the 3 we had before that always go here, equals 39; 5 spells, wanting one.
> This morning put the mill about (about 7 in the morning) but for want of cane stopped again in the evening; because for want of cattle we had but two carts leading home canes and cane-tops too!'.

Salt River Caesar had come not to replace Quacoo, but to spell with him in the mill house. Salt River Oliver, and York who was to join him, would be in the boiling house where the most careful supervision was required; and in the field Quashe would be the supervisory slave driver.

At the beginning of the next week cane grinding continued:

> 'Monday, 3rd February: This morning Old Oliver come again and brings a Negro man named York, to assist in the boiling house, a Grande Copper man.
> In the forenoon, cutting cane in the Breadnut Tree piece, which are old Rattoons;[4] but how old Quashe can't remember, they are now very indifferent, and yield but little liquor.
> 27 cutters in the field
> p.m. Put the mill about.
> Rest of the hands cutting in Coffee Ground Pass piece, and but 20 cutters in the field. About midnight but about 2 loads of cane left, therefore stopped the mill, having ground off 4 coppers of liquor, and potted 2 pots of sugar.
> A great piece of work indeed.
> Three draughts leading home canes & cane tops.'

The next day was a little better. The mill was put about at about 6 a.m. and stopped at about 7 p.m. for want of canes; but they had ground off 5 coppers of liquor and made 16 pots of sugar. The cutters had been:

> 'Employed cutting cane in the Breadnut Treepiece, 20 cutters in the field, and some tiers, and our old and cripple Negroes tying cane tops. Three draught leading home cane and cane tops. It is usual to allow four tiers to 16 cutters, or what is all the same one tier to four cutters, but that is not enough.
> The mule Lucy wanting. Quacoo and Joe seeking her.
> Heard that Colin Campbell Esqr. near Black River died a week or ten days ago. He was sometimes called Counsellor Campbell,

but more often little Colin Campbell, to distinguish him from another of the same name, who lives towards the west end and is usually called long Colin Campbell.'

February was a bad month for illness. The 'northers' were not apparently to be blamed this time, for Thistlewood makes no mention of cold weather, and most of the complaints were abdominal. On Friday 7th, Prue had spent the day at Salt River, sick.

On Thursday 13th, Betty, who had been there for a few days returned saying she was now well. On the next day:

> 'Big Mimber, Old Sibyl, Jimmy, George, and Sampson, all laid up of the belly-ache. Little Mimber and Mirtilla of pains, and Morris of a swelled leg and foot.'

Little Mimber, as we know, was a special case. In mid-March she was down again and said to be '... very ill. Likely to miscarry.' Then, on 22nd February, the girl Lucy fell ill and was sent to Salt River.

There were also two accidents. On Thursday 22nd, Dinah fell going into the curing house and 'displaced' her collar-bone. On the 27th, more seriously:

> 'In the forenoon, the boy Frank let the cattle which he was leading strike him, trample, and the loaded cart which ran over him. He seems much hurt. At noon wrote to Mr Dorrill, and sent him to Salt River on a mule, by Plato.'

Frank seems to have been accident prone. He remained there until the 15th March. On the day before his accident the newly appointed doctor had visited Egypt.

> 'Received a letter from Fookes by one Dr McIntosh, who Mr Dorrill has hired to look after his sick & lame Negroes.'

McIntosh succeeded Dr Horlock who had died in the first week of the month. He dined with Thistlewood 'on yam and salt beef.'

Dr McIntosh visited Egypt six times more before the end of May at intervals of approximately three weeks; but he was called on by letters requesting assistance, for example on:

> 'Tuesday, 17th March: Received by Joe, a letter of yesterdays date from Mr Charles McIntosh, with six vomits, and a phial of liquid laudanum.'

And he borrowed Thistlewood's books. In early April 'lent him Voltaire on the English Nation,' and in late May 'Dr McIntosh here; returned my Petronius.'

'Sunday, 9th February: Had cane tops had home for the mules & cattle, morning and night.

In the morning gave the drivers a bottle of low wines, the Boatswains of the Mill a bottle between them, the 2 head boilers a bottle, the other boilers a bottle, the two potters a bottle, and the stokers a bottle, and some to the cart men.

In the morning I rode over to Salt River and dined there, then home. Strange confusion there, proceeding from bad management, &c. Simms the sugar boiler at Salt River. Above 20 people dine in the hall.'

On Monday 17th Adam and Frank, who had tended the mules and cattle the day before, were 'given leave to go to their ground', and the mules were turned into the recently cut canepieces:

'To fill their bellies in the intervals, ponds, &c. and with the cane-tops. Quacoo 3 boys looking after them.'

The next day Mr Dorrill 'came into the field, &c. &c.' They completed cutting in Potato piece, finished Breadnut piece, and began to cut Marlpit piece. 'Thirty cutters out. Three draughts at work.' Not all the ripe canes would be cut. Some, the first ratoons in three selected canepieces, would be left to provide plants for later in the year. Not all the field slaves could be put into the canepieces every day. There were other occasional labours such as building a shelter at Hill to cover the white lime taken from the kiln.

Robert Robertson and Thistlewood shared spells in the boiling house at nights.

Wednesday, 26th February was Thistlewood's turn, 'All night.' Robert, on his night off was entertaining: 'Dido in R . . . t's house very late, &c. &c.' Next day he noted his dissatisfaction with the crop taking so far that week:

'. . . towards morning, the canes done, cooled the teache with water. Have made since we put about but 20 pots of sugar; so slowly do we go for want of hands, and the badness of the canes together,'

The month of February had carried instances of slave resistance. On the 22nd for unstated reason: 'Broke my English oak stick over London.' And two more fully recorded occasions:

'Wednesday 26th: In the morning seized Sancho by the curing house door, but after a long struggle he slipped off his jacket and made his escape from me. I called for assistance but none came till too late. He got over the river in the fishing dory and went to Salt River. Mr Dorrill gave him a good whipping, and sent him home under the care of Caesar, desiring I would turn him into the field, which I am very glad of, as he is a notorious villain. Reprimanded Robert for not coming to my assistance; and ordered Cyrus to be whipped upon that account, but he runaway.'

Sancho's 'villainous' acts, such as they might have been, were not, however recorded. All we know is that he was the Egypt fisherman, had recently been supplying Thistlewood with some 'very fine' snook, and was soon to discover that he was being cuckolded:

'Monday, 16th March: Sancho found Morris sleeping with Quasheba his wife; complain to me; I advise them to part, which they accordingly did.'

But, on Saturday, 7th April 'Morris & Quasheba quarrell.' Sancho, relieved of his woman, seems also to have been relieved of field-work and put to work in the curing house and with the canoe.

There had also been the comings and goings of whites. On Sunday, 16th February, Andrew Miller who had been Mr Vassall's cattle drover, came to visit Thistlewood. He had left Mr Vassall and now worked for Mr Paul Stevens. He came again on several occasions.

On Monday, 2nd March, nine additional men were sent from Salt River to help with the crop. Thistlewood was able to put 34 cutters in the field even though Will and George, who had tended livestock the day before, had the afternoon off.

On the 4th they knocked out their first sugar: 20 pots yielding two tierces, 'but not perfectly cured yet.' Nonetheless, that afternoon the first shipment was made. Two kegs of rum to Salt River and the two tierces of sugar, delivered on order to Captain Beauchamp. On the 8th, a Sunday:

'Carpenter Robin came here, to put our Mill a little to rights, vizt. Fastened her main roller cap-piece, made some new pointers, &c.'

On Wednesday, 11th March, Thistlewood set out the occupations of the slaves in greater detail than usual. There were many absent from work.

'Employed cutting canes as before, 10 cutters in the field, 3 carts and the canoe employed.
Old Tom and Ambo distilling low wines. Little Mimber, Yabba,

Teresa, Jenny, Chrishea, Old Catalina and Ellin all sick at home. London and Frank sick at Salt River, besides Hagar, Mary, Silvia, Rose, Sibbe, Achilles, Titus, Hannibal. Also, Celia at the hogstyes disabled. Basheba at Town lying. Cudjoe, Old Sharper, Adam, and Nero in the boiling house. Dickson and Plymouth stokers. Quacoo, boatswain of the mill. Quasheba, feeder. Old Sibyl, turner. Hanah and Violet, trash carriers Mirtilla and Lucy, cane carriers. 3 hands in the canoe. 6 hands with the carts. 4 watchmen, 3 watchwomen. Abraham looks after cattle. Phibbah, Dido, Susanah and Nague about the house. Cruddon, Joe, Coffee, &c. &c. drive the mules. Nimini clear the gutters, &c. &c. Rest tying cane, cane tops, and cutting cane.'

Soon there were to be alarms in both factory and field. On Sunday 15th:

'This morning all the water ran out of the 2nd copper. Examined it, found a hole about as long as a sixpence just by the nails sitting in the bottom. Stopped it with a plaster made of wheat-flour and white of an egg made into paste, and spread upon a bit of oznabrig. Stopped in the inside.'

And in the field, about a week later:

'Saturday, 21st March: In the afternoon found 10 or 12 Negro men and women in the coffee Tree Piece, Paradise, stealing rum canes [which had been cut and left for collection later]. Could not catch any of them ... Went to Mrs Hall's and acquainted her about her Negroes. One fell into my hands, says he belongs to Cunningham. Had him choicely whipped. Was about the canepieces and ponds, with my gun, till past midnight, but shot nothing.'

Salt River Ned, the gardener there, '... a white man, but a poor helpless creature' arrived at Egypt one evening:

'He is sent by his master to Orange Bay, to look for a white man, a cabinet-maker, indented servant to Mr Dorrill, who runaway night before last.'

And at Salt River a slave woman lost an arm, ground off in the mill there. On Thursday 19th:

> 'This morning Old Tom Williams called, and made his observations as usual; he once killed a Negro girl of his own that had got looseness, stopping her A – with a corn-stick. And one of the girls cleaning the hall when he thought it did not much want it he shit in it and told her there was something for her to clean. Frequently at home wears nothing but a shirt, and fans himself with the forelap before his daughter, &c. &c.'

And, on 28th March, for what no doubt were much less nasty offences 'Had Quacoo whipped, for several misdemeanours, &c. &c.' Monday 30th was Easter Monday, so 'the Negroes have it holiday.' On the 31st, four more men came from Salt River as cane cutters; and 'In the afternoon, the Negroes being wet, gave each of them a dram in the field.'

The crop taking was now drawing to a close. The cane cutting would be the first operation to come to an end.

> 'Tuesday, 7th April: About 4 in the afternoon finished cutting the Milkwood piece, and as Mr Dorrill thinks we have enough saved for plants before, began to cut off that bit we saved in the Pimento Tree piece.'

By Friday 10th, all cane cutting was over, the last loads in being 'rum canes' to be used for making rum. They had been cut before and left covered in the field.

> 'Friday 10th. Finished gathering rum canes by about 9 in the morning, and ground them all off before noon. Had some tops lead home. Knocked out 31 pots of sugar, which added to the 132 knocked out yesterday equals 163 pots, which have filled the 10 old molasses hogheads and one new tierce. Not quite 15 to a tierce.
> Old Tom and Ambo distilling rum, put 10 small jars into the butt in the curing house.'

About a month before they had bottled 16 quarts of cane juice vinegar and he had noted the size of the rum jars. The small jars took 15 gallons, the large jars took 35, and the capacity of the still was about 140 gallons. That quantity of proof rum, he observed would 'commonly yield 50 or 60 gallons of rum.' But, to return to the business of Friday, 10th April:

> 'Sent Morris to the Sand Ground for cassava, took up 7 roots. Mended the fence around the canepieces, Paradise. Cleaned

out the mill house – heaped up the copper wood.
Made a fence around the horse stable &c. &c.
Last night finished boiling sugar and cooled the coppers with water.
Have made 32 pots, so that the whole produce in sugar stands thus:

1st Week 93	6th Week 71	11th week 32
2nd Week 53	7th Week 84	
3rd Week 56	8th Week 69	
4th Week 65	9th Week 66	
5th Week 42	10th Week 59	
	(Total = 690 pots)	

The whole crop finished in the eleventh week, by 1,189 cutters, in 63 days, which gives 17 ^{18}/63 per day.
If 25 of our pots may be accounted a hogshead, we have made 27 hogsheads and 15 pots over.
In the afternoon sent home by Quacoo, Achilles, Humphrey & Eve 37 mules. Wrote to Mr Dorrill. Keep 2 mules here.'

The same night, the canoe returned from Salt River. It contained:

'. . . a barrel of beef, firkin of butter, barrel of salt, and 4 barrels of mackerel for the Negroes; also 2 shovels and a basket of clay.'

There would be several other deliveries of clay, to be used in claying, or refining, some of the sugar. The same evening Thistlewood:

'Served the Negroes 15 quarts of rum out of the butt a filling in the curing house, and 2 large bottoms of sugar to make them merry, now crop over.'

And, for himself:

'Note: began upon both the beef and butter directly, having none left,'

And, with less pleasure:

'Perceived a whitish matter to appear, though very slowly.'

Gradually the work moved away from the 'works' back into the fields and pastures.

'Tuesday, 14th April: Set Dickson and 4 more hands to help him build a hut, so large as may shelter all the Negroes from a shower of rain. Laid it out, and put up the frame myself, about 18 feet long, 10 broad, 6 ½ or 7 high, &c. &c.'

It had not been a rewarding crop. Not surprisingly, Mr Dorrill decided that Egypt was better suited for the production of things other than sugar. He summoned Thistlewood.

'Tuesday, 2nd June: In the morning went to Salt River, got there about ½ past 7 a.m. Mr Dorrill down at the barcadier. Went to him, and rode over Bowen's plantation with him. He showed me the canes, pasture, &c. &c. there, and told me that he would take the Negroes from Egypt so soon as we had done weeding the canes, for he would make a pen of it, and put them upon Bowen's and that I was to be their overseer there, &c. &c. Was at Mr Richard Bowen's, he at home and his brother Joe with him.'

On the 21st, returning from a visit to Salt River, Robertson was accompanied by 'one Thomas Christy − a Scotchman' who was to live on Egypt and take care of the property 'as soon as the Negroes are moved off.'

'Wednesday 24th: In the morning put 3 mahogany planks in the canoe, my chests, &c. &c. all the Negroes' hoes, bills, axes, provisions, above 20 cripple Negroes, & pickanninnies, &c. &c.'

The able-bodied went by road. Plato, who had complained of being sick and 'absconded' on the morning of Friday 19th, had come home just in time, on the 23rd.

'Set out about ½ past 6 a.m. ... when we got to Salt River, Mr Dorrill and Mrs Anderson at Mr Bowen's which is named Paradise! Proceeded on thither with the Negroes; got there about 10 a.m. He immediately put them to clear a piece of ground to build huts upon.'

Left at Egypt were Old Sharper and Celia, Daniel and Old Phibbah, Tony, Dickson, Glasgow, Old Sarah, Sam, Cudjoe, Phibbah, Abraham, Accubah, Susanah, Nahon, Coffee, Teresa and her children, and Salt River Eve to look after her.

Notes

1 On a first sexual encounter with a slave Thistlewood usually, but not always, mentioned her ethnic group. Where he did not do so I have placed a question mark.
2 Lignum vitae wood was much used in the preparation of medicinal beverages, and was considered to be effective against the 'Clap'.

3 The owner of neighbouring estates, Long Pond and Kirkpatrick Pen. He was later to marry the widow, Mary Hall, at Old Hope. He was then Custos Rotulorum of Westmoreland, that is head of the magistracy and chief civil officer.

4 As distinct from 'plant canes' from newly planted joints, ratoon canes are new shoots from the roots of a previously reaped crop. On some estates ratooning was practised for up to 15 successive years. It saved labour, but the successive yields per acre would decline.

CHAPTER 3   Notes on plantation life: 1752–1754

Introduction

Here we learn something of what life was like, for slaves and for free persons, in the height of the sugar-slave society. Thistlewood records the actions of others who, like himself, took slave women in lasting 'man-wife' relationships, and others still more numerous, whose relationships were obviously more exploitive.

As one would expect, there was resistance. Slave women occasionally braved resistance to the sexual demands of their masters, and were usually punished for their 'impudence'. Slave men sometimes made clear their disapproval of the masters' assaults on slave women. Quashe, the Egypt slave driver, more than once made threatening remarks occasioned by Thistlewood's favouring Jenny with gifts and lighter tasks. Individual slaves assaulted their masters, sometimes in offensive attack, sometimes in self-defence against assault. Usually they suffered dire consequences, but not always.

But the challenges of individual slaves, though often personally dangerous to the master, were, in general, symptoms of a wider resistance which only rumbled under cover until such times as a leader, with a plan and an ability to recruit and to organise the disaffected, rose into action. And, constantly on the road, as Thistlewood records, were the Maroons, in search of runaways, insurgents, and prize-money.

Also on the road, especially following the closure of a crop-season, were a surprising number of whites (European and Creole) in search of employment. Some, like John Filton before Thistlewood, had been fired by their employers. Others, like Thistlewood himself, had severed connections in order to move in search of a better livelihood. As they moved they visited the estates they passed, sometimes finding a welcome beyond a meal because they brought good company and conversation to break the daily round.

But there were other forms of entertainment and relaxation. Thistlewood tells of shopping in Savanna la Mar, visiting neighbours, exchanging news and gossip with others in the Taverns, and of course, welcoming the ships as they arrived in port with goods and

letters, and passengers and crew with the latest news and fashic
from abroad.

And, for Thistlewood now, there was the end of his affair with
Jenny and his taking Phibbah who was to be his 'wife'.

Until December 1752, the Egypt slaves laboured on Paradise. They
began by settling in.

> 'Thursday, 25 June 1752: Was in the field betimes. Salt River
> Negroes weeding canes, loading manure [presumably in cart-
> loads], &c. Paradise Negroes clearing ground to build huts,
> some of Salt River Negroes here cutting fences, &c. White
> Peter (usually called Irish Peter) lopping fences with the
> Negroes.'

On Saturday afternoon, having nearly completed the building, the
Paradise Negroes '. . . went for Egypt everyone except Big Mimber.'
That still was home and that was where some of their children and
their provision grounds were. On Monday morning they were back
at Paradise. Later in the week, Thistlewood located 'Bowen's old
Negro ground' in the bushy backlands. It had 'plantains enough,
and a good soil.' On Saturday 11th the land was shared out between
the Paradise slaves: 'enough and to spare.'

And so the labour continued, at Salt River weeding canes, at
Paradise cleaning pastures and grounds and cutting fences. Thistlewood was overseeing both properties, with Robert Robertson as his
assistant on Paradise, while Thomas Christy supervised the limited
activity at Egypt.

By the end of July the cleaning, trenching and fencing, with
logwood, of the Blue Hole plantain walk was done. On the 30th:

> 'Employed lopping the fence against Blue Hole plantain walk.
> Finished it. This is a prodigious large plantain walk of above 60
> acres, and taking in the Negroes ground far above an hundred.'

A couple of days before, while supervising a party hoeing about the
house at Blue Hole, Thistlewood had met

> '. . . Mulatto Dick belonging to Florentius Vassall. Had some
> discourse with him about the Vineyard, &c.'[1]

A week later, he rode to Sweet River to buy some rum for himself,
and 'saw Marina, and many of the Vineyard Negroes.' He made no
further comment. At Egypt he had taken Nago Jenny into his house
and was involved with her until the end of 1753 when they finally
parted and he began his life with Phibbah. However, he was now 'in
sad pain with the buboes.'

There had been more difference of opinion with Mr Dorrill than was explicitly recorded, for on:

'Tuesday, 11th August 1752:   This morning Mr Dorrill sent for me, and told me as he heard I was unsatisfied in his service he did not desire me to stay against my will, which I gladly yielded to. He said he did not turn me away, but that I turned myself away. He ordered Mr Fookes to remark that my wages ceased today, which Fookes willingly would. Rode over to Paradise, acquainted Robert, &c. got my horse and brought him to Salt River. Gave Quamina a pair of old breeches. In the evening sent Robert, by George, 4 quart bottles of rum. Hercules made me a staple and hasp for my book chest, put a padlock on it, got all things in readiness, &c.'

Next morning, having locked up his things in the house he had occupied and given the key to Billy Mould, he:

'Set out on my horse for Egypt, by Mr Dorrill's approbation, having orders to look over Tom. Breakfasted with Mr Mordiner at the Bridge. Also dined with him there on stewed turtle.'[2]

He intended 'to stay at Egypt till I perfectly recover my health.' Clearly Mr Dorrill did not want to be rid of him.

In these last months of 1752 and the first of 1753 there were the usual comings and goings of visitors to Egypt.

'Wednesday, 1st November 1752 p.m: called here a man (a distiller) servant to Captain Forsyth, just came from the Vineyard; gave him punch, &c. He says Mr Bennett, at Rowe's barcadier at Black River is dead.
Tuesday, 12th December: . . . Mr Mordiner and Carpenter George, who now works with him, called to see me.
Mr Mordiner has been purchasing Quasheba [a Salt River slave]. He gives for her, two new Negroes cost him 48 pounds each, beside duty. He paid 14 pounds per annum for her: he paid in ready cash for her and his two children about 166 pounds — besides what they have cost him in victuals, clothes, etc.'

One morning in mid-November Thistlewood rode into Savanna la Mar to see Mr Storer but he was out. So he went and sat with Mr Barnett, the schoolmaster, for a couple of hours before going home to Egypt. Then on the way:

'. . . overtook a white young woman (riding), she said, to Jacob Allen's. She says she was born at Hull, brought up at

Louth, knows Bucknall very well, having been several times at Mr Dobb's; Knows my brother, cousin Nanny Longstaff, &c. Gave her an invitation to Egypt to rest and refresh herself. She went with me, and stayed an hour or more, I rode to the end of the estate with her. Mary Holmes.'

No particular interest in the young lady was recorded, but she seems to have enjoyed his company, for two months later she sought him out.

'Friday, 19th January 1753: Miss Mary Holmes called to see me. She is going down to the Bay.'

And that, apparently, was as far as it went. The year 1752 was however, to move to a climactic end.

On Sunday, 3rd December, Thistlewood, at the Styx Bridge, found men belonging to Thomas Williams and Colonel Barclay fishing. He confiscated fish, baskets, a fishing net and a line, a knife, some tobacco, and two pairs of breeches. He drove the men off, left the net in the care of Tony in his watch hut, and took the other goods back to Egypt yard and distributed them between Salt River Flora (the knife), Old Catalina (the tobacco), Achilles (a pair of breeches and some fish), Sampson (breeches), Phibbah (a basket), and 'gave the fish to the rest and only kept for myself one basket, the line and 8 tarpons.' But when he sent back to Tony's hut for the net, he learnt that Tony had given it back to Colonel Barclay's men.

'Monday, 4th December 1752. Rode over the estate. Brought over Tony and had him whipped for yesterday's work. In coming home he threw himself into the water by the Styx bridge, and so run into the morass. I stripped and followed him, but was forced to knock him down when I came at him, for he threatened me with his stick he had in his hand; but with much to do I tied his hands behind him and got him home.'

On Saturday, 16th December, Quashe brought word from Salt River that Thistlewood should '... keep 40 hands, and take care the drivers don't cut and slash the Negroes.'

Mr Dorrill had decided that the canes on Egypt should be harvested. Thistlewood was to take charge with John Russell newly employed as his assistant. He picked out 41 of the original Egypt hands, 22 men and boys (including Quashe, the driver) and 19 women and girls (including Jenny). His other current favourite, Susanah, had not been sent to Paradise; nor, or course, had Phibbah, with whom he was later to be involved. Monday morning they began to cut copper wood and the preparations for crop taking began.

Christmas 1752 was spent in the usual fashion with entertainment at Salt River and elsewhere.

> 'Tuesday, 26th December: Mr Dorrill says, by a very good computation, the Negroes in this Parish lay out near 20 thousand pounds per annum.[3]
> Wednesday 27th: At Home most part of the day, in expectation of Mr Emetson and Mr Groves, who promised to come see me.'

They did not arrive, and following his disappointment, Thistlewood went for a walk. He strolled into a struggle:

> 'In the evening, walked to Tony's gate, &c. Killed a black snake by the Styx bridge. Thence walked towards Paradise canepieces, but a little before I got to Cabritto bridge, just at the small causeway end in the little morass (about sunset) met Congo Sam, who has been runaway since the 2nd Instant. Attempting to take him, he immediately struck at me with a backed bill he had in his hand, and repeated his chops with all vehemence, driving me back into the morass towards the river 25 or 30 yards from the road, but through the great mercy of God, his blows either fell short of me or were warded off with a pimento stick I had in my hand, with which I sometimes got a good stroke at him. And although he let on my jacket several times yet, as pleased God, I received no harm; the bill being new was not very sharp. But what the most showed his intention was when I kept him off with my stick saying, "You villain, runaway, away with you, &c.," he answered in the Negro manner, "I will kill you, I will kill you now, &c." and came upon me with greater vigour. I called out, Murder, and help for God's sake, very loud, but no assistance came, so that I had no prospect but to lose my life, till I threw myself at him and fortunately seized hold of the blade of the bill. (Since he made the first chop at me, to this time, might be 5 or 6 minutes). He kept fast hold of the stock or handle. I endeavoured to draw him into the road; he went readily, but would not go homewards. We went in this manner over Cabritto bridge, till we came against the watch-hut then he would go no further. Bella and Abigail there, but would not assist me. (He spoke to them in his language and I was much afraid of them). We might stand against the hut 6 or 8 minutes, nobody came. At last, he suddenly quitted his hold and threw himself into the river. I, being possessed of the bill, leaped in after him, made 3 or 4 chops at him, and the bill flew out of my hand into the water.

He endeavouring to get it, I enclosed him, and a stake
arms, resolving to keep my hold, (up to the breeches wɛ
in water). 5 Negro men, and 3 women, strangers, went ᴄ.ᴠ. ....
bridge and would by no means assist me, neither for threats nor
promises; one saying he was sick, the others that they were in a
hurry. After we had stood in this manner maybe 8 or 10
minutes, London came and assisted me; tied his hands behind
him with my handkerchief; but whilst I was seeking my stick in
the morass, which I quitted when I seized hold of the blade of
the bill, London, having a load of provisions on his head, Sam
got away into the bushes, where he by some means had his hands
loosed, and lost my handkerchief. Presently, London called out
that Sam had seized his machete and would kill him. Two
gentlemen being just rode by towards the bridge, I ran after
them and begged their assistance, being afraid to continue into
the bush, for it now began to be pretty dark. They went back
on the road with me, [London . . .] I secured his hands with my
garters, took [him prisoner] guarded him home, put him safe in
irons [and a] watch put over him.'

That night he sought solace '*cum* Jenny', but there was much in his
head.

'Note: last Friday, in the field, Quashe told me (before all the
Negroes) that I should not eat much more meat here! I, asking
him if he meant to poison or murder me, after a pause he
replied, neither, but he intended to invent some great lie and
go and tell his master, to get me turned away, etc. etc. Am also
of an opinion that London had no good intent when in the bush
with Sam, if he had not heard company coming with me.
Titus with great reason may also be suspected.
Have also reason to believe that many of the Negroes, as
Quashe, Ambo, Phibbah &c. knew that Sam had an intent to
murder me when we should meet, by what I heard them speak
one day in the cookroom when I was in the back piazza
reading.'

Next morning, with Sam guarded by London, Thistlewood went to
make report to Mr Dorrill. Sam was secured, handcuffed, and
thrown in the dungeon. Later in the day, Thistlewood laid charges
against him before Colonel Ricketts and Mr Lewis. He was told to
have Sam at Mr William Cook's at eight o'clock next morning,
Friday. There, Sam was charged and sent to gaol to await trial. At
Egypt, meantime, Abigail and Bella were given 100 lashes each.
They then ran away and Plato was sent in search; but they had gone

only as far as Salt River, to complain, and returned about mid-day, Saturday. It must now have seemed to Thistlewood that there was no doubt that Congo Sam would be convicted.

When he was warned to be in Savanna la Mar on Saturday, 6th January for Sam's trial he summoned London, whose evidence would be required.

'Friday, 5th January: At night London refuses to go with me to Sam's trial: told me he would not go.'

And he didn't. Sam was acquitted.

'Saturday, 6th January: Was down at Savanna la Mar. Mr Lewis, Col Barclay, and Mr Stone try Sam. (Old women). Tuesday, 20th March 1753:   About 7 at night Mr Paul Stevens & Thomas Adams, going to tear Old Sarah to pieces in her hut. Had a quarrel with them. Note, they both drunk.
Monday 26th: Guy, belonging to the Vineyard, a Negro, called here today.
Sunday 8th April: The Captain of Mr Dorrill's new sloop called. Lent him a mule to ride to Mr Crawford's. Came back, dined with me.
Tuesday 17th: Wrote to Mr Dorrill & sent over Quashe very ill of the toothache. In the evening he returned.
Saturday 21st: Am forced to give Celia a weekly allowance of 3 old wives & a bunch of plantains.
"A nut more", an expression used by sugar-boilers when scarce boiled enough − Imagining a string of nuts. Old Simms.
Sunday 22nd: Dined at Mr Mordiner's; Captain Hartley, Mr Baker, &c. there. Quasheba big, she dined with us.
Last night about 10 p.m. Miss Molly Dorrill married to young Mr Cope, Mr Cope's son of Strathbogie (Captain of a London ship), by parson Harris of St Elizabeth. Much doubt if true, but believe will be.'

It was not yet true. John Cope, Jnr, at the time in his early twenties, was however, courting Molly Dorrill who was 'just turned 16.'

'Wednesday 25th: This morning Doctor Cutting called. I rode with him past Mrs Hall's and took leave, he going to Guinea again, (Rhode Island ship, Wilson).
Salt River Guy acted [..?.] his Obia, &c. with singing, dancing, &c. odd enough.
Thursday 26th: 3 Wild Negro men (one of them Capt. Cuffee's son) and a woman, belonging to Cudjoe's town, called to beg refreshment and lodging. Gave them about a quart of rum, a

bottom of sugar, and 8 mackerel, and leave to stay in the plantation all night.'

On Friday, 11th May Thistlewood went to Savanna la Mar to exercise with the militia. The roll was called and the men discharged until Friday, 15th June.

It was now cropover. On Thursday, 17th May news came that the slaves were once again to be transferred to Bowen's (Paradise). Thistlewood recorded:

'The Negroes one and all declare they will not move to Bowen's except I go with them to take care of them. They are instigated to it by Philip for certain ends.'

Perhaps Philip Gudgeon, who had succeeded John Russell, thought that if Thistlewood went to Bowen's he would succeed at Egypt. Thistlewood does not say. Philip was himself recalled to Salt River on 21st May; the Negroes were to go to Bowen's in mid-July, and Thistlewood remained, unsettled, at Egypt. On Thursday, 24th May, in the morning:

'Met Col Cudjoe just by the Styx Bridge. Shook him by the hand. He was afoot, several other Wild Negroes with him. Had on a beaver, feathered, and a large medal hung to chain about his neck.'

On Monday 28th he eventually caught up with Mr Thomas Storer at his house in Savanna la Mar, and was 'well received', but there was, it seems, no further mention of a small sugar works Mr Storer had 'been about purchasing' in the previous November. It was a bad time to be job-hunting. The crop season now being generally over, there were many on the roads seeking employment for the next crop year. When Thistlewood got home from Mr Storer's:

'One William Ward, born at Dublin, wanting an overseer's place, called and dined here. Says about a fortnight ago our Negroes sold 2 pistoles worth of land turtle; that William Slater, distiller, has but one stone, now playing at Bo Peep in Thomas William's plantain walk, &c.

Tuesday, 29th May: This morning Quashe beat Morris in a very bad manner in the field with his whip, &c. He went to Salt River. So did I & Morris, (put Quacoo for driver) Had him given 100 lashes & put in the dungeon.

Thursday, 7th June: Today being a Fast, in remembrance of the great Earthquake, 1692, gave it the Negroes.

Friday 8th: Big Mimber, Little Mimber, Quasheba, Hannah, Yara, Beneba, Yabba, Joe, Teresa, Margie, Rose, & Ellin who

is at Hill [with Yaws] = 12 all sick & home, not at work.
Thursday 14th:　After dinner had Prue & Clara whipped for
going to Salt River last night and pretending sick today.'

As the work went on he observed the birds:

'Cling clings (as the Negro pickanninnies call them) or Barbadoes
black birds have tails stand open down, like a ship's rudder,
very odd.
Thursday 28th June p.m.:　Wrote to Mr Dorrill and sent
Plymouth over to Salt River sick of the foul disease (by Plato),
and above 300 lignum vitae seeds.
In the evening the overseers of Quacoo Hill & of Retrieve
called and drink some punch with me. Looking for above a
score of Negroes that today left Quacoo Hill (Dewsberry) in a
body, going to complain against the overseer to Major Clarke
who has some care of the estate.'

Early in the following week Thistlewood having heard that Mr
Jacob Allen, at Jacobsfield, needed an overseer went there to
enquire. The place had already been filled.

'Tuesday, 10th July: a.m. met Mr Thomas Adams by Sam's
hut almost, in his Troop dress. He asked pardon for his ill
language he gave one night by Sarah's gate, with Mr Paul
Stevens, both being almost drunk, We parted good friends.
p.m. William Ward, who is yet out of place, one Evans who
lives as overseer, and a highlander in Colonel Barclay's service,
all called to beg refreshment. I gave them dinner & punch.
In the evening, Mr Davidson, who some 7 or 8 years ago lived a
short time overseer at Salt River, called to beg refreshment &c.
and stayed all night with me. I liked his company very well. He
has been to Windward seeking employ, but can find none
worthwhile. He told me enough of Mrs Anderson's tricks with
the Scotch doctor, &c. (2 horses & a Negro boy).
And enough about Collgrave, &c. Collgrave used to buy good
clothes for the Negro girls that were handsome, on the estate,
and they were to give him half what they got from any white
person, &c.'

On Monday, 16th July:

'About sunrise in the morning got the Negroes forward to
Paradise. The cripple Negroes and all their victuals &c. in the
canoe, all the rest walk by road − Quashe and 44 other Negroes.
Cruddon is run away long ago. 13 belonging this place already
at Paradise. Left here, Old Sharper & Ellin at Hill, Daniel and
old Phibbah at hogstyes. Tony and Titus. Dickson, Sam and

Celia. Old Sarah. Ambo fisherman, Nimine with him. About the house: Phibbah, Dianah, Susanah, Coffee, Nahon, Old Catalina; most of the Negroes' pickanninnies. Sampson look after cattle. Gave the Negro men each a dram. Phibbah gave me a fine pineapple.
Wrote to Mrs Anderson and sent by Susanah, &c. in the canoe 33 ducks, squabs. Rode over the estate, was at home rest of the day, very dull and lonesome.'

There were, nonetheless, diversions. On Egypt itself, there was the shooting and fishing, and there were visitors and outings.

'Friday 20th: Mr Griffith Williams called and dined with me. Sat a while after dinner.
p.m. I rode to Savanna la Mar. To Mr Clemens for 3 lbs cheese, 4 bitts. Drank tea at Mr Emetson's. Went to see the camels at Wade's (in Wade's yard) about 40 of them, and in very good order. I take them to be dromedarys, though all at the Bay hold them to be camels.'

A few days later, another visitor, and a much more surprising one:

'Wednesday 25th: In the morning, Dianah Jones, who came over in the ship *Flying Flamborough* that I came in, called to see me. She lives on Mr Woodcock's estate, the Delve, has had a child by Mr Thomas Adams the overseer (now living) and has been free sometime. I rode as far as Tony's hut with her.'

He also decided, or had been invited, to visit.

'Sunday, 29th July 1753: a.m. I rode to Delve estate, Mr Woodcock's and dined with Mr Thomas Adams and Mrs Dianah Jones. Was mightily made on. They have a fine child, a girl of about 7 months old. She told me many of her secrets, &c. and is a sensible woman. Showed me a muff of her working, in imitation of Dresden work, admirable. Mr Adams going to leave the Delve.'

There would have been much talk about. It was after dark when Thistlewood got back to Egypt, and he would visit them many times more.

'Wednesday 15th: a.m. Andrew Miller called. He says he hears Forrester is to leave Salt River, Mr Dorrill provided another.
In the evening William Ward called and stayed all night.'

Ward was still in search of a job. On that day also was held the trial of several Salt River slaves who had been charged with the theft of goods from the estate stores.

'Mr Dorrill's Negroes tried today: Oliver's Quaw hanged; Fortune's Quaw both ears cropped, both nostrils slit, and marked on both cheeks; Cheddar's right ear cropped, right nostril slit, & marked on the left cheek. Mr Dorrill vouched Robin was runaway (false) but he punished him himself.'

We are left to wonder, with what greater violence, or with what favoured restraint.

'Sunday, 19th August: Gave a man dinner who is seeking employment. He hás been travelling on horseback ever since the 12th of last month & can't find any place worth anything.'

Other visitors at Egypt included two of Col Cudjoe's men who, on a furlough for nine days, stopped in and drank some punch; and Samuel Matthews, who had replaced Thistlewood and Russell at Paradise. In the other direction, on the 28th:

'Gave Ambo a ticket and leave to go and see his pickanninny who is dangerously ill, until tomorrow morning.'

On Sunday, 2nd September the road through Egypt was crowded with 'an abundance of Negroes', and there was 'a large Negro market by Tony's gate' near the river Styx. On Sunday 19th, 'Cudjoe's men − perhaps the same two − were allowed to sleep in the cookroom for the night.

Towards the end of the month, Thistlewood and the surveyor, Wallace, and his assistant, Blythe, surveyed boundaries between Salt River, Paradise and neighbouring properties. Thistlewood got back to Egypt tired and his current bedfellow caused him some discomfort:

'Thursday, 27th September: Last night Sus[ana]h piss the bed again, makes 3 times, will bear no more.'

But he did.

On the last day of September, Mr Mordiner's Quasheba was brought to bed of a girl.

By the end of 1753 Thistlewood's affair with Jenny was at an end and he was turning to Phibbah. She was very likely a Creole for she had relatives among the slaves on properties in the neighbourhood. Her only child, a daughter, Coobah, was a slave on Paradise Estate and was a frequent visitor at Egypt. So too, was her sister Nancy. As woman in charge of the Egypt great house cookroom she carried the same sort of responsibilities as had the other household Phibbah at Vineyard. But Egypt Phibbah, unlike Vineyard Phibbah, moved frequently between the Egypt cookroom, and the

great house at Salt River where her owner and his househc
She was thus full of information about the goings-on of Thistl
employer and his other employees and his other slaves. Mc
what news she gleaned herself was added to by the information she
frequently received from her widely scattered friends and relatives.
Although we have no picture of her physical attributes, she certainly
seems to have attracted attention. He had first taken her in early
October 1753; but she was not an easy conquest. Not until the end
of November did she spend a night with him, and it was February
1754, before she really yielded.

'Sunday, 6th January 1754:   In the forenoon, a Negro man
belonging to old Tom Williams, named Jinney Quashe (a noted
Obia man) pretending to pull bones, &c. out of several of our
Negroes for which they was to give him money, was discovered
by them to be a cheat, and they chased him out of the estate,
frightened enough. Remember to have seen one Black Lambert
(a noted conjurer) of Wakefield in Yorkshire so chased at
Acworth.
Monday 7th: Mr Mordiner breakfasted with me, also Capt.
Quaque, his son and other attendants. The Capt. had a silver
medal of King George 2nd. hung on a silver chain about his
neck.
Tuesday 8th: Samuel Matthews come over to Egypt as an
assistant to me.
Sunday, 24th February: About noon a white man, with Wild
Negroes armed, and 2 Baggage Negroes, from Trelawny Town,
Vulgo. Cudjoe's Town, called to beg refreshment. I gave them
punch, &c. They are going to bring in Woodcock's Negroes
who are now out, &c. Capt. Ton Ton Panne, and a Lieutenant
with them.
Tuesday, 5th March 1754:   Last night Quashe lit of Salt River's
Roger at our Negro houses and as I hear gave him a whipping.
Wednesday 6th: At noon had Quacoo whipped for beating
Yara in the mill house in a very bad manner last Friday. His
was an old grudge. She has laid in the hot house of it ever
since.
Wednesday, 13th March: I spoke to Mr Dorrill again about
leaving the care and management of this plantation, &c. and
had his approbation, but not consent.
Saturday 23rd: In the morning Sam Matthews come home,
having been at Paradise to see his wife Dido last night.'

And now, although Phibbah was his she was not always at his beck and call.

'Tuesday, 19th February 1754:   At night *Cum* Phibbah, *Sup. me. lect.*
Thursday, 21st February: p.m. *Cum* Phibbah. *Illa habet menses.*
Friday, 22nd February: At night *Cum* Phibbah.
Sunday, 24th February: At night *Cum* Phibbah.
Monday, 25th February: At night *Cum* Phibbah.
Tuesday, 26th February: Phibbah keep away.
Thursday, 28th February: At night *Cum* Phibbah.'

At this time his gonorrheal infection was either cured or dormant. His only complaint was of a long persistent sore 'very much resembling the dry crab yaws' between thumb and forefinger of his right hand. Phibbah, well-informed of these matters, told him that Mr William Dorrill had had the yaws when he was a boy. That might have been small consolation. The little sore did not, however, much alarm him.

'Friday, 1st March: p.m. *Cum* Phibbah ... and, in the evening, *Cum* Susanah in the curing-house, *stans.*'

In March, the ascendancy of Phibbah was clearly established, as was a continuing concern for Jenny.

'Saturday, 23rd March 1754:   Delivered to Phibbah 12 bitts to buy Jenny a coat & frock.
Friday, 3 May 1754:   Hear Mr Cope and Miss Molly were married last night.
Tuesday 7th: In the evening received a letter from Billy by Philip Gudgeon, who came with the canoe. Received 3 sugar tierces. Also come in the canoe a young man who belonged to Mr Cope's ship and I understand is to live here, to learn the plantation business. Let him lie in the hammock in the hall. [Samuel Matthews had been called back to Paradise].
Tuesday 14th: In the evening came here the young man recomended to me by Capt. Cope ... [William Crookshanks] ... put up the bed for him in the N.E. room of the Overseer's house.
Wednesday 15th [At night] Bess became William's bedfellow.'

Upon the marriage of John Cope and Molly Dorrill, William Dorrill allowed young Cope to take over the management of Egypt estate. For the time being, the newly-weds lived at Salt River.

'Friday, 24th May 1754:   This afternoon was the first good shower we have had for four or five months past; which oc-

casioned an excessive drought and scarcity of water; and the country has in most places been over-run with fire, most provision grounds and many plantations burnt up.
Saturday 25th: p.m. Mr Cope sent an Ebo Negro man (a new Negro) he bought today. Our Negroes have named him Hector. I put him to live with London.'

During 1754 the Egypt labour force was considerably increased by new purchases of slaves and by the hiring of jobbing slaves.

'Tuesday 28th: At night Mr Thos. Adams called, and supped with me; says he is to be married to Dianah Jones on Saturday next, and that he is shortly to have the care of Blue Hole and Cambleton estates, and has already left off tavern-keeping.'

Following his departure from Delve Estate Adams had opened a tavern, but he had allowed too much on credit and now was back to overseership in search of financial recovery.

'Wednesday, 5th June 1754: William has a scalding of urine & is afraid he has got the clap.
Hear Philip Gudgeon and William the barber ran away last Monday.
Tuesday 6th: Lent William the dun mule, to ride over to Mr Beckford's Craal. p.m. He returned, and brought me a letter from Dr Walker, who informs me Wm. has got a confounded clap.
Saturday 8th: Wrote to my brother and sent the letter, with a Bill of Lading enclosed, by the *Swinton*, Captain Fullerton, of Hull . . . .
Sunday 30th: A girl took away from Nago Hanah, by Dr Walker. Some say a Mulatto. [Thistlewood had had sexual intercourse with her on September 2nd and October 4th, 1753.]
Sunday, 7th July 1754: Am informed Nago Hanah died today.
Monday 8th. In the morning Colonel Cudjoe, with his attendants, called and stayed about an hour. I gave them a dram each, &c.
Saturday 13th: Gave the Negroes today. Have no provisions for the new Negroes ... Gave [them] 17 bitts amongst them and six shads each.
Saturday 20th: The Negroes had today by Mr Cope's order and are to have every Saturday till provisions begin to be plentiful.'

Rice was now handed out daily for several weeks. Quantities varied, but on most days about 10 to 12 quarts were distributed between the ten new Negroes. On weekend days they got about three quarters of that amount. At the same time, numerous attempts, some successful, were made to purchase provisions in the countryside and on neighbouring properties.

> 'Friday, 6th September 1754:   A little before noon Mr Cope come and stayed dinner with us (pickled herring, bread & butter) . . . [then they went shooting].
> Mr Cope proposed giving me 60 pounds per ann. till we make 60 Hhds and then as many pounds more as we make Hhds more . . . .
> Monday 9th: In the morning accompanied Mr Taffe to Lucea and beyond, almost as far as Mr Hautton's [Haughton's] whom we met in the road. Returned to Lucea, Mr Phil. Hautton Snr offered me 70 pounds per annum to go live at his estate near Montego Bay, to live & eat at his table, and have the liberty of killing fowls or a shoat when I pleased if he was not upon the estate, &c.
> Thursday 12th: Mr Cope here from noon till almost night. I acquainted him what offer Mr Hautton had made me; upon which he offered me 80 pounds per ann. till we make above 80 Hhds, and them 20s per Hhd for every one over. I agreed to stay.'

At the beginning of October they began to put the Egypt great house in readiness for occupation by Mr and Mrs Cope. By Wednesday 9th, Thistlewood had been required to move into the 'old Overseer's house'. In December, he would move again, into a newly built Overseer's house.

> 'Tuesday, 8th October 1754:   Mr & Mrs Cope, Mrs Gorse, Miss Bessy Storer, and Mr Hungerford dined here. A second table in the back piazza. Mrs Anderson gave me 26 black crabs. William very officious about the house, but no concern about the field. 2 fine mahogany tables &c. brought from Strathbogie in a cart. Great enquiry whether I keep Phibbah.
> Sunday 13th: For 300 corn, to Col Barclay's Negroes, 6 bitts.
> Sunday 17th, November: For 350 corn, 7 bitts, and 75 plantains, 3 bitts.
> Thursday 28th: Guliemus & Mirtilla *primus somnus-a nocte*.[4]
> Tuesday, 10th December 1754:   In the night Mr Mordiner called me up twice going for Drs Graham & Smith. He says he does not expect to find Mr Dorrill alive when he goes home.'

William Dorrill died between 7 and 8 a.m. on Wednesday, 11th December 1754, and was buried at Salt River on the following day in the presence of 'a multitude of company'. Minute guns were fired at noon.

'Tuesday 17th: This morning I found Adam dead in the hot house. Had a grave dug and buried him by the cherry trees, not far from the old barcadier.'

Notes

1 Mulatto Dick, a slave, had been the 'Driver' on Vineyard while Thistlewood was there. Shortly after his departure Florentius Vassall had sold the Pen with all its livestock and transferred the slaves to his properties in Westmoreland.
2 Mr Mordiner was at the time engaged in repairing the Cabaritta 'big bridge'.
3 Edward Long, planter and historian of Jamaica, and others, made similar claims. The slaves, as we shall see from Thistlewood's accounts, were very much involved in petty trading or higglering. A main source of their money income was sales in the Sunday roadside markets of the surplus produce of their provision grounds.
4 William Crookshanks had now taken Mirtilla to be his 'wife' – for the first time they now slept together.

CHAPTER 4   Notes on plantation life: 1755–1759

Introduction

In the Jamaican slave society the sugar plantocracy were supreme. They were white, they were wealthy, and they were the better educated in the formal sense since they could afford a schooling in England. Moreover, they controlled the island legislature since they had the property qualifications to support them either as voters or as candidates for election, and free persons of colour, however wealthy, were legally barred from both those categories. The slaves, of course, as the property of others, had no rights at all except those allowed by their masters; and it was the planter-controlled legislature which enacted the Slave Laws which purported to protect the slaves against abuse. In such a society, obviously, the behaviour of the masters was largely ungoverned, except by general consensus of opinion of what might be done without incurring the disapproval of one's peers, and by the state of mind of the individual at the given moment.

Through these years of his diary Thistlewood records excesses of behaviour beyond anything previously described, and indeed, he is himself guilty of the worst. We do not know if he was following the examples of others, or simply displaying a personal, sadistic disregard for the feelings and sensibilities of fellow humans. Perhaps he later felt remorse, perhaps he was admonished by his employer or his peers, or even by Phibbah, herself a slave, with whom he was now closely and obviously affectionately joined. For whatever reason, he was to exercise a greater control over his behaviour in the future. It is, in a sense remarkable that in these same years he displayed to the full the warmth of his relationship with Phibbah and his apparently friendly attitude towards many of the slaves under his management. Apparently, because he does not tell us, and we have no certain means of knowing, what the slaves thought about him and how they reacted to his 'apparent' friendly concern.

The diaries for this period bring much else of interest to

our notice. We read of food scarcity in the area, of rice-planting in the Egypt morass (precursor to the enterprise of the later twentieth century); of slave 'plays' and other ceremonial rites; of fights and quarrels, often over sexual relationships, among the slaves themselves; and of the apprehensions following the outbreak of the Seven Years War (1756–1763) between England and France with Spain as a late entrant ally.

And there were more particular events such as the surprise with which the slave woman, Doll, recognised the newly acquired man, Achilles; the arrival, but by no means the first, of a large box of books for Thistlewood who would lend out several to his friends; and his observations of a now famous comet.

But these and other happenings would soon be overshadowed, for in the north-central parish of St Mary a leadership of slave resistance was in the making.

'Saturday, 4th January 1755: In the forenoon, myself, William Crookshank, Ambo & Daniel, walked through our Sand Ground Plantain Walk, westward, to a large sand ground, and came to a piece cleared lately, now in corn and cassava. In going saw a logwood fence Daniel says he planted, runs nearly NW & SE. Returned through marooned grounds, by where Sarah Ward lives. Eat some breakfast of buttered toasted cheese and roast plantain with her (Homer Jackson come here). We got home about noon.
p.m. *Cum* Phib.
At night Phibbah slept in the hammock in the hall; would not come to bed. She was rather too saucy.'

On the 28th January, Thistlewood put the mill about in commencement of the year's crop taking.

'Thursday, 30th January 1755: At night *Cum* Phib.
Friday 31st: Nancy, Phibbah's sister, here tonight.
Saturday, 1st February: About 2 p.m. *Cum* Phibbah. At night she slept in the cook-room.
Sunday 2nd: Phibbah did not speak to me all day.
Monday 3rd: About midnight last night I fetched Phibbah from her house. Had words with her again in the evening. At night *Cum* Phibbah.
Friday 7th: Phibbah denied me.'

While Thistlewood and Phibbah were having their temporary differences, Mrs Anderson at Salt River was becoming more involved with William Mould.

'Sunday, 19th January 1755: 'At night had a deal of private discourse with Mr Cope about Mrs A[nderson] and Mr W[illiam] M[ould]. He is well acquainted with the affair.'

The affair blossomed into matrimony. In early February 1755, one of Mrs Anderson's slaves, Mason Quashe, hired to Egypt, was away helping to move his mistress's goods from Salt River to a house in the Savanna. She had now forfeited her Dorrill inheritance.

'Monday, 17th January 1755: Hear Mrs Anderson was last night married to Wm. Mould, who was apprentice to Mr Dorrill, and served as book-keeper boy in the counting-house, & was a Blue Coat boy.[1]

About 8 a.m. when Mr Cope heard the news of Mrs Anderson's marriage he immediately discharged all her Negroes except Mason Quashe.

Wednesday, 22nd January 1755: Last night William Crookshanks and Mirtilla at the Negro houses, quarrelled, made a prodigious noise, &c. Wm. cut his own thumb with his machete.

Thursday, 13th February, 1755: Mirtilla very ill, it is thought going to miscarry. William cries sadly, the more fool he, as it is probably for Salt River Long Quaw.'

Mirtilla belonged to Mrs (Anderson) Mould, and, a few dyas later she went off to Mrs Mould's house in the Savanna. Crookshanks visited her there every night.

'Sunday, 23rd February 1755: Mirtilla is here, (William says he has hired her of Mrs Mould at 20 pounds per annum), sick in William's house.'

At the beginning of March she had recovered and went to work in the field at Egypt. Mr Cope would pay Crookshanks 2 bitts per day for her hire. That would just about meet the £20 a year if she worked regularly.

In 1755 and 1756 ground provisions were scarce and dear and Thistlewood noted the usual heavier incidence in such circumstances of slaves moving beyond their grounds to find subsistence. The vicious responses of their masters were also noted by Thistlewood who in 1756 would calmly record his own disgraceful excesses.

'Tuesday, 25th February 1755: At dinner-time rode over the plantation to see who would be eating canes. Found Hector & Beck. Had them whipped.

Sunday, 2nd March 1755: Bought plantains for the new Negroes, house Negroes, &c. &c. at nine hundred for 27 bitts.'

The plantocracy, as distinct from their white employees, differed from the latter only in their greater possession of resources and authority and, therefore, of responsibilities which Mr Cope at any rate seemed unable to bear. He was always in financial distress, and frequently in other predicaments, often of his own making.

> 'Monday, 17th March 1755: This morning Mr Cope took all Mrs Cope's china, glasses, &c she brought here when he was last at Town, and smashed them with all his force against the floor, and broke them in pieces; believe they were given her by an old sweetheart, J. Thoms^n. Then he went out and stayed the night, &c. &c.
>
> Friday, 11th April 1755: Our Negroes have this week had but 3 plantains each per *diem*, and none on holy days or Negro days (New Negroes).
>
> Sunday, 13th April 1755: Rode over the estate. The canes mostly destroyed by the cattle. Mr Cope talks of renting it out, or throwing it up.'

This was in the height of food scarcity and in the dry weather the cattle, even more than the slaves, were moving into the canefields in search of sustenance.

> 'Tuesday, 15th April 1755: Sent Port Royal with a mule and bags to Dr Frazier's at Negril, for corn. [He got a bag full].
>
> Monday, 19th May 1755: Although Whitsun-Monday, Mr Cope made the Negroes work as a punishment (he says) for eating canes so much.
>
> Sunday, 8th June 1755: In the morning rode into the Savanna to the Negro market. Plantains 5 bitts per hundred; Corn 4 ditto. Bought none. William Crookshanks with me.'

Three days later London was sent with two mules to Paradise to buy plantains. He got only a few and the price there was the same. On the Sunday, Thistlewood tried the Negro Market at Hatfield gate. Again, he 'bought some' at the same high prices. In the next few days:

> 'I give our New Negroes a pint of Norward [from the American mainland] Corn each for a meal, three times per day, & a herring each day. Quaw, Cubbenna, Moll, Melia &c have but three plantains or a pint of corn each per day.'

On Sunday 22nd, at Hatfield, prices were down 1 bitt per 100 on each item; but on the 29th plantains were up to 5 again, and 'scarce'. Not until the end of July did prices begin to decline. On the first Sunday in August plantains were still at 4, but corn was being offered variously at 2, 2½, and 3 bitts per 100. Thistlewood planted corn at Egypt.

By this time, Mr Cope had changed his mind and re-employed Mrs Mould's slaves; but Mr Mould still seemed to carry some resentment, and perhaps with good reason for John Cope seemed never to be in good financial standing. When, in early April, Mr Cope offered to pay him for the slaves' hire with an order upon Mr Gardiner in Savanna la Mar, Mr Mould refused to accept it. It might even have come to blows.

'Wednesday, 23rd April 1755: Being St George's Day, Mr Cope dined out, and at night came home seemingly in liquor, and bloody, his lips seem bruised, &c. W[illiam] C[rookshanks] sent to Mr Mould's to enquire.'

No more was recorded, but time apparently mended differences.

'Sunday, 15th June 1755: Mr Cope dined out. Mrs Cope told me how much Mr Cope wants her to cut the entail off and settle upon him for life. Or, as it is going to be a war, he must go home and try to make his fortune that way, if she don't.

Wednesday, 13th August 1755: At night Mr Cope come home in liquor; wanted Silvia very much and was like a madman almost.

Had my supper sent into my house to me.

Monday, 6th October 1755: Mr Cope and Mr Christopher Senior went and took possession of Salt River and Paradise estates last Saturday p.m. and have agreed to pay the debts off if possible before they make any dividend.

Wednesday, 15th October 1755: Mirtilla has been at home all this week, ails little or nothing, only resolved to put William to a needless charge through spite.

Sunday, 28th December 1755: Mason Quashe had a feast here tonight'.

And in January, 1756, Thistlewood recorded a striking co-incidence:

'It is remarkable that one of the last New Negroes, named Achilles, is he who took Doll and sold her; and that having some clothes, some tobacco, dram & a gun, &c. was robbed going home, &c.'

And now, as a consequence of an increase in assault on the canefields by slaves who were by his own account on very short rations, Thistlewood inflicted punishments which seem to have gone even beyond the accepted bestiality of the time. One of the chief consumers of young canes was Derby.

'Wednesday, 28th Jan 1756:   Had Derby well whipped, and made Egypt shit in his mouth.
Tuesday, 24th February 1756:   Mirtilla went away into the Savanna. It seems her time is up. Hear her neck is to be put in the yoke. She has worked 244 days in her year and earned William Crookshanks £15 15s. At night William Crookshanks abused Mr and Mrs Mould in an extraordinary manner in the Savanna, at their own house; afterwards crazed went down [on] his knees & begged their pardons, &c . . . . Mirtilla the cause.'

Mirtilla was now pregnant, near childbirth. In mid-March she was sent to Paradise where Crookshanks went to see her.

'Saturday, 13th March 1756:   Hazat catched Derby last night stealing cane. Derby wanting this morning.'

Two days later he was caught, escaped, and a short while after recaptured and put in the bilboes. For days, said Thistlewood, he remained sullen, not eating or drinking, and not seeming to care when he was whipped.

'Monday, 15th March 1756:   In the morning W.C. went to Paradise, Mirtilla in labour all day. At night Dr Robinson sent to her, who delivered her of a girl (a mulatto) after supper. Mr and Mrs Mould also came over to see her, and returned again in the night. W.C. came home & cried. She is in Egypt Lucy's house.' [At Paradise]

On the 19th Thistlewood went to visit Mirtilla and her daughter. About a week later Crookshanks was transferred to Paradise, Mirtilla was to remain there and Sancho would be sent to Egypt in her stead. At Paradise, William Crookshanks (according to Thistlewood) continued to pamper Mirtilla.

On Monday, 5th April 1756, the Moulds left Jamaica for England. For a while, before their departure, they had stayed at Egypt. It was also cropover time.

'Mr and Mrs Mould went away into the Savanna this morning. Wrote a letter to Mr Henry Hewitt, by Mr Wm. Mould . . . p.m.
Mr and Mrs Cope went into the Savanna to take their leave of Mr and Mrs Mould. Egypt now seems very dull. However, I had a bottle of good ale at my supper, which I mixed with sugar & water & grated some nutmeg over it. Roast beef, roast turkey, cold tongue, cheese, &c. to my supper.
At night *Cum* Phibbah.
Sunday, 2nd May 1756:   Sometime in the middle of last night Mr Cope come home and Mr McDonald with him. They sat

drinking for sometime, then went to bed; Mr McDonald had Eve to whom he gave 6 bitts, and Mr Cope made Tom fetch Beck from the Negro houses for himself, with whom she was till morning.
Wednesday, 5th May 1756: p.m. Egypt Susanah & Mazerine whipped for refusal last Saturday night, by Mr Cope's order.[2] Little Phibbah told Mrs Cope last Saturday night's affair. Mrs Cope also examined the sheets and found them amiss.'

Mrs Cope had been away on the Saturday night spending a few days with Dr and Mrs Gorse. She had returned to Egypt on the morning of the 5th.

On Wednesday, 26th May, the Egypt slaves planted rice in the morass behind the mill house; but that, like much of the corn planted, would be eaten by the birds rather than them. And Derby was again:

'. . . catched by Port Royal eating canes. Had him well flogged and pickled, then made Hector shit in his mouth.'

This sadistic and degrading punishment seemed to appeal to Thistlewood.

In June, 1756, came an interesting instance of an unusual domestic event. Nancy, Phibbah's sister, was then a house slave at Egypt and she had an infant son. Rose, an Egypt field slave who had been sent to Salt River at the end of February '. . . to be salivated for the bone-ache' now returned to Egypt.

'. . . and is to live with Nancy who is to give Mr Cope five pounds per ann. for her.'

Unfortunately, Thistlewood made no further comment on the arrangement by which one slave was hiring another from the owner of both, but the reason for it seems clear — little Davie was ill. About noon on 18th July he died.

'Saturday, 24th July 1756: Nancy's play tonight.[3]
'Sunday, 25th July 1756: Nancy's play ended, much music & dancing all day, &c.'

In July, Port Royal, who had run away, was taken and brought home.

'Gave him a moderate whipping, pickled him well, made Hector shit in his mouth, immediately put in a gag whilst his mouth was full & made him wear it 4 or 5 hours.'

Next day, the 24th, a woman slave, Phillis, caught breaking canes, was similarly treated, but spared the gag. On the 31st her punishment was repeated. The reason was not stated, but perhaps she had run away after the 24th; for on the 30th two other runaways had been apprehended and punished.

'Friday, 30th July 1756:   Punch catched at Salt River and brought home. Flogged him and Quacoo well, and then washed and rubbed in salt pickle, lime juice & bird pepper; also whipped Hector for losing his hoe, made New Negro Joe piss in his eyes & mouth &c.'

On 1st August, another runaway, Hazat, who had absconded in early April was caught.

'Put him in the bilboes both feet; gagged him; locked his hands together; rubbed him with molasses & exposed him naked to the flies all day, and to the mosquitoes all night, without fire.'

On the 4th, Derby was again caught, this time by the watchman as he attempted to take corn out of Col Barclay's Long Pond corn-piece. He was severely chopped with a machete, his right ear, cheek, and jaw almost cut off. On the 27th of the same month, Egypt was whipped and given 'Derby's 'dose' [that is Derby was made to shit in his mouth] for eating cane. On Thursday, 5th October, Hector and Joe and Mr Watt's Pomona were similarly punished for the same misdemeanour. Thereafter, for unmentioned reason, Mr Thistlewood shed his depravity of 1756 and resorted to the usual whippings and chainings.

Late in 1756 the monthly musters of militia, perfunctorily attended, were more regularly held and additional guard duties instituted.

'Friday, 10th September 1756:   Being warned, in the evening rode to the Bay, supped at Mr Emetson's .... I watched in the Fort from 8 till 10, and from 4 till daylight, Mr Stecher the Pilot with me, but 6 more & the Sergeant besides ...
Saturday, 4th December 1756:   Martial Law has now been sometime. Rode down to the Bay and entered upon guard at 8 o'clock.'

But it was all still very much like play. A body of the militia had, a few days before, been formed into a troop of Dragoons, headed by Mr Crawford, who was appointed as their Colonel.

'The Troop mounted today. At night Col Witter, Mr Cope &c. come into the Fort, &c, all drunk, &c. Young Mr Gooding, our Officer, gave the guard 14 bitts to spend at night. Carr, the wire-dancer, our Sergeant for the day.

Friday, 10th September 1756:   Last night Mr Mould's Scotland was shot and cut with a machete till he died, in Col. Barclay's Negro ground, by Old Jenny's, by the watchman. He was stealing corn, plantains, &c. This morning Mr George Cummins came to acquaint me, and I rode with him to the place where he lay dead. Did not meddle with him, came home and acquainted Mr Cope.'

No more is mentioned of the Moulds themselves until late March 1758, when William Mould, returned from England.

'. . . came here, supped and slept. Mrs Mould dead. He had a Mulatto by her, &c. Phillis christened Pegg, &c.'

He subsequently went to live in Kingston.

'Saturday, 25th September 1756:   Many reports about Mr Wm. Crookshanks, particularly in regard to his humouring Mirtilla, and about some rum sent to Mr Mordiner to sell, &c.'

Samuel Matthews was now sent back from Paradise to Egypt to replace Crookshanks.

'Sunday, 26th September 1756:   p.m. Samuel Matthews come here as Driver. They are weary of him at Paradise, so I spoke to Mr Cope for him to come here. He lives where William lived.'

Matthews, while at Paradise, had hired Dido from Mr Cope at £15 a year commencing in mid-April, 1756. At the beginning of October she came to Egypt to live with him. For an unstated reason, she remained only 2 months.

'Tuesday, 7th December 1756:   Dido went to Paradise, and Samuel Matthews also went to deliver her up to the Overseer. Mr Wm. Crookshanks sent me a piece of cheese by him.'

A week and a half later another white employee was taken on at Egypt, Thomas Fewkes. His employment lasted only a few months, during which he was housed with Matthews.

'Saturday, 9th October 1756:   Mr C. in his tantrums last night. Forced Egypt Susanah in the cookroom; was like a madman most part of the night, &c. Mrs Cope very ill today. p.m. Dr Gorse come to her & stayed all night.

Sunday, 7th November: About 4 in the morning set off in Mr Mordiner's canoe to go a shooting to the seaside with him. Stephen Vidal steered us. James Perrin, Davie, Sussex & Lincoln rowed us. I shot a white curlew sitting on a mangrove. Mr Mordiner shot a sort of blue golding. We also got 21 young crab-catchers off the mangrove trees which grow out in the sea off Robin's Point, many conches, &c. We went to the Creek westward of [the point] then returned towards the river mouth, went ashore, struck a fire, and made a fine breakfast of broiled herrings & plantains which we brought with us, as also salt, pepper, sugar, rum, limes, water &c. Broiled many young crab-catchers, very fat & sweet, broiled conch buttered, &c. During breakfast we hooked a young shark (the bait was crab-catcher's guts). I laid Mr Mordiner 4 bitts that he was 2 ft 9 ins long, but he proved only 2 ft 8 ½ ins, so I lost. Then, we rowed to Mr Mordiner's house at Salt River and dined there. About 4 p.m. set out for home again, and got home before supper.'

Early in December a domestic disturbance ended in death.

'Wednesday, 8th December 1756:   At dinnertime, Mole being jealous of Mr Mould's Lydde with Cobenna, she beat Lydde so that we were forced to have her carried home. Moll afterwards went to Cobenna's house, took out his clothes, &c. and made to the river's side.

p.m. Sent Cobenna and Dago to look for her. They could see nothing of her.

Thursday, 9th December: In the morning Sancho the fisherman found Moll in the river drowned wilfully (we imagine she thought she had killed Lydde). Hauled her upon dry land, and at night gave Cobenna leave to bury her. Have been very much afraid of Cobenna & Quamina's making away with themselves, they seem to be so much concerned, & by their looks.'

But Thistlewood gives no explanation of his remark about Quamina who seems not to have been involved in the unfortunate triangle.

Christmas Day 1756 passed uneventfully. The Copes dined with Col Barclay; Thistlewood dined at Egypt, sumptuously; and Mirtilla arrived at Egypt, from Paradise, with her daughter Sukey Crookshanks.

'Sunday, 26th December: Gave Mirtilla's Sukey, for a Christmas box, 3 bitts. In the morning served our Negroes 6 herrings each, drivers 12 each, children some two some three each …

In the morning Mr Crookshanks rode over here (gave him a glass tumbler) then he prevailed with me to go to Paradise with him.

Called at Mr Mordiner's going, dined at Paradise, Mr Wm. Maddin, Mr John Bell, Mr Blanch, Mr Samuel Mordiner, his wife [Quasheba] & children also dined there. [These were all of

Thistlewood's and Mordiner's class. No large landed proprietor was there]. In the evening got home. Samuel Matthews at Paradise all day and night.'

His wife, Dido, whom he had hired at £15 a year, had recently, on 7th December, been recalled to work on Paradise. Thistlewood himself should have gone to do guard duty with the militia on the 26th, but 'ventured not to do so, as we are going to keep guard upon Cabritto Bridge' where, earlier in the month, two Egypt slave women, going over the bridge at night had found it almost covered with smuggled goods. Although the Seven Years War had begun, it was not until the following year, 1757, that Thistlewood's notes begin to display some apprehension.

In mid-January 1757:

'Sam and Thomas parted their house, broke down a door at the end, &c. &c.

Sunday, 16th January 1757:   Thomas Fewkes and Little Lydde made up a match.

Wednesday, 19th January 1757:   Thomas Fewkes says Little Lydde has clapped him confoundedly.

Friday, 18th February 1757:   Thomas Fewkes burnt Little Lydde's coat, a continual noise all night in their room, &c. Last night this happened.'

Since Dido's departure Samuel Matthews had been unmatched. At the beginning of March, 1757, he took Mrs Mould's Franke (not to be confused with Phibbah's close friend or relative, House Franke). Soon he would, for a time, replace Thistlewood as Egypt overseer.

'Tuesday, 1st Feb 1757:   The chain and collars struck from Quacoo and Charles neck, Cobenna & Quamina being bound for Quacoo, & Plato for Charles.'

The meaning is not absolutely clear, but it would seem that Cobenna, Quamina, and Plato were 'standing surety'. This, remarkably, was the first mention of any punishment in the year, and there had been no record of any runaway. Perhaps he had been challenged by his conscience, or by Phibbah.

'Wednesday, 16th February 1757:   Heard great guns fired out at sea.'

But the crop taking had begun on the 7th and, for a few weeks it was that and other estate business which primarily occupied Thistlewood's attentions.

'Monday, 7th February 1757:   In the morning, at turn-out time, put the mill about. Was to have put about at the rising of

the morning star, but did not [though I] strictly ordered Ambo to do so, for which gave him a good flogging, also one to his wife Agnes for her impudence.
Tuesday, 22nd February: Paradise and Salt River not about, can't make good sugar. (Ours very good yet, thank God.)
Wednesday, 23rd February: New Negro Quacoo seen in the morning, wanting all day.'

On Tuesday, 1st March he delivered two large pots of sugar from the curing house – one for Dr Gorse and one for Mrs Winn – and delivered ten hogsheads of 'molasses out of the boiling house cistern' to a party of sailors to be put on board ship.

'Saturday, 2nd April: Cobenna catched London and Rosanna (Cobenna's wife) at work upon London's bed. London got a good thumping as I hear. This was after the coppers done cooling.'

But already ominous rumours of war and insurrection, were spreading.

'Saturday, 26th March 1757: At night Mr Cope received a letter from Mr Antrobus, suspecting the French intend to invade this island, by the men-of-war arrived at Hispaniola, and their having took the Greenwich man-of-war of 60 guns.
Thursday, 31st March 1757: Reported: Bowman that murdered Priddie, his own child, Mrs Dunbar, &c and some of Cudjoe's Negroes, at last killed by them.
Thursday, 7th April 1757: p.m. Some French prisoners went by, well-guarded, towards Savanna la Mar, belonging to a French privateer in Little Bay this week.'

The capture brought its special rewards. On Sunday 10th, Thistlewood had guests for dinner:

'Had roast beef and plum pudding to dinner (as it is Easter Day), also mangrove oysters. Good porter to drink, and very good claret wine bought out of the French prize at 5 pounds per hogshead [about 22 dozen bottles]. A bottle of this claret now sold in the Taverns at Savanna la Mar at 10s per bottle, and at other times at 15s per bottle ...'

It served also as a pre-cropover celebration, for on the 13th: 'Finished our crop this forenoon ...'; but it had not been an outstanding one. They had made only 991 pots of sugar.

The Martial Law instituted in late 1757 had, apparently, been relaxed, for on Wednesday, 27th April 1757:

'Martial Law commenced the 19th Instant in Town, and here today.

Thursday, 28th April 1757:   Capt. Quacoo and some of his attendants dined here.

Friday, 29th April: A report that ... the French have dispossessed us of all we had on the coast of Guinea.

Sunday, 5th June 1757:   About 8 at night, many (10 or 12) great guns fired at the Bay.'

But soon, he was to be for a time removed from the sounds of guns and the guard house carousings at the Fort in Savanna la Mar.

'Saturday, 18th June 1757:   In the morning rode to Paul Island, and agreed with Mr John Parkinson [to whom Mr Cope had addressed "an extraordinary letter" of reference] to live at Kendal. Am to have an hundred per ann. the first year and afterwards to have my wages raised, 4 barrels of beef, one of flour, 2 firkins of butter, a box of soap & a box of candles, rum, sugar, plantains, &c. and to raise fowls.

Returned Mr Cope his law books which I have had a long time lent me.'

With him, went his own personal slave whom he had purchased from Mr Mason at Hertford on 3rd January 1756, for £43. As he had noted then:

'He is an Ebo, about 16 years of age, measures 4 ft 9 $\frac{2}{10}$ inches. Named him Lincoln.'

Nowhere in his diaries does Thistlewood state explicitly why he made the move, but there were two possible explanations. In 1756 he had suffered another painful recurrence of veneral infection. He first mentioned notice of the symptoms at the beginning of September. At the end of the month he was taking an electuary made up for him by Mulatto Will.[4]

'He says it is Rhubarb, Cassia & Balm Capivi and some Jollop scorched to make it mild over the fire.'

And, early October, Cobenna seeming to be cured, he took some of another mixture made up for Cobenna by Dr Gorse. That one contained 'Jollop, Rhubarb, Gum Guiacum, Balsam Capivi and Mercury.' Neither seems to have brought complete cure. But if he hoped to elude further infection by removing himself from Egypt he was to be disappointed.

More likely an explanation was his constant bickering with Mr Cope over the terms of his employment. He might have felt that he was getting nowhere near to a fortune. There is some suggestion that he would have preferred the overseership at Salt River, if he had been offered it at an increased wage; but Cope made no offer of that. So, on 23rd June 1757, Thistlewood and Cope settled their accounts, in a fashion. Cope owed him £92 9s 9d, and there was still an outstanding £15 12s 7½ d due from his short stay with William Dorrill at Salt River in 1752. Now, he received an order on a Savanna la Mar merchant for £8 9s 9d, was promised a puncheon of rum valued at £14, and was given Cope's promissory note for £70, currency, payable with interest at some future, unstated date. On the Salt River account he was paid a little over £14. Next day he left, after a hard parting from Phibbah.

'Sunday, 19th June 1757:   Phibbah grieves very much, and last night I could not sleep, but vastly uneasy, &c.

Wednesday, 22nd: Took up of Mr Gardiner [in Savanna la Mar] 10 yards of brown oznabrig, 20 bitts (which oznabrig delivered to Phibbah for a certain use). Gave Phibbah 2 pistoles in money, mosquito net, 3 cakes of soap, about 3½ yards of cloth . . . out-door lock, &c. Begged hard of Mrs Cope to sell or hire Phibbah to me, but she would not; he was willing. Gave 8 bitts for little Quaw,' 4 to Damsel, 2 to Silvia, 4 to Ambo, 1 to Mazerine, 8 to Franke, and 8 to Nancy.

Mr Cope dined and supped out. Come home in the night and had Little Mimber.

At night *cum* Phibbah.

Thursday 23rd: Phibbah gave me a gold ring, to keep for her sake.

At night *cum* Phib.

Friday 24th: In the morning parted with Phibbah and set off for Kendal.'

Now was the testing time. His offer to hire or purchase Phibbah indicates that he thought he wanted her with him. But he was now to be away from her for a prolonged period, and there were women to be had at Kendal, and it was not beyond possibility that he would find a new 'wife' there.

On Saturday, 25th June, he sent Lincoln to Egypt with a letter for Mr Cope. He was, he noted, 'mighty lonesome'. Sunday, Lincoln came back with Thistlewood's trunk, and among the things, 'a fine land turtle Phibbah sent me'. At the following weekend Lincoln was despatched again, this time with some plantains. Shortly after his departure, Thistlewood began his Kendal amours:

'Friday, 1st July 1757:   About 7 p.m. *cum* Phoebe, the cook, *Sup. Lect* in North Room.'

Next morning Lincoln was back:

'... and little Quashe with him. Franke sent me 2 bottles 'of porter. Phibbah sent me some biscuit, cheese, bread, 6 naseberries, and 7 fine mudfish, &c. In the evening Sam Matthews [now Egypt overseer] come, rode on Mark Mule and Phibbah with him, rode on Sam's mare, a good while after sunset; come vastly unexpected; was sent to persuade me back to Egypt. At night *cum* Illa, *Bis*.'

Sam Matthews, we are told, lay in the south room bed.

'Sunday, 3rd July: About 10 a.m. Sam and little Quashe set out for Westmoreland .... Gave Sam a little sugar in his handkerchief. He rode on his mare. Lent Quashe a bag and filled it with plantains, which he carried home on Mark Mule. Also gave Quashe 2 bitts.
In the morning walked about and showed Sam and Phibbah the garden, all the works, &c. &c.
p.m. walked with Phibbah to the Negro houses, plantain walk, &c. &c. and discussed about various affairs, &c. At Egypt, the curing house has been broke open since I came away; by Port Royal and Pero &c. Nancy brought to bed of a girl about a week ago, had a very hard labour, the child dead.
At night *cum* Phib.
Monday 4th: Lent Phibbah my horse to ride home on. She set out before sunrise. Made Lincoln go with her. He carried some plantains in a basket, and a few French beans for her to plant. Sent Mrs Cope some roses. I wish they would sell her to me. (She had Nancy's side-saddles). Tonight very lonely and melancholy again. No person sleep in the house but myself, and Phibbah's being gone this morning still fresh in my mind.'

Next day Lincoln returned with Thistlewood's horse, Toby. He brought gifts from Phibbah: 'a fine large pumpkin, 12 cashews, and 12 crabs, & a piece of soap. They got to Egypt in very good time yesterday'. The next week, Lincoln went back to Egypt. He took plantains for Phibbah. She sent back a land turtle, dried turtle eggs, biscuits, a pineapple, and cashews. 'God bless her!'

'Sunday, 17th July 1757:   In the morning about 8 o'clock, little Quashe and Dover come from Egypt. Had a mule with them. Brought me a fine turtle and 18 crabs Phibbah sent me. Quashe says she is sick, for which I am really very sorry. Poor girl, I pity her, she is in miserable slavery.'

On Saturday 23rd, Phibbah came again, unexpectedly, and was joyfully received. She brought gifts, a letter from John Cope, and news. Plato and little Dover were with her. Monday morning, about seven o'clock, she set out for home with foodstuffs and a letter to Mr Cope. In it, Thistlewood said he would return to Egypt if Mr Cope would pay him £100 a year, as he had at Kendal. Lincoln provided escort. He came on the Tuesday with more foodstuffs from Phibbah for Thistlewood: 'So good a girl she is. I only sent 2 bitts by her to lay out in fish.' And so it went on every weekend. If Phibbah did not visit, Lincoln would be sent, and in any case there was the exchange of gifts.

On Wednesday, 3rd August, Thistlewood himself paid a visit to Egypt. He set out from Kendal at about seven o'clock in the morning.

'Rode down to Storer's barcadier, afterwards called at Dr Roberts in Camp Savanna, drank some wine and water, then rode on to Egypt. Got there just before shell-blow, dined with Mr Cope & Mr Deeble there. Supped and stayed all night, slept in my own parlour, and, at night, *Cum* Phibbah, *bis*. Gave little Quaw 2 bitts. Mr and Mrs Cope very glad to see me.'

On Saturday 13th, Phibbah returned the visit. She arrived at Kendal escorted by Lincoln and accompanied by Little Quashe and Egypt Susanah. She brought a basketful of goodies; and, as usual, news. 'Abraham is turned in the field at Egypt'. Poor Egypt Susanah, a frequent sex-partner with Thistlewood, and at Egypt 'kept' by Lincoln was neglected. Lincoln don't seem to look good upon Egypt Susanah, he has got Gordon's Polly here.'

'Friday, 26th August: Sent Lincoln with my horse to Egypt for Phibbah tomorrow, if she can come. He carried her some plantains, and Mrs Cope some roses.'

She came. And, in the same way, she came again on Saturday, 10th September, Saturday, 23rd September, Saturday, 8th October, and Friday, 4th November. In between, Thistlewood had once more visited Egypt, on Monday, 24th October. On her previous visit to Kendal Phibbah had complained, and they had quarrelled, about Thistlewood's association with Aurelia, who seems to have been *la femme fatale* of the Kendal slaves. But, as usually happened, by next day they had made it up, and she and Thistlewood 'walked . . . as far as the cave at the head of Green Island River, &c.', and so to bed.

Then, once again, a new infection. Phibbah's remonstrations

notwithstanding, Thistlewood had gone again with Aurelia on Thursday, 10th November, and on Saturday 12th another woman, Fanny, had spent the night with him. On Monday 14th: 'Headache, feverish, feel oddly, a small running, &c.' By the 17th he was quite certain that he was once again in trouble.

On the 18th he sent Lincoln with his horse to Egypt, and, on Saturday 19th Phibbah arrived. As usual she went back to Egypt on the Monday morning. On Saturday, 3rd December she returned to Kendal. On both those occasions there was the usual exchange of news and gifts. Phibbah must have been well aware of Thistlewood's condition, but there is no mention of complaint or quarrel. Nor is there any mention of sexual activity.

On Saturday, 10th December Thistlewood agreed to go back to Egypt to work for Mr Cope and Mr Dorwood at the Hill barcadier. On Tuesday 20th he made the final gesture at Kendal.

'In the morning *cum* Sabina, *Sup. seat, in Parv. Domo.* A burning of the seed in coition.'

On Thursday 22nd he visited Egypt to make the final arrangements for his return. He slept there and Phibbah came to him. On Saturday, 24th December 1757 he made the move:

'. . . got to Phibbah's house late at night, where I supped and slept, as Mr and Mrs Cope had long been gone to sleep.'

There is no doubt that now he knew he needed her.

On his return to Egypt Mr Cope offered Thistlewood half the profits of operating a new wharf near the mouth of the Cabaritta:

'. . . provided I find 5 Negroes, attend myself, and give him the hundred per annum I should have from Dorwood; but I would not run the risk.'

This was a rather different proposition from one previously made. On December 10th, he had agreed with Cope and Dorwood, who were in partnership of the wharf, to live at Hill, to find 5 slaves and to feed himself (but his slaves would be fed), to manage the business of the wharf, and to receive £200, currency, per year, of which, apparently, Cope would pay half and Dorwood half. Now Cope seemed to want to sell his share of the profits (or losses) to Thistlewood for the fixed £200 a year. It was certainly not a tempting offer, and, in fact, the venture did not prove successful.

Thistlewood, however, set about preparing himself for eventuality. He stayed, restlessly, at Hill, in a house built there for him. On 3rd January he rode to Savanna la Mar and, among other purchases, acquired 'a silver mark TT with which he would brand his belongings. He was offered an overseership by Mr Dorwood at Mountain Spring at £120 a year and salt provisions. He refused. Mr John Parkinson proposed a joint venture in tanning. Again he refused. Next day:

> 'Tuesday, 21st February 1758: p.m. Rode to the Bay. Bought of Mr Samuel Lee, an *Essay Upon Plantership*, by Saml. Martin, Snr Esqr. 3rd Ed. Antigua, 1756 . . . 5 bitts.'

And, on the same day:

> 'Bought of Mr John Parkinson two New Negroe men, at 51 pounds each, and a New Negro girl at £46 pounds = 148 pounds. Mr Parkinson would have no note or bond.
> Monday, 27th February 1758: My two new Negroes in Egypt field. The one I have named Johnie lives with Samuel Matthews, the other named Simon with Coffee, & the girl, Abba, in the cookroom.'

As the weeks passed Thistlewood undertook the receiving and shipping of goods from the Hill barcadier. Continuing restless, and sometimes denied visits by Phibbah because of disagreement with the Copes, he was job-hunting, and performing in his usual various ways.

> 'Tuesday, 7th March 1758: Was Exercised at Salt River by Adjutant McGuire . . . Exercise day first Tuesday every month.
> Tuesday, 21st March: Write a Memorandum, how Mulatto Will's goods are to be disposed of at his death. His wife's shipmate Silvia to have his cow; her daughter Hester, the heifer; Damsel his wife (Jimmy Hayes's wife) the filly & rest of what he has. He desires to be buried at Salt River at his mother (Dianah's) right hand, and that no Negroes should sing, &c.'[6]

Mulatto Will must have known that his time was at hand. He died at Egypt on Easter Monday, 27th March 1758 at about 2 p.m. Thistlewood does not record whether his last wishes were honoured.

At the end of March he 'gave no answer' when Mr Cope, dissuading him from 'going to Honduras' made another offer of the overseership at Egypt.

> 'Wednesday, 19th April 1758: About 2 p.m. *Cum mea* Abba, *Sup Lect*, (*sed non bene*).'

That was his first occasion with one of his own.

On the following Sunday Mr Cope arrived with another offer at Egypt.

> 'With great promises, which refused; and told him about his

readiness to assist Cunningham [at Salt River] and Crookshanks [at Paradise] and of his opposing me in many ways, &c. about the mosquito net, feeding Lincoln, giving Phibbah no time, &c.&c.'

In May, he went the round of estates, but without success. Places had been filled, or offers were unacceptable. Plagued by mosquitoes and jiggers [chigoes], and with an itch which he claimed had been given him by Harry Weech with whom he had shared his bed one night, he was 'vastly lonesome and disagreeable . . . .'

> 'Sunday, 11th June 1758: . . . rode to Mr Mordiner's, dined there. (Read in the Humorist several entertaining things. This was the 2nd vol.) Stayed at Mr Mordiner's till the evening then rode home . . . Mr Mordiner says, reported, Mrs Cocker has made free with one of Michigan's Negro fellows! Strange, if true, but scarce to be doubted.'

On Tuesday 27th June he agreed with Mr Cope. He would go back to Egypt for:

> '. . . £120 per annum certain, and 20s per hhd for all above 120. He is also to hire my Negroes.'

On the 30th he moved, and on 8th July the Copes moved out of Egypt back to Paradise. It is not improbable that that was part of the deal; not that Mr Thistlewood should occupy the great house, for he didn't; but that he should have no interference in his management of the estate.

There is little room for doubt that Mr Cope was glad to have Thistlewood back in charge at Egypt. Early in October 1758:

> 'Mr Cope told me to send to Hyndman's of Saturdays for 6 bitts worth of beef, and when crabs are good to buy a bitts worth of a Sunday . . .'

and, having thus expressed his appreciation, he departed, only to return:

> '. . . at night in liquor, after bed time, slept here and had Silvia. He gave her a cobb.'

On Sunday 19th, November, there was a repeat performance.

> 'In the night Mr Cope and Mr Stephen Coppige come & stayed all night. Mr Cope had Silvia. Mr Coppige had Egypt Susanah, gave her 6 bitts. She pissed the bed.'

Mr Thistlewood was well and minutely informed, no doubt by Phibbah. But, as we have also already learned. Phibbah's great house duties, perhaps with good reason, sometimes led Thistlewood to conjecture.

'Saturday, 2nd December 1758: a.m. Mr Cope and Mr John Dorwood come; dined here. (Suspect Phib.) p.m. They went away.'

On the last day of that year he recorded in detail an account of another kind of excessive behaviour, in which as a mere overseer he could not yet himself indulge.

'Cost of an entertainment given his Excellency the Lieut. Governor at the Court House at Savanna la Mar, by the Gentlemen of the Parish & furnished by Messrs Hayes and Brooks.'

The event had occurred on 2nd July 1757, and the Lieutenant Governor and his hosts had had at their disposal 6 dozen claret at 15s a bottle, 3 dozen old hock at £3 10s. a dozen, 3 dozen Span [Spanish?] at 30s a dozen, 1 dozen champagne at 17s 6d a bottle, 4 dozen madeira at 45s a dozen, 8 dozen cider at 30s a dozen, and dinner for all for £35.

On the same day, 31st December 1758, turning to an entirely different subject of immediate importance to him, he listed the titles of eighteen publications, some in several volumes, which he had received in a case sent by Mr Hewitt in London. They included:

'*Religion, a poem* ... *from the French of the younger Racine.* (London, 1754)
The 2nd Edition of the *Court and City Register* for 1757, corrected to 19th January ... Printed for J. Barnes.
The Gardiner's Dictionary abridged from the last folio edition. Ed. Phillip Miller. (Lond. 1754)
Observations in Husbandry by Edward Lisle, Esqr. (Lond. 1757)
Select Essays on Commerce, Agriculture, Mines, Fisheries, &c. Translated from the Journal Oeconomique, Paris. (Lond. 1754)
Horse-hoeing Husbandry: or an Essay on the Principles of Vegetation and Tillage. by Jethro Tull, Esqr. of Shalborne in Berkshire. (Lond. 1751).'

And, he had been lent, by Mr Cope, two Caribbean works:

'... *a Treatise upon Husbandry or Planting*, by William Belgrave, a regular bred and experienced planter, of the Island of Barbadoes, printed at Boston, in New England, 1755, small 4 vo. as bound; [and]
Instructions for the management of Drax Hall & the Irish Hope

plantations; to Archibald Johnson by Henry Drax, Esqr.'
[The latter about 15 pages Ms.].

From both of these, he made copious notes.

On Saturday, 20th January 1759, there was another festivity in
which he could not share, a ball at Paradise, hosted by Phibbah's
sister Nancy, but the occasion was not explained.

'At night lent Phibbah my horse to Paradise, to Nancy's ball.'

Then, 'betimes' on Sunday morning, Phibbah returned bringing him
'a bottle of wine, &c.' During her absence, he had risked a wetting
'*Cum* Egypt Susanah, *Sup. Lect. (Ter).* Gave her 2 bitts'. But on
Sunday night he made it up '*Cum* Phib.'

On Egypt, preparations were in hand for the 1759 crop, and on
12th February he put the mill about.

A few weeks later, a white employed at Paradise was murdered.
Suspicion fell on Salt River Duke, who ran away. Then on the night
of Friday, 30th March, Paradise great house was broken into. No
damage was recorded, but here suspicion fell on Prince, a Paradise
slave. The Copes decided to move. Next day, Sunday, 1st April,
they went to Egypt and remained there until the last week of April.

'Monday, 2nd April: Saw a large comet this morning to the
eastward.'[7]

Next morning he saw it again.

'Sunday, 8th April: Last night Salt River Duke, at Old Sarah's
gate, seen by Old Sarah and Pero. He had a machete in his
hand, and enquired if any Salt River Negroes were this way. He
drank some of Pero's cane liquor he had in a calabash, went
towards Top-Hill.'

Thistlewood made no mention of any attempt to capture Duke, and
for the time being, things quietened down.

'Monday, 9th April: My Johnie wanting. In the evening
returned very loose with yaws.
Observed the comet (whose tail rather increased I think), it
rises about 2 hours before the sun. Its course is retrograde,
moves to the Southward. Began to give Simon a diet drink
again, of lignum vitae, sarsaparilla and senna; believe I shall
lose him, he is so meagre, &c, distempered.
Friday, 27th April: Observed the comet about 8 in the evening to the south, about 25 degrees high with a bushy tail &c
eastward.

Monday, 30th April: The comet resplendent tonight, making its way to the westward of the north somewhat (about 50 degrees high in the south, before 8 p.m.) Tail about 20 degrees. Tuesday, 15th May: About 8 p.m. saw the Comet again, in the south-west, about 60 degrees high (Faint). This evening some clouds in the west, of a greenish colour.'

And he recorded it twice again, on Wednesday 16th and, for the last time on the 22nd: 'Saw the comet at night, faint.'

In mid-May, after the Copes had returned to Paradise, Little Mimber was brought out of the field and put to sewing in Egypt great house.

'Saturday, 19th May: At night Mr Cope came. Slept here, had Little Mimber; but suspect he has the clap.'

Nonetheless, and indeed he had little reason to worry whether or not, five nights later:

'In the evening, *Cum* Little Mimber, a Creole, *Sup. Lect. in meo domo* parlour.'

Indulging other interests, he had also been discussing some of the books going the rounds among the planters.

'Lent Mr Parkinson the Oeconomy of Love, a poem (said to be wrote by Armstrong, a Scotsman). Mr Parkinson praises Tom Jones, said to be wrote by Fielding, Joseph Andrews, by Fielding's sister (Harvey's meditations). Roderick Random & Peregrine Pickle, by Smollet, not quite so good, though praised by the Scotch. (Maryland, said to be wrote by Chesterfield).'

On 21st June the Cope's daughter, Polly, was christened at Paradise. Phibbah went over to help cook dinner. It was a busy afternoon for Thistlewood.

'About 1 p.m. the canoe came. Received by her, 2 firkins of butter from Meyler's wharf, a small barrel of herrings, and half a barrel of beef; also received an old grindstone about 22 inches & a half dr. from Mr Wheatley. Received a note from Mr Stokes; a hog from Joseph Williams Esqr. – wrote to him. They also brought Abba in the canoe, flogged her well.

Having thus attended to her, he turned to others.

'About 2 p.m. *Cum* Mazerine, *Sup. Terr.* old Curing house cane-piece. Gave her a bitt.
About 3 p.m. *Cum* Warsoe, in the boiling house. Stans: Backwards.'

Later, he settled down to a supper sent to him from Paradise by Phibbah who returned next day bearing gifts from the Copes – a leg of mutton, cheesecake, pine tarts, &c. There is no indication that she was told of his capers during her absence; but she soon caused him a good deal of anxiety which he apparently attempted to hide behind an unconvincing display of indifference. In the evening of Friday, 3rd August, Mr Cope, Mr Stephen Coppige and his brother Tom Coppige arrived. Mr Cope had Mimber, the others had Rosanna & Mazarine.

'I reprimanded Phib. for going in the house.

Sunday, 12th: a.m. *Cum* Little Lydde, *Sup. Terr.* [in a cane-field]. Gave her a bitt.

Wednesday, 15th: Phibbah last night at the Negro house. p.m. Mr Parkinson called to see me; told me he saw Mr Peter Collgrave in town, who enquired much after me.

Phibbah sleeps in the great house, I take it.

Thursday 16th: Phibbah yet away.

Friday 17th: At night *Cum* Mountain Susanah, *Sup. me lect.* gave her 2 bitts. Phibbah, I don't know where, at the Negro house, in the cookroom, or great house, &c., with Dago, &c.

Saturday 18th: Phibbah yet away. Received 6 lbs. beef from Mr Hyndman.

Gave our Negroes today.

p.m. Rode to the Bay, drank tea with Mrs Emetson, in the evening rode home.

In the evening (but after I was gone to bed) Mr Cope come, had Mimber or Venus. Phibbah in the great house also; what about I can't tell.

Tuesday, 21st: Put Betty and Clara in steep for the crab yaws. Phibbah sleeps yet in the cookroom, or great house, Dago also.

Wednesday 22nd: a.m. *Cum* Violet *Sup. Terr.* [in a cane piece]. Gave her a bitt.

Thursday 23rd: In the night Mr Cope come. (Phib. I don't know where).

Friday 24th: a.m. Mrs. Cope, Miss Polly Cope, &c. come to stay here awhile.'

And, perhaps in consequence, he enjoyed a Sunday dinner of 'roasted bullock's tongue, very good'. For the next day or two, there was no mention either of Phibbah, or of his interference with any other; then, on:

'Wednesday 29th: p.m. *Cum* Mould's Lydde, in the Curing house, Stans! Backwd. Made Phib. run for her impudence.'

Next day he took 'Daphne, a congo, *Sup. Terr* . . .' and on the 31st
he noted: 'Phibbah yet away, very saucy and impudent.' And so,
until:

> 'Tuesday, 4th September: In the evening *Cum* Egypt Susanah,
> *Sup. me lect.* Gave her 2 bitts. Sent word by her to Phib., she
> might come if she would, and accordingly she did. At night
> *Cum* Phib.'

Towards the end of the year, Mr Peter Collgrave came and
dined with Thistlewood at Egypt and they discussed the difficulties
of overseership. Mr Collgrave remarked that

> '. . . the three essential qualifications of an overseer are Lenity,
> Industry, and Honesty, supposing him to have common sense
> also.
> That the warm sun and blue skies in this country are all that is
> agreeable.'

The conversation must have been interesting. Thistlewood was in no
doubt of his own excellence and never hesitant to record the failings,
and the merits where he saw them, of others who supervised the
work of slaves. On the neighbouring Long Pond Estate, Mr Reid,
formerly at Salt River, had recently been employed by Col Barclay
in the place of Mr Cummings who had been 'too easy with the
Negroes'. On Egypt there had been, and would continue, a rapid
turn-over of white 'Drivers', or 'Book-keepers' as we refer to
them – but Thistlewood seldom used that term. At the end of July
1759, for instance, Thomas Beard (apparently too lenient) had been
replaced by Robert Lawrence. In early 1760 Lawrence was replaced
by John Groves, of whom more anon.

Thistlewood himself was never really happy working in someone
else's employ. He had successively quarrelled with Florentius Vassall,
William Dorrill, and John Cope of whom he seemed to have the
least opinion. In mid-September he addressed himself to Mr Vassall.

> 'Egypt Plantation, Savanna la Mar, Westmoreland, Jamaica,
> September 13th 1759. To Florentius Vassall
> > Sir, I have lately been informed that it is imagined you are
> > not yet provided with a person in Mr John Brown's place
> > altogether to your liking, if not, and that you think me a
> > proper person, I should be glad to serve you, which am in
> > hopes I should to your satisfaction. The place I am in with
> > Mr Cope, is as good as an hundred pounds, sterling, per
> > annum, all necessaries found me, and no expenses, which
> > is indeed as much as it can afford, therefore shall not leave

it except something offers very considerably to my advantage, as I imagine your employ would be; where I should also hope to be fixed for many years, having a great dislike to often changing, which must be very disadvantageous to the owners of estates, as I have observed it is not uncommon in these parts for a man to leave his place, by the time he is acquainted with his business. I am, Sir, yr. most humble servt., Thos. Thistlewood.'

This was not simply a shot in the dark. In conversation with others a few days previously Thistlewood had been told that Mr Vassall would like to have him, though others were trying to persuade him otherwise. In any case Mr Vassall's reply was not recorded.

There were few remarkable events in the next two months except Phibbah's announcement on Monday, 22nd October that 'she suspects she is breeding'. In the same week, Thursday:

'Phibbah behaved oddly tonight, conscious of guilt in the great house with J.C. this afternoon, &c.'

Since the incidents of late March and early April there had been occasional rumours of restlessness among the slaves of one estate or another, but there had been no great alarm. Such apprehensions as there had been were of a more personal and domestic nature, and had alarmed the planters rather than the slaves; but the year ended with two events of a kind not previously recorded. One morning at the end of September, some of the Egypt slaves had 'chased some runaways from off an island in the morass ...'. Among those chased was Egypt's Cambridge; and, in the afternoon he had been found, by himself, 'in the Dunbar ground'. Brought home by Jackie, Cambridge had been well flogged and secured in the bilboes. Later in the year:

'Sunday, 2nd December 1759: About one p.m. Little Quashe come and told me, that Cambridge was found dead, in the morass, back of the cotton tree where we cut copper-wood last year, in the water, by Daniel and Jackie, &c. The cattle boys say they heard him holler last night, but thought it had been canoe-men in the river. Imagine he was murdered by runaways who, it seems, threatened to murder him the last time he was runaway if he did not leave them, least they should be found out upon his account, by our looking for him. Wrote an account to Mr Cope, per Prince.'

Next morning, Thistlewood went to Savanna la Mar and reported the death to Mr Theodore Stone, the coroner. Then he returned to

Egypt, and only then did they fetch Cambridge's body out of the morass and examine it. No mark of violence was discernible, but the examination was rapid and perhaps perfunctory because of the state of the corpse. Nonetheless:

'... I and the Negroes think he was forcibly drowned by runaways.'

Again, Thistlewood reported to Mr Cope and to Mr Stone, and, on the authority of the coroner, Cambridge was buried.

Exactly a week later, another Egypt runaway, Mould's Hazat, came home, this time alive and voluntarily. Hazat had been runaway for some time. Once, on 1st December, he was spotted by other Egypt slaves working at Hill, but he had not been taken.

'Sunday, 9th December 1759:   Received a letter from Mr Henry Weech [Paradise overseer], per Mason Quashe, with whom comes Mould's Hazat, come home of his own accord. He says he was afraid of being murdered in the woods; has been shot at 3 times since he has been out.'

Notes

1 A blue-coated soldier.
2 They had refused to go to Cope and McDonald who had then summoned Eve and Beck.
3 The beginning of the wake, which continued through Sunday.
4 A slave 'doctor' at Salt River.
5 This was Thistlewood's son borne by Nago Jenny. He would later be referred to as little Thomas. He died in childhood.
6 This is not clear. Jimmy Hayes (colour unknown) was a tavernkeeper in Savanna la Mar. Mulatto Will was a slave. Damsel, clearly, had been one, and perhaps still was. Perhaps she had originally been with Jimmy Hayes, either as his property, or simply as his 'wife' though belonging to someone else. If Hester was Damsel's daughter she seems not to have been Mulatto Will's. Perhaps she was Jimmy Hayes's.
7 Halley's Comet on its first predicted return. It had first been sighted elsewhere in December 1758.

CHAPTER 5   1760 – following Tacky

Introduction

Thistlewood's many complaints about the slaves under his charge
reflected in large measure the constant acts of individual resistance
to bondage. Running away; pretending illness; planting potato slips
in the wrong way, and similar 'mistakes'; maiming animals, and
other 'careless' acts; damaging or losing tools and equipment; allow-
ing livestock in the canefields; poisoning foodstuffs; and on occasion,
direct physical assault – all were used as means of protest. These
individual resistances were annoying and sometimes dangerous to
the master concerned, but posed no real threat to the general
society and economy. For that to be achieved, a wider planning and
co-ordination of resistance would be necessary. Of such larger and
more ambitious attempts in eighteenth century Jamaica, Tacky's
Rebellion of 1760 was undoubtedly the most formidable.

Tacky, an Akan Negro from the Gold Coast (and so described
as 'Koromantyn'), was representative of an ethnic group described
by Bryan Edwards as distinguished by their:

'... firmness both of body and mind; a ferociousness of disposition; but withal activity, courage, and a stubbornness, or
what an ancient Roman would have deemed an elevation of
soul, which prompts them to enterprises of difficulty and danger;
and enables them to meet death, in its most horrible shape,
with fortitude or indifference.'

The understood aim of Tacky's rebellion was the destruction of the
whites and the establishment of Akan controlled states in which
Akan leaders and their supporters, Akan or other, would enslave
their defeated opponents and continue in the production of sugar
and rum as well as foodstuffs.

It is not always easy to assess whether any particular act of
resistance, individual or larger, was successful. Success means the
achievement of an objective. The purposes of slave resistance were
various: the annoyance of a particular master on a particular occasion;
the removal by discharge, resignation or death of a master; the

hindrance of a successful crop; the destruction of a building or canefield; and many others. One might go so far as to argue that if an individual slave carried out an act of resistance intended to annoy, and was subsequently lashed by an infuriated master in an apoplectic fit of rage, he would have, at some cost to himself, achieved his aim. But in the all-embracing objective of island-wide takeover, such as Tacky's was said to be, there is no doubt. The outcome would prove success or failure.

The failure of Tacky's attempt resulted from three main disadvantages: the lack of a closely co-ordinated strategy of attack throughout the island; the superior fire-power and battle tactics of the regular troops, the militia, and the Maroons, once they had been mobilized; and the 'Achilles heel' in the power of Obeah which protected the charmed person from death, and if death should come it would signify the weakness or unworthiness of the charmed rather than of the charm. The death of a leader thus not only removed his leadership, but also threw doubt on the wisdom and propriety of his leadership.

In Jamaica, as elsewhere in the Caribbean, the eighteenth century was punctuated by many acts of slave resistance and rebellion; but in Westmoreland the year 1760 opened in a quite ordinary way.

'Tuesday, 1st January 1760:   Quaw at Hill making trash baskets. Job and Dago in the canoe cutting grass for the cattle; brought 24 bundles wild scotch grass, at 3 times.
Began to wear new neckcloth, [No.] 6.
Flanders hewing staves.
Sent to Paradise five young pigeons per Warsoe.
In the evening shot a night-walker by the great pond side.
Sent the Negro man to Mr Stone this morning, per Jackie, who robbed his girls last night. He belongs to Colin Campbell, Esqr.
In the morning billed bushes in the pasture, then took 40 hands upon the road. Plato and Coffee watching the canes. Rest of the hands carrying trash into the pens.
At night cleaned out the hogsheads.'

Preparations were being made to take the crop.

On the domestic scene, Mrs Cope was brought to bed of a girl on the night of Saturday 26th; Mr Cope was paying frequent nightly visits to Egypt where he would summon Little Mimber, for whom he had a passion until mid-April when he transferred his attentions to Sancho's wife, Cubbah.

Phibbah was pregnant, but still at work in the great house cookroom. Her baby was not due until April. Meantime, she occasionally overstepped Thistlewood's view of her proper authority.

'Friday, 11th January: p.m. Reprimanded Phibbah for inter-meddling with the field Negroes business with me, &c.'

As we know, she was a woman of some property, and now she disposed of some of it. On 27th January she sold her filly for £4 10*s* to William Rickett's slave, Coffee, and wanted to give Thistlewood a present of 33 bitts (a little over £1) '. . . which I being at present scarce of accepted, but shall make myself debtor to her for it'. (And so he did, but he did not repay her till September). Some weeks later on April 5th, she:

'sold her mare Patience to the Negro man of Col Barclay's named Crossley for seven pounds. He paid her £5 10*s* down, and is to pay the remaining 30*s* in three months.'

Then, on the 28th, Old Daphne came over from Salt River to attend to her, and at about 8 o'clock in the morning of Tuesday, 29th April 1760, she was delivered of a boy.[1] House Franke was sent over from Paradise to look after her for a few days, and Egypt Lucy was kept at home 'giving Phibbah's child suck'. For a day or so Phibbah was unwell with 'a bad looseness' and, on hearing of it from Thistlewood, Mrs Cope sent her flour, wine, cinnamon, &c. At the end of the week House Franke was recalled to Paradise and went laden with gifts, a Cuba teal and a diver for herself, and a roasting pig for Mrs Cope. In her place, Mr Mould's Franke came to take over the Egypt cookhouse until Phibbah was up and about again.

There was, it seems, no heavier than usual incidence of slaves running away or of punishments inflicted. There were accidents and ailments:

'Thursday, 28th February: Coffee coming over the bridge, to bring the cart home, with a load of cane-tops, somehow or other let the cart jam him against the post & rails, tore one of his legs in a bad manner, and he tumbled into the river. Wrote to Dr Gorse by Abraham. He soon came and sewed up the wound, &c. Beck is sometimes light headed today. The doctor and I went to Hill to visit Celia who has the ague and fever. I had the canoe ready to take us over.'

But old Celia did not recover. A week later she died at Hill and was buried by Old Sharper and Morris.

In late March Lincoln and Violet 'made a match'; and, as the cane cutting declined, the field hands were increasingly employed in other tasks.

'Tuesday, 4th March: Transplanted star-apples, oranges and shaddocks out of the garden into Top-Hill interval. Also planted lignum vitae seed and the horse lilac seed in d*°* interval.'

Provisions, it seems, were scarce. On Sunday, 20th April, Thistlewood spent most of the forenoon on the road westwards 'looking out for plantains'. He got 100 for 4 bitts. And so hands were employed planting corn and plantain suckers in the provision grounds, vegetables (cauliflower, broccoli, cabbage, lettuce, parsley, spinach, beets) in the garden, and, in the pasture, aloes.

On some Sundays, as the pressures of the crop taking became less heavy, special relaxations were allowed, such as fishing in the great pond. On Sunday, 4th May, for instance, Ambo, Daniel Dago, Cubbenna, Little Quashie and Jackie were given permission to fish. They got 20 large tarpons between them.

As for Thistlewood himself, he contentedly followed his various interests.

'Wednesday, 20th February: In the morning, rode by Mr Hungerford's, away to the Bay, and had our large canoe meet me at the westmost wharf. Went on board the ship *Earl of Effingham*, Capt. Joseph Bellamy (but he was not on board). Was detained a long time, they were so busy, and at last went down into the hold myself and found my 2 cases, which received and gave receipt for them. Breakfasted and dined with Mr James Foot who is Mate, and Dr Priest, young Cave, &c.&c. Then went to the Bay again. Bought of Mr Francis Gallagher 4 new puncheons at 35s. each = £7 0s 0d. Gave him an order on Mr Cope for the money, and had his receipt. Brought them home in the canoe. Mason Quashe, Lewie, Quaw, Lincoln & Flanders in the canoe. I rode home & the canoe got home soon after dark.'

The next few days his spare hours were spent opening his two cases and cataloguing and packaging their contents – mostly flower and vegetable seeds. Catalogues and sample assortments were then sent to interested people: Col Barclay, John Parkinson, Dr Gorse, Mr Cope, Randolph Donaldson, and others.

A lingering 'clamminess' notwithstanding he had also, by early May, returned to his sexual exercises with accustomed vigour.

'Friday, 9th May: In the morning *Cum* Warsoe *Sup.* Ladder top by the corn-loft side in the curing house. Stans! Backwd ... In the evening *Cum* Amelia (belonging Miss Sally Witter) *Sup. Lect.* She had been in the country selling soap, and would sleep in my house.'

And there were visitors. On 19th May, for instance, Samuel Say and Joseph Roberts dined with him and enjoyed 'one of Phibbah's pigs, roasted, Madeira wine, porter & punch.'

Of slave unrest there was no word. The usual militia exercises were, as usual, rather infrequently attended; the maroon parties were scarcely seen at Egypt, having paid only one visit, on the morning of Friday, 1st February when they were entertained with some grog; and the restrictions on the slaves were not always observed.

'Friday, 14th March, 1760:   Sold Old Sharper the gun I bought from driver Quashe many years ago. He gave me only 10s. for her but paid ready money. He will soon shoot aligators &c. enough at Hill.'

On Sunday, 20th May, Thistlewood rode to Paul Island estate and dined with Mr John Parkinson. While there:

'About 4 p.m. Mr Roberts come home from his mountain, and brought news of a supposed insurrection tomorrow, when 3,000 Negroe men were to muster in a certain place, from Hanover and this Parish, &c. Told him by a strange Negro man who came to him in the mountain. In the evening rode home.'

There was not, it would appear, much credence given to Mr Roberts' account. It had been a peaceful crop season, just over, and now was the time for relaxation. Perhaps, hopefully, it was just another of those rumours which, from time to time, lent excitement to the conversations of the whites. But was it?

Not so many days before, at about 1 a.m. on Easter Monday morning, Tacky, a Coromantee slave on Frontier Estate in the parish of St Mary, had led a small band of his fellows from Frontier and the adjacent Trinity Estates down into Port Maria. There, they had attacked the fort, killed the sentinel, and captured a large quantity of arms and ammunition. They then moved inland attracting increasing numbers as they went firing through the estates − Trinity, Frontier, Ballards Valley, Esher, and Haywood Hall where they stopped to rest, to celebrate, and to eat. Meanwhile, 'about 130 Whites and trusty Blacks, tolerably armed' had been mustered and were following in pursuit. News had also been sent to the Governor in Spanish Town and two companies of regular troops and a band of Maroons from the central Maroon settlement at Scotts Hall had been despatched in aid.

Militia, troops, and Maroons attacked Tacky's forces and eventually scattered them into nearby woods where Davy, a Maroon sharp shooter, shot and killed Tacky. His followers were soon defeated.

The revolt was discovered to have been part of an island-wide plan and before all the fighting was over in late September there had been uprisings in St Thomas in the East, St John, Kingston, St James, Hanover, and, on a scale almost equal to that of St Mary, in Westmoreland. By then, over 50 whites had been killed and nearly 400 slaves had lost their lives in battle or in terrible punishments including mutilations, gibbetings, and slow burnings.

The rebel slaves, strengthened by charms provided by obeahmen had fought and died with great courage. Tacky had been killed, but:

'... some others of the ringleaders being taken, and a general inclination to revolt appearing among all the Koromantyn Negroes in the island, it was thought necessary to make a few terrible examples of some of the most guilty... [of three found guilty killing the whites employed on Ballard's Valley] one was condemned to be burnt, and the other two to be hung up alive in irons and left to perish in that dreadful situation. The wretch that was burnt was made to sit on the ground, and his body being chained to an iron stake, the fire was applied to his feet. He uttered not a groan, and saw his legs reduced to ashes with the utmost firmness and composure; after which, one of his arms by some means getting loose, he snatched a brand from the fire that was consuming him, and flung it in the face of the executioner.'[2]

By the end of May the revolt had broken out in Westmoreland. Mr Robert's news was accurate. For the next weeks we take Mr Thistlewood's record of events in that parish.

'Monday, 26th May 1760: Soon after midnight Messrs Say, Bowen, Walker & Rumbold called me up and told me of Mr Smith at Capt. Forest's being murdered by the Negroes (Mr Smith shot about ¼ before ten o'clock); Capt. Hoar sadly chopped, &c. Capt. George Richardson, and Thos. Barnes, &c. running to the Bay on foot, a narrow escape they had. When we reached Col Barclay's I galloped back immediately to Egypt, and secured my keys, writings &c. which had before neglected in my fright, because those who called me were some almost without clothes, and rode bare-back, telling me I should probably be murdered in a short time, &c. &c. Soon returned after I had put my things in order as well as I could, and was down at the Bay about 2 o'clock. Did duty till daylight then was set at liberty by Mr Antrobus to go home and take care of the estate. John Groves, the madman, shot at several Negro boys, wounded Oliver, Mr John Cunningham's waiting-boy. Went to the bay without my orders., &c. but in the evening he returned. The soldiers were soon despatched after the rebellious Negroes. Sailors and militia halted at Egypt, gave them 6 or 8 pails of grog, had a silver spoon stole in the hurry &c. &c. This happened about 9 a.m.

Gave our Negroes today. Strange various reports with torments & confusion.

Mr Walker dined at Egypt. Gave one John Turge, belonging to the [ship] *Peter Beckford*, Capt. Lovelace, also, dinner. p.m. Mr Walker went away, but John Turge, John Groves, and a sailor who had fallen asleep in the bush and lost his arms, had supper and kept watch by turn all night.

Had 4 Negro men kept watch at the Hothouse door, pen gate, wash house door, and curing house door, & had the words "all's well" passed.

Vast numbers of people belonging to the Troop, Militia, called, &c. Frequent alarms fired, &c. Vast number of dispatches passing, &c.

Tuesday, 27th May 1760: Gave Morrice a new hoe as he is now in the field. Employed carrying the trash out of the Mill-house into the pens, cleaning up about the works, &c.

Wrote to Mr Forbes, and sent a suspicious Negro to gaol per Coffee.

The soldiers remaining that could be spared rode by through Egypt to Leeward about 1 p.m – most of them it seems come from St. Elizabeth. The sailors commanded by Capt. Watson returning, called and had grog again. Gave the Capt. and officers punch & bread and cheese. The sailors drunk, &c. Lewie, Quamina, Lincoln, &c. got guns, &c. Sad work amongst the sailors, &c. About 9 or 10 a.m. part of the Troop and Militia also halted here.

A report of a party of the rebellious Negroes are near us in the Salt Savanna, that they stopped a canoe loaded with sugar, &c.

Gave Morrice, Prince, Adam, Venus, Abba, Plato, L[ittle] Doll & Phibbah each a new dung basket – Egypt Lucy and Simon, Little Mimber.

Broached last year's puncheon of rum for to make grog for the Troop &c.

Our Hector wanting. p.m. come home. In the evening Col Barclay, &c called and drank porter.

Let our Negroes sleep till p.m. turn out time, that watched last night.

Lent the mate of the *Earl of Effingham* my horse to the Bay, made Job go with him.

Sent Dido to Paradise, her belly big, almost at her time.

In the evening 2 gentlemen from Hanover begged for a mouthful of salt beef and plantain, and a drink of toddy, all which I gave them.

Had 4 Negroes armed watch all night, John Groves also. I lay down sometimes with my clothes on and slept little.

Wednesday 28th: Employed carrying dung out of the great pond and lying it upon heaps in the pasture by the pond side. Put up the sugar pots in the Curing house, &c., had a broken chain took off.

a.m. *Cum* Mazerine in the Curing house behind the butt, Sup. Mule Collar. Gave d° 2 bitts.

A guard of soldiers (about 8 a.m.) called and had grog. They guarded 21 Negro prisoners to the Bay. *Vizt.* 19 men & 2 women. Amongst the men was one of their grandees, his hair shaved in form of a Cap on his head. He was said eat the heart & tongue of one of the white people murdered. Was to have been King.

Gave grog to a party of Militia going into the Country & to many others. Gave Mr Wheatly & 2 more gentlemen and Mr Collins some broiled fish & plantains, &c. Strange confused reports. Some of the Old Hope & Colin Campbell's Negroes gone.

Gave a sailor dinner who was going with the militia but is left behind. (John Dufharty [?]) he stayed all night and helped to keep watch, &c. Had strict watch kept, and the words "all's well" passed from one Negro to another. When the report was of the Old Hope Negroes being rose, perceived a strange alteration in ours. They are certainly very ready if they durst, and am pretty certain they were in the plot, by what John told me on Sunday evening, what they had said in the field on Saturday in the Pawpaw tree piece, that he, what signified him, he would dead in a Egypt &c.&c.;[3] and from many other circumstances, Lewie being over at Forest's that night, &c. Coffee & Job also very outrageous.

Thursday, 29th May 1760: Employed carrying out pond earth for dung as before. Flanders [the cooper] as usual. Benjamin at Paradise.

In the morning *Cum* Barnett's Nancy, *Sup. Cot, in Mag. Dom.*

About 2 p.m. a Mulatto boy and 2 Negro men-boys come running from Jacobsfield, the late Mr Allen's, and reported that some Negroes come with a shout and fired 4 or 5 guns, and began to tear the great house in pieces, before they escaped. I immediately wrote to the Commanding Officer at Savanna la Mar, and sent Job on horseback express with it. A party of 14 horsemen were soon sent there.

Immediately armed our Negroes and kept a strict guard and sharp look-out; all the afternoon and night being under dreadful apprehensions as Mr Joseph Johnson told me we had but bad success, being defeated and some of our people killed; of which perceive our Negroes have good intelligence, being greatly elevated, and ready to rise, now we are in the most imminent danger. Saw Mr John Jones's house burnt tonight, &c. Many parties of soldiers, and other persons passed by to Leeward in the dusk of the evening. 4 Footmen called in the evening, I gave them refreshment. One of them could not bear the mosquitoes and went away in the middle of the night. The others lay in the great house piazza till daybreak.

Gave a party of the militia porter to drink, who were guarding 6 prisoners down the Bay.

'Friday 30th: Negro men under arms, as yesterday. Negro women pulling up weeds about the Negro houses, &c.

Several of our wounded came by this morning, and multitudes of Negroes carrying goods down to the Bay from Col Ricketts's, &c.

Mr Reid from Long Pond came to see me. He says great fear of Crawford's Negroes rising. Hid my old coins, &c. Secured a golly-pot in the curing-house.

John & me kept strict watch all night, passing the words "all's well" almost continually. 2 Negroes in the Mill house, 1 at the hothouse door, 1 at Mule pen gate, 1 at wash house door, one at the Curing house door, and me to walk the round. John and I are both almost spent.

Saturday 31st: a.m. part of the Troop called and had grog. a.m. a guard carrying prisoners to the Bay called. Gave them grog. Mongst the prisoners are Mr Foot's Coffee who formerly worked here. Mr Reid come over to see me.

p.m. *Cum* Barnett's Nancy *Sup. Me. Lect.*

p.m. Several Troopers, &c. call. The attack put off till Monday, waiting large reinforcements from distant parts. Arrived a Man-of-War with soldiers, at Savanna la Mar Road. In the evening Mr Reid came and slept on my bed. He was warned by one of their Negroes to go off the Estate as one of their Coromantees was expected to come in the night, with a party of the rebellious Negroes to take all they could with them. Many of the well-affected Negroes left the estate lest they should be forced to join the rebels. Salt River Long Quaw[4] burnt yesterday to Leeward, & Paradise Dover hanged. Our Negroes had today. Gave Egypt Lucy and Syphox tickets. Kept a very strict watch all night.

Sunday, 1st June 1760: Gave Jackie, Lewie, Johnie, Margaritta & Phibbah tickets to go to Roaring River to buy provisions. Also to Hector & Peter – Pero – Sarah, Cubbah, Abba, Eve – Dover to Paradise. Egypt Susanah – Quamina, Simon, Punch, Phillis, Primus, Rosanna, Beck, Juno – Little Mimber, Abigail – L. Quashe – Egypt Lucy – Derby, Morrice – L. Lydde, Betty – Achilles, Phillip – Toby, Ellin, Adam – Plato – Princess – Big Lydde – Cloe.

Many people called with Mr Cope, &c. Gave them grog and porter.

p.m. Mr Mofatt, Donaldson, Blakeney and Wilson, guarding provisions and ammunition called. I fitted them out with many things as pads, ropes, crooks, &c. Gave them grog & porter. A young goose died.

At night kept a strict watch as before.

Monday 2nd: Lincoln beat Violet again, and is very impudent & ill-minded. Achilles told Daniel if he did not take care he would cut his head off in the bush. Witness Egypt Lucy, Chrishea, Hazot, Pero & Margarine.

p.m. He run away.

Mr Henry Weech dined with me, just come from Moreland, almost spent.

p.m. went away. Cleaned about the works, threw up the wood hoops, carrying out pond earth, &c. p.m. *Cum* L. Mimber, *Sup Me Lect.*

Gave Abraham a ticket to Savanna la Mar. Gave many people porter & grog.

p.m. Mr Solomon Cook called, wounded in the left shoulder, with a slug, in the engagement today which was very smart. Several of the rebellious Negroes killed, their provisions and town took, also most of their powder, and a great deal of plunder as ruffled shirts, laced hats, shoes, stockings, cravats, &c. &c., and fine mahagony chests full of clothes, &c. &c. They had fortified themselves with palisadoes and sundry walls, but we took it. Col Cudjoe's Negroes behaved with great bravery.

The Black Shot[5] from Hanover, &c. had not much resolution.

At night kept a very strict watch as before.

Tuesday 3rd: Employed carrying out pond earth, &c.

a.m. a serjeant of the regulars called, very ill. Lay all day upon the cot and all night also. Ordered Abraham attend him. Wrote to Mr Robert Baker at Savanna la Mar per Job. Kept a strict watch all night.

Achilles yet away. Many people called as usual, but not much done against the rebellious Negroes today.

Wednesday, 4th June 1760: Employed as before. Wrote to Lieut Preston, and doctor Cooper, of His Majesty's 74th Regiment about the serjeant who is sick here (per Coffee). Had a fowl killed for him.

Some people who wanted to press my horse, or exchange a bad gun for a good one threw a Madam Fating bottle of Rum[6] down at the Curing house door, broke the bottle & spill the rum. Many people called all day long.

a.m. Moved 48 pots of sugar into the Curing house = 947 pots. Mr John Parkinson, Mr Saml. Say, James Lawson, Mr Lauderdale, and Mr Williams of Quacoo Hill, and a young man from North Side, named Odel or Parr, I think. Had stewed fish, crab, a boiled pigeon, and two broiled fowls. Punch, grog, porter, &c. (Mistake! His name was Enniss and he was driver at Midgeham, Jacob Ricketts's estate). When a Negro belonging Will Ricketts's estate, norward, p.m., was going to be burnt at the Bay, he told Mr Thos. Tomlinson's Jnr book-keeper that if he would let him escape (he being of his guard) that he would give him 14 pistoles, all the money he had by him, and make him overseer of Midgeham. This Negro, although burnt by degrees with a slow fire made at a distance from him, never flinched, moved a foot, nor groaned, or cried "oh!".

At night kept guard as usual.

Just in the dusk of the evening Capt. Forsythe and his company (just arrived from St Mary's having quelled the rebellion there) halted at Egypt, and had grog, then marched to Leeward, when, having got about an hundred yards along the road past Col Barclay's canes, 2 guns were fired at them out of the woods, and Captain Forsythe immediately made all his company fire at the place, but cannot tell if they did any execution. They had Abraham for a guide to show them the near way to Mr Crawford's. Messrs Emetson, Leister, Gallagher, &c. called going to the Bay. Took a bag of powder, some cartouches [cartridges] cutlasses, &c. out of a house just by John Steward's. The Negroes ran away at the sight of them.

Thursday 5th: Employed as before. Gave Cubbenna a ticket

to Paradise. Gave Lincoln & Syphox, Dago & my Johnie, tickets to go sell crabs. Dr Parkinson called and breakfasted with me. Served our Negroes a pint of salt each, and gave them a pail of molasses amongst them.

p.m. *Cum* Phibbah *Sup. Lect.*

Admiral Holmes has wrote down to the gentlemen of the parish, that if they think it necessary he will pick the choice men out of the whole fleet, bring them down in the *Cambridge*, and head his men himself, to keep them in order and under command. Very pretty indeed! Gives great satisfaction

Mr Walker from Jacobsfield dined with me. (Bookkeeper). Also supped and slept in the yellow room.

Achilles yet out. Abraham not returned from Capt. Forsythe.

At night kept a strict guard, heard a noise in the water between us and the Salt Savanna, in the part between the islands, seemingly like a multitude of horsemen in a hurry, but conjecture it must be cattle chased by some of the rebellious Negroes, about ⅓ of a mile from us.

Friday 6th: Employed as before. Gave our Negroes a pail of molasses. Hear yesterday a soldier was shot by the rebellious Negroes, and one of the militia named David Lander.

Received a letter per Waterford, from Mr Robert Chambers, at Mr Cope's request, write to Mr Cope per d°.

a.m. John Witter, John Hutt, Thos. Coppige, &c.&c. called and drank porter, eat herrings, &c. Also a great many more almost continously. The sick serjeant here yet. Gave him a vomit last night. Seems to have done him some good. Had a fowl killed to make him broth.

Mr Walker come, supped, and slept here.

Kept a strict guard at night.

p.m. Wrote to Mr Cope, sent Coffee, Cubbenna, Quamina, Dago & Lincoln in the canoe to the Bay.

p.m. A suspicious person come here under pretence of seeking employ, going to Leewards unconcerned, wanted to stay all night, but I made him go back. (Take him to be a French man disguised). He says he has been long a prisoner amongst them; perhaps he is a person appointed to stir up the Negroes, &c. A Jesuit very likely.

Saturday 7th: Employed as usual. Gave our Negroes the afternoon. Received by our canoe a barrel of beef, a firkin of butter, and a bag of mashed biscuits − all which opened and begun upon immediately.

Strong party of Cudjoe's Negroes went by to Leeward.

This morning the sick serjeant rode to the Bay, on a strange horse.

Gave Syphox a ticket, and made him attend him, but they pressed the horse as he was coming back.

Abraham not yet returned. Mr Bevil, one of the officers belonging to the company he guided told me he very believes he was killed in Thursday's engagement, but cannot be positive (Mr Antrobus & Capt. Forsythe prest him).

Gave John Groves a fine thread red handkerchief spotted with white. Also gave Little Mimber one.

Mr Samuel Say dined with me. Gave 2 of the militia dinner, &c.

Caesar come home from Paradise this afternoon.

Mr Samuel Say and Mr Walker supped and slept here.

About 9 p.m. Mr Hayward called and says we have destroyed about or near 20 of the rebellious Negroes today.

Kept a strict watch all night.

Was alarmed in the night by a canoe coming up the trench, but made them stop when about half way up, by threatening to fire at them. All the Negroes in the island, it is said, were to have rose at Whitsuntide, but by mistake Negroes in St Maries [St Mary] rose at Easter, and a Negro carrying the wooden sword adorned with parrot's feathers (being the signal of union some part of Guinea) was discovered by a Capt. of a Guinea man who saw it carrying in a procession at Spring Path, had the fellow seized, and he discovered the affair. Fire was to have been set to the Towns in many places at once, and all the whites who came to help extinguish them were to be murdered in the confusion, whilst the estate Negroes engaged their overseers, &c. at the same time.

Sunday, 8th June 1760: a.m. *Cum* Phibbah *Sup. Lect.* Gave near 30 tickets to our Negroes to go buy provisions, &c.

a.m. Mr Thos. Reid, Long Pond overseer, came to see me.

Lincoln gave me two fine large mountain cabbages.

Killed one of the young pigs and had pork for dinner.

Note: Wm. Crawford's estate name is Albany, Jacob Ricketts's, Midgeham, and Wm. Ricketts's, Ridgeland.

Gave a great many grog today. Gave Mr Martin Bowen some dinner.

One of the militia supped and slept here.

Kept a strict watch at night.

Monday 9th: About 2 a.m. a party of soldiers (about 22)

going to Leeward called. Gave them each a pint of strong grog.
a.m. *Cum L.* Mimber *Sup. me Lect.*
Employed carrying earth out of the great pond, as last week.
Abraham not come yet from Capt. Forsythe. He passed through
the estate yesterday and today, but would not come home. He
clearly loves a lazy life.
Achilles yet out. Port Royal wanting this morning, catched &
flogged him.
It is said the rebellious Negroes took Jerusalem plantation
yesterday. It is also said that Salt Spring Negroes in Hanover
refuse to work and that a company of soldiers is gone there.
p.m. a fire broke out between Coffee Ground and Coffee
Ground Path pieces in the morass, but luckily we stopped it
before it reached the canes. Occasioned by the crabbers setting
fire to the stumps. At night kept a strict guard as usual. Many
people called for refreshment.
Tuesday 10th: Finished getting earth out of the great pond.
Turning up the mule pen, and the pickanninnies cutting and
heaping samphire for bedding the pens, &c. (Received a note
from Mr James Mariat.)
Sent Daniel and Cubbenna to look for Achilles.
Gave Lincoln a new hoe.
Juno & Daphne wanting all afternoon.
Run off the 42nd cistern of liquor, got 18 small jars of weak low
wines.
In the evening Mr Parr (late overseer of Midgeham) came here,
supped and slept.
At night kept a strict guard.'

Next morning Thistlewood went into Savanna la Mar. There,
news was to be had and, also, rumour was rife. Large numbers of
prisoners, many of whom were women, were now being brought in,
by soldiers and militia. It was said that the day before many of the
rebellious Negroes had passed through Glasgow estate moving eastwards towards the Cabaritta river, that they had been pursued and
engaged, and that Wager the rebel leader, (otherwise named Apongo)
had been killed by Captain Furre of the Moroons. That certainly
was rumour. Thistlewood later recorded:

'Thursday, 3rd July 1760: Wm. Grove's Apongo, took and
carried by, prisoner this evening. He was King of the rebels,
but despised of late since wounded.'

Apongo, clearly, was a remarkable man. Stories about him were many.
According to one source, unfortunately unnamed, (but probably

John Cope from whom Thistlewood had received much other information that day):

> 'Wager, alias Apongo, was a Prince in Guinea, tributory to the King of Dome [Dahomey]. The King of Dome has conquered all the country for 100 miles around him. Apongo came to visit the late John Cope [of Strathbogie], my employer's father, when governor of Cape Coast Castle, attended by a guard of 100 men. well-armed. He was surprised and took prisoner when hunting, and sold for a slave, brought to Jamaica & sold to Capt. Forest. In Jamaica, Mr Cope knew him again, and Wager used, when a slave, sometimes to go to Strathbogie to see Mr Cope, who had a table set out, a cloth, &c. laid for him; and would have purchased him and sent him home had Capt. Forest come to the island. Wager came to this country 6 or 7 years ago.

There is a basic credibility in some of this. In Tacky's rebellion his fighters had been protected from harm by a powder given them by the obeahmen. It is quite possible that Apongo and his people had been given similar protection, which, if it failed, would bring loss of confidence, not in the obeah, but in the man.[7] The Kingdom of Dahomey had been greatly expanded under the leadership of Agaja who reigned from 1708–1732; John Cope, Senior, buried at Savanna la Mar in February 1756 in his 55th year, had at one time been Governor of Cape Coast Castle; and Apongo would seem to have reached Jamaica about 1753/4. But it is difficult to see how Captain Forest's absenteeism could have prevented the purchase of one of his slaves. John Cope, the son, if he was the relator of all this, was perhaps making excuses for his father. But there was a slightly conflicting story from Stephen Parkinson, who said that Apongo had been with Captain Forest, in England, in the [ship] *Wager*, which was how he got his name.

It was also rumoured that Wager's original intention had been to wait until the ships in the Savanna la Mar roadstead had sailed before launching his attack, but that he and his wife quarrelled in the Negro ground, she had threatened to disclose his plans, and so he had immediately gone into action. But there were other things which Apongo himself, reportedly, had said:

> 'Wednesday, 30th July: Dr Gorse says Wager told them, when tried, that the night they broke out he advised coming directly to the Bay, but the others were afraid too much.'

On the day before, he had been sentenced.

'Today, Mr Antrobus, Messrs Gallagher, Lister, &c. guarded Wager, the King of the rebels to Captain Forest's. He is to hang in chains in 3 days, then be took down and burnt. I gave them grog. Asked Wager if he knew any of our Negroes. He said he knew Lewie & wished him good bye.'

Wager died before they could take him down for burning. So too did Capt. Forest's Goliath, who:

'... gibbetted alive Tuesday noon was alive when I went down about 10 a.m. but dead by noon [Thursday, 19th June]. He cut off Mr Rutherford's thigh & pulled out his eyes whilst alive.'

In July, on Friday 11th, in Savanna la Mar, Thistlewood:

'Saw Forest's Davie put up alive in the gibbetts. They gave him bread and cheese & grog before he was hoisted up.'

Thistlewood and others watched:

'Last Friday [this was Thursday 17th] Davie, who is gibbetted alive, seeing David Lopez & another white person fighting, said "Tha's good, me love for see so"; and seeing a monkey leap upon a pail of water a Negro wench was carrying on her head, laughed heartily and said: "That monkey damned rogue, true", &c. &c.'

Davie died on Friday 18th at about 11 a.m.

Others who led, or notably contributed in the rebellion included:

'... Aguy [who] was a hunter for his King in Guinea. Simon was one of the said King's captains. He frequently reprimanded Aguy for his immoderate love of women.'

Aguy, who belonged to Thomas Williams' estate, was reported shot on the 31st July. Simon was not among those killed or captured. In late September he was reported as having led a party of the rebels 'to high Windward' away from the plains of Westmoreland.

Some, such as Cardiff, suffered the full torture:

'Tuesday, 3rd September: Mr Cope says Cardiff, who was burnt at the Bay told him and many others present, that multitudes of Negroes had took swear ... that if they failed of success in the rebellion, to rise again the same day two years, and advised them to be upon their guard; and was going to make further discoveries, but accusing Col Barclay's Tackey & others, put the Col in a rage, so that he called the Marshall "Villain" for not making a fiercer fire, &c. A sad mistake.'

Thistlewood had no sympathy with the 'rebellious Negroes'. He wished them all the direst punishment, and had little use for any who seemed to show leniency:[8]

> 'Thursday, 17 July 1760: Yesterday evening Capt. Forest's Fortune (a principal offender) came in to Col Witter, who gave him a ticket to go home to Masemure; policy or something else.'

And on the same day, more approvingly:

> 'Col Spraggs off's with the heads of all the rebels who fall into his hands, immediately. He says he is sent to destroy the rebels & destroy them he will to the utmost of his power, except women and children.'

Whatever may have been behind Colonel Witter's apparent leniency, however, it was not to be allowed.

> 'Thursday, 21st August: Yesterday in the evening Major Cope and several troopers went to Savanna la Mar with Forest's, Campbell's & Old Thos. Williams' Negroes (such as were notorious, but had come in of themselves and had tickets from Col Witter) seized unawares ...'

While, earlier in the day, about noon, there had been another group of Moreland Negroes similarly escorted.

At the end of September the imprisoned Negroes were still in Savanna la Mar, and it was said that they would be transported. Quacoo and Abraham, two of only three Egypt slaves who were suspected by Thistlewood to be actively engaged in the rebellion, were sent to join them.

> 'Tuesday, 30th September: Quacoo & Abraham head down to the Bay in the large canoe, to Mr Meyler, to be transported with the rebels, also Mould's Hazat (out of Salt River dungeon) several of Paradise Negroes, Sawyer, Cudjoe, Duke, &c. from Jacobsfield. (Mason Quashe, Mulatto Davie, Pompey, Sharper, Humphrey, and our Plato in the canoe.)'

And, at Savanna la Mar, they perhaps saw:

> 'One of the St Mary's rebels now in gibbetts at the Bay. He looks about him.'

The proposed transportation did not take place. At the beginning of October the prisoners were still in the Fort at the bay, and it was the hope of Mr Thistlewood, and others, that they would be executed.

It would seem that only a couple of the Egypt slaves were

directly involved in the rebellion, though Thistlewood had suspected that several were aware of the intention to rise.

'Saturday, 18th October: Note: at the beginning of the rebellion, a shaved head amongst the Negroes was the signal of war. The very day, our Jackie, Job, Achilles, Quasheba, Rosanna, &c. had their heads remarkably shaved. Quasheba's brother fell in the rebellion ...'

The only one who was actually hunted as a rebel was Achilles who had run off the estate after threatening Daniel in early June.

'Saturday, 9th August: In the morning betimes, John Groves, Mason Quashe, Jackie, Job Coffee, Quamina & Daniel, went armed with 5 guns, cutlasses, &c to look for Achilles & his companions. Found many huts, cuttakans, raw cassava, cassava dokunu⁹ in the fire a-roasting, &c. but no Negroes. Plenty of water in calabashes, rum in one, &c. Made prize of all & burnt the huts. Found many beef bones, some ropes, &c. so that they were beef stealers. I stood ambushed in the morass armed with my gun pistols, &c. in case any had come that way.'

Achilles remained at liberty until Saturday, 6th December when:

'About 3 p.m. our Achilles (alias Hercules) and Paradise Achilles come home together, of their own accord. I secured them in the bilboes.'

Two days later, Egypt Plato and Jackie escorted them to the Salt River dungeon. Abraham, it will be recalled, had been sent off as a guide with Captain Forsythe, also early in June. He simply failed to return. At one time he was thought killed, but on Monday, 25th August:

'Mason Quashe & Daniel brought home Abraham whom they found helping to haul the seine at the Hope barcadier. Secured him in the bilboes.'

There were, of course, other runaways from Egypt during the year. Egypt Quacoo, for instance, was away for a prolonged period, and, on one occasion was spotted and shot at:

'Tuesday, 26th August: Mason Quashe and Daniel come up with Quacoo & 4 more runaway Negro men in Punch's ground, both shot, and Quashe says he believes hit one of them, but got none, only their cuttakans, crabs, &c.'

And, obviously, there were, on the other hand, those such as Mason Quashe, Daniel, Old Sharper, and the members of the Black Shot groups, who, like the Maroons but for different reasons, sided with the masters.

'Thursday, 4th September: Our black party was out in the morning again, and before noon brought home 3 Negro men they catched in the Salt Savanna islands. All pretend to be fishermen, one says his name is Gloster & belongs to Colonel Ricketts, the 2nd, Batchwell to Midgeham Estate, the 3rd, Pompey, to Forest's. Wrote to Mr Cope and sent them to him.'

In times of rebellion it would be risky to be a non-combatant runaway.

The Maroons, as we have seen, were much involved. It was said that Colonel Cudjoe had long before 'wrote to Col Barclay & the gentlemen of this parish ... to warn them of this that has happened'. Maroon parties were constantly on the move, and Thistlewood had occasion to entertain:

'Sunday, 20th July: Col Witter, Mr Cope, Mr Douglas, Mr Ferris, Mr Coppige, Mr John Tomlinson all dined at Egypt (also Col Cudjoe. He has a prodigious hump on his shoulders or back, and not so tall as me. Capt. Quaw, &c. with him).'

And they, the Maroons, were paradoxically an inspiration to the rebellious slaves at whom they shot on sight:

'Friday, 1st August: Dr Miller says the rebels give out they will kill all the Negroes they can, and as soon as dry weather comes fire all the plantations they can, till they force the whites to give them free like Cudjoe's Negroes.'

But by the end of June the rebellion had been broken. On the morning of Sunday 22nd, the warships sailed from Savanna la Mar roadstead. Mr Thistlewood went into his garden and 'drew some radishes, which I had for dinner', and then '*Cum* Warsoe', in the curing house corn loft.

The alarms and excursions, however, continued, and the torturous punishments of rebels captured, as did the excesses and excitements of the soldiery.

'Tuesday, 24th June: Last night about eleven o'clock, Messrs Say and Walker called me up requesting me to be upon guard, as the Negroes was driven from the mountains, and were come into Peter's Plain about 2 miles from us. Immediately fixed a watch as usual, and called "all's well". Both John and me set up all the rest of the night.'

In mid-November, one evening just after dark, Captain Forsythe arrived at Egypt 'with 20 Rangers (mulattoes and Negroes), besides

6 or 8 baggage Negroes & some Negro boys'. They stayed overnight before going into the Salt Savanna to search out rebels and runaways. Forsythe occupied Mr Cope's bed in the great house.

'Two white people that were with him & all the Negroes, &c. laid in the NE room of the great house, &c. The Negroes served a gallon of our rum, they got drunk, and attempted to break open the Negro House doors to come at the girls. I was obliged to get out of bed, take my pistols, and go to quiet them, which soon effected; but they fought after, one amongst another, till almost midnight.'

The movements of the Negroes between the various estates was watched and discussed. 'Thos. Williams' Negroes were at Paul Island last night [Monday, 30th June], have not learned the reason.' And, about a month later, 'Lewie of Egypt at Masemure almost every night'. Thistlewood did not on this account limit his own issue of tickets, but he seems to have warned the Egypt slaves not to move off the estate without them. On Saturday, 23rd August, for instance, he:

'Gave our Negroes extraordinary charge to work in their fields.'

He issued no tickets the following day; but on Sunday 31st he 'Gave out tickets as usual'. Not all other estate owners or overseers were being so careful. As the threat of immediate danger had diminished, so they had begun to relax controls.

'Sunday, 27th July: Negroes began to ride and walk about in the night again without tickets. Suspect something is a brewing amongst them.'

Whether or not his suspicions were alarmist, he maintained through the rest of the year the managerial policy which may well have saved him great distress in the harder days. He kept the Egypt slaves as busy as he could; he tended them when sick; he flogged them when he thought they erred; he regularly gave them their allowances of food and clothing and liquor, and sometimes extras for unusual labour or good performance; he allowed them, even in the midst of rebellion, their Sunday tickets to move about; but he held them in strict control:

'Wednesday, 24th December: Driver Johnie drumming at the Negro house last night. Flogged him for it.
Thursday, 25th December: Being Christmas Day, gave it to the Negroes. Gave strict charge to the Negroes to make no noise, &c.'

Meanwhile, instructions had been received by the Custos, Col

Barclay, from the Governor, that the militia, horse and foot, should be on patrol from the middle to the end of December, and should ensure that no Negro moved off his plantation without a ticket.

It is difficult to illustrate the views of the whites on the possible causes of the rebellion. They were certainly aware of Tacky's struggle (and defeat) in St Mary, and some had received letters telling of thwarted uprisings elsewhere, even as far away as St Thomas in the East. But Thistlewood gives no hint of awareness of a plan for a general uprising throughout the island. Nor did they seem to think that any such uprising could be engineered solely by slave leadership.

'Saturday, 12th July:　Mr Parkinson, &c. called. He suspects some of those who pass for Jew distillers to be Jesuits, and stir up the Negroes, or perhaps there may be Black Jesuits in the island amongst the Negroes.'

Nonetheless, they knew an old rhyme which seemed to suggest that the blacks had an objective, not necessarily inspired by Jesuits of whatever colour:

'Friday, 24th October:　Mr John Stewart called and dined with me. He says there is an old saying, or proverb, which frights many people:
"One thousand seven hundred and sixty-three, Jamaica no more an Island shall be."
(Not for the whites).'

In the latter months of the year conditions on Egypt estate returned to normal. There were fewer alarms and invasions by troops in search of food and shelter, and fewer instances of news of attacks and reprisals.

Several of the slaves went down in an epidemic of measles. They included Little Mimber, who had recently become Thistlewood's No. 1 girl. Phibbah, his 'wife' and their child (to whom he still referred as Phibbah's child, and who was in fact, like Phibbah, the property of John Cope, Esqr.) also suffered. Phibbah, tending little John who had the measles, herself had 'a hard swelling on one of [her] breasts, but don't hurt much she says'. Lincoln, seemingly unhappy with Violet with whom he occassionally fought, had 'got the Clap. He says from little Doll'. The information must have interested Thistlewood who was himself uneasy in his private parts and had recently been entertained by Little Doll. And, except for the final entry, the diary jottings for the last day of the year carried nothing of the recent troubles.

'Wednesday, 31st December, 1760:　Employed junking and

getting out copper wood. Received home 13 cart loads, which equals 107 loads now home in all.

Flanders hewing headings. Mason Quashe repairing under the coppers.

Pero & Neptune making mortar & tending him.

David sawing laths. a.m. Plato, &c. sifting lime. Received home a cartload of sift lime.

a.m. Broke in the Cotton Tree piece corn, 168 good dung baskets, brought it home in the canoe & put up in the corn loft. Had Quashe & Davie with me.

Pickled some samphire today.

Running continues, stains but little, seems waterish. Urine scalds yet. Urethra sore & somewhat inflamed. Weakness of parts continues.

Took Balsam Capivi.

Have given out since the beginning of June 767 tickets.

Mr Crawford's Jackie condemmed, and burnt, by a slow fire.'

Notes

1 Thistlewood's son, Mulatto John, of whom much more anon.
2 Bryan Edwards, *History of the West Indies*, 5th Ed. London, 1819. Vol. 2, pp.78–79. As a young lad of 16, Edwards had been sent to his uncle Zachary Bayly, owner of Trinity Estate in St Mary and other properties. He was there in 1760, and, according to him, it was his uncle who had mustered the first body of men against Tacky.
3 Thistlewood is here apparently reporting a phrase which the slaves might well have used: 'him would a dead eena Egypt', i.e. he would die in Egypt.
4 Long Quaw, of whom we have heard before in reference to Mirtilla, had some time previously been listed by Thistlewood as one of the best field slaves on Salt River.
5 See Cassidy (1971) p.164. As in some other instances, this is an earlier use of the term than that (in a printed work) noted by Professor Cassidy. The Black Shot were bodies of trusted slaves who were sent out as a sort of 'rangers', distinct from the regular soldiery and the militia.
6 Presumably with intention to hinder work on the estate. 'Madam Fate', a poisonous weed, mixed with other plants and steeped in rum, if applied to arms and face, was supposed to induce a profound indolence. See Cassidy & Le Page (1980) p.286.

7 Immediately following Tacky's rebellion the Island Legislature imposed a penalty of transportation or death on anyone practising or claiming to practise obeah.

8 How, we might wonder, would he have reacted to the activities and the punishment, in 1820, of his nephew Arthur Thistlewood, of Tupholme, who was the leader of the Cato Street conspiracy to assassinate members of the British Cabinet of the day and set up a new provisional government. Arthur Thistlewood's plan was divulged by one of his fellow conspirators, and, following his information, the Duke of Wellington, then Prime Minister, and the other ministers took steps to thwart the plotters – one of whom, William Davidson, was said to be a West Indian. Thistlewood and his associates were cornered and after a fight in which a Bow Street runner was killed, eventually captured and tried. Thistlewood and four others, including Davidson, were executed. Others were imprisoned or deported.

9 Cassidy (1971) p.193 '... the *duckanoo* ... another African delicacy [first referred to in 1740].' Plantain, green-banana, sweet potato, or other food seasoned, wrapped in plantain or banana leaf and boiled, or less commonly baked.

CHAPTER 6   Preparing his own

Introduction

As we know, Thomas Thistlewood had not come to Jamaica to spend his life as a sugar estate overseer, and now after ten years of it, he began to make positive moves towards his own independent proprietorship.

He had also abandoned any idea he might have entertained about becoming a sugar planter. His experiences with William Dorrill and John Cope led him to the opinion that the social prestige enjoyed by that class could not compensate for the problems of financing and operating a sugar estate and profitably marketing its produce. One suspects too, that his wide botanical and horticultural interests would not have been satisfied by a pre-dominant concern with the sugarcane. Above all, perhaps, was the fact that he lacked the large capital and credit-worthiness necessary to purchase, or to establish a sugar estate of viable size and suitable situation.

There were, as he had observed, profitable though less prestigious alternatives. At the Vineyard he had seen that money could be made by cutting and chipping logwood for export, raising cattle for the local market, and sending slaves out on the road higglering imported small consumer goods. On Egypt he had already established a thriving garden of vegetables and flowers which found ready markets, and he had established connections with the store-keepers and taverners of Savanna la Mar who would be his customers. He had also built up a steady export (from his allowances of rum and sugar) and import (of books, textiles, foodstuffs, and other items) business with Mr Hewitt, in London, as his chief metropolitan agent.

He now began to acquire the slaves and to look for the land he would need to establish his own proprietorship. A visit to the site of his Breadnut Island Pen (now called Rock Dondo) leaves the observer amazed that here, on the dry rocky hillocks of poor pasture and wild thorn and rosemary bushes, there once flourished a horticultural show-place; but Thistlewood was wise in his decision to purchase. Lying in a curve of the Cabaritta river, swamps and morasses provided a suitable habitat for fish and wildfowl, the

higher ground of the 'island' pen pastured livestock, and in the
hollows, which were cooler and covered with alluvial deposits, the
most delicate plants could be nursed into bearing. But there, too,
was the potential danger. In times of more than usually heavy
rainfall those hollows could become ponds. Such were, and are, the
encouragements and the apprehensions of the gardener.

All these preparations were undertaken in a period disturbed
by continuing threats and outbreaks of slave rebellion, though none
of the magnitude of that of 1760, and the local effects of international
conflict. But Thistlewood clearly was confident and optimistic. Following
his own successful career as an overseer he had encouraged the
arrival in Jamaica of his nephew John, perhaps to follow in his
footsteps; but that was not to be.

The slave uprisings of 1760 were of greater threat to the whites
since they occurred in the middle of the Seven Years War which had
begun between Britain and France in 1756, with Spain later joining
France. During this war nearly all the French West Indian colonies
fell to British attacks, but the most notable conquest was the capture,
in 1762, of Havanna, Cuba, by a large British naval and military
force including ships and men (whites, Free Coloureds and slaves)
from Jamaica. Curiously, Thistlewood makes little mention of these
large events, and the Treaty of Paris by which the war was ended in
1763, and by which Havanna was restored to Spain, and Guadeloupe,
Martinique, and St Lucia were restored to France, passed with little
note. By the Treaty, Britain gained New France (Canada) from the
French and acquired Dominica, St Vincent, Grenada and the
Grenadines, and Tobago, in the Caribbean. From his immediate
concern with rebellion around him, Mr Thistlewood had returned to
his primary, long term concern – making his name and fortune.

He had begun to make a record of his assets and liabilities on
the 1st January in each year. On Thursday, 1st January 1761, his
affairs were as follows:

Assets

Ready money	£ 12	13*s*	1½*d*.
Mr Cope owes me about	329	0	0
Mr John Parkinson [for seeds] owes	3	0	0
Mr Hamilton [for pins] owes	4	5	0

Mr Green [for cloth] owes   3   14   2
Brigadier-General Barclay [for books] owes   5   15   0

                    £358   7*s*   3½*d*

During 1759 and 1760 he had consigned 8 puncheons of rum to Mr Hewitt and he had received, in part payment, sundry goods valued at (Stg) £38 10*s* 6*d*. Dr Drummond, Mr Mould, Mr Barnett, Mr Atkinson, Mr Blythe, Mr John Parkinson, and Mr Emetson each had one of his books on loan; and Mr George Goldring had one of his handkerchiefs. He owned 4 slaves: Lincoln, Johnie, Abba and Simon. He also owned a horse, a considerable number of books, and other personal items.

Liabilities
He owed Mr Robert Baker [for a pair of pistols]   £4 15*s* 0*d*
Phibbah [who had lent him money]   10 17*s* 6*d*
And uncertain amounts to Dr Gorse and to Mr Hewitt.
He also had Mr Emetson's 4 volumes of Tom Jones.

From that account we can gather some of the sources of his income. There was his wage, but this was usually much in arrears. John Cope had little ready cash and a dubious credit rating. He imported a variety of commodities from England for sale locally. He exported his share, taken in part payment of wages, of Egypt's produce. He hired out his slaves; but here again he was mainly dependent on payment by Mr Cope to whom, at any given time, the majority were hired. And additionally, though not indicated here, he bought locally at wholesale, and then retailed articles such as beef, flour and cloth. This enterprise he had seen successfully operated in his early days at Vineyard, when Vineyard Phibbah and Scipio used to take to the road with clothes and thread for Mr Vassall's account.

The year opened unhappily. On Sunday, 4th January:

'Gave our Negroes many tickets.
a.m. shot a hawk from off the cotton tree.
Finished the rice today.
p.m. Angled in the river, got mudfish and a drummer, and in the evening got some good drummers and small tarpons at the Styx bridge. Phibbah complains of a violent pain at the bottom

of her belly. She also has a running which stains yellowish, suppose it is Fluor Albies, or I rather suspect a venereal infection. Gave her a mercury pill at night.'

It was indeed a venereal infection.

Among the other slaves Coffee, Julina, Jenny, Cudjoe, Little Charity, and Jude all caught the measles.

John Groves, who before coming to Egypt had been at Roaring River Estate, gave up his job at Egypt for the same reason that he had been fired from Roaring River.

'Tuesday, 6th January: Note: Yesterday afternoon John Groves like a madman amongst the Negroes, flogging Dago, Primus, &c. without much occasion.'

And, when reprimanded, he decided to leave the estate. His successor, John Orman, hired on Friday 16th, was apparently a man of prodigious appetite. 'Our white man eats as much as four moderate people would do.' In April, though confined to his house, sick, he was still eating heartily. On the 17th, he died.

The plantocracy were behaving in their usual style. On the evening of 12th January, Mr Cope and Mr Thomas Coppige arrived at Egypt. Mr Cope had Coobah (that is Egypt Coobah, not Phibbah's daughter). Mr Coppige wanted Little Mimber '... but Mimber would not go to him' and Egypt Susanah was roughly taken to him in her stead. And they still faced the aftermath of the previous year's rebellion and the height of local effects of the current war abroad.

On 6th January, Thistlewood apparently had thought of elevating himself from the ranks of the militia foot to the status of mounted trooper, but the costs were not inconsiderable. He would have to find:

	£		
1 Red Coat	£ 9	10s	0d
1 Jacket & Breeches	7	0	0
1 Laced hat	4	15	0
1 pair boots	3	11	3
1 pair spurs	3	0	0
1 horse [this he already had]	35	0	0
1 demy pick saddle, with furniture	10	0	0
1 bucket, bitt & sword	7	10	0
1 pr pistol [he had 'pocket pistols']	10	0	0
1 carbine	4	0	0
	£94	6s	3d

He went no further with the idea. It is clear that there were apprehensions of further open hostilities by bands of those who had escaped capture during the rebellion; but it is doubtful that Thistlewood was moved by a large desire to ride into combat. Much more likely he was after mounted appearance rather than mounted assault. On Wednesday, 14th January he noted, with wry comment:

'It is said a law is passed that no overseer shall go off the estate he lives upon a Sunday, under fine – then he can't go to church.'

Notably, however, he began once again to record the issuing of tickets to those slaves who wished to go abroad; though he seems not to have tried to limit the number given out.

Saturday 24th, he rode into the Savanna and spoke to Mr Cope, and then to Savanna la Mar 'to see Mr Carr's Negroes'. There were many buyers and the prices were 'very dear'. He bought none.

'In regard to buying of Negroes, I would choose men-boys[1] and girls, none exceeding 16 or 18 years old, as full grown men or women seldom turn out well; and beside, they shave the men so close & gloss them over so much that a person cannot be certain he does not buy old Negroes. Have observed those with cut faces (Chamboys, I think, they call them[2]) do not do vastly well at Egypt, yet as that may only be by chance, have no great objection to them. Those Negroes that have big bellies, ill shaped legs, & great feet, are commonly dull and sluggish & not often good; whereas those who have a good calf to their leg and a small moderate size foot, are commonly nimble, active Negroes. Many Negro men are bursten [i.e. ruptured] and are always the worse for it, therefore one would not buy them if perceptible. Have also observed that many new Negroes, who are bought fat and sleek from aboard the ship, soon fall away much in a plantation, whereas those which are in a moderate condition hold their flesh better and are commonly hardier. Those whose lips are pale, or whites of their eyes yellowish, seldom healthful.'

In late March he was visited by 'Lawer Stancliffe, one Mr Robinson, and one Dr Robinson very curious people'. He later described them more fully. Mr John Robinson, FRS, was a linguist, a personal friend of the Governor, and the owner of a 'polink' in Clarendon – presumably on property belonging to the planter-historian Edward Long; for Dr Anthony Robinson, Thistlewood believed, lived with Mr Long 'as he speaks much of him'. Dr Robinson, he recorded, was paid by the Royal Society in England, through the Governor, £200 a year for 'collecting curiosities and making remarks, &c. in this country'. He and Thistlewood subsequently had many a discussion, and he instructed Thistlewood, who was a very interested student, 'in drawing birds, plants, &c.'. The new interest was, however, interrupted in early April by the arrival of a vessel with freight on board for Thistlewood. It was by no means the first such, but it brought an illustrative variety of cargo.

> 'Monday, 6th April ... called on board the *Earl of Effingham*, Capt. Bellamy, and received my bundle of trees, marked TT No. 1 The rest of my things could not be come at. Gave a receipt for this.'

Two other vessels, the *Westmoreland* and the *Adventure*, were also in the roadstead and he boarded them for Mr Cope. The *Westmoreland* had brought '2 bundles of hoops'. The *Adventure* was to take 5 tierces of sugar.

> 'Tuesday, 7th April: Dr Gorse here, let him have his trees, according to account. Some of them seem to be alive.
> Thursday, 9th April: Received [from the *Earl of Effingham*] my cask garden seeds, box of ketchup, chest of books, &c., and case of arms.'

He also received letters from his brother and sister.

> 'Saturday 11th: carried my 4 puncheons of rum, had of Mr Cope, on board the *Westmoreland*, Capt. Hore.'

The puncheons contained 444 gallons at 3s per gallon, after paying excise duty of 10 per cent.

> 'Monday 13th: Gave out my Scotch check handkerchiefs to Phibbah to sell for me. They are 28 inches square.'

And on the same day he sampled a bottle of his mushroom ketchup which 'seems very good'. He also noted with satisfaction:

> 'A rebel Negro killed not far from Glasgow Estate lately, (one of those who was at Mr Thomas Torrent's) and the other took by his Negroes after a desperate engagement with two Negroes, and another took in St Elizabeth, both brought to the Bay.'

On Egypt, the slave population remained relatively undisturbed. There were few instances recorded of runaways or punishments meted out for other alleged misdemeanours in the field or at home.

On Sunday, 19th April 1761, he noted that Driver Johnie and Little Mimber had 'made a match'. On the 20th, Thistlewood took Little Mimber on his bed, and perhaps in acknowledgement of her new status, 'Gave ditto a cobb'. Four days later there came a new turn to an old matter. Nago Jenny now had two sons, Quaw, the mulatto, whom Thistlewood had acknowledged only by gifts of clothing, money, and so on; and the recently born Cudjoe of father unknown to us. Thistlewood must have grown fond of young Quaw, and perhaps had even begun to entertain thoughts of his manumission, for on 22nd April, a Wednesday:

'Jenny's mulatto Thomas bad of the small pox at Paradise.'

There was no further mention of him until early December, Saturday 5th.

'Received a note, *per* Little Beneba, from Mr John Thompson acquainting me to send over Jenny to Paradise, as Thomas lies a-dying.'

Inexplicably, Jenny was not sent until the next morning. She returned on Friday 11th. Mulatto Thomas had died the day before.

In April, 1761, Thistlewood began to dispose of his goods. He:

'Wrote to Jeremiah Meyler Esqr. and sent (*per* Plato) my Simon, who as he is good for nothing, I have sold to Mr Meyler, for 35 pounds, to send off.'

Simon would be a re-export.

At about the same time, he made up catalogues of his imported flower and vegetable seeds and sent copies to individuals and to Jimmy Hayes' and Mr Emetson's taverns for display. There were numerous buyers, and his ketchup, too, which went at 3s 9d per pint bottle was well taken. In May he sowed varieties of seed in the Egypt garden and in boxes.

On 5th May he received £2 2s 6d from Mr Emetson for cloth sold for him; on 2nd June he received £1 11s 3d for the hire of Abba for 5 weeks; on the 19th, Lincoln who had been sent out on the road with a basket of seeds returned with 10s worth sold. In the first week of July he was out again and returned with £2 10s. On both occasions he was accompanied by Jenny, belonging to Mrs Sarah Bennett, who was teaching him the arts of higglering. Mrs Bennett, who lived at Robin's Hill outside Savanna la Mar, was the owner of Paradise Pen which lay to the east of Egypt just across the Cabaritta river and was managed by Thomas Eddin. She was a well-to-do woman, and though the relationship was unexplained by Thistlewood, she was a close friend of Phibbah.

The first week of June also brought further concern about roaming bands of 'rebels' said to be at Morelands. Colonel John Cope[3] and others had gone there to try, unsuccessfully, to persuade them to surrender and be transported. More troops were sent into the area, but no action immediately followed. John Cope went home to Paradise Estate and thence to Kingston on business.

'Monday, 6th July 1761:   [Rode to Salt River] and received three new Negroes Mr Cope bought for me in Town, at £50 per head, and 3 suits of clothes at 7s 6d = £151 2s 6d. To which add for provisions 7s 1½d = £151 9s 7½d. A girl which I named Nanny, one boy Solon, and the other Caesar. Quamina took Solon, & Flanders, Caesar.[4]

Caesar seems to be about 14, Solon 16, and Nanny 21 years old.

Tuesday 7th: For 150 plantains, 6 bitts, to feed my new Negroes.'

On the 14th, all three were at work in the field. Solon, at first, seemed to be a doubtful purchase. He had the belly-ache, and then, two weeks after his arrival, Thistlewood sent him to Dr Gorse, 'as he had a film growing on one of his eyes'. Dr Gorse gave him 'some powder' to blow into the eye. The cure whatever it might have been, was successful; but he was soon to endure another ailment.

'Wednesday, 5th August 1761:   Ellin weeding in the garden, having a bad sore on her thigh.

Thursday 6th: In the morning, *Cum* Ellin, in the garden, by the Indian-arrow bed, Stans: Backwd. Gave ditto a bitt.

Monday 17th: a.m. Rode to the bay, gave Mr Samuel Lee some grass seeds. Abba is left Dunlop, received a pistole for her time there. She is now hired to Mr Samuel Lee at £14 per annum. Neptune at Mr Emetson's is her husband, and it is said she is with child.

Tuesday 18th: Mr Cope, Mr John Dorwood, Mr Alexander McDonald dined here, also supped and got very drunk; disturbed me sadly in the night, but I would not let them into my house. They had Eve and Margaritta amongst them.

Monday 24th: It is said Phibbah's Coobah, Mrs Cope's waiting maid at Paradise, is with child; but whether for Mulatto Davie her husband, or J.C., in my opinion is doubtful.'

He appears to have been right. The child, a Mulatto, and certainly not Davie's, died soon after birth.

'Tuesday 25th: My Solon has got a guinea worm. Wound some of it out upon a quill.

Saturday 29th: My Johnie sick today, dressed his yaws.
Sunday 30th: Sent some of my salt beef to sell in the Leeward road, to the Negroes *per* Egypt Lucy. Received 11*s* 3*d*. Gave her a little beef for her trouble.
Monday 31st: Received more of Phibbah to take care of for her £14 12*s* 6*d*; which with what received April 21st. £52 4*s* 4 ½*d*, equals £66 16*s* 10 ½*d*. Sent Job to Mr John Weech's store at Savanna la Mar with a mule. Received 2 rolls of osnabrig, Nos. 109 & 139.
Thursday 3rd September: a.m. Dr Gorse here. Showed him Solon's leg much swelled with the guinea worm, altho' it all seemed to come out this morning. He advised a poultice of roast calabash guts to be applied to it.
Friday 4th: Served our Negroes cloth, who have not had this year before. Had 25 yards for my Negroes at 1*s* 3*d* per yard.'

During August and September Thistlewood had received several offers of employment. Mr Bernard Senior had proposed that he go to Mint Estate; Mr Emetson had told him that there was a vacancy at Three Mile River Estate for which he should apply; Parson Atkins wanted him at George's Plain Estate; and there were others. Perhaps for that reason, Mr Cope arrived at Egypt early in the morning of Saturday, 3rd October and determined Thistlewood's account up to the 30th September. He owed £246 18*s* 11 ½*d*. He promised to so arrange matters that Thistlewood would be 'quit in regard to the militia'; and also he promised 'to free Phibbah's John'.

Nonetheless, Thistlewood went off in the next week to look over George's Plain. Parson Atkins had come to Egypt and offered him £160 per annum, to hire his Negroes, and to make him joint attorney until 1763 when Atkins would be leaving Jamaica. Then Thistlewood would act for him and receive £200 a year. Thistlewood did not accept, but seems to have been invited to visit, for on Wednesday, 7th October:

'About 8 a.m. set off from home, rode thro' the Savanna and Three Mile River Estate to George's Plain Estate, belonging to the Revd Dr Robert Atkins. Found him at home, was treated very generously, rode round the estate with him, &c., dined with him & Mrs Atkins. Had a duck stewed in claret, a roast turkey & ham & greens, fryed ortolans, cheese & bread, oranges & a very fine shaddock, punch, madeira wine & claret.
About ½ past 5 p.m. set forward for home, where I got by grass-throwing time. Moody, from the Old Hope, comes there

as overseer tomorrow. Out of 22 overseers offered their service to him, but 2 English, the rest Scotch.'

During dinner they had, apparently, discussed books, or plantership, or both; for a few days later Thistlewood left Mr Richard Beckford's *Instructions*, and Martin's *Essay on Plantership* with Mr Baker at the Post Office in Savanna la Mar, to be delivered to the Reverend Dr Atkins.

Back on Egypt, Clara had got the clap and blamed London for the infection, Quamina had caught Quasheba in the act with the new white employee, James Rogers, many of the other slaves were down with fever, Phibbah was sadly clapped, and so too, was Thistlewood. Unbelievably, his most recent sexual activities had been on Thursday, 10th September: '*Cum* Mountain Susanah, *Sup* Chest Lid T T No 2, Books & wearing apparel, *in me. dom.* and then with Phibbah on the 13th. His next was to be with Princess, on 11th November when he noted 'emission painful' and subsequently went into another period of semi-retirement.

In mid-November, James Rogers left Egypt after a reprimand for assaulting the slaves in the field when he was drunk. And John Cope, too, was in a sense reprimanded.

'Thursday 11th: At dinner Mr Cope and me had various discourse and proposing to come and live here, I desired him then to provide himself, for that I should not stay with him.'

On the last Sunday of the month, Thistlewood observed: 'Several Negroes from Midgeham, &c. to court my Nanny today.'

On the night of Wednesday, 2nd December 1761, a party of Frenchmen raided the Negril guard house and captured some Negroes. The war was getting close. Undeterred, on the 7th Thistlewood paid Mr John Hutt £112 for two men and £200 for one boy and three girls. Mr Hutt accepted an order on Mr Cope for the full amount, and gave Thistlewood a receipt. The new Negroes were soon branded with Thistlewood's mark \TT/ on the right shoulder, and he described them as follows:

Coobah: 4 ft 6 6/10 ins. tall, about 15 yrs. old, Country name Molia, an Ebo. He put her to live with Egypt Princess.

Sukey: 4 ft 8 8/10 ins. tall, about 14 yrs. old, he put her to live with Job.

Maria: 4 ft 11 1/10 ins. tall, about 15 yrs. old. Country name Ogo. She was put with Egypt Lucy.

Pompey: 4 ft 9 9/10 ins. tall, about 16 yrs. old, Country name Oworia, a Coromante. Put to live with Plato.

Will: 5 ft. 3 ²/₁₀ ins. tall, about 25 yrs. old, Country name
              Abasse, an Ebo.
Dick: 5 ft. 7 ³/₁₀ ins. tall, about 22 yrs. old, Country name
              Sawnno, alias Dowotronny.

He calculated the cost of feeding them:

> 'Note: I give my new Negroes 3 pints of rice each per diem,
> (and allowing 3 pints for a bitt) it is dearer than feeding them
> with plantains if 10 bitts per hundred and allowing them 3
> plantains each meal, or 9 per day. (Just dearer than at 16 bitts
> per hundred if only 6 plantains per day each).
> Sunday 13th, December: For 400 plantains 12 bitts, for my
> new Negroes.'

Next day they were put in the field.

On the night of the 30th his Abba was brought to bed of a girl
at Mr Lee's at Savanna la Mar. At first said to be Mulatto, she was
Negro. Among the Egypt slaves, Little Mimber was ill at the Negro
house: 'It is said she miscarried last week.'

On 1st January, 1762, therefore, Thistlewood listed among his
assets 12 slaves and Abba's girl recently born named Mary. In ready
cash he had £58 14s 4½d, and he was keeping £66 16s 10½d for
Phibbah. Various people owed him about £10. On the other side, he
owed a total of about £20. There was something due to him on rum
sent to Mr Hewitt; and, of course, he had his horse, his books, his
watch, his pistols, &c. And no doubt he also counted it as a credit
that Mr Cope had not moved to Egypt to interfere in the running of
the estate. On Monday, 18th January he 'Put the mill about' for the
crop taking, but he was also busy about the garden.

> 'Wednesday 20th: I have now a white narcissus in full flower
> in the garden, a pretty large bunch of 12 or 13 flowers in it. This
> is probably the first that ever flowered in this island. It opened
> about a week ago.'

A week later, another bunch opened.

On the 25th, a Negro man, named Witte, came to Egypt
boiling house from Mr Bernard Senior at Mint Estate. 'He is a
famous boiler.' His reputation stood the test. When he left, on
Saturday 30th, Thistlewood gave him 4 bitts and 2 bottles of rum,
and commented: 'He is a very good boiler.'

Early in February the militia were mustered, round-the-clock
guard duties were established at the Bay and all were ordered to be
in readiness to march for Town at a minute's notice. 'People greatly
alarmed.' On Monday 8th Thistlewood's company escorted the

prisoners, 72 Spaniards, 5 French, 1 Italian, and 1 Maltese, by canoe from Savanna la Mar to Bluefields, and then by road to Parker's Bay, where they were handed over to Captain Gordon and his Company. While at Savanna la Mar, the prisoners had been fed once a day on 'boiled plantains and saltfish'.

While Thistlewood and Lloyd (a new white employee on Egypt) were away, another body of soldiers coming from Midgeham had stopped at Egypt and 'frightened our Negroes into the morass, &c. (being no white person upon the estate).' They had commandeered a cart to take their equipment to Savanna la Mar. They were to board the warship *Centurion* at Bluefields to go to Kingston. Through the year there were to be alarms and the sounds of naval engagements off-shore; and in November another raid on shore.

On the first of April, 1762, Thistlewood bought yet another slave:

> 'Bought of Mr Jeremiah Meyler, a Congo girl, 9 or 10 years old, 4 feet and 1 inch high, give 42 pounds cash. Had a receipt, named her Sally, and intend her for a semptress.'

Accordingly, Sally was sent to learn sewing from Mrs Blake's Doll. Thistlewood was to feed her while she worked as Doll's apprentice, and when she had learnt, he was to pay Doll a doubloon.

In November and December 1762, the enemy raids and the scare intensified.

> 'Tuesday, 2nd November: The French or Spaniards last night, 2 or 3 hours before day, went up to Col Barclay's polink[5] on the other side the Hope, 3 or 4 miles, and about a mile and quarter within land, and took 15 (some say 20, others 27) Negroes, men, women and children clear off, besides some fishermen, &c. There were but 19 in all at the polink, so only 4 escaped, Old Coffee one of them, who I saw today about noon, been acquaint his master.'

Next day, guns were heard at sea to the west, and on the 4th:

> 'The Spaniards (above) 33 men, 2 carriage and 8 swivel guns taken yesterday a.m. by the *Westmoreland*, Capt. Lake, and carried into Bluefields.
> Sunday 28th: Got up last night and stopped a play at driver Johnie's house, and had Hazat flogged. Much afraid of the Spaniards, walked till almost day. They have robbed Bluefields lately.
> p.m. Rode to Col Barclay's, Mr Antrobus, John Williams & another gentleman with him. I sat about half-an-hour and drank

some excellent claret. The Col agreed to send 2 hands every night to watch Cabritto bridge, and we 2.
Begin tonight. I sent Cubbena and Dago, and Colonel Barclay, 2. One of his and one of ours watch at a time, have each a gun which, should the enemy appear, they are to fire, and then run each home to give notice, &c.
I went to the bridge twice in the night.
Monday 29th: Mr Thos. Eddin come to see me and consult about the Spaniards.
Today Mr and Mrs Cope come to their house in the Savanna again [they had purchased the Mould's house] for fear of the Spaniards, altho' a serjeant & 6 soldiers at Paradise.
Tuesday, 30th November: Flogged Prince and Kent for making a noise last night, and reprimanded Robert about it.'

Robert Gibbs, a Barbadian, was the new driver at Egypt, and, with Thistlewood's assent, had taken the much courted Nanny as his wife. On 1st December, a second white driver, an Irishman, Christopher White, was taken on. He soon 'made a match' with Egypt Susanah.

'Tuesday 7th: ... yesterday evening Dr Gorse, Mr Randolph Donaldson, Mr Abraham Lopez, &c. conducted the Spanish prisoners thro' Egypt towards Savanna la Mar.
The Captain and another rode in a Kitterine, the common men walked. The Captain looked very thoughtful, I could not help pitying them, altho' they are the people who plundered Mr Thos. White's house at Bluefields, last Friday night was a week, of his plate, furniture, wearing apparel, &c; the girl he kept, &c., even made him help carry his own things down to their canoe, stripped him naked except an old dirty check shirt they gave him. She was took by Captain Cuffee's vessel (belonging Mr Meyler) off Hanover somewhere.'[6]

That was the last enemy action of any significance recorded by Thistlewood; and, indeed, the war was drawing to a close with the Peace of Paris to be agreed in 1763.
On Thursday, 13th January, Mr Lee paid £10 wages for Abba for 1762, £4 having been deducted for the periods of illness and laying-in. Thistlewood sent to Mr Emetson's and bought 4 bottles of Madeira at 5s each. On the 14th he entertained.

'Mr Richard Hungerford, Mr Chambers, and Mr Samuel Barton dined with me and sat the afternoon. Had stewed snook & ketchup sauce, boiled salt beef and broccoli, a roast squab, a roast teal, roast coot & roast snipe, soft crabs & others, cheese, oranges, honey, water melon, wine & punch.'

That evening he caught Lydde eating canes in Potato canepiece. Perhaps because he was contentedly satiate he did not dish out 'Derby's dose'; instead *'Cum Illa, Sup. Terr.* in ditto piece.' On the 17th, he put the mill about for the crop of 1763. On the 18th he sent to Mr Cope 'a honey water melon, raised from seed, from Martinico'. On the 24th, he went off to 'Exercise' with the entire regiment of militia, horse and foot. In future, they were to meet the first Monday in every month.

In late February there was another set to with Mr Cope. Thistlewood had delivered 2 puncheons of rum to Mr Anthony Morris, the store keeper at Hungerford and Antrobus' wharf. They had been returned as 'not proof', and Mr Cope had written a chiding letter, to which Thistlewood had hotly replied.

Clearly, Mr Thistlewood was of the view that Mr Cope could not easily dispense with his services, and that if he did other employment would be readily available. His long regime at Egypt seems to have been most unusual for the times, and was in great contrast to the rapidity with which his subordinate white drivers came and went. Six days after his employment, Patrick May, the latest such arrival, was said to be 'in his house all day, drunk'; and towards the end of May, he too was dismissed.

'Monday, 23rd May 1763: Yesterday evening Patrick May went to Savanna la Mar and came home sometime in the night in liquor, quarrelled with Nanny whom he kept, and shot her with small shot, one of which struck her head near the top, and the other her ankle, both these shots seem to be lodged. Today I told him to go about his business, & he went.'

March and April had been marked by illnesses. Thistlewood himself endured another bout of heavy venereal infection, so too did Phibbah. Sally at Mrs Blake's had chickenpox, Abba's Mary caught the smallpox and was blinded by it, and in early April:

'Am well informed that Mr C-p- has been bad with Venereal disease for near a year past and has but lately got well.'

And in April, after a very long period in which there had been no mention of them, the Maroons were reported back in the field.

'Tuesday, 12th April 1763: The Wild Negroes (Cudjoe's I mean) lately came up with eleven runaways in a hut in the mountains. Killed 3 and took the rest, who were tried today at Savanna la Mar. One is kept as an evidence against others which may be taken, and the others, some of them hanged, and the others burnt alive, by a slow fire, in the morass behind the Court House. Those Negroes confessed to have murdered Mr Wright at Mr Grizzle's, &c. &c. at Round Hill, in Hanover, &c.'

Thistlewood had been informed of all of this at first hand, for on that day he had gone to Savanna la Mar and:

'... received of Mr Chambers a lawyer the receipt for John's manumission, it not being recorded yet, so backward in their books at that office.'

At the end of April, the *Earl of Effingham*, Capt. Jesse Carling, brought him another case of goods, wearing apparel, from which he selected gifts for Phibbah and Little John.

'Friday, 3rd June: Capt. Toby, from Cudjoe's Town, and 2 boys slept in the cookroom. Gave them supper, &c.
Saturday 18th: Mr George Mercy called in the afternoon. Says he hears amongst the Negroes that Mr Say's Vine is kept by Mrs Bennett's driver, Sam, a Negro, and she went to his house lately to see him. (Mould's Lewis kept Mr Smith's Grace, brought her a coat from Town when he came last.)'

Mr Samuel Say was a good friend of Thistlewood and Vine was one of his house slaves, but she was not apparently established as his 'wife' in the same way that Phibbah was Thistlewood's. Though there seems little doubt that Phibbah from time to time went, voluntarily or otherwise, to other men there is no doubt at all that she was 'kept' exclusively by him. Mould's Lewis, for a long time a hired slave on Egypt, had gone to Kingston with Mr Mould on his return to Jamaica.

In early September, Samuel Hayward went off to Kingston on business. He left his money bag, containing £469 13s 9d, in Thistlewood's care, and asked him to keep an eye on the property – Hatfield. In return, Thistlewood asked him to try to extract John's manumission paper from the Secretary's Office.

'Sunday 11th: Rode with Mr Say & Solomon Cook to Mrs Bennett's pen. p.m. Rode to Mr Hayward's at Hatfield. All well. Returned.'

On the 25th, Mr Hayward came home. He had not succeeded with John's manumission paper.

In October, as his house was now repaired, and Mr Cope was coming to stay at Egypt for a fortnight, and as the great house 'yellow room', in which he had slept 'leaks abundantly', Thistlewood moved back into his own. On the 13th he set out for Savanna la Mar, where:

'Mr Moffatt's Negroes sold; many Mandingoes, &c. I bought none, as Mr Moffatt refused to take Mr Cope's bond; but he would let me have what I would upon my bond.'

He was not yet ready.

'Wednesday, 14th December: Received a note from Mr Samuel Hayward (*per* James) with *New Experiments and Observations on Electricity, made at Philadelphia in America*, by Benjamin Franklin, Esqr. &c.

Thursday 15th: Carried a dozen bottles of ketchup from home to Mr Robert Baker's store for him to sell it for me; also two dozen from Mr John Week's store to Mr Baker's. Billy Hartnole says he has sold seven bottles for me, which are upon the books. I gave him the remaining five bottles. (Mr Baker has 3 dozen bottles).

Bought of Mr William Antrobus & Co. a barrel of flour, 237 lbs at 25s = £2 19s 3d. Paid for it.

Received from Mr Fitzgerald's wharf, a case marked TT, Savanna la Mar, which came by the *Neptune*, Capt. Robert Kaye. Paid 2 bitts wharfage.'

The case contained:

78 yards brown linen at 15d (33 ins wide, nearly)	£4 17s 6d
100½ yards white oznabrig at 10d (28 ins wide)	4 3s 4d
100 yards brown oznabrig at 7¼d (27 ins wide)	3 11s 0d
24½ yards Russia drab at 12d (28 ins wide)	1 4s 6d

It also contained seven fairly new publications including works on Chemistry, Optics, Natural History, Husbandry, Physick, and 'The Most pleasant & Delightful History of Reynard the Fox & Reynardine, his son ...', and half a ream of folio paper. He was now acquiring reading material for Mulatto John.

In the first week of January, two more cases arrived for him. They contained more cloths and a 'Magic Lanthorn' which he wanted to show to his new assistant Nathaniel Tackle − but Nathaniel was not to be found, he had gone to the Negro houses. Nathaniel, indeed, was a disappointment. On Friday 2nd, he came in the night took his gun and belongings '... and went away privately: like a scoundrel.' He had received his pay the day before.

On the 3rd, Mulatto John was ill with a violent fever and Dr Wedderburn was sent for and prescribed 'some cooling powders'. Later, he 'had a glister put on John's neck'. Then:

'At night, about 11 o'clock, broke Job's banjar [banjo] to pieces in the mill house.'

During the next three weeks, he, John, and Phibbah were all ill, sometimes violently, and he seems to have lost some of his usual control of affairs.

'Friday, 12th February 1764: Myself and Mulatto John much as before: Phibbah somewhat better. Note: I took 15 drops of laudanum tonight, as well as last night. Both the white people in liquor. Driver Johnie, &c. drunk. The Negroes make a noise, at the Negroes houses, &c.'

Next day, as the mill was put about to start the crop taking, Neptune, greasing the side-roller gudgeons had his left thumb ground off. He was immediately sent off to the doctor. As for Driver Johnie, he was flogged 'for last night's work', as was Quashe for leaving his watch-post in the yard, and Lincoln for being off the estate.

On Thursday, 23rd February, 1764:

'Received a letter from Mr John Thistlewood, Jnr dated Kingston, Feby, 16th, 1764. Paid postage 2 bitts.'

This was his brother's son, and Thistlewood who was now clearly on the way to acquiring his own property must have encouraged his arrival, to follow him at Egypt, perhaps, and thence by example, into independence.

John Thistlewood had voyaged in the *Earl of Effingham*. The vessel called at Morant Bay, Kingston, and put in at Old Harbour to take refuge from a squall, before arriving at Savanna la Mar. He too kept a diary.

'February 25th 1764: This day came on shore at Savanna la Mar and thence I went to Egypt and got there about 2 p.m. where my uncle kindly received me, but was in poor state of health; but everything in the best order. Things seemed odd, but yet very pleasant.'

And, from his uncle's side:

'Saturday, 25th February 1764: I had something of the fever last night. John [that is his son, Mulatto John] rested badly last night. He is not so well as yesterday. About 2 p.m. my kinsman John Thistlewood Jnr came here from Savanna la Mar, walked. Received by him a letter from my brother, dated October 24th 1763. My kinsman slept in the green room bed.'

The diaries of John Thistlewood, the nephew, are disappointingly uncommunicative. Not once, in his daily accounts, does he mention little Mulatto John, or Phibbah, or his uncle's relationship with either, or his uncle's frequent attentions to other slave women. Nor for that matter, does he say much about his own personal affairs. He relates, in detail, the daily activities of the crop taking and other estate work; he describes expeditions in search of runaways; he makes bare notices of visits and of visitors; he occasionally refers to the sexual activities of Henry MacCormick the new estate book-keeper; but not once does he openly admit his own. It is, indeed, from his uncle's diaries that we learn about his deep involvement with one of the women slaves, Little Mimber.

In late 1764 or early 1765 John Thistlewood, the nephew, began a liaison with her which was strongly resented by her 'husband' driver Johnnie. Thomas Thistlewood also raised objections, seemingly unwilling to allow Johnnie to be deprived of his woman. Several times he warned his nephew to keep away, and, on each such occasion he severely punished Little Mimber. On the morning of Saturday, 30th March 1765, nephew John took the dory and went on the river. His uncle recorded subsequent events:

'p.m. Rode to Sav la Mar ... Being in Mr Emetson's tavern with Mr Hayward, drinking some punch, Neptune rode down on Phibbah's mare (this was something after 11 o'clock) and told me my kinsman went upon the river a shooting and was not returned, but the canoe found overset, &c. I rode home as fast as I could, and was informed about 9 o'clock he called Henry out of the Millhouse and desired he would look after the boiling a little, till he walked to the river side to try to shoot a coot or two; and although Henry and Phibbah persuaded him to take somebody with him, yet he would not, but got into Cyrus's little dory (properly belonging Mr John Barry) and paddled himself into the river where he shot once or twice, was met by Kinsale & Old Sharper, of whom he inquired if they saw any coots. But not returning, Henry and the Negroes began to think he stayed long, when, somewhat after 10 o'clock, Mr Meyler's boat going up the river with a load of boards, met the dory overset going down the river, somewhere against the wild canes, with his powder horn & a coot. Presently after, they met his hat floating down the river, which convinced them somebody was drowned. Therefore they carried them up to the Estate & then Neptune was depatched to me. Searched all afternoon, but discovered nothing of him or his gun.'

Next day MacCormick and others went again in search. Lincoln and Plato swam and dived in the river.

'Henry says my kinsman told him but a day or two ago that he had strange bad dreams about himself, &c. About 11 p.m. our white man [Henry MacCormick] discovered my kinsman floating down about 150 yards below the old barcadier. Soon made hands get him out. Oh: how strangely he looked. I rode and acquainted Mr Stone, the coroner, but he thinks it needless to have an inquest over him. Flanders made a coffin, and Mr Hayward, who spent the day, read prayers over him when we buried him in the evening, about 15 yards NE of my house. Davie & Quashe here at his burial.'

And on the night of Thursday, April 4th 1765 between 8 and 9 o'clock

'. . . heard a shell blow on the River, and afterwards in the night, 2 guns fired with a loud Huzza after each, on the river against our Negro houses, for joy that my Kinsman is dead, I imagine. Strange impudence.'

As the tragic relationship between John Thistlewood and Little Mimber developed business went on around them in much the usual way. Thomas Thistlewood made his first approach to Mrs Sarah Bennett about the possible sale to him of her property, Paradise Pen. In September, 1764 he bought 'at the public Vendue' in Savanna la Mar '49 Norward hams' for which he paid £2 5s 7½d.

'Made 50s and a bitt of them; besides the 4 or 5 I eat, and gave several to my Negroes.'

He was not the only entrepreneur. In early June, for instance, Cubbenna had sold 2 hogs for 42 bitts.

Earlier in the year, Mr Hayward had appointed Thistlewood his attorney during an absence in England. He returned in early January 1765 bringing a variety of gifts, including books, for Thistlewood, and an electric machine with which they and friends played for some time being 'electrified'. One of the gifts was a key-ring, on receipt of which Thistlewood 'gave Phibbah my old one given me by Patty Hatchard' – another sentimentality abandoned, and indeed he had even forgotten the name, Hatcher.

'Saturday, 5th May 1764: A Negro wench hanged at Savanna la Mar today. She was concerned in cutting out the sailor's tongue lately, &c. Cudjoe's Negroes brought her down, and another who is with child, and a vast deal of Obeah of different kinds.[7]
Hear there is an information against Mr Samuel Say of Cabaritta Estate for permitting a Negro play (for Vine's mother who is lately dead) last Sunday Afternoon.'

Little Mulatto John had been put to board with Mrs Bennett in order to attend Mr Hugh's school in the Savanna. He was looked after by Mrs Bennett's Old Leandra. From time to time he suffered slight injuries and ailments (including yaws). Usually, Phibbah would go to see him; and Mrs Bennett had sent a 'Negro wench name Bess' to live with Phibbah.

In August Thistlewood, who was a keen alligator hunter from his Vineyard days:

'Saw a crocodile at Savanna la Mar, about 5 feet & 1 inch long and 30 inches girth, his eyes large, iris sea-green, pupil very dark colored, long and narrow. Head shorter than an alligator's. Skin yellowish in some places. Made much like a croaking lizard. This was brought by Bob Mitchell's vessel from some of the Quays [cays], and had got away into the morass. No musk.'

He had always been descriptive of flora and fauna new to him; but perhaps here we can detect the influence of Dr Anthony Robinson's tutorials.

In November there were rumours of slave revolts and killings on estates in northern Westmoreland and southern Hanover, including Kendal. Thistlewood thought them highly exaggerated, and allowed no rumour to disturb his immediate concerns. Achilles and Plato were long runaway; his Caesar was caught by Rose eating dirt,[8] and on Wednesday 21st, Daniel brought home a hired woman slave named Cubbah, whom he had found on another estate. Thistlewood, for reasons which we can only surmise, again displayed his occasional excessive and sadistic brutality. Next day, he: 'Picketted Douglas's Cubbah on a quart bottle neck, till she begged hard'.

In December he flogged Egypt Lucy for leaving Daniel and going to Quashie. 'Quashie beat Daniel last night also about her, &c.'; and, on Thursday 6th, 'Today first heard that Colonel Cudjoe is dead some time ago'. Cudjoe's men, however were still around. In January 1765 a body of them under Captain Toby, were much about in search of runaways.

In April Thistlewood sent off more puncheons of rum on his own account; old acquaintance Derby ran off again and came home of his own accord and was flogged; Little Mimber was in the hothouse, soon to be sent to Paradise; Princess had got the clap; and on Monday, 29th April 1765:

'... about 8 o'clock Mr Haughton and me set out for Lucea, got there 10 o'clock. Immediately went aboard the Guinea ship, and the sale began. I got together 10 new Negroes into Mason Quashe's hands, who was with us on board, and bought them off Mr Cuthbert at the following price: 2 men at £56 per head, 2 men-boys & 2 young women at £54 per head, 3 girls at £52 per head, and 1 boy at £51 = £535. The Bill of Parcel is in my name with a receipt in full. Mr Cope gives his bond, and Mr Moffatt joins him.'

With Mason Quashe and Lincoln in charge, the newly acquired slaves were sent off to Egypt as quickly as possible, arriving there by 8 p.m. ('Note: the smallpox is prodigiously at Lucea.') Thistlewood gave the sailor who brought them ashore 4 bitts, and provided them with 14 bitts worth of bread and saltfish. On June 19th he listed them.

'*SYPHOX*,	a Negro man (a Temne donco)[9] about 19 or 20 yrs. old, 5 ft 5 ½ ins several rows of punctures across the belly, & thus on the face.
CUDJOE,	a man (coromante) about 20 yrs., 5 ft 6 ins bow-shinned, 3 spots on his right cheek, 4 on his left.
CHUB,	a boy, about 13 or 14 yrs., 4 ft 10 ³⁄₁₀ ins, 3 perpendicular scars down each cheek.
BRISTOL,	a boy 5 ft 1 in, (Soco Country), about 17 yrs, several perpendicular small & one diagonal scar on each cheek.
JIMMY,	a boy, about 10 or 11 yrs, 4 ft 5 ⁶⁄₁₀ ins (Coromante or Shante).
MYRTILLA,	a woman, 4 ft 8 ins, (Soco), about 19 yrs. Two black marks descending obliquely from her eyes, and her belly full of her country marks.
PHOEBE,	a woman-girl, about 12 yrs old, 4 ft 7 ins Coromante. Very black eyebrows.
PEGGY,	a woman, 5 ft 1 ⁹⁄₁₀ ins, Scar on her left cheek, back & belly full of country marks, holes through her nose. About 16 or 17 yrs old.
FRANKE,	a woman-girl, 4 ft 9 ¹⁄₁₀ ins, her face all over Champherred, about 13 yrs.
DAMSEL,	a woman-girl (Chamboy) on her face 3 long strokes down each cheek, 2 small oblique, &c. Her belly full of country marks, & in arch between her breasts. 4 ft 8 ⁹⁄₁₀ ins, about 13 yrs.'

All were branded on the right shoulder⟍TT⟋.

New Negroes were, it seems, soon infected. In early May, Simon had the clap. By late May Peggy was full of yaws, and Chub was full of boils. Thistlewood had also in his own way begun to initiate the females.

In May, he began to go in search of landed property. He visited Mrs Bennett again, and, on the 11th, he;

> 'Rode to Savanna la Mar, and attended at Mrs Frazier's to see the late Wm. Cunningham, Esqr., his lands sold, to the best bidder, by Gibson, Mr Stone, &c.'

He does not say whether he made an offer, but on Sunday 26th he went back to Mrs Bennett. She wanted £1000 for Paradise Pen. Two days later, he went to discuss the matter with Mr Say. On the 30th, they both rode over the Pen and 'found it extreme rocky, &c.' On the 13th June, Mrs Bennett sent him the Plat of Paradise Pen and he took it over to Cabaritta Estate where he and Say made up their minds. Mrs Bennett had nearly halved her original price. By an indenture made on the 3rd July 1765, between Sarah Bennett, gentlewoman, and Thomas Thistlewood and Samuel Say, planters and co-partners, the property was transferred at a price of £550 currency. William Antrobus officiated, and Charles Cooke and George Lowther were the witnesses.

Paradise Pen had once been the property of William Cunningham, from whom Sarah Bennett had, in unstated way, received it. About 300 acres, it was bounded on the west by the Cabaritta river, on the north by the river and lands belonging to George Goodin Esqr., on the east by Kirkpatrick Pen and lands belonging to Goodin and Thomas Hall Esqr., on the south-east the property extended beyond the King's road and on the south it was bounded by the King's road to Savanna la Mar and lands belonging to John Prynold. Most of these surrounding lands were morass.

Even before the sale, Thistlewood had moved to take over the property.

> 'Monday, 24th June: p.m. Went to Paradise Pen and put Lincoln to watch the house, provisions, &c. Gave Lincoln a ticket for him to carry a machete. A Negro man of Mrs Bennett's there, named Tim.
> Tuesday 25th: Opened one of my barrels of flour and delivered it to Phibbah to sell at a Bitt per quart. It is No. 116, 240 lbs net, cost about 67 bitts, or a very little more. Made of it 69 bitts, and served my Negroes 73 quarts out of it I believe.'

And in the afternoon he and Phibbah went to look over the Pen.

In July, Solon, who had the yaws, was sent to stay with Lincoln at the Pen. At Egypt, Thistlewood's Franke had the clap. There were rumours of a slave revolt in Hanover, and, on the 16th of that month:

'About 40 of Long Pond Negroes going home this morning, having been at the Savanna & at Cornwall, with complaints of the overseer flogging too much, &c. &c.'

On Sunday 21st, Phibbah went to see Mrs. Bennett, and on the same Sunday, the latest Egypt white driver, John Hartnole, also went out, but he over indulged.

'Monday 22nd: Last night J. H. rtn.1. having overeat himself in the Savanna, sh.t in the great house, &c. &c.'

During the summer months of 1765 the weather was dry at Egypt and obviously the food crops failed. Between 22nd July and the end of August Thistlewood recorded 14 instances of slaves eating canes (Derby, not surprisingly, was one), breaking the fowl house, the boiling house, killing meagre cattle, robbing provision grounds, and such like. As he also noted, he gave them the afternoon of Saturday, July 6th 'to help themselves for they are very hard set'. Nonetheless, those he took were flogged, in some instances severely.

On 24th July, Mrs Bennett's Bess, who had previously been sent to spend time with Phibbah, was now sent back, permanently:

'This evening Mrs Bennett sent a Negro wench named Bess, whom she has given to Phibbah for life, and then to John after her. She brought a paper as underneath: "Received this 24th July of Mr John Thistlewood, a free Mulatto, the sum of Five Shilings in full for a Negro girl sold him. Sarah Bennett." '

Bess was about 11 years old, Nago country, 4 ft 9 ^{8}/$_{10}$ ins tall, with large yaws scars on the back of her right calf and the front of her right knee. She was branded with Thistlewood's mark and put to live at Paradise Pen 'to look after the stock'.

At the beginning of October, Nago Jenny, at Cope's Paradise, produced another son; but there was neither charge nor claim of paternity. Thistlewood was chiefly engaged in investigating his own property. His Sally, placed with Mrs Blake's Doll to learn sewing, was not minding her work and Doll sent her home. Thistlewood put her in the bilboes, and sent her into the field. By the end of November, 1765, John Hartnole had the clap; and John Cope, in the Marshall's custody, had set out for Kingston, with nearly £2,000, raised somehow, to pay some of his debts and stay out of prison. The year closed with further 'great suspicions of the Negroes intending to rise now about'.

About mid-month a rare note of slave conversation was recorded:

'Saturday, 11th January: Margaritta today in the Trash-house telling how a Buckrah wanted her to go in the bush with him near the Styx bridge, after mentioning how he spoke to her, began thus: "Me bin say, heh, no me go, bin say warrah", &c.'[10]

On the 22nd he received more boxes of goods from England, including books, and a 60 lb Cheshire cheese from a Mr Ellis by whom he had been appointed to collect monies due in Jamaica.

'Wednesday, 26th February: Reprimanded Mr Hartnole & Harry for always getting together when I am out of the way, and neglecting minding the Negroes, &c.'

Next morning, Harry MacCormick went off affronted, to complain to Mr Cope. He apparently received no great satisfaction:

'Sunday, 2nd March: Mason Quashe being very ill, p.m. Phibbah went to Paradise to see him. At night sent Prince on my horse for her. She got home between 3 & 4 o'clock Monday morning. Franke sent me a bottle of cordial of some sort, I don't know what, & I sent them 30 tallow candles.'

On Tuesday, Mason Quashe was brought to Egypt 'on a horse, just alive & that's all. He has the bellyache, gout, &c.' On the Sunday, House Franke and Phibbah's Cubbah came to see him. On Thursday 13th, he was sent 'to Mr Bossley's at Amity Hall.' No further explanation was given, but by early April he was back at Paradise Estate. Two months later:

'Tuesday, 3rd June: About 3 p.m. Egypt Lucy, Phibbah & my Pompey went to Paradise to see Mason Quashe, who is very low and weak and is going off to the Northward very soon. I sent him a blue duffle surtout coat, warm & fit for him when he comes into a cold climate. At 8 p.m. sent Neptune with my horse to Paradise for Phibbah to come home.'

But she stayed with Mason Quashe for a few hours more, and did not get home until 5 o'clock next morning.

Sometime later in the year Mason Quashe did go to North America. The circumstances of his departure were not noted, but on Thursday, 1st January Thistlewood observed: 'Hear Mason Quashe got to North America alive.'

At the end of the 1766 crop, Thistlewood noted the Egypt production 'since Mayday 1754 that Mr Cope has had it.' The figures reflect the comparative unsuitability of Egypt, in terms of soil and climate, for sugar production; the heavy dependence on hired slave labour which was not always dependable in either attendance or performance; and the unreliable condition of the Egypt mill. There was hardly a year in which production was not stopped,

Year %	Pots made	Sugar (lb net)	Rum (gallons)	Molasses (gallons sold)
1755	114	8 322	234	–
1756		No crop was taken		
1757	991	72 343	850	2816
1758	2669	194 837	700	7000
1759	1114	83 659	1417	2948
1760	947	71 800	1710	1161
1761	793	56 053	1240	1402
1762	2054	147 348	5700	–
1763	1945	147 228	5000	–
1764	2021	148 693	4800	–
1765	884	58 546	2250	–
1766	1381	100 192	2607	1003

more than once, and the millwrights called in to carry out repairs. It is also clear that neither Mr Cope nor indeed Mr Dorrill before him, had the large financial resources to enable the proper equipment and maintenance of three sugar-producing properties, none of which was ideally situated on good cane land.

'Monday, 12th: a.m. Mr and Mrs Cope come here. Settled with Mr Cope to the 31st March last. After this day I take my Negroes away, and prepare to leave the place myself, as soon as convenient.'

But it would be more than a year later that he moved.

At the end of May, Nanny and Chub were put to live in one of the Negro houses 'upon the hill' at Paradise Pen to watch boards and shingles purchased and stored there. On the 30th, Lincoln, Johnie, Dick, Will, Caesar, Cudjoe, Pompey, Maria, Chubbah, Sukey, Mirtilla, Franke and Damsel were sent up to clear the bushes around the houses on the hill. Nanny and Chub were already at the Pen, they were in the 'great house'. Jimmy and Bess were about the house at Egypt. Solon, Syphox, Phoebe, and Peggy all had yaws. Sally was at Mrs Emetson's, she had been taken out of the field at Egypt. Abba and her two children were at Mr Samuel Lee's.

And so the next weeks were spent by Thistlewood's slaves, who still lived on Egypt but went daily to the Pen, clearing up bushes around the slave houses and clearing the path from the house to the King's road. Lincoln was driver, and Thistlewood paid daily visits of inspection. At Egypt, Phibbah's Cubbah, who had leave to hire herself out at 12 bitts per week, had been employed by Thistlewood to sew for him. She arrived with her husband, Nagua, 'a free man' who came with her and was given leave to shoot in the Egypt morass. Derby, at month's end, 'has got the clap very bad'. At Paradise Estate, Little Mimber, on Monday, 16th June, was brought to bed of a mulatto boy 'for Mr Miller'.

On 3rd July, exactly a year after the purchase, there came the first large transport of goods from Egypt to Paradise Pen. With great difficulty, Lincoln, Dick, Will, Johnie and Cudjoe moved up the hill from Cunningham's trench, along which they had used the canoe, and stored the goods in the room next to that occupied by Nanny.

But Nanny was in advanced pregnancy so she was: 'Sent to Paradise to lie in, as Mrs Cope is so good as to promise to take of any I send.' And she was replaced at the Pen by Maria and Peggy, who still had yaws.

The able-bodied now began 'bushing round the island', for the Pen was very much an island in the morass, 'for our readier traversing round it'. He and Samuel Say were about to begin a survey preparatory to dividing the property between them. And, in the days that followed, through July, more household equipment and other articles were sent up; Thistlewood began planting at the Pen, aloes, Indian Kale and Guernsey lilies to begin with; and logwood was cut and chipped and stored for sale.

On 15th July he paid Mr Abraham Lopez (with rum) £113 8s of his debt. He had borrowed £275 at 6% p.a. from Mr Lopez in order to purchase his land.

'This forenoon, one of Cudjoe's Negro men (named Appea), very saucy because I would not give him a bottle of rum.
Monday 21st: Flogged Ambo & Johnie for permitting a singing, &c. at the Negro house last Saturday night. Also reprimanded Henry MacCormick for frequenting the Negro houses in the night, &c.'

Of his own slaves, Cudjoe had the clap, Peggy seemed 'disordered in her senses, but am not certain yet', and on the 26th Maria was brought back to Egypt, sick and Chub was sent to replace her at the Pen. Maria soon returned, however, to stay with him.

'Monday, 4th August: Flogged Jimmy & Bess about meddling with my watch and telescope in great house piazza. Watch hour hand bent crooked.
Tuesday 5th: Let Mrs Bennett's Jenny have my Franke to

carry a basket of gingerbread, &c. into the country with her Sunday 10th: Received of Mrs Bennett's Jenny, 6 bitts for wages for Franke.'

On the 11th, Bess was sent to Mrs Emetson's to learn to be a sempstress, 'as Sally won't do'. On the 12th, Henry MacCormick left Egypt 'as he does not choose to stay under Mr Hartnole'. It would appear that on Thistlewood's departure Hartnole would become Egypt overseer, which he did. It might have been simply that MacCormick (whose age we do not know) did not wish to continue subordinate to John Hartnole who, as Thistlewood recorded, was now only 19 years old. On Saturday 16th August: 'This evening in the height of the bad weather' Nanny was delivered of a daughter at Paradise Estate. On Tuesday 19th, his 'girls' were weeding Phibbah's garden at Egypt, his men were thatching her house, Chub had got the clap, and Thistlewood and Say completed their survey of Paradise Pen. On the following Sunday:

> 'Mr Say and me tossed up who should choose his part of the Pen, according to a division we had made. I lost, notwithstanding which, Mr Say gave me my choice & I picked upon the north division, (which is to allow another £50 for his part of the house, &c.). Advantages & disadvantages attend each part.'

Now that he had acquired it, Thistlewood set about extensive repairs to his house. With hired carpenters the work began in early September on the cookroom and buttery. On Monday 29th, he again noted the disposition of his own. Maria had been sent to Paradise, pregnant and near her time; Nanny who now had yaws, had come home with her daughter, little Phibbah, and was employed weeding the garden at Egypt; Damsel and Caesar were now in residence at the Pen; Abba and her two children were still with Mr Lee; Jimmy was about the Egypt house; Bess was with Mrs Emetson, Sally had yaws; Cudjoe was 'bad of the clap again', but was nonetheless employed with others billing and bushing around Paradise Pen; the hired carpenters were squaring rafters preparatory to putting up the piazza posts.

During the past few months there had been rumours and actual instances of slave revolts on nearby estates. On Tuesday, 7th October, Thistlewood went into Savanna la Mar for duty as a juror, but the Court was adjourned, and:

> 'I was ordered out in a party immediately, without going home for arms, &c. Mr Hayward [now living in Savanna la Mar] lent me a gun, powder & ball.'

After dining at Mr Hayward's Thistlewood set off in a party of ten, under Mr Baker, with his waiting-boy Jimmy carrying his gun. They moved through Hatfield, Strathbogie, Amity Hall, Hartford, Petersfield, 'and thence to Mr Wm. Witter's at Dean's Valley Dry Works' arriving there at about 3 p.m. There they complained bitterly about the poor hospitality. The patrol continued through the estates north-east of George's Plain where, from the high ground, they could look over the mountains towards Savanna la Mar, Green Island and Lucea, circling round Blackheath and Frome estates 'a very large extensive valley, or rather level, with little risings ...'. Then back down to Dean's Valley. There, they spent their second night out. They had seen no rebels, but:

> 'Hear Mr Ralph Hambersley's party has killed 4 rebel men & took 2 women prisoners. Two of our party guarded 2 prisoners from Dean's Valley to Savanna la Mar ... through Houghton's Ferris, Paradise, Salt River, &c.
> Friday, 10th: Note: 2 of the Rebel Negroes were tried yesterday and one of them burnt with slow fire (alive) near the gallows at Savanna la Mar, yesterday evening; and the other, this morning at Cross-Path, where they killed Gardiner.'

Near the end of October, Thistlewood's Coobah was sent to Paradise Estate, where Maria still was, as she too now 'begins to be very big'. Will, suffering from a swollen finger, was sent to stay a few days at Dr Wedderburn's.

> 'This evening Maria brought to bed of a girl at Paradise Estate. A stout Negro man of Dr Lock's is now gibbetted alive in the Square ... a resolute rebel.'

On Wednesday 12th it was Coobah's turn. She also had a girl; and on Tuesday 18th, Abba produced her third, another boy. Cubbah's child was a Mulatto.

In December, planting began in the garden 'in the valley before the house' at Paradise Pen − corn, peas, and some flowers. On the 20th, Thistlewood rode over to Paradise Estate. En route, in Savanna la Mar, he saw Florentius Vassall, just returned from England and staying overnight at Mrs Emetson's. At Paradise:

> '... discoursed with Mr. Cope on various subjects. He, by the Governor's leave, has laid down all his posts civil and military ... Mr & Mrs Cope had high words about selling Paradise Estate & Negroes, &c &c.'

Mr Cope's appraisment of Paradise Estate had been as follows:

35 acres of plants & land for ever, at £30	£ 1050	0	0
20 acres of first ratoons & land for ever, at £20	400	0	0
58 acres of ratoon canes & land for ever, at £15	870	0	0
40 acres of land & barcadier rented, at £100 p.a.	1400	0	0
1147 acres of woodland, pasture, provisions, *et al* at £4	5788	0	0
120 Negroes at £50	6000	0	0
Stock	1000	0	0
	16508	0	0
Works — a water-works of 200 hhds being allowed to be £7000 more valuable than a cattle works, Paradise at 50 hhds will be £1750, and buildings added	3000	0	0
	£ 19508	0	0

Thistlewood made no comment. Of his own, he was about to suffer his first loss. Since early November Syphox had been ailing of an unspecified illness, but it might have been yaws. Mid-November, he was sent to Savanna la Mar to stay with Little Mimber, then living there, 'so that he can wash in the sea'. But, on 24th December he died, and was buried by Lincoln and Dick.

1767 was the year of the move and Thistlewood perhaps had a new, special and slightly excited feeling as he drew up his balance of account on that 1st January. His ready money was small, but John Cope owed him money, and as we have learned, Phibbah provided supplementary financial resources; and of course he now owned land and 28 slaves:

Lincoln	Nanny and her Phibbah
Johnie	Maria and her Lucy
Dick	Coobah and her Silvia
Will	Abba and her Mary, Johnie; & Neptune
Caesar	Sukey
Solon	Damsel
Pompey	Franke
Chub	Mirtilla
Cudjoe	Phoebe
Jimmy	Peggy
	Sally
	Bess

'Saturday, 3rd January 1767: Paradise Quasheba (the grannie) here today. Gave her 3 cobbs for looking after Nanny, Maria & Coobah.

Sunday, 4th: Cumberland, a Negro carpenter, whom I have hired of Mrs North at £20 per annum come to work. I am to feed him. Gave him 2 bitts & 7 herrings for his week's allowance, put Solon with him & set them to pull down the old fowl-houses, &c.'

Cumberland replaced Old Ninevah, a previously hired carpenter. Through January the carpentry continued, the majority of Thistlewood's slaves worked on clearing and preparing land for planting, and he and Phibbah visited (he daily) and supervised the storage of more and more furnishings and other goods sent up.

'Tuesday, 5th February: A great horserace today, upon Camp Savanna, New Market Course. Vast many people passed through Egypt. Mr Johnson's horse won.

About 8 a.m. Franke ran from the Pen, and gave an account that Sukey was very bad, Lincoln having beat her terribly. I rode there & found her speechless, and Lincoln run away. Returned to Egypt and got Mr Hartnole to go with me to the Pen to bleed her, which he did, also rubbed her with hungary water &c., and gave her some hartshorn drops in water, &c. after which she was a little better. Then had her brought to Mr Say's trench, where was Flanders in Cubbenna's canoe in which he brought her to Egypt, where had her well rubbed with spirits of turpentine, a few drops given her inwardly, also a drink of sea punch. p.m. She could talk, & in the evening walked to the Negro house.'

Next morning Lincoln came back with a note from Mr Hayward. He had apparently gone to ask Mr Hayward to write a letter begging him off. It did no good. Thistlewood: 'seized him, had him to Egypt, flogged and pickled him well, then put him in the bilboes'.

In March, work began on the provision grounds and on Thistlewood's 'intended garden', an area 'fenced' round with penguin plants. Trees in the area were felled; and, from the largest of the young cotton trees, Mulatto Davie was hewing him a small canoe. Davie had hired the Egypt cooper Flanders and his assistant, Job, to help him.

Early in May, Phibbah's Coobah, having left or been left by Nagua, was at Egypt and 'made a match with Mr John Hartnole'. The honeymoon was brief. On Friday 8th she was at Egypt, and she 'slept with Hartnole'. On Saturday 9th, she 'took her leave this morning'. She was soon to sail on the *Henry*, Capt. George

Richardson, to England with young William Dorrill Cope. On the 13th, Capt. Richardson sailed. At the end of the month, there was another 'match' between Egypt watchman, Harry, and Thistlewood's Damsel.

On June 1st, there was sad news. Thistlewood, in Savanna la Mar heard that Mason Quashe had died in North America. Why he had gone, where exactly he had gone, and precisely when he died, were not recorded.

The little canoe had been finished by Davie, Flanders and Joe in mid-April. They had worked on six successive Sundays, but, said Thistlewood, 'frequently did but little'. They had asked 50*s* for making it. Thistlewood thought it far too much for 'she is scarce worth a fourth part', but he does not say that he refused to pay. It was, in fact, small: 14 ft 7 ½ ins long, 27 ½ ins wide, and 15 ½ ins deep. He found it necessary to acquire a larger 'battoe'; and it was in this that Phibbah went to the Pen in June to plant yams and plantains, and 'many things' besides, in the Negro ground. This planting both in grounds and garden, continued into July.

'Sunday 5th, 1767: All last night & today, a vast of company, with singing &c. at the Negro houses, with Franke, for the loss of her husband, Quashe. She killed a heifer, several hogs, &c. to entertain her company with. Delivered Franke a jug of rum, 8 gallons or more.
Friday 17th: Mountain Lucy miscarried, having I am told drank Contrayerva[11] lately every day on purpose.
Tuesday 28th: This morning rode to the Pen and planted some euphobias... My Negroes not up, &c.
Wednesday 29th: p.m. Went to the Pen, took Job with me with a whip, flogged Lincoln & every one of the field Negroes for impudence & laziness, &c.'

Late in July, Thistlewood's Will had been sent to stay at Dr Wedderburn's. He had the dropsy. Maria went to look after him. On August 7th she came home to tell Thistlewood that Will had died about breakfast time that morning. 'Sent Cudjoe & Solon to bury him.'

'Tuesday, September 1st 1767: Cumberland ... & part of my Negroes at the Pen [working] as yesterday; but had the greater part of Negroes at Egypt, and p.m. carried my Book-case, in the battoe, to the Pen, and the books in baskets upon Negroes' heads, &c. I went to the Pen & put all up safe, except *Human Prudence*, which Mirtilla let fall in the dirt by accident, but not much hurt.

p.m. Had my desk carried to the Pen in the battoe, and drawers carried upon Negroes' heads. I had also a copper tea-kettle and earthen tea-pot, old long ketchup box with brown paper and sundry other things in it.

Thursday 3rd: a.m. Lincoln, &c. carried in the battoe to the Pen: cask of muscovado sugar, 196 lb net; cask of rum, 28 galls net of the strong proof; manchioneal table; 3 old chairs; pisspot; 8 empty bottles, &c. And on Negroes' heads, &c. guns, pistols, machete or cutlass, shot bags, machine stick, &c. thermometer, old saddle, whip, &c. &c. I rode to the Pen and stowed them away.

Note: Mr John Hartnole stayed at home, watching me as it were.'

That afternoon, with Flanders' assistance, he took up plants, mostly fruit trees and suckers, and transported them to the Pen in the battoe. He also sent over his chest and some of his bedroom furnishings. Then:

'p.m. Rode in the field (the Potato Piece) told the Negroes I was going away & had nothing more to do with them, that Mr John Hartnole (who was present) was their overseer, that I hoped they would behave well & I did not doubt but he would use them well, &c. and that I desired no body would come to me upon any account whatever.

(Now at Paradise Pen or Breadnut Island.)

At 40 minutes past 5 in the evening, took my leave of Mr Hartnole, having first showed him everything; given him the keys, &c. Jimmy rode Prince horse and I Mackey. Jimmy was drunk. Got to the Pen about sunset. Supped on bread & cheese. About quarter past 7 Phibbah come, Prue with her. At night, *Cum* Phib: *Sup me lect.*'

His admonitions notwithstanding, Egypt and Paradise slaves visited him at Breadnut Island Pen. Phibbah arrived early in November to live with him following Mr Cope's agreement to hire her out to Thistlewood. Thereafter, her slave friends came a-visiting: and it was on one such occasion that he was told:

'Egypt Negroes privately called me ABBAUMI APPEA, i.e. "No For Play". Mr John Hartnole they call CRAKRA JUBA, i.e. "Crazy Somebody."'

Notes

1 Men-boys, i.e. teenagers of about 14 years and over.
2 Cassidy (1971) p.134. 'Chamba', meaning cut up or disfigured, in

the case of slaves by their 'country marks' or tatooing; from the Bight of Benin.

3 Thistlewood's employer, now a Colonel of the Militia, to replace Alexander Barclay now Brigadier-General.

4 We have seen similar instances, previously recorded, of newly acquired slaves being housed with those of longer residence on an estate. This was for a 'seasoning' period, during which the new slaves would be made aware of their new conditions of life and labour, learning from those with whom they were lodged. It is worth noting that Thistlewood himself, the only white on the Vineyard Pen during his first year in Jamaica, had himself (though in rather different circumstances) been 'seasoned' by the Vineyard slaves who introduced him to the local scene.

5 A smallholding, a provision ground, a 'mountain' where foodstuffs were grown.

6 Captain Cuffee was, it would seem, the slave (possibly free coloured) captain of a coastal vessel belonging to Mr Meyler.

7 Cassidy (1971) pp.241 ff. 'Obeah', by which spells could be laid, 'was once counterbalanced by Myal', by which the powers of obeah might be resisted or overcome; but even by Thistlewood's time, according to his contemporary, Edward Long, it would seem that there was some assimilation by the obeahmen of the practice of myalism.

8 Among the greatest causes of slaves' mortality were tetanus ('lock-jaw') especially among the newly-born; yaws, a contagious disease of the skin; and more usually among the older slaves, 'dirt-eating'. Bryan Edwards (see chapter 5, footnote 2) opposed a view prevailing among slave-masters that the practice should be severely punished. He correctly described it as an ailment [now known to be symptomatic of infestation by hookworm] rather than a crime. (*History of the West Indies*, 5th Edition, Vol. 2, p.167.)

9 Thistlewood's writing of this is cramped and blotched in the bottom corner of a page, but with the help of Professor Phillip Custin's *The Atlantic Slave Trade* (Univ. of Wisconsin Press, 1969) pp.184-5, I hope I have got it right, except that I have found nowhere any interpretations of 'donco', if that be the word. 'Temne' '... probably meant almost anyone from coastal Sierra Leone.'

10 'Warrah' — what a thing! what is this! See Cassidy & Le Page (1980) p.462, 'warra'.

11 A herbal drink used as an antidote and remedy for stomach ailments. See Cassidy & Le Page (1980) p.119.

CHAPTER 7   Settling in on the Pen

Introduction

Now at last on his own, and with Phibbah and son Mulatto John, Thistlewood's accounts allow us closer glimpses of his household life. We are told of evenings' entertainments, of visitors to him and to Phibbah, and of ailments in the family.

And, as might be expected, much more detail of horticultural and other money-earning enterprises on his Pen. The term 'Pen' was, in the British Caribbean, peculiar to Jamaica, and it carried several meanings. We have already learned of the main activities on Florentius Vassall's 'Vineyard' which was a sort of intermediate type of Pen property. On Vineyard, the main products were logwood for export, and beef for the local market; but there was also, importantly, the rearing of cattle to be supplied to his sugar estates in Westmoreland.

Some 'Pens', indeed, were little more than livestock raising properties maintained to supply draught animals to the sugar estates to which they were attached by ownership or location, or both. Others, more like Mr Thistlewood's, supported a wider range of products – lime (used in the boiling of sugar); grass for animals (the eighteenth century equivalent of today's petrol for motor vehicles); foodstuffs; spices; and a variety of other commodities, not necessarily entirely for local consumption. And, still another kind of 'Pen' was the large residential property, usually in or near to an urban centre – for instance, Admiral's Pen, Rollington Pen, and others in the environs of central Kingston which, in the eighteenth century was bounded on the north by North Street, on the east by East Street, on the south by the sea, and on the west by West Street.

On Pens such as Mr Thistlewood's, but less so on the other types, one considerable source of income was the hiring out of slaves, and now we find him yearly in search of some not-too-distant planter who needs to hire additional labour for the harvesting of the sugar crop.

We are also able to trace in greater detail the fortunes of the slave population of the Pen, for the slaves with whom he now daily associates are his own property. We begin to learn of their household arrangements; their tasks in domestic and field-labour, and in the always unfortunate role of 'fisherman' for Mr Thistlewood's table. And we find Mr Thistlewood caught in the dilemma of all slave owners who dealt with their slaves as people, and, at the same time, as more or less valuable pieces of property, that is, as livestock.

Obviously by previous arrangement, and probably to save Mrs Bennett, or themselves, the cost of an official survey, Thistlewood and Say on 18th December 1767 sold back to Mrs Bennett for the original price of £550 currency all the land they had jointly purchased from her. On the following day, she sold it back to them in the individual holdings they had agreed on in their survey. Thistlewood's share, consisting of 66 acres of dry land and 78 acres of contiguous morass, cost him £275 currency. This new indenture was witnessed by Samuel Hayward and William Parr.

On his newly acquired Pen, there were his 27 slaves. By his listed distribution of iron pots to households on Tuesday, 29th September 1767 we can tell how they were then accommodated. Abba and Sally lived together and with them, Abba's children Mary, Johnie and Neptune. He had given no estimate of Abba's age when he acquired her from John Parkinson in 1758. Sally, bought in April, 1762, would now be about 15 or 16 years. Mary would have been 6, Johnie nearly 4 and Neptune just over a year. Abba's 'husband', the father of Mary, was Mr Emetson's Neptune, and it is tempting to assume that he had also fathered the two boys of whom the second bore his name. On the Pen, Abba, home from her long service at the Emetson's, was chief domestic slave, with special duties as laundress. In September 1767 she was teaching Egypt Silvia how to iron clothes. The main references to her during 1767—8 dealt with a brief illness at the end of October, 1767; and the building of a house for her on the Pen, in which work Cumberland, with assistance, was employed off and on between mid-December, 1767 and late February, 1768 when it was finished. It was a wooden house with thatched roof. Then, towards the end of 1768 Abba's Neptune, together with two other small children, was weaned from the breast.

'Abba, Maria & Nancy, took each a pill last night & physick this morning to prepare them, because they give suck to their children.'

iday 16th December:

> 'Sent little Lucy (Maria's pickanninny) to Egypt to Hagar, to wean from the breast.'

And, supposedly, Neptune and Nanny's Phibbah were similarly detached from their mothers, though not necessarily at Egypt. Sally's story to the end of 1768 is more complicated and much more unhappy. Unlike Abba, whom Thistlewood apparently left unmolested, Sally was much troubled by him; but the attraction, perhaps to his disappointment and annoyance, seems not to have been mutual. On 7th March, 30th May, 18th June and 1st July, 1768, Thistlewood recorded sexual intercourse with her and in every case commented '*Sed Non Bene*'. Then, on Monday, 4th July, he 'Made a match between Chub and Sally'. There is no indication whether the match was at the request of either or both the parties involved or simply imposed by Thistlewood. No further mention of Sally until Monday, 22nd August when:

> 'Note: Phibbah send Sally yesterday forenoon to Savanna la Mar for a bitt's worth of bread, and she is not returned since. In the evening a Negro woman of Mr Blake's took up Sally at Southfield, and brought her home. I gave her 4 bitts.'

Sally was immediately put in the bilboes and there she remained until the next morning when she was violently punished, even though (or was it because?) she had suffered assault during her absence.

> 'Put a collar and chain about Sally's neck, also branded her with ⟨TT⟩ on her right cheek. Note her private parts is tore in a terrible manner, which was discovered this morning by her having bled a great deal where she lay in the bilboes last night. Being threatened a good deal, she at last confessed that a sailor had laid with her while away. Mr Say's Vine undertook to doctor her.'

Between then and the end of 1768 there was only one other reference to Sally:

> 'Thursday, 20th October: p.m. *Cum* Sally, *mea, Sup. Terr* at foot of cotton tree by New Ground side, West north west from the house (*sed non bene*).'

Considering her earlier attempts to run away and this latest assault it seems a reasonable assumption that she was not one of the more contented of Thistlewood's slaves.

Lincoln lived with Sukey, with whom he had made a match on Saturday, 6th April 1765. The relationship between him and

Thistlewood is interesting. He was often rebuked, sometimes, as we have already seen, with severe violence, and yet he remained close to Thistlewood, was often given preferential treatment, and was to outlive him on the Pen. At first, on the Pen, he was driver and fisherman.

'Friday, 4th September 1767: [Lincoln] got me some good mudfish for dinner, after he had set the Negroes to work, &c.'

Next day, Thistlewood gave him an old coat. About a month later, on Friday, 9th October, he was sent off, with a ticket, to take to John Filton's man, Will, a mare which Phibbah had been entrusted to buy for Will. He returned on the 12th, and: 'brought me (sent by John Filton's Will) a large yam & a good deal of coffee'. He also brought the mare back to graze on the Pen. Not long afterwards Lincoln was again in disfavour.

'Wednesday, 9th December 1767: Did not send Lincoln a fishing again, as he spends the whole forenoon and brings next to nothing, a few small drummers or loggerheads.
Chub brought fish.'

But, on Christmas Eve, he was allowed a ticket to go to see his countryman Will in Hanover. Through the second half of June, 1768, he was ill – feverish with pains in neck, wrists, and knees, which were only temporarily relieved by a 'bleeding' given him by Mr Hartnole at Egypt, to whom he had been sent on horseback. By the beginning of July he was up, but not in the field, and again, complaint was recorded:

'Saturday, 2nd July: Received 9 bitts for grass today = 350 bitts.
Note: Lincoln does not give a clean account of 7 bitts worth, which was sent more, and he pretends he could not sell, &c. &c. cannot trust him. However, told him he might have what he could get for it.'

On the 6th 'a little better' so he was back in the field; but on the 13th he was said to be 'sick again', it seems only for a day or two. On Sunday, 4th September, Will came to see him; and on the last Saturday of October he 'set out with Will's young mare for Richmond Estate'. Then, early in December, the 5th:

'Broke Lincoln from his drivership and made him work with the rest: He is notorious headstrong and roguerish.'

But he would be reinstated.

Sukey, his woman, suffered occasional brief illnesses in

September, 1767, when she was 'said to be breeding', but apparently was not, and again in May, 1768, when she returned home 'with a sore foot' from Masemure Estate, where Thistlewood had hired out some of his slaves. Otherwise, she featured only as a frequent object of Thistlewood's attentions.

Dick shared a house with Bess. He was a field worker whose most notable accomplishment in this period was the felling of a large cotton tree. The tree, measured by Thistlewood, was said to have been 80−90 feet high and 40 feet in girth near the ground 'including its irregularities'. It took Dick eight days to bring it down, and it came with a tremendous crash that frightened Thistlewood and all the others on the Pen. In mid-November, 1767, he suffered a bad stomach-ache and was given a 'Vomit'.

Bess, who had replaced the uninterested Sally at Mrs Emetson's, did not arrive to live on the Pen until early 1768. Then, she was put to sewing clothes for the others.

'Friday, 5th February: My Bess has got a sore in her nose. Wrote to Dr James Wedderburn & sent Maria with her there. Received an answer and 4 pills, 2 purges & a syringe.'

Hopefully it was not all for Bess's relief. At the end of May, she was accused of stealing from a neighbour. On Monday 30th:

'Phibbah told me of Bess stealing 3 cobbs from Egypt Lucy, and of her denying it stiffly; but 15 bitts of it found upon her this morning, being met by Abba & searched when going to the Bay.'

On Monday, October 3rd, she was sent back to the Emetsons.

Solon lived with Maria. He made fishpots, fished, and was sometimes employed in the garden. He was one of those hired out on Masemure, and like many others he came home lame.

Maria's daughter Lucy was less than a year old when the move was made to the Pen, and Maria was lightly employed tending the horses and doing 'sundry small jobs'. Thistlewood took Maria twice, in late June and again in mid-December 1768.

Cudjoe and Caesar shared an iron pot. They both worked for spells on Masemure; but when the gang first went at the start of February, 1768, Caesar was kept at home to look after Peggy who had smallpox and had been moved to a specially constructed hut. Cudjoe, at the end of November, 1767, was said to be 'laid up of the pox' and Thistlewood dosed him with 'a Ward's pill'. On 1st February 1768, he was sent to Masemure.

'Monday, 8th February: In the evening Cudjoe come home ill of his old complaint, brought a note from Mr David Kinlock [then Masemure's overseer].

Tuesday 9th: Flogged Cudjoe, Nanny and Coobah, for misdemeanours &c.'

Later in February Cudjoe was sent back to Masemure; but on 1st March he was once again home 'sick'.

Coobah, with her mulatto daughter Silvia, aged about a year at the end of 1767, shared a house and pot with Peggy. The next year began unhappily for her. In February, as we have noted, she was flogged 'for misdemeanours'. On the same day, the 9th she was sent to Masemure 'to go in the field tomorrow'. Her child was left in Nanny's care.

'Monday, 14th March: In the evening received a letter from Mr David Kinlock, by Coobah, whose child is sick.'

Two days later, Thistlewood made the laconic and impersonal note: 'Coobah's child Silvia died. Had it buried'. Then, in mid-May:

'p.m. Chub came home, sent by Hannibal [the slave-driver at Masemure] to acquaint me that Coobah is going to have the smallpox. Wrote to Mr Grant [who had replaced Kinlock] the overseer, and sent Mackey horse for her.'

She came home next morning, with 'a good many smallpox upon her face.' In mid-June, her recovery was noted. In September, she was twice on the road selling fish for Thistlewood, bringing him 6 bitts on each occasion; and on 14th December, '*Cum* Cubbah *mea, sup. terr* ...'. It was not the first time.

Peggy, Coobah's house-mate, had been the first of the smallpox victims on the Pen in 1768 and she had been isolated.

'Monday, 25th January: Dick digging in the garden. (Rest of Negroes getting thatch and putting up a hut for Peggy, behind the hill, west from the house, &c.)'

Next day, under Caesar's care, she was moved in.

'Sunday, 31st January: Dr Pugh gave me a bottle of something to give Peggy a spoonful every 2 hours. Peggy is much afraid of dying, she says she shall kikrevou [sic]; but I hope not much danger.'

She recovered, and on 1st May Thistlewood resumed his attentions. She was one of his favourites.

Pompey, who shared an iron pot with Chub, was employed during late 1767 looking after the livestock. In late October he had a short bout of fever. Then, no mention of note until:

'Sunday, 31st July 1768: It seems that yesterday evening my Pompey, with Mr Say's Jimmy, and [Egypt] Devonshire, took my battoe down to the sea-side a crabbing, where they completely left her and can't find her again.'

Next day, Lincoln and Cudjoe were given tickets and sent in search. They returned, unsuccessful, on Tuesday 2nd. On the 3rd, another search party was sent out, but again they returned without her. There were later attempts. On Monday, 15th August, Lincoln, Dick, Cudjoe, Say's Jimmy, and Devonshire went out again:

'... as I hear she is hid in some of the cricks or ponds near Robins Point by runaway Negroes; but they did not find her.'

The search was then abandoned.

'Thursday 25th: [Sent Lincoln, Dick and Cudjoe] to the sea side for an old thrown up canoe, formerly belonging to Paul Island. She is square sterned, about 26 feet long, near 4 wide & 3 deep. She is very leaky, however they brought her up Mr Say's trench.'

Pompey, remarkably, seems not to have been punished for losing the battoe, but for what might seem a far less serious irresponsibility, he was.

'Monday, 19th December: Finding many corn cut up by the roots, and the corn stole, flogged Pompey well.'

Pompey had been the watchman.

Chub, also, had been a livestock attendant before he was sent, in December 1767, to Egypt: '... to go awhile with Kinsale a fishing, to learn how to strike & set fish pots, &c.' Then for a time until Johnie and Solon took over he replaced Lincoln as fisherman. In both occupations he sometimes fell short of Thistlewood's approval.

'Monday, 21st September 1767: Chub tending the horses, but by neglect let [a strange, stray] grey or white horse before mentioned get at them, and almost kill Mackey, before the Negroes could get to his assistance. Flogged Chub well, and small-shotted the grey horse thrice.'

The grey horse had attacked once before, and was to return next day

when Thistlewood finally loaded his gun with a slug and shot t
Its owner was unknown.

'Monday, 4th January 1768:   Chub fishing. Flogged him for
neglect & roguery.'

Not much else about Chub, except that in July he was matched with
Sally; and in September he suffered a common complaint, the yaws.
Mirtilla, whose husband was driver Johnie at Egypt, was another
of Thistlewood's favourites. At the beginning of November 1767 he
took her: '*Sup.* board and matted bed in Dick's house' and he took
her four times more before Christmas 1768. She seems to have been
allowed to remain on Egypt until mid-December 1767 when, on the
15th, she was sent home by Mr Hartnole with a note.

'. . . she having been fighting with her husband, driver Johnie,
at Egypt last night. Wrote to Mr Hartnole and [put] Mirtilla in
the bilboes.'

But she was not separated from Johnie, and seems to have been
allowed to visit him.

'Friday, 2nd July: In the evening I rode over to Egypt. Coming
home, *Cum* Mirtilla *mea, sup. terr.* in the old Boiling house
piece, by the morass side, over Cabritto Bridge. Gave [her] a
bitt.'

Mirtilla's cook-pot sharer, Franke, was another of Thistlewood's
more frequent sex-partners. For instance:

'Friday, 13th November 1767:   *Cum* Franke *mea Sup* large
cotton tree root west from the house (which Dick fell a little
while ago). Gave [her] a bitt.'

She was a field slave, one of those sent to Masemure, but was
sometimes sent a higglering.

'Wednesday, 11th November: Received by Damsel 3 bitts for
pr. of Cuba teal, and 2 bitts for sugar beans; and by Franke 7
bitts for the 3 ducks. . . .'

Of Johnie, one of the three bought by Thistlewood ·from John
Parkinson in February 1758, there was no mention of particular
interest. He and Solon often fished together. He appears to have
lived alone for no one is recorded as sharing his cook-pot.
Phoebe and Jimmy shared a pot; but there is nothing to suggest
a match. Jimmy, a Coromante, in 1768 about 13 or 14 years old by
Thistlewood's estimate, was his houseboy, attendant, and general

messenger. Phoebe, purchased at the same time, and also Coromante, was perhaps a year older. On the move to Breadnut Island she had been left at Egypt, ill with yaws and ringworm. She came to the Pen on October 12th. On Saturday, 26th November 1768, she made a match with Egypt Neptune. In December, her yaws broke out again and Thistlewood felt 'obliged to make her lay up'. Next day, the 17th, he recorded: 'Last night gave Phoebe and Sally each a mercurial pill, and this morning each a dose of salts'. There was no specific mention of Sally's ailment, but perhaps she had been infected with the yaws by Chub.

Jimmy, constantly in Thistlewood's shadow about the house or on the road, was consequently under close observation. One day, mid-March, he 'wore a collar all day for lying'. Late May, he was again flogged and collared, but, on the same day, the 21st, was sent to Mrs Bennett's 'to bring John home' for the weekend, and to Masemure with 18 bitts for provisions for Thistlewood's slaves there in the following week. On 23rd November he was made to sleep in the bilboes; and on the 30th he brought Thistlewood 9 bitts received by the sale of peas (5 bitts), ochroes and Indian kale (3 bitts) and toyer callaloo (1 bitt).[1]

Damsel was a little older than Phoebe and Jimmy. On 31st May 1767 she had made a match with Egypt watchman Harry, and perhaps for that reason was one of the last to be moved from Egypt to the Pen. She was a house slave and Thistlewood's chief higgler. On the 30th September 1767 she:

'... sold at Savanna la Mar for me, 14 eggs, 2 bitts; Indian kale, 2 bitts; cabbage & savoys, 3 bitts. ...'

And there were many other such records. As we have seen, she was not the only higgler from the Pen, but she was the most frequently mentioned in a growing activity. After each sale and return of cash, Thistlewood noted the amount then received and the total so far received by higglering through the year. Two entries are illustrative of the growth of the business. On the last day of December 1767, he noted the receipt from Damsel of 2 bitts for Indian kale, making a total of '212 bitts in all'. It is true that most, but by no means all, of this had been earned since the move to the Pen in early September. Then, on 4th May 1768, he received another few bitts from Damsel for the sale of lime beans. The total for that year so far was then 211 bitts.

Nanny, one of the three bought for him by John Cope in Kingston in 1761, was now, at the beginning of 1768, about 26 years old. She did not move to the Pen until the end of January, 1768. A week later, she was one of those flogged for 'misdemeanours'. She lived with her daughter, little Phibbah, born 16th August 1765, and she has already been mentioned. She too, was a victim of yaws, and of Thistlewood's attentions.

The first nine months at the Pen were spent putting the place in order. Cumberland, with the help of others, was kept busy moving between new building work and repairs in Thistlewood's house, the slave houses, the out-buildings, and in making furniture and sawing palings for the garden fence. By August, he was finishing off. He made benches and a little table for Thistlewood's piazza. In November he was put to work repairing the Cabaritta bridge. During all this period he seems to have spent most nights at his owner's, Mrs North, and from time to time she took him away from Thistlewood for a few days to work for her. Also, in July 1768, he was absent for about a week, ill.

The move from Egypt had not completely severed Thistlewood and his slaves from that estate and its population. As we have seen, Thistlewood's Damsel, Mirtilla and Phoebe had connections there; Phibbah had many friends across the river and was frequently visited by them; and, for all his harshness, and his farewell warnings Thistlewood was himself the object of many visits from Egypt slaves.

'Saturday, 5th September 1767: Egypt Lucy come brought me a present of some potatoes & a pineapple; Mulatto John come with her & stayed till the evening, that I sent him home by Jimmy.'

Phibbah, as we know, did not come to live on the Pen until November. In February 1768, Egypt Lucy lent him £10. He repaid her in August. In September Egypt watchman Harry had sent him, by Prue, a gift of 2 young cats for the Pen. In October, Egypt Susanah gave him three pineapples, and in mid-December she and Driver Johnie came over to visit: the latter also very likely in search of Mirtilla.

Among other visitors from Egypt were driver Cubbenna, who, in late May 1768 '... called, going home from Paradise to Egypt, being got well of the smallpox'; Mountain Lucy, who in January had 'brought Jenny's Hanah, and her own Flora, to stay here awhile', but three weeks later they were sent home as 'they want to run away'; Old Sharper and Kinsale, who came over to see him in May; and Port Royal, in search of help.

'Thursday, 17th March 1768: This evening when I got home [from Savanna la Mar where he had voted in the local election of Vestrymen and Churchwardens] found Port Royal, who was run away from Egypt, waiting to get me to beg for him. I gave him a letter to Mr John Hartnole.'

There were visits, too, from slaves he knew at Paradise, most frequently Paradise House Franke, a long standing friend [perhaps a relative] of Phibbah.

'Sunday, 27th September 1767: a.m. Phib., Paradise House Franke & Stephen Parkinson's Betty come here, & dined here. p.m. We walked about, &c. Mulatto John also with them, and in the evening the 2 latter and John went away. Gave Franke the 2 coots I shot. At night *Cum* Phib.'

In the morning, Phibbah went home to Egypt.

Late November, House Franke, Egypt Lucy and Egypt Neptune (recently matched with Phoebe) paid a visit. And, in December, Dido once at Egypt now at Paradise, brought him 'thyme, sage and rosemary' which he planted. Little Mimber, too, was remembered. In mid-October, 1768, Thistlewood sent her '4 squab ducks, raised from her old duck', and two days after Christmas she, 'and her little Mulatto' visited the Pen.

But the most interesting of all the arrivals occurred on Sunday 31st January, 1768.

'Capt Richardson came in today. About 5 p.m. Coobah got to Paradise. She walked from the barcadier. She looks very well.'

This was Phibbah's Coobah, back from England. Thistlewood had gone to Paradise to Mr Cope and had thus been one of the first to see her. On 3rd February she arrived at the Pen. 'She rode. Quamina with her.' In the evening she went to Egypt where her man, John Hartnole, was. On the 4th, her box arrived at the Pen and she distributed gifts. Only one was recorded by Thistlewood:

'Coobah came home this morning [from Egypt]. She made me a present of 6 pretty china tea cups, 3 saucers (the other 3 being broke) &c.'

She seems to have been a practical business-woman, for, on the 7th: 'To Phibbah's Coobah for 24 yards of coarse sheeting, 60 bitts.'

Coobah spent the following few days between Egypt and Breadnut Island. If only Thistlewood had recorded some of her accounts and some of the questions which must have been asked, by him as much as any other, of her experiences abroad. On 15th February she came over from Egypt, borrowed a horse, and 'rode into the Savanna to see Mrs Bennett.' Next day:

'Coobah came home this morning from Egypt and as Paradise Quamina is come for her with a horse, she went with him. She is to call at Mr Barton's and there be innoculated by Dr Pugh for the smallpox.'

So, back to Paradise into the service of Mrs Cope. But she was allowed to visit Egypt and Breadnut Island.

'Sunday, 28th August 1768:   Phibbah's Coobah here, stayed all night. She and Mr Hartnole had disagreed.'

She was at the Pen again several times in September, and, presumably, also visited Egypt, but there is no mention of a reconciliation.

'Saturday, 1st October: Phibbah's Coobah marked on [Egypt] Silvia's smock bosom. D T S J H, for Dago, her husband; Mr Meyler's Tom, her sweetheart; and John Hart . . . e, who she is supposed to love best; and other ornaments.

[A sketch follows]:

D T S J H

(all that heart love best)

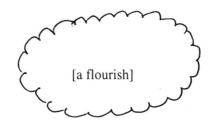

[a flourish]

Here's meat for money
If you are fit, I'm ready
But take care you don't flash in the pan.'

On the night of Wednesday, 14th December 1768, Coobah, at Paradise, was delivered of a girl, a mulatto.

Across the fence-line of penguin plants which separated the properties, Mr Say's woman, Vine, had moved in early June 1768 'to live at his new house'. Her relationship with Mr Say was not explicitly stated, but she had a 'husband', Mr McArthur, a white employee on Roaring River Estate. She was a very frequent visitor to Thistlewood's household, where she and Thistlewood exchanged entertainments.

> 'Wednesday, 14th September: Showed Vine the Magic Lanthorn this evening.
> Sunday 17th: Mr Say's Vine told many diverting Nancy stories[2] (as Negroes call them) this evening at my house. She tells them very cleverly.'

Vine's repertoire of Ananci stories must have been extensive, or she must have told them so well that they bore repetition, for:

> 'Tuesday 20th: In the evening Phibbah's Coobah came here. Vine told many Nancy stories.
> Wednesday 21st: At night Vine and Abba told Nancy stories, &c.
> Friday 23rd: Vine here this evening and told Nancy stories, &c, &c.
> Saturday 24th: Vine here, told Nancy stories, entertaining enough.
> Tuesday, 27th September: Vine told Nancy stories, &c.'

Whether in the hearing, or in the recording, there seems to have been a declining appreciation on Mr Thistlewood's part. He had certainly had a concentrated exposure. No more story-telling was recorded, but in December, to illustrate the still close relationships at least between the slave women:

> 'Wednesday 14th: Egypt Lucy's Little Quashe being very ill, p.m. Phibbah and Vine went over to Egypt to see him, and in the evening returned.'

On the eastern side of Breadnut Island Pen was Kirkpatrick Pen, one of the properties of the late Colonel Barclay. Kirkpatrick people also, but far less often, called on Thistlewood. Chief among them were Kirkpatrick Old Quashie who was a fairly frequent visitor, called upon by Thistlewood from time to time to treat livestock. He was welcome. Another, also comparatively frequent but unwelcome visitor, was Kirkpatrick Sissoo Sambo who, between November 1767 and November 1768, visited the Pen five times, armed, shooting at birds in Thistlewood's morass; and twice at Thistlewood himself, but without scoring. On 2nd November 1768, Lincoln, out shooting by the pondside saw a Negro fire at some teal, '. . . and presently after Lincoln fired at him with a ball in his shot. Did not see him again'. Ten days after Old Quashie confirmed that it was Sissoo Sambo 'whose backside was well-peppered on the 2nd

...'. On the 13th Sissoo Sambo was back at the ponds and Thistlewood spotted him and fired, but the range was too great for small shot.

Of the Maroons, little was seen on the Pen. In 1768 none of them appeared. In 1767, late September, Captain Toby had come once, and Thistlewood had bought 2 bitts worth of tobacco from him. Among the more interesting of other occasional visitors was Stephen Parkinson's Betty. On the afternoon of Thursday, December 1st, 1768 she:

'... came here to look vervine and other herbs, as Mr Lopez has put her to look after the hothouse at his estate. She says she hears Mr Stephen Parkinson died at the Commanders.

I bought her cassava baking iron for 10 bitts, she says Mr Lopez's estate, Flamstead, is very unpleasant and sickly and unwholesome for the Negroes, &c.'

She left the following morning.

And there were occasional notes of interest about some who did not visit.

'Saturday, 2nd July 1768: Hear Stompe, the Mial Man, was burnt alive this evening, and his wife, (Dr Frazier's Polly, a mulatto) hanged. (She was Robert Paton's daughter, who lived with Billy Cunningham.)'

During 1768 Thistlewood arranged one large hireage of his slaves to Masemure Estate, the property of Captain Arthur Forest. Following a visit to that property on 31st January, he:

'Ordered Lincoln, Cudjoe, Solon, Pompey, Chub, Johnie, Sukey, Franke, Mirtilla & Phoebe, to be at Capt. Forest's Masemure Estate this evening as I have hired them there at 3 bits per day each for the crop, to take spell every third night.'

On their first day of labour, 1st February, he visited them. Thereafter, he regularly sent the agreed 2 bitts per week, in advance, for each slave thus at work; but because of illnesses among the gang, the number varied widely from time to time. Thistlewood was worried. On 2nd May he rode to Masemure: '... to enquire about the Negroes lying up so much, &c.' He spent some time at the house with the overseer then rode: '... into the field and talked with Hannibal [the Masemure slave driver].' Nonetheless, the 'lying up' increased. The number at work steadily declined during the crop taking: 13 on the 5th of March, 11 on 5th May, 9 on 16th May, 7 on 25th May; and then Sukey and Mirtilla were sent back so 9 remained for the last week of work.

'Saturday, 4th June: In the evening, Hannibal, who is christened Frank Gale, called with my Negroes last week's account; and as crop is now done I gave him a doubloon for looking after my Negroes.'

Apart from that general hireage, the activities on the Pen were various, as the following excerpts illustrate. We begin with Phibbah who, in late 1767, visited Thistlewood almost every evening and remained with him till early next morning when she would return to Egypt. What with the visits and the gifts sent, it was like Kendal all over again, except that there was much greater frequency. While she still lived at Egypt so too did their son Mulatto John.

In November, 1767, John Cope yielded.

'Tuesday 10th: Rode to Egypt about 10 a.m. to meet Mr Cope who came by water. Carried with me a Cuba teal and some bread, had Jimmy with me. Dined and drank tea at Egypt.

In the evening rode to Top Hill with Mr Cope and Mr Hartnole, then rode and saw Mr Cope safe in the Savanna. Got home at darklins. Mr Cope gave me some stock to begin a breed with, and condescended to hire me Phib. at £18 per ann. to go to my place next Monday.'

On the Saturday he sent for his 'stock' − two geese and a gander, two turkey pullets and a turkey cock, two ducks and a drake and two guinea fowls. The battoe also brought Phibbah's chest.

'Monday 16th: In the morning sent the battoe to Egypt, by Lincoln & Pompey, in which came Phibbah and many things belonging to her.'

On the last day of December, Thistlewood noted 'things sold from the Pen this last year'. The earnings had been from sugar beans, 10 bitts; Indian kale, 12 bitts; peas and fish, 16 bitts each; capons, 24 bitts; cabbages, &c. 26 bitts; eggs, 49 bitts; and duck and teal, 59 bitts: Total 212 bitts, or £6 12s 6d. He also noted 'at night *Cum* Phibbah: equals 87 times this last year'.

'January
Sunday, 3rd January 1768: It is said a horse keeping at Savanna la Mar stands in between 45 and 50 pounds per ann. in grass and corn; 3 bitts worth or more of grass per day.
Tuesday 5th: In the evening planted 25 cabbage plants in the garden, which Dido sent me from Paradise.
Saturday 9th: To Capt John White for 6 Windsor Chairs at 17s 6d = £5 5 0. Paid him at Mr John David's. Settled with Mr

Samuel Lee, and received of him £2 11*s* 8*d* in full for Abba's wages, after deducting one pound for loss of time in laying in, £1 3*s* 9*d* he paid the grande, &c. &c.

Sunday 10th: Three mason Negroes, Duke, Quashie & Prince, came and underpinned an end and a side of my house. Solon, Pompey, Caesar & Cudjoe attending the masons. I fed the masons today. They are Dr Gorse's people.

Monday 11th: Sent to Paradise for John [who had been sent there after innoculation against smallpox] by Sukey and Damsel, a basket of yams, 6 quarts of rice, a dozen eggs, &c.

Tuesday 12th: Between 8 and 9 o'clock a.m. Dick and Solon came and told me they heard somebody cutting wood upon my land. Immediately took my gun and went. When just behind the first logwood fence, found 2 Negroes felling a large White Wood, Quashie belonging to McLeod, &c. runaway, upon which I fired a couple of balls amongst the trees over his head. The other Negro named Cyrus, stood, and we brought him, his bill, ax, &c. home. About noon received a note from McLeod and Lesley, wrote an answer. p.m. Rode to Savanna la Mar and had Dick & Solon take Cyrus with them. Called at Mr Meyler's but he was not at home. Thence went to Mr Hayward's, but as no magistrate could be conveniently come at, let the Negro go about his business. Afterwards, Messrs McLeod and Lesley came to Mr Hayward's where we had high words and ill language, &c.[3]

Wednesday 20th: p.m. Lincoln, Phibbah & me went through the morass, to the westward of the lime kiln, and looked at some small islands in the morass, having some thoughts of making a Negro ground there.

Thursday 28th: Negroes billing bushes. Also put up an arbor for granadillas and grape vines in the garden between those for lima beans, and one for choatas [cho-cho][4] over the cotton-tree root.

February
Wednesday, 3rd February: Dick, Maria, Coobah & myself employed planting the English trees, [received the previous day by the *Henry*, Capt. Richardson].'

More planting followed. During the next few weeks he planted crocuses, narcissi, tulips, jonquils, all of several varieties; lucern, clovers, timothy grass, french furze, Saint Joan, melongena, turnips, cabbages, parsley, nutmeg, coconuts, coffee, and much more.

'Sunday 21st: Mr John Hartnole sent me some mudfish. Wrote

to him. He came, dined and drank tea with me, as did also Miss Nancy Bell and her 2 daughters Miss Bessy and Miss Jenny Brown. Note: They sat at table at dinner.

March
Tuesday, 15th March: Bessie making Vegetable Soap, some by boiling, & some by insolation.[5]

Monday 28th: a.m. Mr John Hartnole rode over. Received 32 bitts for sewing work, to be done by Phib. and Bess, for Wm. Brown, the white man at Egypt ... p.m. William Brown come over for Phib. to take measure of him.

A girl of Mr Meyler's came to buy garden stuff. Wrote to Mr Meyler, and sent 2 water melons, some tomatoes, green peas, dry peas, and dry kidney beans to plant as a present.

April
Monday, 4th April: Mrs Bennett's Old Leandra here. Gave her 8 yards of brown osnabrig as she looks after John a great deal.

Friday 8th: Took up of Mr Hayward about 13 feet iron wire, about 8/10 of an inch circumference, 8 bitts; 2 dozen of gilt picture hooks, 12 bitts; 6 hooks for hanging hats, 6 ditto for clothes, 2 for a glass, 12 bitts.

Saturday 9th: Having received 790 ft of boards at £10 per thousand, 2,000 shingles at 40/− of Captain Hagleton, and carried my logwood [5½ canoe loads] to Fitzgerald's wharf, returned Mr Hayward's canoe.

[He later had to sue Fitzgerald for payment.]

Since I left Egypt, Park has left Mr Williams at Moreland; Monteith, Mr Stone at Long Pond; Messrs John and David Kinlock & trustee, overseer to Capt. Forest at Masemure; Kenny, Rickett's estate Ridgeland; and it is now reported that McDonald has left Petersfield. The overseer of Lincoln gone away; Otty from the Retrieve; and Peterkin from Crawford's.

May
Tuesday, 10th May: Sowed clover, lucern, burnett, timothy grass, sainfoin, french furze, angelica & borage seed under the vine arbor.'

On Thursday 12th, after another day of planting in which he 'sowed above 30 sorts of seeds in the garden', he heard from Mr Hayward of the death of Dr Anthony Robinson. For days, he was greatly upset. He penned a eulogy.

'His enquiries were not for curiosity alone. He endeavoured to search for such properties in plants as might render them serviceable to mankind, and not above 7 or 8 months ago received a hundred pistoles from the Assembly of this island, as a gratuity for his discovery of the Vegetable Soap, and was promised a further reward. When he lived in this parish he spent a good deal of his time at Egypt with me, and I was never happier than in his company.

Monday 16th: Phibbah gave me £6 for speckle, &c. she sold of mine, having scarce saved any for clothing herself.

Friday 20th: Mr Say's Vine here today. Mr Lawrence Oliphant and his little boy dined with me. p.m. Mr Samuel Barton came, they stayed till 9 p.m. and saw the Magic Lantern shown, &c. Note: I gave Mr Oliphant, Lady M. W. Montague's Travels, 3 vols. 12 mo., which I had 2 or 3 years ago, those sent me by my brother being a better edition.

Saturday 21st: a.m. Robert Perrin came to look at my book-case, to make one like it for Mr Oliphant.'

On the following Tuesday morning, Thistlewood rode into Savanna la Mar and posted letters with bills of lading and lists of things he wanted, addressed to Henry Hewitt Snr, Henry Hewitt Jnr, and his brother John Thistlewood. He also wrote to his sister, Anne Haddon and in her letter enclosed 'the wings of a long-tailed humming-bird ... 2 inches & a half long'. And then: 'As I was coming home they were hanging two Rebel Negroes'.

'Wednesday 25th: Wrote to Mr Anthony Morris and received by Cumberland a firkin of butter, 66 lb at 1*s* = £3 6*s* 0*d*. p.m. Planted in the garden, mahogany seed, cocoa or chocolate nut, and 4 of the best sorts of Mr Barton's cashews. Also planted a South Sea rose layer.

June

Sunday 5th June: Dined at Egypt, (as did also Phibbah), rode home in the evening, much not well.'

On that week-end, having finished the Masemure crop, all of Thistlewood's slaves were now back on the Pen. On Monday, 6th June, Solon, Pompey, and Phoebe were all laid up lame. Johnie was dressing crab yaws on his hand. Coobah had smallpox and Caesar was attending her. Abba, Damsel and Jimmy were 'about the house'. Cudjoe, Nanny, Sally, Sukey, Mirtella, Peggy, Franke, Maria, Chub and Dick were all at work in the garden. Lincoln, left at Masemure with Forest's canoe returned at noon.

'Tuesday 7th: The stalk of a bunch of bananas being thrown to the hogs, found it chewed like a heap of thread, in long fibres. This deserves further notice.

Saturday 11th: Planted out borage & pot marigold plants, cucumber, &c. &c., also slips of sage and marjoram, &c. &c. Sowed 4 rows of English peas.

Tuesday 14th: Sowed celery, fennel and caraway seed. The hard rain this afternoon laid great part of my garden under water, washed up the peas, seeds, &c. and made sad havoc.

Wednesday 29th: Sent Sukey, Maria, Franke, Mirtella, Peggy, Cudjoe, Chub & Caesar, to Savanna la Mar with 16 bundles of Scotch grass to sell, for which received 16 bitts. Phibbah and me sat up till past 10 o'clock, to see the moon totally eclipsed. Could still perceive her dark parts through my achromatic telescope.

July
Friday 17th July: Flogged my field Negroes for laziness, scolding, quarrelling, &c.'

On the 23rd, he was paid in bills of exchange upon Arthur Forest, in London, at 90 days sight, £78 3*s* 4 ½*d*, stg, or £109 8*s* 9*d* currency, 'in full for my Negroes hire 1167 ⅓ days at 3 bitts per day'.

'August
Friday, 5th August: Negroes fencing in the intended Negro ground by the standing lime kiln, planting logwood sets, &c.

September
Sunday, 4th September: Received preparatory powders, pills & physick, by Mr Say, for my Negroes. Gave each a pill this evening and the children powders . . .

Monday 5th: Gave the 17 Negroes intended to be innoculated physick this morning. Rest of Negroes hoeing in the garden, &c.

Tuesday 6th: Wrote to Mr Cope, by my Coobah, and sent him . . . 2 water hens, some green peas, radishes and a large land turtle which I took in payment from Egypt Negroes for work done by Phibbah. [Coobah returned bearing gifts from Mr Cope] . . . a leg of fresh pork, a black pudding, a piece of coconut cake, and an excellent pineapple.

Thursday 8th: Johnie & Solon setting the Negroes' fish-pots. Caesar watching the new ground. Coobah & Peggy pulling up weeds. Rest of the Negroes took pills last night and physick this morning.

Friday 9th: Between 9 and 10 a.m. Dr Drummond came and innoculated 17 of my Negroes, on each arm between the elbow and shoulder; just raised the skin with a lancet dipped in the matter and let it dry.[6]

Monday 12th: Gave Johnie, Neptune, Lucy and 1. Phibbah each a preparative powder last night, and physick this morning; and the upgrown Negroes each a pill last night, but no physick.

Tuesday 13th: As Abba, Nanny and Maria took each a pill last night, gave them physick this morning. Note: They have had the smallpox, but this is on account of their children sucking.

Wednesday 14th: As Dick and Cudjoe had the fever yesterday afternoon, gave each a pill last night and physick this morning. Pompey, Sally, Damsel and Franke had the fever this evening. Gave each a pill.

Thursday 15th: Gave the 4 Negroes physick this morning, who took pills last night.

Friday 16th: Lincoln, Bess & Phoebe, having the fever yesterday, gave each a pill last night and physick this morning. a.m. Dr Drummond here. The smallpox is come out on several of my Negroes, indeed all except Jimmy, Chub, Sukey and Mirtilla.

In the morning rode to Egypt where was Mrs Cope and Mr Chambers, Mrs Cope yesterday having desired that I would meet her there, she having something to say to me. When, lo! it was for to pay £18 ready money to her for a year's wages for Phibbah's hire, although it will not be due till the 16th day of November, and Mr Cope still greatly in my debt; but she says Mr Cope tells her she must receive the wages of the house Negroes hired out, strange meanness − but Mr Cope is capable of any meanness whatever.

Monday 19th: Solon and Johnie setting fish-pots, &c. Coobah, Peggy &c. billing bushes, and those who have the smallpox walking about, &c. Mr Weech says, take a green sour orange, and with a grater or knife scrape off a little of the outside rind, which scrapings laid to a sore or place wherein is maggots that could not be got out any other ways, and they will soon come out.

Tuesday 20th: Dr Drummond came and examined the Negroes. Says they are in extreme good way, and that he need not come again. He thinks Jimmy, Chub, Sukey and Mirtilla have certainly had them before.

Sunday 25th: For 600 plantains, 20 bitts.

Monday 26th: Solon & Johnie fishing. Caesar watching Negro ground, that is the New Ground I mean. Chub, Peggy and Coobah billing bushes. Sukey and Mirtilla laid up with sores, the rest of smallpox. Wrote to Dr Drummond, by Sukey,

received 20 doses of physick for up grown Negroes, and 4 for children, to take after the smallpox, also ointment to dress their arms. Made Jimmy go out and bill bushes. He is ruined with laziness.
Tuesday 27th: Smallpox begins to dry, made the Negroes turn out and bill the pasture; Jimmy also.'

On the 29th, Thistlewood wrote to Mr Hayward and returned some books he had borrowed. Hayward replied, and lent him two more: *The Freemason's Pocket Companion*, 2nd Edition, Edinburgh, 1763, and *The Gentle Shepherd, a Scots pastoral comedy*, by Allan Ramsay, Glasgow, 1758.
The last day of September was the day of final medication as the smallpox was now dry, and in the first days of October, except for Johnnie sick and Sally and Sukey home lame, normal work was resumed. It was not, however, too strenuous. The garden was weeded, the causeway leading from the house to the cookroom was cleared, and lands around the buildings and on the path to the King's road were bushed. Towards the end of the month the garden trenches were cleared of silt; and on the 27th Solon, Sukey and Franke were sent crabbing. They got 56 – Solon 20, Sukey 20, and Franke 16.

'*October*
Friday, 28th October: Doctor John James Gorse, Capt'n Binder, Mr Hugh Duncan, Mr Anthony Morris, Colonel John Cope, Mr James Crowder, and Mr John Hartnole dined with me. Dinner: roast beef, green peas, cucumbers, a roast turkey [apparently given him by Phibbah], stewed snook, stewed crabs, boiled crabs, shrimps, 2 roast teal, a boiled pudding, ripe pawpaw, cheese. Punch, grog, porter, French brandy. They went away about 5 p.m. – pretty merry.
Monday 31st: Mr Hughes says he knows Johnson the author of the noted dictionary very well, that he was a tall stout man, and a great sloven, that his beard would frequently be 1/2 or 3/4 of an inch long, and did not put on a clean shirt perhaps above once in 2 or 3 weeks, in which condition he would frequently go and dine with noblemen at their houses; that he was reserved till he had drank about a bottle of claret, but then became excellent company; that he was allowed £500 pr ann. by the noted booksellers in London during the time of writing his dictionary; that after 2 years, being talked to by Osborn for having got no further than the letter C, he knocked Osborn down with a book and stood astride over him, telling him he

scorned to strike him while down, but when he got up he would have a knock or two at him, to which Osborn replied then he did not intend to get up. However, it is said Johnson was more diligent after.'

On the same day on which he penned that long entry, Thistlewood supplied 15 of his Negroes to work on repairs to the Cabritto Bridge. It would take them 22 days, with the assistance of Cumberland for 1 day, and on completion on Friday, 25th November Thistlewood noted, 331 days − £31 0s 7½d earned for him, at the usual 3 bitts per day each.

November was a month of illnesses in his household. For most of it, Mulatto John was ill and had to be kept away from school until Monday 21st. Phibbah also was unwell. On the 18th he recorded:

'About midnight last night Phibbah was so restless and violently ill of the pain in her left elbow, &c. that I thought she would have died. I got up and tended her, had her arm rubbed with British oil, &c. I got no rest this night past.'

John Hartnole was sent for, and he came from Egypt and bled her in the right arm. The relief was short-lived.

'Sunday, 20th November: Many Negroes came to see Phibbah. House Franke came in the afternoon and stayed all night with her. She had a bad restless night. Vine is very good in assisting about Phibbah, &c.'

Next day, House Franke, rewarded with 'a mess of green peas & a roast duck', returned to Paradise and was replaced by Dido, who arrived with a note from Mrs Cope.

'Tuesday 22nd: a.m. Shot 5 red headed coots in the great pond north of my house. Gave Vine 2, Ellen and Venus who were come to see Phibbah one each.'

On the 23rd she was a little better, resting in the hammock in the 'red or mahogany room'; and on the 24th p.m. *Cum* Phib. *Sup. Lect.* John's room'. On 3rd December Dido returned to Paradise. He gave her '2 bitts and a basket of pumpkins, &c.'

'*December*
Sunday, 18th December: Gave my Negroes tickets as it is near Christmas.'

On the following Monday morning they started breaking in the corn crop. Much had been stolen, but, said Thistlewood, the crop was still 'much as I expected'.

'Sunday 25th: Mr Hayward, Mr Morris, Capt. Cheeseman, and Mr John Hartnole dined with me. Had stewed mudfish, and pickled crabs, stewed hog's head. Fried liver, &c. quarter of roast pork with paw paw sauce and Irish potatoes, bread, roast yam and plantains. A boiled pudding, very good. Cheese, musk melon, water melon, oranges, French brandy said to be right Cognac, punch and porter. We walked into the New Ground, upon the hills, &c.

Sent to Egypt for Mr Hartnole, a fine loin of pork. This morning I gave Lincoln a bottle of rum, Abba ditto, Dick and Solon a bottle between them, Cudjoe and Johnie ditto, the girls a bottle among them, Pompey, Chub, and Caesar each a drink. Also about 9 herrings each Negro, and above a pint of dry salt to everyone.

p.m. Gave Kirkpatrick Old Quashe a bottle of rum.

For mudfish, a bitt. Mr Hartnole sent me some mudfish; I sent them to Mrs Bennett.

At night, *Cum* Phib.

Monday 26th: Gave my Negroes today.'

On Saturday, 31st December 1768, he made his final sale for the year, eggs for 2 bitts, and he summed up the sales of 'sundries' for the twelve month.

Phibbah's sewing	128 bitts
Wild fowl	124 bitts
Fish	57 bitts
Eggs and domestic fowls	31 bitts
Scotch grass	93 bitts
Vegetables, &c.	322 bitts.

The vegetables, &c. included peas, beans, cucumbers, pumpkins, turnips, Indian kale, ochroes, callaloo, melons, paw paws, sweet gourds and parsley. The total earning, 755 bitts, was the equivalent of £25 11s 10½ d; and, additionally, there had been his earnings from the hireage of his slaves.

Notes

1 This probably refers to young dasheen leaves.
2 Folk stories, of West African origin, relating the sly exploits of Ananci the spider. See Cassidy & Le Page (1980) p.10.
3 McLeod and Lesley (or Leslie) were now in charge of Kirkpatrick Pen.

4 A vine fruit eaten as a vegetable. Texture somewhat like marrow squash. In the east and south Caribbean called Christophene.

5 A process discovered by Dr Anthony Robinson. His work in this, and other practical experiments, was rewarded by the Jamaica Assembly. Some of his drawings, etc., are to be found in the archives of the National Library of Jamaica.

6 Dr Drummond, who innoculated Thistlewood's (and others') slaves against smallpox was up to date in his treatment. He followed practices only that year introduced by Mr John Quier in Lluidas Vale. See Donald Monro (Editor) *Letters and Essay on the Smallpox and Innoculation* ... [etc] London, 1778, including letters from Mr John Quier and discussion of recent treatises on the subject. See, also, Richard Sheridan, *op. cit.*

About 20 years later Edward Jenner (1749–1823) would show that innoculation with the fluid of cowpox, rather than with the smallpox itself, would protect against the latter. Thus 'vaccinations' from the Latin word 'vacca' meaning 'a cow'.

CHAPTER 8 Unhappily labouring on the Pen

Introduction

In any account of life and labour during slavery we are at a tremendous disadvantage. The slaves, the vast majority of whose activities we set out to describe or to discuss, are silent except by report. And the report is for the most part given by their masters.

How much can we accept what Thistlewood tells us about his slaves, as persons, or even as property? In 1760, for instance, he and his white associates speak of Negro 'Rebel' leaders. Would the slaves have described them in the same way? This is not to say that Thistlewood lied. He was simply recording his view of the matter. Indeed there is much in his diaries to suggest that he was forthright and honest — but it is doubtful whether he always understood what the slaves did, or said, or thought.

We can, therefore, accept without much hesitation his statements of *what* occurred, but we have always to be wary when he attempts to say *why* something was said or done by them. At the same time, as we have seen, Thistlewood's diaries are for the most part, a recording of *what* rather than of *why*.

Equally, for in fact we are in a different way removed from the slaves of the eighteenth century, we should be wary of putting *our* interpretations on what they said and did. In simple illustration, neither they nor Mr Thistlewood would have had the same understanding of 'labour relations' as we do today. Nor would they have regarded the infliction of punishment by the lash with the same repugnance and sense of personal humiliation that we feel today. It was then a common form of penalty served on the free as well as the slaves.

Nonetheless, we must use what information we have, and there is much to be learned about Mr Thistlewood and his slaves from his accounts. There are few other sources which allow us so intimate an introduction to individual men and women among our enslaved ancestors, and in the case of some, to feel that we begin to know them as persons, not just as names.

On 1st January, 1770, Thistlewood owned 26 slaves, of whom four (Abba, Bess, Damsel, and Jimmy) were house and personal attendants, 16 (Lincoln, Solon, Dick, Cudjoe Ceasar, Pompey, Johnie, Sally, Sukey, Maria, Mirtilla, Franke, Phoebe, Peggy, Nanny, and Coobah) were field slaves, Chub was fisherman (a job which no one seemed to keep for long), and five children (Abba's Mary, born December 1761; Johnie, born April 1764, and Neptune, born November 1766; Nanny's Phibbah, born August 1765; and Maria's Lucy, born November 1766).

As might be expected, most of the information about individuals concerns the house slaves and those field slaves who were more intractable. Of the other adults, mentions are made of their illnesses, their labours on particular days, their misdemeanours and punishments, and their running away. The children almost entirely go without notice except for births, illnesses, and deaths. In the following account all notices of serious illnesses, punishments, and running away are recorded. Comparatively minor ailments, and the details of every day's work are illustrated by the occasional references below. More specific information about births, match-making, and deaths is given in the subsequent accounts of the individual slaves.

'Saturday, 13th January 1770:   Gave my Negroes today.

Thursday, 25th January 1770:   Carrying penguin plants from the garden to fence in the old Negro ground once more and enlarge it somewhat.

Monday, 19th February 1770:   Hoeing over the old Negro ground, digging holes for goat house posts, and bringing plantain suckers from Vine's garden to plant in the provision ground.

Sunday, 25th February 1770:   Wrote to the overseer of Friendship Estate, by my Negroes whom I got away at 3 p.m. Mr Hayward's Negroes are to meet them there, to work at 3 bitts per day. Sent 16 Negroes ....'

On Monday 30th April 1770, he kept all his people at the Pen for the week and sent them to Hill, at Egypt, where he had been given permission to cut and carry as much thatch as he needed.

'Sunday, 13th May 1770:   They have done with Mr Hayward's Negroes and mine at Friendship it seems, but did not acquaint the Negroes, so they had to go back to fetch their tools. 1682 days at 3 bitts = £157 13s 9d. Mine, 921 days = £86 6s 10½d. Cudjoe lost me 2 days, Johnie 5, Caesar 1, Nanny and Coobah ½ day each.'

Early in June the goat house was ready and he bought 33 goats from Mr Hayward for £23 15s. Pompey was put to look after them.

'Monday, 2nd July 1770: Sally tending the corn. Sukey and Mirtilla weeding the garden. Pompey has the day and Caesar is minding the goats, Maria and Dick lame, Coobah run away and Lincoln given a ticket and sent in search. Chub fishing: "but brought none". Cudjoe, Solon, Johnie, Franke, Phoebe, Nanny and Peggy cleaning pasture.
Wednesday, 11th July 1770: At noon served my Negroes some salt.
Saturday, 14th July 1770: Gave my Negroes today as they are starving.
Sunday, 22nd July 1770: On this day Johnie died.
Saturday, 22nd September 1770: a.m. Finding a vast of corn sticks pulled up by the roots, and the best of the corn gone among the crab thatch by Lime-Kiln provision ground side, flogged all my field Negroes well, except Phoebe, Franke, Mirtilla and Peggy, whom don't so much suspect.
Monday, 24th September 1770: a.m. set traps of nails in boards, in the paths through the crab thatch against Lime-Kiln provision ground. Acquainted all my Negroes of them.
Friday, 19th October 1770: This morning shared the Lime-Kiln provision ground amongst my Negroes thus: stuck a line from the southmost stile post to a young alligator pear tree in Abba's line (Abba's ground remains the same), beginning at the stile, south side: 1. Jimmy, Damsel, Bess and Sally 2. Lincoln and Sukey 3. Solon and Maria &c. 4. Dick and Mirtilla 5. Franke & Phoebe. North side, returning 6. Peggy 7. Cudjoe and Chub 8. Nanny, &c. 9. Caesar 10. Coobah & Pompey. Gave the Negroes the rest of today and tomorrow, to plant and put their grounds in order.
Saturday, 10th November 1770: At night served my Negroes 10 Jumpers [much like herrings] each & gave Lincoln, Solon, and Cudjoe some rum and a bitt apiece as some reward for their loss of time. [The others had had the day, but these three had been sent off to try and find Thistlewood's bull, Roger, which he had small-shotted the night before in the provision grounds. It had run off into the morass.]
Sunday, 11th November 1770: Fourteen hands sent to work at Friendship. Pompey at home tending the goats. Dick too full of the yaws to be sent. Abba, Bess, Damsel and Jimmy about the house.'

On Monday, 3rd December, Dick and Bess were minding the go
Cudjoe, Franke and Mirtilla were ill; Mirtilla had been whipped ₒₗ
not coming home with the others on Sunday, and then given a
Ward's Red Hill. Coobah was still runaway and Solon was out, with
a ticket, looking for her, 'So only 9 at Friendship'. On the 17th,
Coobah having returned was sent off to Friendship, but eight hands
were employed on the King's road by the Styx bridge. After the
Christmas break, the roadwork being done, all who were fit were
back at Friendship, and on the last day of the year there were 14
there.

> 'Monday, 29th April 1771: Lincoln at home digging in the
> garden. Chub dressing for crab yaws. Pompey minding the
> goats, & Dick of the yaws. Eleven hands at Friendship.
> Wrote to Mr Hayward, by Jimmy, and sent Coobah to have a
> collar and pot-hook[1] put on her.... p.m. sent her to Friendship,
> by Jimmy.
> Planted a bed of English (marrow-fat) peas in my garden. Also
> planted an acorn.
> The morass coming down this evening, some water in my
> morass duck pond. Sent John to school, on Mackey, by Bess.
> Last night when I went to bed, perceived a pain in my left side,
> which increased in the night. Feel it yet, am much not well.
> At night, *Cum* Phib.'

On Thursday, 8th August, Solon, Dick, Cudjoe, Chub, Franke,
Sukey, Peggy and Coobah were sent to Savanna la Mar to bring
home lumber purchased for the Pen.

> 'The Negroes having loitered very much time away, and not
> coming till late, flogged them all.'

Two days before, the whole field gang had been flogged 'for laziness,
&c.' On the 4th September they were again flogged, this time 'for
making a path through the penguins I lately planted in the line
between Mr Say and me.

> 'Tuesday, 1st October 1771: a.m. Rode to Savanna la Mar. A
> sale of Negroes on board a ship today by Mr Hewy; but I could
> not get on board, and it's no matter as Vassall, Wedderburn,
> Meyler and Graham are to have the pick, &c.
> Wednesday, 2nd October 1771: The remainder of the New
> Negroes brought ashore. Mr Hewy asked me £50 and the duty
> each for a little boy and girl, near children. A poor choice, so
> bought none.
> Monday, 13th January 1772: The Negroes at home making

mortar, pulling up weeds in the pasture, &c. Breaking in corn in the Rockhole provision ground (2 sorts of guinea corn, and Barberry wheat); but it is in a manner all eat up by the Cling Clings, Parroquets, Pea & ground doves, Vine's fowls, &c. A cattle has also been in last night.'

In mid-September, inbetween two sessions of labour at Retrieve Estate, the field slaves were again at home. Abba, Bess and Damsel, the three house slaves, were all lying-in at the Negro house. Abba had recently had Jenny, born 25th August; Bess was with Bristol, born 29th August; and Damsel with Nelly, born 11th September. Old Leandra was attending them. Solon and Sally had yaws, and Franke, Maria, Cudjoe and Peggy were all, in some degree, unwell.

'Monday, 21st December 1772: Rode to Savanna la Mar, went aboard the Guinea Snow, but Mr Murray sold his Negroes too dear. Mr Herring gave about £64 & duty (which is 20s) for 35 Negroes. Mr Leslie gave £68 pr head for 4 privilege Negroes.[2] They asked £60 for the women and £52 & the duty for girls not 10 years old, and got it also. Eboes.

Sunday, 18th April 1773: Served my Negroes their oznabrig, year cloth, or Master's thank ye.'

In May, 1773, Mr Thistlewood got rid of his goats. They had proved a dreadful nuisance, running all over the place, through gardens and provision grounds and through the penguin fence 'on to Mr Say's land after Vine's ram'. Moreover, they had not brought him any profit and the flock was declining. He advertised 20 remaining at £10 each, cash, and got it. One sick one he let the purchasers have 'for broughta'.[3]

'Saturday, 12th June 1773: In the evening flogged Nanny, Maria & Cudjoe for walking thro' my corn piece, & Chub & Caesar for hiding Cudjoe.

Monday, 2nd August 1773: My hogs get lamed and cut, almost every day, which is very surprising who does it, and where. The lame hog now missing also.'

So, on two Saturdays, 31st July and 7th August, he refused to give his slaves their time off 'as they will not confess about the boar, nor who lames the pigs, &c. Can keep nothing for them'. In his view, July/August had been an almost ruinous period.

'Tuesday, 17th August 1773: Within this month past, have lost as follows:

A young boar gone (never learnt how) worth say £1.

A young barrow, his back broke and killed (can't tell how), 10s.

Phoebe's child, jaw fallen £5 [b. 27th July 73]
Abba's Neptune, near seven years old, £35.
A fine ewe, fit to lamb, found dead in a rock-hole, £1 5*s*.
Rachael's [the cow] young calf, say 40*s*, and young steer £8.
Nanny's young child, jaw fallen £5. [b.13th August 73]
Total £57 15*s*.
God's will be done.
Sunday, 13th February 1774:   Served 15 Field Negroes [working at Bluecastle Estate] 5½ lbs saltfish each instead of 2 bitts apiece....'

It was very seldom that saltfish was mentioned in Thistlewood's diaries as having been issued to the slaves; the issue had always been herrings, shads, or jumpers. Apparently, there was little advantage for him in the issue.

'Sunday, 3rd April 1774:   Served my Field Negroes 19 bitts and 11 bundles of salt fish of 2 ¼ lbs each. So that my hundred weight of salt fish which cost 40 bitts just made 41 bitts out again. So no profit, only saves silver.
Tuesday, 24th May 1774:   My Negroes now get great quantities of snooks, tarpons, mudfish, &c., the morasses being full of new water. Plenty of crabs also run o'nights.
Monday, 13th June 1774:   Served 13 of my Negroes 2 bitts each ... gave them a ticket, and ordered them to be at Paul Island early tomorrow morning, to work with Mr Hartnole's and Mr Dobson's Negroes.
Saturday, 23rd July 1774:   'Gave my Negroes today. Gave them plenty of cabbage, savoy & broccoli plants to plant in their grounds.
Saturday, 13th August 1774:   'My Negroes have scarce done an hour's work in the whole day, in the evening flogged them.
Saturday, 17th December 1774:   'Made them work as they will never mind their work as they ought; and don't intend giving them any day till they do better.
Sunday, 25th December 1774:   'Christmas Day. Served my Negroes 18 herrings each, likewise gave Lincoln, Dick & Abba each a bottle of rum, Cudjoe & Solon a bottle between them, Caesar & Pompey d*°*, Chub & Strap d*°*, Fanny, Damsel & Bess d*°*. Rest of the women 2 bottles among them. Phib 5.
Gave Abba 4 bitts for Christmas.
Gave my Negroes tickets.'

And, for himself, 'a.m. *Cum* Egypt Little Doll' on the bench in the garden shed. And for her, 2 bitts.

The general routines have now, perhaps, been sufficiently indicated. Thistlewood continued his attempts to increase his labour
force,.without success.

'Monday, 15th July 1776: . . . attended the Negro Sale, in the
house [in Savanna la Mar] where Jimmy Hayes formerly kept a
Tavern. A very unfair sale, as Mr Salmon permitted Mr Goodin,
Dr Walker, Bessie Murray, Fanny Duncan, &c, &c, to pick
before the sale began, and whole parcels placed ready for
particular people, besides above 20 of the best left aboard,
picked out before they come ashore. The sale not opened till
past noon & held in a dark room. The men exposed first, & the
women afterwards. How could a Negro be examined when 200
people at least in a small room & the door next the sea kept
shut.'

On Friday, 19th July, the Birch Tree provision ground was allotted,
and the account is of interest because it suggests changes of households
since October, 1770. The allotments were as follows: 1. Caesar 2.
Dick and Mirtilla 3. Maria 4. Jimmy and Phoebe 5. Nanny 6.
Jimmy [an extra bit] 7. Peggy 8. Abba 9. Bess 10. Solon and
Damsel 11. Cudjoe and Fanny 12. Sally 13. Lincoln and Sukey
14. Strap and Franke 15. Pompey. Next day, Saturday, they had
the day to work for themselves. In early August Thistlewood distributed eight quarts of peas between them, and in late September they
began to reap.

'Monday, 12th August, 1776: . . . about 10 a.m. went aboard
Mr Watt's ship . . . with Mr Beckford, Mr Bossley, &c. &c.
Agreed to give £55 & the duty. Mr Watt could not abate of £59
& duty; so, Mr Beckford, Mr Bossley, Mr Hugh White, Mr
James White, Mr Sterling, Mr Boyd, myself, &c. in all about a
dozen came away before the sale was opened. However, others
stayed & he sold a good many. Mrs Cope wanted an Ebo girl,
about 12 years of age, with small feet, not bow-legged, nor
teeth filed, small hands & long, small taper fingers, &c. for a
sempstress for Miss Peggy.'

At the end of 1776 Thistlewood had 29 slaves. Around the house
were Abba, Damsel, Bess, and Joe, a boy attendant purchased in
1775; in the field gang there were now 17, (including the fisherman).
Johnie had died in 1770 and Chub in 1775, and Coobah had been
sold in 1774, but he had relegated Jimmy to the field and in 1773 he
had purchased Strap and Fanny. Of children, there were now eight
alive, Abba's Mary, Jenny, and Phibbah; Maria's Lucy; Phoebe's
Tony; Damsel's Nelly and Quashe; and Bess's Bristol. Abba's Johnie

and Neptune, and Nanny's Phibbah had died. Thistlewood's journals allow us a fairly detailed view of the lives of some of them.

We are able to establish at least some of the man-woman relationships. In September 1767, by the distribution of cooking pots to households, and by other information about individuals, we can identify couples.

Person	Matched with	Housed with	Children
Abba	Emetson's Neptune	Sally	Mary, Johnie, Neptune
Bess	Dick[?]	Dick	—
Damsel	Egypt watchman Harry	—	—
Sukey	Lincoln	Lincoln	—
Maria	Solon	Solon	Lucy
Mirtilla	Egypt driver Johnie	Franke	—
Phoebe	Egypt Neptune	Jimmy	—
Nanny	Egypt driver Cubbenna	—	Phibbah
Coobah	—	Peggy	Mulatto Silvia
Sally	Chub	Abba	—

This last match had been ordained by Thistlewood on Monday, 7th July 1768, and obviously was not successful. Franke, who lived with Mirtilla, also had a husband in Egypt, Egypt Lewie. The other four of Thistlewood's slaves were Pompey, with whom Chub was housed, Johnie, who lived alone, and Cudjoe and Caesar, housed together.

When, in October 1770, provision grounds were distributed, there were a few differences. Abba now lived in her house with her three children. Sally was temporarily with the other house slaves Jimmy, Bess and Damsel who slept in the cookroom or about the house. Bess having moved elsewhere, Dick now lived with Mirtilla. It is not clear that they were 'matched', for there was no word of a break with Egypt driver Johnie, but in fact Dick and Mirtilla remained house-mates until 1786, so a 'match' is a reasonable assumption. The new arrangements were as follows:

Person	Matched with	Housed with	Children
Abba	Rickett's Cudjoe (Dec.70)	(Mary, Johnie, and Neptune)	—
Bess	—	Jimmy, Damsel, Sally	—
Damsel	Egypt Harry Mrs North's George (1771)	(as above)	—
Sukey	Lincoln	Lincoln	—
Maria	Solon	Solon	Lucy

Mirtilla	Dick	Dick	—
Phoebe	Egypt Neptune	Franke	—
Nanny	Egypt driver	—	Phibbah
	Cobbenna		
Coobah	Pompey [?]	Pompey	—
Sally	—	(see Bess)	—

Of the others, Johnie had recently died, so, too, had Coobah's Silvia. Cudjoe and Chub were now housed together, and Peggy and Caesar were on their own. Franke was still matched with Egypt Lewie.

In July 1776, according to another distribution of provision grounds, there had been a few more changes.

Person	Matched with	Housed with	Children
Abba	Mr Johnson's Jeremy	(Mary, Jenny, Phibbah)	—
Bess	Mr Wilson's Jimmy	—	Bristol
Damsel	Solon	Solon	Nelly, Quashe
Sukey	Lincoln	Lincoln	—
Maria	Mr Wilson's Peter (Jan 1776) Egypt Cubbenna (Sept 1776)		Lucy
		—	
Mirtilla	Dick	Dick	—
Phoebe	Jimmy	Jimmy	Tony
Nanny	—	—	—
Sally	—	—	—
Franke	Strap [?]	Strap	—
Fanny	Cudjoe [?]	Cudjoe	—

Coobah had been sold, and Caesar, Pompey and Peggy lived on their own.

Of these 29 slaves, 24 were still on Breadnut Island Pen when Thistlewood died in December 1786. Ten others were their children. We can now trace the fortunes of several of them in some detail during the period 1770 to 1776. A few are well documented, the majority are mentioned from time to time, we can take them in the order of their acquisition by Thistlewood.

Lincoln — An Ebo, purchased at Hertford in 1756, Lincoln would have been about 30 years old in 1770.

During these six years he apparently suffered less from illnesses (chickenpox, fevers, belly-ache and in 1776 a 'bloody flux') than from the often severe punishments inflicted by Thistlewood; in spite

of which, one senses a mutual understanding which might even h
touched upon affection.

'Monday, 16th July 1770:   a.m. Lincoln refused to trim some
trees; knocked him down with my stick. He is very deceitful,
lazy & impudent, &c. Sent him to weed with the rest.'

Lincoln was not a large man. After another episode in the following
week Thistlewood described him:

'Sunday, 22nd July 1770:   Yesterday, noon, Vine and Nanny
come with a complaint of Lincoln's stealing their fowls, &c.
When he came out of the morass in the evening had him seized
by Solon, and made Jimmy take him to Old Jenny's hill. I went
with them, and Mr Say's Nancy. Hanibal affirmed that Lincoln
had brought a hen to his house in the night of Saturday 14th
Instant, dressed it and eat it, then went and fetched a pullet
which he wanted to sell him; told him of Nancy's hog, which he
wanted Bacchus to assist him to catch. He also spoke several
threatening words, &c. Took him back, flogged him, and upon
his promising payment let him go.
He is an Ebo, about 5 ft 2 %10 ins high; his teeth not filed, crab
yaws on hands and feet, so tenderfooted; ⧵TT⧸ on each cheek,
and each shoulder; some weals on his back.'

In February, 1771, Lincoln was reported to have stolen a mare
belonging to one of Three Mile slaves.

'Wednesday, 20th February 1771:   p.m. I rode to Savanna la
Mar, had Jimmy with me, and brought home Lincoln out of Mr
Hayward's bilboes, and secured him safe in mine. He has not
been at work this week at Friendship Estate, but skulking
about, and Dick secured him on Monday evening at Friendship
Negro houses, suspecting he would run away, about the mare.'

He remained in Thistlewood's bilboes until Sunday 24th when:

'Took off Coobah's collar and put it upon Lincoln. Gave him a
good flogging, and ordered him to his work with the rest.'

He wore the collar until the following Sunday.

Lincoln, as we have already seen, was not a one woman man.
In addition to earlier involvements with Egypt Susanah, Egypt
Violet, and Egypt Mountain Lucy who had borne him a daughter,
Mary, he was now matched with Sukey, mating with Abba, and
there was at least one other current attachment:

'Monday, 6th May 1771:   Note: Lincoln went out yesterday,
and did not come till today noon, and then brought a note from
Mr Hughes begging I would forgive him, he having been at the
Prospect Estate to see his wife, and overslept himself.'

In punishment, he was ordered: 'To bring me 24 crabs, this morning [the 7th]. . . to pay for the loss of yesterday forenoon, which he promised to do, but never troubled himself to perform . . .' so Thistlewood took away a great coat which Mr Thompson had given him 'and sold it (before his face), to Egypt Daniel, for 2 bitts, to mortify him.' He then ran off to Savanna la Mar, was brought back by Jimmy and Solon, and again secured in the bilboes, and next day, flogged.

At the end of November, a month in which he had really excelled in duck-shooting, he was sent out to search for Coobah, run away. On Monday, 2nd December he was still out 'although strictly charged to come home on Saturday evening'.

Tuesday 3rd, Thistlewood rode to Masemure Estate to check on his slaves then at work there. At Retrieve Estate, through which he passed, he was told that:

'Lincoln was at a play, at the burial of a Negro at the Retrieve all Sunday night.'

On Monday morning he had arrived at Egypt saying that he was on his way to the Old Hope, where Coobah was said to be at the seaside, but later he was observed going in the other direction towards Savanna la Mar. Thistlewood sent letters all around soliciting aid in the re-capture of both Lincoln and Coobah.

'Wednesday, 4th December 1771: About noon, received a letter from Mr Samuel Say, by Lincoln, who also brought home Coobah. She was catched among the Old Hope canes by one of their watchmen, and carried to Mr Say. p.m. Flogged Coobah, put a chain about her neck. Wrote to Mr Peter Richardson, and sent her to Masemure by Lincoln. Both to go in the field tomorrow morning. Gave each a bitt to buy provision with.'

Lincoln seemed to hold no grudge against old Hanibal:

'Monday, 5th May 1773: The dogs catched a hog in Birch Tree ground, and Lincoln & Jimmy brought it home.
Tuesday 11th May 1773: Flogged Lincoln well for going last night and telling old Hanibal about his hog, &c.'

And he apparently liked music; but Thistlewood's reaction, presumably to the time and place rather than to the actual performance, was spiteful:

'Saturday, 20th November 1773: About 10 o'clock this night, got up and went to my Negro houses, where found Mrs. North's George playing upon the Banjar to Lincoln. I chopped all up in pieces with my cutlass, & reprimanded them.'

On the night of Friday, 13th September 1774, unluckily, Lincoln on housewatch fell asleep on a table in the cookroom, fell off, and displaced his right knee-cap. Thistlewood tried, but could not set it back, so he sent for Doctor Allwood who came in the morning with his associate, Doctor Rock. They fixed it. 'It stood up edgeways somehow, it seems in a very uncommon manner. Paid them £2 10s for this visit.'

And, in 1776, the see-saw of opinion was very plain, though, as we shall see, it was of Lincoln the fisherman as much as Lincoln the man.

'Wednesday, 10th January 1776:   Lincoln brought most excellent fish today.

Thursday, 25th January 1776:   Lincoln scarce brought any fish. Put him in the bilboes.

Friday, 26th January 1776:   Took him out, flogged him, sent him fishing again.

Monday, 29th January 1776:   About 11 p.m. Lincoln come with fish, but did not bring enough for a cat. Ordered Pompey to take hold of him in the cookroom, but while I was getting the bilboes he escaped from Pompey & ran into the morass & Pompey after him; but he could not come up with him.'

Not surprisingly, for Lincoln was apparently small and nimble and Pompey suffered from incipient elephantiasis.

'Tuesday, 30th January 1776:   Lincoln brought fish again today pretty good.

Tuesday, 7th May 1776:   About half past noon Lincoln came, but did not bring ¼ of a bitt's worth of fish; which has been his practice a good while past, and when he perceived I would punish him, he threatened to make away with himself if I troubled him. However, gave him a good flogging & put him in the bilboes. He sells all the fish that he ought to bring me, cannot be kept fishing in my own morasses, or the rivers, but will go out to sea, &c. and does not come at all until past dinnertime; is extreme impudent, &c.'

Thistlewood found 6 bitts in Lincoln's purse 'which makes some small amends for his loss of time; this suspect for fish he sold Tuesday'. Next week, Solon was put to fish and Lincoln was sent to dig in the garden.

Johnie – Bought from Mr John Parkinson in 1758, Thistlewood did not estimate his age. A field worker, he was almost constantly ill, of stomach troubles, in 1770, and on Sunday, 22nd July he died. Solon and Cudjoe dug his grave, and he was buried on the Pen 'near where Coobah's child was buried [Silvia, b.12/11/66 d. 16/3/68].

Simon — Also bought from Parkinson in February 1758, Simon had been sold to Jeremiah Meyler in April 1761.

Abba — The third listed of the three bought from Parkinson, she was one of those who survived Thistlewood on the Pen. The main notices of her in the period January to November deal with her health (in April and May she was 'sadly plagued with boils' and was being given mercury); and her negligencies.

'Sunday, 3rd June 1770: Gave Abba a ticket for herself and Solon, who carries her barrow [pig] to sell (worth 5 cobbs). They killed him in the path, and scarce made 3 off him. She is very wrong-headed and obstinate.

Wednesday, 11th July, 1770: Warned Abba and Damsel, this morning, with a manatee strap,[4] for laziness in cleaning the house, &c.

Thursday, 13th September 1770: In the morning flogged Abba and Damsel for neglect in cleaning the house.

Sunday, 23rd September 1770: For corn and plantains 12 bitts; corn 3, and plantains 4 bitts per hundred today; but Abba is a very negligent market woman.'

In December, Abba made a match with John Rickett's Cudjoe. They did it 'slyly', said Thistlewood; but on the 30th:

'Abba's new sweetheart, Cudjoe, at the Pen today and asked me leave to have her, which I consented to.'

This in no way affected Thistlewood's proprietorship. Between 26th November and 31st December he took her four times; but twice '*sed non bene*' because '*Illa habet mensam.*'

In 1771 Abba's Johnie died. His ailments began on Saturday, 5th January.

¦a.m. Abba's Johnie fainted, or had a fit. His mother almost out of her senses. Vine bled him, &c. and he come to himself; but complains of a pain in his stomach, &c. and much not well.

Tuesday, 8th January: This morning sent Abba to Savanna la Mar with Johnie to the doctor, (made Bess go with her) and I rode down to the Bay also and went to Dr Panton's; but he not at home. Got a phial of mixture from his assistant to give him, for which I paid 4 bitts; but he died, before they got home, about 10 o'clock; ... his disease was a spasm, or locking of the jaws. Abba quite frantic & will hear no reason.

For rum, a bitt. Gave Abba rum to entertain her company at the burial. Made Lincoln dig a grave for Abba's Johnie, near her house. At night they buried him. I gave some boards, nails, &c. to make him a coffin, which Mrs Bennett's Sam and Cumberland performed. Venus, Johnie, Shalle, Mr Say's Vine, several of Egypt and Kirkpatrick Negroes, &c. at the burial. Sang, &c.&c.'

Johnie would then have been about 6½ years old. Within the next three weeks both Abba and her Cudjoe gave Thistlewood presents. Cudjoe brought him oranges and Abba gave him 'a fine roasting pig' which he had roasted for dinner and sent his horse for Mr Hayward to come and eat with him.

Cudjoe did not apparently hold Abba for long.

'Note: it is suspected that Abba keeps Jimmy, for he is asleep and stupid all day, & the Negroes remark the reason.

Friday, 3rd May 1771: A little before day this morning, a crab making a huge noise in the piazza, called Jimmy, but he was not in the cookroom. Therefore got up, and took Pompey with me to Abba's house, and catched Jimmy sleeping with her. He endeavoured to escape, but I laid hold of him. Put them both in the bilboes, and when light flogged them. One of the children was upon the bed with them, full of the yaws, although Jimmy has never had them; and the cookroom left to itself, although all the utensils in it, and all the clothes in this week's wash.'

But this was not a 'match'. Jimmy, as we shall see, was playing the field, though Abba was for a time his favourite, as she was Thistlewood's. In the course of the year Thistlewood took her 39 times, and in these seven years 155 times, often in his house, sometimes in the fields, and on the well worn garden bench. On nearly every occasion, as with the other women, he paid her 2 bitts. On at least one occasion he seemed to display a jealousy of her association with Jimmy. On the night of Saturday, 17th May, 1771, Coobah, who had runaway, was brought home. Getting out of bed to put her in the bilboes:

'Jimmy not to be found. Said to be gone a fishing ... I went and searched Abba's house for him. *Cum Illa, Sup. Lect. in illa Dorm*. Also searched the other Negro houses, but did not find him.'

On Sunday, 7th July, Abba was given leave:

'... to Throw Water (as they called it) for her boy Johnie who died some months ago; and although I gave them strict charge to make no noise, yet they transgressed, by beating the Coombie loud, singing high, &c. Many Negroes there from all over the country.'[5]

On 17th October 1771, Abba was brought to bed of a girl 'very yellow it seems'; but the baby died a week later 'jaw fallen; had it buried.' On 11th November Abba returned to work. Most references to her in the diaries deal with his sexual relations with her, with occasional illnesses, pregnancies, the death of Neptune; and indications of special attention by Thistlewood, partly, perhaps, because she was chief domestic slave, partly, perhaps, because she was his most prolific child-bearing female, and perhaps also because he liked her.

'Thursday, 13th February 1772:   A stray hog in Rockhole provision ground this morning. Made Jimmy catch it, with the dogs, cut its throat & gave Abba.

Sunday, 19th April 1772:   Egypt Lewie here all day, hangs after Abba, Bess, Damsel, &c.

Friday, 3rd July 1772:   Abba has a little of the fever, occasioned by a waxing kernel, it seems. Gave her a wine glass of Tinctura Sacra.

Saturday, 22nd August, 1772:   Gave Abba leave to keep a sow.

Sunday, 23rd August, 1772:   a.m. *Cum* Abba . . .

Tuesday, 25th August, 1772:   Abba brought to bed of a girl between 1 and 2 p.m.

Sunday, 30th August, 1772:   Gave Abba a cobb as I have nothing to assist her with now she lays in.' [On the 21st September she came out.]

The baby girl was Jenny. No mention was then made of paternity; but later word indicated that the father was neither Jimmy nor Thistlewood, but Lincoln.

From time to time, Abba's remaining son, Neptune, had been unwell, but there had been no suggestion of a dangerous complaint until 2nd August, 1773. Two days later:

'About 4 this morning, Abba's Neptune died, complained of pains all over him. &c., a most violent cold, got I suppose by the water running thro' her house [recent heavy rains] & making the floor wet. Had a fir coffin made for him by Mr Say's Quacoo, also had a grave dug, and at night they buried him, This is a great loss.'

On the 4th May in the next year Abba was ill of a violent pain in her belly. 'Miscarried, it seems.'

'Wednesday, 15th June 1774: For rice, 2 bitts, for Abba's Jenny, who is sick.

Saturday, 4th February 1775: As Abba's sow eats up all my young lambs, in endeavouring to catch her today she somehow hurt her, so that at night she died. As this sow was the support of herself and children, gave her 32 bitts to lessen her loss.

Tuesday, 2nd May 1775: Gave Abba 10 bitts against her laying in.

Saturday 20th May 1775: Gave Abba 2 bitts for her honesty in bringing me some bitts I had lost out of my pocket.

Sunday, 28th May 1775: In the evening, *Cum* Abba *(mea) Sup* Bench, under shed in New Garden. Gave d*°* 2 bitts. Also gave d*°* 8 red herrings, equal 20 bitts, besides what eat, &c.

Friday, 9th June 1775: About 3 o'clock this morning, Abba brought to bed of a boy ...'

This child also died about a week later, ('jaw fallen. Had it buried').

'Friday, 26th January 1776: a Mason Negro here, named Jeremy, who has, or is about making a match with Abba, He belongs to Mr Johnson. It is said Abba is with child already, suspected for Jimmy or Lincoln.'

And, perhaps for Thistlewood.

In March both Abba and her daughter Mary, and in April little Jenny, had chickenpox. On Friday, 19th April 1776 Abba was ill, close to labour, and on the night of the 21st she was brought to bed of a girl. This was Phibbah, whose parentage was acknowledged by Lincoln.

Nanny – purchased by Mr Cope for Thistlewood in July 1761 in Kingston, Nanny, a 'New Negro', would have been about 30 years old in 1770. Bought at the same time, and therefore probably her shipmates, were Solon and Caesar. She was a field worker and, as with the other mothers, her child went with her whenever she was hired out.

'Friday, 30th March 1770: My Nanny brought home [from Friendship) (little Phibbah ill) Nanny returned immediately. The child is griped sadly'.

Phibbah would then have been nearly five years old. On this occasion she recovered.

In the first week of June, Thistlewood bought 2 young hogs from Nanny for 10 bitts each. They were small. Of the first: 'the 2 sides just weighed 12 lb. It is but meagre'.

'Saturday, 30th June 1770: This evening Nanny stole one of my squab ducks (Caesar saw her catch it) found it upon her, in her room. She held it so fast under her coats that she killed it. Flogged her.'

In July 1770, Little Phibbah was again ill 'of a sore backside, &c. Gave it physic. Nanny at home minding it'. And Nanny herself suffered in 1771 from crab-yaws and from a cut on her left hand accidentally received while working at Friendship. This kept her away for a few days so that she could be sent to Dr Panton.

'Wednesday, 16th January 1771: ... Received ... some Cerate[6] & purge for her.

Thursday 17th January 1771: Laid a poultice to Nanny's hand last night, this morning took it off, laid on dry lint, and made her sweat over the steam of boiling water all day. Gave [her] a dose of physic.'

In April she had crab-yaws again, badly, on her hands. Thistlewood had them dressed 'with Black Dog'[7] and then put her in the bilboes, presumably to ensure that she did not use them.

In September 1771, after a long illness, Little Phibbah died. Mid-July, Nanny and Thistlewood had taken her to Dr Panton.

'He says her bloating is owing to the yaws striking in, and that I ought to have given her brimstone when first perceived. He now gave me equal quantities of Flour of Brimstone and Venice Treacle [?], to be given her, as much as will lie upon the small end of a teaspoon, 3 times a day in a little sugar and water.'

Nanny stayed at home to mind her daughter, and doses of Jallop[8] followed. Thistlewood supplied rice and chicken broth. On 22nd July she was still ill with Nanny tending her. At the beginning of August she was given 'a small mercurial pill, as she is troubled with worms'.

'Thursday, 8th August 1771: This morning, gave l. Phibbah 2 spoonfuls of warm water as she has voided some lately by the mouth; and about 2 p.m. Nanny brought her to me with her belly swelled monstrously. Wrote a note to Dr Panton and sent her immediately by Nanny. They did not return this night.'

They had waited all night 'without seeing Dr Panton' and little Phibbah was 'rather worse if anything'. Thistlewood had her bathed in warm water and oil; and on Saturday 10th, he and Nanny took her back to Dr Panton, who examined and again prescribed. But to no avail. Little Phibbah died about 8 p.m. on Monday, 9th September. Next day she was buried in a grave dug by Lincoln and Dick.

There was not much more about Nanny beyond the routine labour. She was flogged once for showing unwillingness to carry a length of board from Savanna la Mar to the Pen. In mid-1772 she had 'ringworms on the side of her neck'. In May, 1773, she was 'lame of a breaking out on her legs'. On 28th July she bore a girl who died on August 17th, 'Jaw fallen'. He had 'it' buried. On Sunday, 21st November 1773: '*Cum* Nanny (*mea*) ... *Stans*. Backwd ...' It was the fifth and last occasion in these seven years. Nanny remained generally unhealthy throughout 1774, but she was back in the field. In August 1776 she was again flogged 'for refusing to let Peggy go with her yesterday to look provisions'. In late November she was 'laid up of a looseness', but she recovered.

Solon – must have been about 25 years old in 1770. For a time, he appears to have taken Lincoln's place as driver, until he was himself succeeded by Dick. He was frequently sent out in search of runaways.

'Thursday, 6th December 1770: In the evening Solon come home, but no news of Coobah. Suspect he misspends his time, had him flogged, then gave him a fresh ticket & sent him out again.'

Like all the others, he suffered from yaws which broke out from time to time, and there were other occasional ailments, but he appears to have been comparatively healthy.

Late in 1773 he was one of the watchmen, and twice was flogged for negligence or absenteeism; and on Monday, 20th December his house was destroyed by a fire which 'began in Maria's room, owing to her carelessness'.

'Note: although my Negroes were all at work, close, yet no one saw it till I discovered it.'

At the time, Solon and Maria were having domestic troubles.

'Sunday, 14th November 1773: Flogged Maria for cuckolding Solon at the Retrieve, and stirring up quarrels, &c .... The Retrieve stable man, Quashe, called in the evening, on his way home from Ackendown, preached a sermon, &c.'

In August 1774 he had the misfortune to be appointed as Thistlewood's fisherman.

'Thursday, 6th September 1774: At night flogged Solon, for neglect, in bringing fish.
Saturday, 31st December 1774: At night flogged Solon, and reprimanded John [Mulatto John, at home for Christmas holidays]

for leaving my canoe in Mr White's trench, so that Taylor, the pilot's, Negroes took her to Savanna la Mar, under the pretence of their lines being stolen, &c. However, John & him fetched her back from the Bay.'

Again, on 23rd April, 11th May and 13th June, 1775, Solon was flogged for bringing no fish or poor quality fish. On 16th June, 'no fish brought, nor sign of Solon'. Understandably enough, he had run away. Next morning he returned with a beg-off note from Mr Hayward. It did not help. He was flogged, a collar and chain put about his neck, and sent out to fish. 'He brought mudfish today.' But a month later he was flogged again.

Then, to compound misfortune, he lost Thistlewood's canoe.

'Thursday, 20th July 1775:   Solon came and told me my canoe has gone from her place. The scoundrel has lost her. He was out all day but could not find her.'

Solon was given a ticket to go in search, but, not finding her, he stayed out. Sunday 23rd, Dick brought him back from Savanna la Mar. Solon was, perhaps to his great relief, sent off to Retrieve to work, and Chub, perhaps to his dismay, was put back as fisherman. But only for 2 days; for on the 35th Lincoln was appointed to the job. Several searches failed to recover the canoe.

'Thursday, 28th September 1775:   Flogged Solon about the canoe again; as he would not tell how she was lost but first one lie then another.'

Lincoln, as we have seen, suffered as fisherman, and in June 1776 Solon was back to the task and the whippings. On 20th June, 2nd September, 4th September, and again on the 5th, he was flogged and, not for the first time, collared.

'Brought bad fish. Flogged him again & put a collar about his neck.
Note: he started from Lincoln, Jimmy, Strap, Caesar & Pompey when going to be put down, but they catched him again in the morass.'

More complaints followed, and on the 9th Solon disappeared. Lincoln brought him back on the 10th. Put in the bilboes, he remained till the 14th when, taken out, he ran off again. Dick, Strap, and Lincoln were sent in search.

'Wednesday, 10th October 1776:   This morning Solon was brought home by Egypt Quamina who catched him last night. He attempted to stab Quamina, & did wound his arm a little.

Gave long Quamina a dollar for his trouble. Flogged Solon,
a chain on the collar about his neck, brand marked him in tl
face, & sent him in the field.'

Caesar — would have been about 23 years old in 1770. There was
comparatively little special mention of him.

'Wednesday, 26th September 1770: Caesar catched stealing
corn last night out of the Lime-kiln provision ground, by Solon.
Flogged Caesar well, and put Solon to watch d° piece.'

In each year, Caesar suffered some ailment, and there were
occasions when Thistlewood thought that he was pretending.

'Sunday, 17th October 1773: Caesar worked last Monday forenoon only, and laid up all the rest of the week in the Retrieve
Negro houses; threatened Dick about it well and made him
fetch him home, then had Caesar flogged. He has no fever at
present, but perhaps may not be well.'

Next day he was given a Ward's Red Pill.

Towards the end of 1776 he was sick '. . . at home of the clap'.

Coobah — was one of the six slaves bought from Mr Hutt at
Savanna la Mar in December 1761. She was an Ebo, and would
have been about 24 years old in 1770. Her child, Silvia, born in
November 1766, had died in March, 1768. She was, in the terms of
the time, 'an incorrigible runaway'. Between 1st January 1770 and
18th May, 1774, when Thistlewood sold her, she ran away fourteen
times. During the first five months of 1770 there was little beyond
routine mention of her. Then:

'Saturday 30th June, 1770: Coobah wanting. Sent Solon to
look for her; but he found nothing of her.'

Sunday, 1st July 1770: 'Heard of my Coobah's robbing a Negro
wench of Mr Bossley's of rice & young pigeons, about a fortnight
ago, in the road, under pretence of carrying her load for her,
marched away with it.'

On July 2nd she was sent home from Paradise where she had been
found. Thistlewood put her in the bilboes, and next day took her
out, collared and chained her, and sent her to clean pasture.

'Friday 6th July 1770: p.m. Coobah wanting; but about 4 o'clock
Jimmy and Damsel coming home with water from Barclay's
river, met her going that way and brought her back. Flogged
her well & brand marked her in the forehead. She has broke

open Mr Say's Nancy's house, since noon, stolen rice, beads, calabashes, &c. I was forced to pay Nancy a bitt for her rice.'

On Wednesday 11th she was off again but caught the same evening by Solon in the Egypt canefields. Thistlewood sent her back into the field to work, but locked her in the bilboes at noon and at night.

'Monday, 23rd July 1770:   At the intercession of Egypt Lucy (by my desire) did not put Coobah in the bilboes at night but ventured her again.
Thursday, 26th July 1770:   Found Coobah had got her collar loose, so took it off for good, once more.'

But he collared and chained her again after another day's absence in early August. Three days later, on the 6th, she was off again.

'Tuesday, 7th August 1770:   Lincoln out looking Coobah yet. Note: She was in Goodin's Pen's bilboes yesterday, but pretending to faint as one of Mr Goodin's Negroes was bringing her home, he left her and she went away.'

On the 9th, Lincoln brought her home.

'Friday, 10th August 1770:   Flogged Coobah & sent her in the field; but she presently fainted and dropped down and they brought her home, but believe she shams it. She says Lincoln beat her on her breast in the field; but all the rest of the Negroes say not.
p.m. Sent her out again by way of trial.
Monday 13th August 1770:   Gave Coobah a mercurial pill last night (as she has the venereal disease it seems very bad) and moved her into the cookroom to prevent her getting cold, where secured her in the bilboes, and take her out into the field in the days. Gave her another pill at night.
Saturday, 29th September 1770:   Last night, the garden gate being locked, Coobah climbed over it and grubbed up the potatoes. Flogged her this morning for it.
Thursday, 4th October 1770:   A punch strainer hanging up against the buttery, Coobah sleeping in the cookroom last night took the strainer and shit in it, wrapping it up and covering it with a piece of board. This breakfast time had it rubbed all over her face and mouth. But she minds it not.
Thursday, 1st November 1770:   As my Coobah has took a great many mercury pills, gave her a Ward's Red Pill today, which worked her well.'

On Tuesday 27th, Coobah ran off again. Solon was sent in search.

'Saturday, 8th December 1770:   Last night Solon brought home Coobah. He catched her near the Cave going to Bluefields where she says she has a shipmate. Secured her feet in the bilboes, in the stable, allowed no fire.

Sunday, 9th December 1770:   Set a chain to Coobah's collar and delivered a padlock & key to Solon, to fasten her every dinnertime & night; and sent her to work with the rest.'

At this time the field gang were working at Friendship with Solon as driver. On Christmas Eve Coobah got away again, but was caught the same day. Assistance in catching her cost Thistlewood 5 bitts, which he duly noted.

For the next 3 or 4 months, except for a day's absence, following which she was again chained and collared, Coobah stayed put. Then, on 23rd April 1771, she ran away again. Five days later Solon brought her home from Roaring River Estate 'where she had broke open a house, &c.' This time, Thistlewood sent her to Mr Hayward to have a collar and a pot-hook put on her.

On 13th May she went again. Once more Solon was given a ticket and sent in pursuit. On the 18th, at night, he brought her back from Bluecastle Estate. She was, apparently, still wearing collar and chain, and pothook, for on the 29th the collar and chain were taken off but the pot-hook left on. During the next few weeks of quiet that too must have been removed.

'Friday, 1st November 1771:   Last night Coobah was detected by Bess stealing her corn, but neglecting to secure her, this morning she is wanting.

Sunday, 3rd November 1771:   One of Kirkpatrick Negro men brought home Coobah this morning. Made Bess give him 4 bitts, as she neglected securing her and flogged Coobah very well.'

On 25th November Coobah ran off again. She was caught in the Old Hope Estate canes and brought home by Lincoln, she was flogged and sent, with Lincoln, to field work at Masemure Estate.

'Tuesday, 10th December 1771:   This evening my Cudjoe come from Masemure to let me know that Coobah got out of the hot-house last night and is runaway again.'

Dick brought her home on the 14th. Back in the field, she was accidentally cut on the arm with a hoe and consequently sent home. By this time Thistlewood had determined to get rid of her.

'Tuesday, 24th December 1771: p.m. Wrote to Mr Hayward, by Jimmy, and sent down Coobah for Mr Gilbraith to see; but he did not like her.

Sunday, 29th December 1771: For plantains tor my Coobah, 2 bitts.'

And that became a regular weekly allowance.

'Friday, 10th January 1772: Gave Coobah a Ward's Red Pill this morning. She has took many mercury pills lately, till her mouth begun to be sore.

Wednesday, 15th January 1772: Flogged Coobah for stealing potatoes, &c, out of Rockhole provision ground.'

Towards the end of March, when the field slaves were sent to labour further afield than usual, at Mount Pleasant Estate in the parish of Hanover, Thistlewood 'Did not send Coobah, she is so troublesome in running away, &c.' She was kept at home weeding the gardens.

'Saturday, 28th March 1772: p.m. Wrote to Mr Hayward, by Jimmy, and Coobah; but Coobah was not liked, so come back .... I would have let her gone at £30.'

In August she was at work with the others at Retrieve Estate, but she had been continually unwell, and on the 4th:

'p.m. Sent Jimmy on Mackey horse to the Retrieve to bring home Coobah; which he did. She is very bad of the clap, or rather pox.

Monday, 8th November 1773: Coobah still at home ill of a dropsy & venereal running, &c. and I think is rather worse if anything.'

Since August of the previous year, Coobah had been frequently ill; and now, on 10th November she was sent to Dr Drummond's to remain there for treatment. She seems to have stayed until early April, 1774, when she was again among the field gang being sent out to work.

On 18th April she ran away. Thistlewood sent word all round that she was missing. Solon was sent in search. He couldn't find her. On 8th May, Thistlewood heard that she had been to Mr Chambers, in the Savanna, to get him to beg for her. Mr Chambers had given her a note; but she had not brought it home. Chub and Strap were sent after her. Again, no success. On Monday 16th May she was brought home by Paradise Jack who caught her on that estate. He was rewarded with 6 bits and a drink. There was no mention of punishment for Coobah; but on the 18th May, Thistlewood took her to Kirkpatrick Pen:

'. . . where I sold Coobah to Mr George Lesley for £40. I made Dick take her down to Savanna la Mar, where went myself & delivered her to the Captain of Mr Lesley's vessel going for Georgia. Mr Bean, the wharfinger, present.'

On Saturday, 21st May 1774, the vessel sailed for Savanna, Georgia. Coobah was on her. So too was a Mr William Pommells, on a visit to Georgia, whom we meet later on.

Sukey – who was Lincoln's wife, had been one of the six bought from John Hutt in December 1761. Thistlewood then estimated her age at 14 years and he paid £50 for her. Hers was a comparatively quiet record in these seven years. She reportedly bore no children; suffered no illness more serious than a bad belly-ache in March 1775, and chickenpox in April, 1776; never ran away; and was flogged only once, in April, 1771, for lending out her hoe and so losing time on job-work. The most frequent mentions of her relate to sexual activity with Thistlewood; 26 times, at 2 bitts a time.

Maria – also a field worker and one of the six bought from John Hutt, would have been about 23 years old at the beginning of 1770. In November 1766 she had borne a daughter, Lucy. Her husband was Solon, whom she deserted for a lover at the Retrieve, followed by Mr Wilson's Peter mentioned as her husband in January 1776, and Egypt Cubbenna in September 1776. Thistlewood took her only thirteen times in the seven years, and, whether because she was less demanding, or he less impressed, her usual recompense was only 1 bitt. At the beginning of February 1770 she was big-bellied and said likely to miscarry. Nonetheless, Thistlewood took her on the 20th. Again, in early May, she was reported likely to miscarry, and Vine came over and bled her in the foot. On 11th June she was 'Laid up, complaining of her belly'. But she was at work in the garden that week.

'Tuesday, 26th June 1770: p.m. *Cum* Maria (*mea*), *Sup Illa lect.* in Solon's house.'

On 9th July, she was at the Negro house 'big-bellied' again. In that month Thistlewood took her twice. On Monday, 6th August she was delivered of a boy. On the 13th, the child died: 'Jaw fallen. Had it buried.'

On 20th February 1771 Maria was once more said to be breeding.

It was an early assessment, for it was not until 23rd September that she produced a daughter. Phoebe was put to attend her after the departure of Kirkpatrick Old Phibbah.

'Sunday, 29th September 1771:   For plantains, 2 bitts to assist Maria & Solon.'

This child was Rachael.

In July, 1772, Maria's older daughter, Lucy, was ill of a fever, and Thistlewood dosed her with 20 grains of Jallop and 'Give Lucy annatto every morning'. Lucy recovered.

Late in 1773 Maria's match with Solon began to break up as she flirted with a new-found love on Retrieve Estate:

'Monday, 17th December 1774:   In the morning flogged Maria for leaving Solon and running to her sweetheart at the Retrieve.

Thursday, 26th January 1775:   Maria's Rachael is troubled with a falling down of the anus, owing to weakness, I imagine, occasioned by the yaws.

Sunday, 5th March 1775:   Flogged Maria for quarrelsomeness at Glen Ilay, &c.'

In August, little Rachael was still bad with yaws, and Maria had for sometime been laid up lame with a bad sore on her leg.

'Sunday, 27th August 1775:   Rachael (Solon and Maria's child) died, occasioned by the yaws, having had them exceeding bad a long time; also troubled with a prolapsus ani, &c.'

In 1776 Maria matched first with one of Mr Wilson's slaves, and then with Egypt Cubbenna who had previously been Nanny's husband. In November of the same year little Lucy, asleep in the cook-room, tumbled from the table and broke a bone in her thigh.

'Friday, 8th November 1776:   p.m. Dr Samuel Bell came & rolled up Lucy's thigh, &c. The bone was broke short, but in its place before he came.'

This was lucky for her because the accident had occurred on the 5th, three days before the doctor arrived.

Pompey − a Coromante, also bought from Mr John Hutt, would have been about 25 years old in 1770. He began 1770 in the hazardous job of fisherman.

'Thursday, 8th February 1770:   Flogged Pompey well for roguery and laziness. He brought 27 shrimps for 24 hours work.'

Four days later Thistlewood sent for him and 'turned him in the field'. Chub was made fisherman. But Pompey had a bad leg and was never to be a strong field worker. In June he was taken out of the field gang and put as goatherd.

'Thursday, 7th June 1770:   Flogged Pompey for letting the goats stray all about.

Tuesday, 12th June 1770:   Pompey after the goats. Note: He was robbed of his provisions last night in the thatch walk; he fought stoutly, and has a cut in his face.

Saturday, 4th August 1770:   This morning Plato brought Pompey home, catched last night stealing corn and breaking cane at Egypt. Gave Plato a bitt, a dram, and a piece of tobacco.'

Between mid-February, 1771, and the end of June, 1772, Pompey was flogged eight times for 'negligence' in minding the goats and the horses. On some occasions Thistlewood noted dissatisfaction without punishment, as on:

'Sunday, 8th September 1771:   Died an ewe goat and her wedder kid through Pompey's neglect, & feeding them on wet ground.'

His bad leg apart, Pompey appears to have kept comparatively healthy, but in July 1772 he had fever and Vine bled him and Thistlewood gave him a Ward's Red Pill. Chub was temporarily appointed goatherd. In August Pompey was dosed with 'a mercurial pill'. In September, on the 15th:

'Pompey and Mackey horse missing this morning. It seems he said he was going into the country to sell his fish and look for victuals, last night.'

Coobah was put to tend the goats, and Jimmy was given a ticket and sent to the gaol to see if Pompey had been apprehended. He had. He and Mackey horse were brought home and he was flogged and once again put into the field gang.

Thereafter, the main entries concerning him are of treatment for a bubo which had to be lanced; and his swollen leg.

'Monday, 10th July 1775:   'Pompey at home [from Retrieve] of his big leg, now greatly swelled, &c.'

In 1776, Dr Drummond was of the view that 'nothing can be done for Pompey'. Thereafter, he was usually kept on the Pen from whence he made occasional raids on the Egypt canes; and towards the end of that year we leave him, flogged for having stolen a chicken from a watchman on Egypt.

Will — also purchased from Mr Hutt, had died before Thistlewood's move from Egypt to Breadnut Island Pen.

the sixth listed of Thistlewood's purchases from John Hutt
.iid to be an Ebo, about 26 years old in December 1761 when
hc as acquired. For some time he and Bess were matched, but by
1776 he was with Mirtilla with whom he remained.
Dick was a fieldhand, sometimes acting as Driver, and sometimes put to help one or other of the skilled slaves whom Thistlewood
from time to time employed or hired.
In mid-1770 he was for nearly two months ill of stomach troubles
from which he only slowly recovered in August. Then, in 1775, he
was down with yaws. But there is little else of particular interest
recorded about him.

Sally – a Congo, had been purchased from Mr Jeremiah Meyler
in 1762. In 1770 she would have been only 17 or 18 years old.
Thistlewood's matching of her with Chub was not successful and for
the most part she lived either alone or with the house slaves.

'Monday, 2nd July 1770: Last night, when Jimmy, &c.
fast asleep in the cookroom, Sally took a young fowl out of a
basket, where covered up, by the cookroom side on the outside,
boiled and eat it, carried the feathers and threw behind where
Nanny lives, &c. Then came and waked Jimmy, telling him
somebody had come and stood a long time looking upon her
then took out the chicken & went away, and that she endeavoured to wake Jimmy but could not. However, some of the
feathers were found in the pot in which she boiled it, this
morning, and she soon confessed. Flogged her.'

She was then sent back to her job tending the corn in the provision
ground:

'Tuesday, 3rd July 1770:   *Cum* Sally *(mea) Sup Terr* . . . .
Tuesday, 7th August 1770:   As Sally steals everything left in
the cookroom, and eats it if eatable, Phibbah had her tied with
her hands behind her naked for the mosquitoes to bite her
tonight. She bawled out lustily, but before 9 o'clock in the
evening broke loose and ran away. I got up, and all hands went
to seek her. I catched her near the Rockholes, in ditto provision
ground. Her hands were tied up so tight that the string hurt her
very much. Brought her home and secured her for this night in
the bilboes.
About 9 in the evening, *Cum* Sally *(mea) Sup. Terr.* in Rockhole
provision ground.
Saturday, 18th August 1770:   This evening, Sally being sent on
an errand to Egypt, made away with a new handkerchief driver
Johnie gave her to bring to Phibbah.

Tuesday, 2nd October 1770: p.m. *Cum* Sally *(mea), sed non bene ....*'

In 1771 Sally ran away three times: first from 7th to 9th February when Solon brought her home from John Ricketts's mountain. She was put in the bilboes and, next morning, flogged and chained about her neck. The chain was not removed until Sunday, 3rd March; but a week later collar and chain were put back on 'as she lost me an afternoon this last week', being absent from jobwork. She remained collared and chained until the 24th.

On 20th May she ran away again. This time she returned of her own accord on the 22nd. Next day she was whipped, kept at home, and sent to weed in the garden with Lincoln and Mirtilla.

On Saturday, 2nd November 1771, Thistlewood again recorded sexual intercourse with her. She apparently ran away immediately after and Lincoln was sent after her. She was not, however, brought in until the 6th, when Pompey found her, and it would appear that Lincoln had let her go after hearing that Thistlewood had taken her.

'Thursday, 7th November 1771: Flogged Lincoln for not bringing Sally Saturday evening, and Sally for running away, and news carrying. Phibbah highly displeased.'

Nonetheless, he took her twice again in early 1772.

In August, 1772, Sally was badly taken with yaws, from which she had previously suffered; but this time it led to the amputation of a joint of one of her toes. Late 1772 and early 1773 she was generally lame, and Thistlewood sometimes provided her with foodstuff. She did not go back to field gang work until Monday, 10th May 1773 when she was sent to Bluecastle Estate. In December, Thistlewood resumed his sexual attentions: on the 4th, and again on the 23rd when once more '*sed non bene*'. And, as he would have put it, on Tuesday, 6th June 1774, 'ditto'.

In September 1774 Sally once again ran away. Mulatto John was sent after her and found her at Long Pond gate and brought her back, and 'I had her flogged'.

'Sunday, 20th November, 1774: 'Sally has the clap very badly.'

In June 1775 the sequence was repeated. Another occasion '*Sed non bene*', another runaway, returned of her own accord this time, and again flogged. But now Chub, who had been sent after her, had failed to come home.

In April 1776 Sally came home from Bluecastle, lame. A few days later Thistlewood again took her, and afterwards told her to go back to Bluecastle. She set off, but not for Bluecastle. On Wednesday, 1st April she was brought home by Solon who found her in the Savanna. Mr Goodin's penkeeper had harboured her. She was put in the bilboes, flogged next day, collared, and sent to work with Jimmy and Pompey carrying pond earth into the garden. That evening she was sent back to Bluecastle.

'Saturday, 22nd June 1776: Took the lock collar from off Solon [unsuccessful fisherman], & put it upon Sally as she will not help herself, but attempts to run away.'

In July she went twice. On Monday 8th for the day, and again on the 15th when Jimmy found her at Spring Garden Estate. The punishments followed.

On Saturday, 3rd August Thistlewood led her to the bench in the garden shed and took her again.

On 28th October she ran off again and was brought home by Egypt Quamina two days later. He got a bitt and a drink. She got the chain about her neck. On 2nd November she, Fanny, Mirtilla & Dick were 'flogged for [unstated] evil doings'.

'Sunday, 17th November 1776: It seems Sally pretended to be sick yesterday afternoon & Dick, like a fool, let her come away before the rest [from Bluecastle]; so that she went to a Negro house at 3 Mile River, where a Mulatto daughter of old Mr John Thompson lives, & told her she was sent from Egypt by Jenny Young to buy plantains, &c.; and while the woman stepped to another house, not doubting the truth of her story, not mistrusting her, she stole her work basket with several valuable cloths, &c. and got off clear with them. This Mulatto woman was at my house as soon as I got up this morning, with this complaint. I sent out immediately, but heard nothing of her.

In the evening Bessie, Miss Bessie Calam, Thompson [sic] come & brought home Sally whom she catched in Betty's house at Mr Goodin's Pen, with part of her things; but there is wanting a silver thimble with a steel bottom; 2 cambric bed gowns at a pistole a yard; 2 children's shifts at 12 bitts per yard, 4 yrds; 2 white handkerchiefs with end borders, 7 bitts each. Put Sally in the bilboes.'

On Monday morning a search warrant was obtained and Thistlewood:

'... gave to one Isaacs, a Jew constable, & lent him my horse. He rode to Mr Goodin's Pen and searched Monday's [the penkeeper who had previously harboured Sally] & Betty's houses, but found nothing. Paid him 10s for his trouble.'

Sally, back in the bilboes, was flogged, chained, and sent out to work in the garden. Thistlewood gave Bessie Calam who 'lamented so much and behaved so mildly' £3 13s 6d, to make amends in part.

Syphox – bought on board at Lucea in April 1765, had died before Thistlewood moved to the Pen in 1767.

Cudjoe – a Coromante, with eight other shipmates, was one of the lot purchased from Mr Cuthbert on the slave ship in Lucea. In 1770 he would have been about 25 years old. His record in that year was mainly of infirmity. In mid-February he was flogged for stealing pumpkins out of the provision ground. In April he was unwell, for Thistlewood gave him a Ward's Red Pill, but on the same day he was sent off to Friendship to join the rest of the gang. The next notable reference was in August.

'Wednesday, 1st August 1770:   Cudjoe wanting. Come home about noon. He got drunk at Kirkpatrick at a burial last night.'

No punishment was recorded.

'Tuesday, 4th September 1770:   Cudjoe complains of his side & hip. Gave him a Wards Red Pill, and rub his hip, &c. with camphorated rum. Suspect he has had a stroke there, altho' he wont confess to have received any hurt there.

Thursday, 11th October 1770:   'Hear my Cudjoe eats ashes.'

In November, when the gang was once again working at Friendship, Cudjoe came home 'lame of his hip'. Vine was summoned to bleed him, and he was sent back to work. A week later he was home again with a pain in his back. But he continued in the field gang.

'Friday, 10th September 1771:   About one o'clock this morning, was called up by Lincoln, &c, who said Cudjoe had fallen into the fire in a fit. Got up, and found him brought into the cookroom, senseless, the Negroes thick about him. Made them stand off, to give him air, applied spirits of hartshorn, &c. Suspected his being drunk, which all to a single one denied; but Egypt Harry [Damsel's husband] told me the truth, for which they hate him. It seems Cudjoe had been selling grass at the Bay, and brought home rum; drank a good deal by itself, then more in hot punch, &c, till it overcame him; after which the Negroes called me, and joined to impose upon me. He went to his work this morning.'

He was flogged, not, it seems, for his escapade, but 'for using my shingles to wedge his hoe with'.

In August 1774 Cudjoe's health really began to fail. He had suffered occasional ailments in 1772 and 1773; had run away once and been caught by a Retrieve Estate slave and brought home to a flogging; in June, 1773, he had suffered painful boils under his arms, for which he had been given the panacea, a Ward's Red Pill; but his serious complaint was yet to come.

'Thursday, 18th August 1774:   Cudjoe has got the clap. Gave him a Mercury pill.

Tuesday, 15th November 1774:   p.m. Cudjoe come home from Masemure, ill of the clap again. He pisses blood, &c. p.m. Gave him a dose of salts.'

He was sent to Dr Drummond's for treatment and remained there for some time early in 1775. But the cure was certainly not complete.

'Monday, 23rd October 1775:   Cudjoe pisses blood. Wrote to Messrs Drummond and Ruecastle & sent him to them.'

On the next day Cudjoe returned with a box of pills and half-a-dozen bougies. At the end of November he was still laid up wearing a bougi.[9]

On 28th January, 1776, Nanny came home from Bluecastle Estate sick, and Cudjoe was sent out to take her place.

'Wednesday, 31st January 1776:   My Cudjoe come home from Bluecastle; can't stand it.'

At the beginning of February he was taken back to Dr Drummond's hothouse and left there. He remained for four months.

'Friday, 7th June 1776:   About 2 p.m. Cudjoe come home from Dr Drummond's greatly mended, if not quite well.

Tuesday, 11th June 1776:   Dr Bell called to see me. Got him to look at Cudjoe, his rupture being down. Advised me to give him a wine glass of a strong solution of salts (till he had a stool) every hour, made sweet with sugar or molasses.'

Through the remainder of the year Cudjoe suffered from his rupture, and two days before Christmas, he was put into a newly-built watch-hut in Birch Tree provision ground 'for good'. He survived Mr Thistlewood.

Chub − one of the ten shipmates bought at Lucea, then a 'manboy', he would have been about 18 or 19 years old in 1770. At first in the field, he was taken out in mid-February and put as fisherman under the supervision of Egypt fisherman Cyrus. He suffered the fate of all Thistlewood's fishermen.

'Monday, 26th February 1770: Trimmed Chub well for not coming till past one o'clock, and bringing very little even then.'

In March, Thistlewood wrote to Mr Hartnole, at Egypt, complaining of the 'villainy' of Cyrus and Chub who brought no fish, or very little, 'about enough for a cat'. In May, and twice in June, Chub was severely beaten for bringing no fish. In July, Chub and Cyrus both ran away.

Nearly a week later, on 1st August, Chub was brought back from Delve Estate. He was flogged, put in the bilboes, and given Johnie's [recently died] hoe and put to field work.

In 1771 he suffered an attack of 'the measles, or some such disease', but recovered and continued as a field gang member.

'Thursday, 15th October 1772: Received a letter from Mr John Hartnole acquainting me of Chub being very ill. I wrote to Dr John Drummond .... Rode to the Retrieve Estate, got there about ½ past 10 a.m. Went to see Chub, &c.'[10]

Chub remained in the Retrieve hothouse. On the Saturday, Thistlewood wrote to Hartnole to enquire about Chub (and Sukey also there with fever). He was said to be a little better. They both recovered.

In October, 1775, Chub's final illness began. On the 19th he came home from Retrieve Estate with 'a violent cold, fever, headache, &c.' The weather had been very wet and cold. Next day he was 'very ill indeed', and Thistlewood had him bled. That night, he died.

'Saturday, 21st October 1775: At night the Negroes buried poor Chub. I gave them a bottle of rum.'

Bristol − not to be confused with Bess's son of the same name, was one of the ten purchased from Mr Cuthbert at Lucea. He died before 1767.

Jimmy − a 'Coromante or Shanti' was the youngest of that list, and would have been only 15 to 16 years old in 1770, but he was already sowing his oats. He was not one of Thistlewood's favourites.

'Sunday, 20th May 1770: Flogged Jimmy for getting drunk last night, burning a hole in my piazza floor, impudence, laziness, carelessness, lying, &c. &c.'

In June, Jimmy was given mercurial pills and salts, and for a violent itching (see next chapter) was given brimstone and grease.

'Sunday, 4th November 1770:   At night flogged Jimmy for misbehaviour, impudence, laziness, &c.

Friday, 23rd November 1770:   p.m. sent my Jimmy, on Mackey horse, to Friendship to charge my Negroes [on coming home] to keep the King's road. He galloped as if for life & death, like a madman. At night, put him in the bilboes.

Saturday, 24th November 1770:   a.m. Jimmy and Damsel an intolerable while in fetching water. Strapped them both with a manatee.

Wednesday, 6th June 1771:   Jimmy is daily becoming more careless, stupid & impudent, through Abba's encouragement.

Thursday, 24th October 1771:   Locked Jimmy up in the cookroom, else no resting in the night, such a noise going out and in all night long of him and the wenches, &c. Attribute the death of Abba's child [born 17 Oct] to his disturbing them in the night. Also locked him up again tonight when he spoke many impudent words, &c.

Friday, 1st November 1771:   Jimmy throwing the fire about the cookroom, and being otherways very impudent, saying if this be living he did not care whether he lived or died, &c, put him in the bilboes.

Saturday, 2nd November 1771:   This morning took Jimmy out of the bilboes and gave him a flogging.

Friday, 15th November 1771:   Kept up all day, and eat a little, but very uneasy, &c. Take the bark at night, rested very poorly. Jimmy made me some warm beverage (lime juice, sugar & water) at night, and an hour or two after I had been in bed, taking a drink, verily thought I had been poisoned, as I really believe I should, had drank much more; tasted so strong of sublimate. Suspect him very much, he is very impudent, lazy, sly and sullen.

Sunday, 12th January 1772:   Gave Jimmy two pr of Russia drab breeches, not yet half wore, that did not fit me; and began to wear 4 pr new Russia drab d*o*.

Saturday, 31st October 1772:   As Jimmy did not come home until 5 p.m. [he and Chub had been sent out selling] and then drunk, and has lost his flour, &c. put him in the bilboes, and gave Chub a bitt for selling the wild ducks.

Monday, 2nd November 1772:   Took Jimmy out of the bilboes about 8 a.m. flogged and pickled him, then sent him to work with the field Negroes.

Thursday, 17th June 1773:   Catched Jimmy making up the [asparagus] bunches much too large, suppose to part in the path. [I] had 4 bundles made into 5, and they rather too large! He makes a fool of Phib. just as he pleases, and so do they all.

Saturday, 4th December 1773: In the evening I shot 4 Cuba teal, yet got but 2 of them. Jimmy let one get away & stole another; for which I had him flogged.

Friday, 28th January 1775: Jimmy left the cookroom and in the middle of last night at the Negro houses.

Saturday, 9th April 1774: This evening perceived Jimmy has the smallpox out upon him, which only discovered by accident. He says his head aches a little, but he has no fever. He was innoculated with the rest of my Negroes, but did not take the infection, so we concluded he had them before.

Thursday, 8th September 1774: Flogged Jimmy for staying at Sav la Mar till near 2 p.m. and being in liquor.

Sunday, 11th December 1774: Understand Jimmy wants to throw away Abba, he having long kept Phoebe slyly; Phoebe has also thrown away Neptune (or wants much to do it) upon Jimmy's account. A hopeful chap!

Wednesday, 14th December 1774: Flogged Jimmy and Phoebe for Crim. Con. &c.

Wednesday, 4th January 1775: Gave Jimmy a cobb, to buy me a piece of beef for corning, this morning. He brought me 8¾ lbs, but said it cost the whole 10 bitt; but on enquiry of Mr Thos. Tomlinson, find he gave him a bitt back, and that it weighed 9¼ lbs.

Wednesday, 1st February 1775: As Jimmy was out last night, he says at Egypt (but doubtful) suspect his riding my horses; therefore fixed a chain &c. to lock my pasture gate o' nights.

Thursday, 6th April 1775: Gave Jimmy a dose of salts as he pretends to be not well, owing to his being up last night, about his tricks with Phoebe, &c.

Wednesday, 21st June 1775: Flogged Jimmy for being from 7 to 2 p.m. selling 2 bitts worth of fish & 2dᵒ lima beans.

Wednesday, 5th July 1775: Jimmy come home about 2 p.m. in liquor.

Tuesday, 22nd Aug 1775: Jimmy came home ½ past 2 p.m. drunk, newspaper all frumpled, and suspect one of them lost. [A few days before he had lost Thistlewood's letter and newspaper bag]. He walked away again towards Savanna la Mar, and I saw him no more that night.

Thursday, 24th August 1775: Jimmy at home this morning. Had him flogged, then gave him a new bill & new hoe, and sent him, by Lincoln, to the Retrieve Estate, to work with the rest of my Negroes. Wrote to Mr John Hartnole, by Lincoln, gave each a ticket, and gave Jimmy a bitt to buy provisions till Sunday. Fresh branded him on the left shoulder \TT/ . He measures near 5 ft 3 ins high.

Thursday, 26th October 1775: Jimmy has got the yaws, it seems. He is a lazy scoundrel, and dare say he has infected himself purposely.'

In 1776 he remained with the fieldgang, out of Thistlewood's way, and was now seldom mentioned except for two more outbreaks of yaws, one in April, and another in October-November.

Mirtilla – a Soco, bought on shipboard from Mr Cuthbert, she would have been about 24 years old in 1770. Her husband in 1767 had been Egypt driver Johnie; but in 1770 she lived with Dick. She was a field slave.

'Saturday, 30th June 1770: Mirtilla dropped down in the field, about ½ past 10 a.m. Imagine she fainted for more want of victuals, by what I can hear.
She was drunk, I understand, having stolen Dick's rum.'

On Monday, 3rd December she was flogged for not having come back with the others from Friendship Estate on the previous morning. She was, apparently, ill at the time for she was given a Ward's Red Pill. Also, it seems, she was put in the bilboes because Thistlewood thought she was pretending.

'Thursday, 6th December 1770: This morning, Mirtilla begging to be let out of the bilboes, and that she found herself well enough to go to work, let her out and sent her to Friendship.'

In May, 1771, Mirtilla 'has got the clap and it's very bad upon her' so she was kept on the Pen and put to weed the garden. She was also, from time to time, seized with fits.

'Wednesday, 18th November 1772: ... Mirtilla took with a bad fit; but in about an hour's time came to herself somewhat. Complains of a violent pain in her neck, and of 3 somebodys stretching her there, who want her away, &c.
Thursday, 19th November 1772: Mirtilla complains much of her neck, &c. and is very low-spirited. Her courses, or time as the Negroes call them, flows abundantly today.'

For the remainder of November she was ill. Vine bled her.

'Friday, 21st May 1773: a.m. *Cum* Mirtilla (*mea*) *Sup. Terr* ...'

This was the second of only three times in these seven years. In

June, she was again briefly 'sick', but in November, 'Mirtilla has got the clap badly'.

> 'Tuesday, 26th July 1773: About 2 p.m. Mirtilla took with a fit, such as she has had before, which held near 3 hours before she could speak.'

On these occasions she seems to have been left to recover, as she now did, and then later given medicine, usually a dose of salts. Except for one more flogging in August, 1776, 'for impudence', we can leave her.

Peggy − also purchased at Lucea in 1765, would have been about 21 or 22 years old in 1770. Her history during 1770 to 1776 was comparatively unremarkable. She was not reported as having a husband or sweetheart; she bore no children. Between 23rd November and 30th December 1775 Thistlewood took her 5 times (he had until then ignored her), and he took her only once again in July 1776. She suffered relatively seldom, and then with very minor ailments. She seems not to have caught the clap. She never ran off, and only one flogging was recorded, at the end of August, 1774 when:

> 'Flogged Peggy for eating dirt. Sukey catched her in the fact.'

Phoebe − a Coromante, would have been about 17 years old in 1770. In 1767, when only about 14, she had been matched with Egypt Neptune, and in 1770 was still his wife, though Jimmy would later take her from him.

Her history in 1770 was generally unremarkable. In the course of that year Thistlewood took her 5 times. Towards the end of the year she developed a sore on her leg, for which, in 1771 she was occasionally treated.

> 'Wednesday, 10th July 1771: At night gave Phoebe a mercurial pill as her leg is breaking out again.'

In 1771 Thistlewood took her only twice. The next year was more eventful for her.

> 'Tuesday, 21st January 1772: Discovered by accident that Phoebe's sore leg is broke out (which she concealed). Had her flogged and put in the bilboes.
> Tuesday, 11th February 1772: Phoebe's sore being healed over, let her out of the bilboes, and put her to weeding in the garden.'

Early in that year Thistlewood's field gang were sent to work on Mount Pleasant Estate, Orange Bay in Hanover. He visited them from time to time. On one such visit:

'Friday, 17th April 1772:   Phoebe ill of a pain in her side, and they all look very poorly. Mr Hayward's all well. The Estate's Negroes excessive sickly, the hot house full.'

Phoebe was then about 6 months pregnant, presumably for Egypt Neptune who had set out from Egypt on Saturday, 23rd May to visit her at Mount Pleasant. He lost his way, was seized on Half-Moon Estate by a driver and locked in their stocks. There he stayed until report of his misfortune reached the Mount Pleasant Overseer, Mr James Wedderburn, who had him released on the 31st.

Meantime, on another visit to Mount Pleasant, on 29th May, Thistlewood had ordered Lincoln and Phoebe to return to Breadnut Island on Saturday 31st. They were delayed by Neptune's arrival, and on the 1st June, with a note of explanation from Mr Wedderburn, all three arrived at the Pen.

On Sunday, 5th July, Phoebe had a son. He died on the 11th of the common cause, 'Jaw fallen'. In July 1773 the story was repeated. Another son, born the 27th, died 2nd August. In the same year, her sore leg broke out again.

'Monday, 18th October 1773:   'Phoebe's leg not yet well, so she is at home yet, doing sundries in the garden.'

Two days later, Thistlewood visited her there. He had left her alone in 1772, taken her once in January 1773, and he now resumed more frequent attention. Between 20th October 1773 and 4th August 1774 he took her eleven times more.

At the end of 1773, and again in April 1774, Phoebe was reported ill of stomach trouble for which she was given a Ward's Red Pill; and 'of a bloody flux' for which she was given a dose of rhubarb. Again, in May, she complained of pains in her belly, not surprisingly for she was then again five months pregnant.

'Saturday, 3rd September 1774:   Sent Phoebe & Fanny for Mrs Edwards to see, who thinks they are near their time.
Monday, 5th September 1774:   As Phoebe & Fanny are now very big, sent them to Mrs Edward's this evening, to lay in. Am to give her two pistoles each.'

About noon, on the 9th, Phoebe was delivered of a boy at Mrs Edward's. This was Tony.

'Wednesday, 19th October 1774:   Gave Phoebe 3 bitts to buy 1½ yards of oznabrig for a Tie-cloth.'

The laying-in over, Phoebe went to garden work.

'Friday, 30th June 1775: a.m. *Cum* Phoebe (*mea*) in Garden. Stans Backwd. behind the indigo. Lincoln, Str Sukey sticking beans, covering beds, &c.'

In July, the gang were at Retrieve Estate. Phoebe came home with her child ill. She remained on the Pen for the next couple of months during which Thistlewood took her three times before noting on 22nd September that she seemed to be breaking out with yaws again. In February 1776 Phoebe was home again [from Bluecastle Estate] with her Tony, and they both went down with chickenpox. In April, Thistlewood noted another assault upon her. In July, he flogged her 'for wishing she was dead already, &c.' She was again lame and was laid up until Monday, 9th September when she returned to work

Franke − Another of the 10 shipmates, Franke, about 18 years old in 1770, was also in the field gang. Her husband was Egypt Lewie; and she was also a favourite of Mr Thistlewood, who had her 33 times in this period. Others, as we shall see, also found her attractive.

'Thursday, 8th November 1770: Egypt Lewie brought me 13 crabs as a present. (He keeps my Franke).

Thursday, 8th August 1771: Last night, about midnight, Egypt Lewie catched Mr Hayward's Tom come to Franke; fought before my door till I parted them, &c. They disturbed me very much.'

In September 1772, when Abba was lying-in, Franke was taken into the house to assist Phibbah.

'Sunday, 1st November 1772: Sent Franke to Savanna la Mar and gave her a bitt for her loss of time. She found what Jimmy had lost [his flour, &c], at Old Celia's at Kirkpatrick, and brought them.'

Up to this time, Franke had reportedly suffered only occasional aches, pains and fevers. But in November 1772 she was ill for a longish period.

'Monday, 30th November 1772: Franke laid up again of her belly. Suspect she has the clap. Gave her a mercurial pill in the evening.'

In May, 1773, she was ill again, and had to come home from gang work on Bluecastle Estate. Thistlewood had her bled, but for some days she continued unwell with 'a pain under her right breast'. On 8th December Thistlewood took her in the garden 'among the lima beans' and it was perhaps then that he first observed 'Franke's, sore worse, made her lay up'. By the beginning of 1774 the sore was 'plainly the yaws', so he made her go out to work with the rest. They were off to Bluecastle again. The ailment persisted.

'Friday, 29th July 1774:   Began to give Franke sarsaparilla diet drink, &c. for the yaws. Some of them beginning to dry naturally. Monday, 19th September 1774:   Franke in the gardens weeding, &c. She is now almost well; has a small sore on one leg, which was the yaws mother; but has now no visible yaws about her, and looks well; however, still continues to drink the sarsaparilla, &c.'

So, although he was himself complaining of a bad headache, an outbreak of boils, and 'not near well', on the 22nd they went to the garden bench, and, as was almost always the case with any of the women, he gave her 2 bitts.

'Thursday, 1st February 1776:   p.m. Franke come home from Bluecastle Estate; pains in her back, she pretends.'

She was flogged and put in the bilboes.

'Tuesday, 13th February 1776 [she was back at the Pen] ... can't cut cane she pretends for her back. Set her to burning off dry logwood in the pasture.'
The price of Logwood when he was at the Vineyard had been £12 or £13 a ton.'

Now, since mid-1775, it 'will scarce fetch a third of that price'.

On Friday 1st and Saturday 16th March. '*Cum* Franke (*mea*) ...'; and late on the night of the 24th Franke miscarried. 'Her belly was pretty big.'

Damsel — a Chamboy, and a house slave, was reckoned to be the same age as Franke, her shipmate. In May 1767 she had made a match with Egypt Harry. She apparently left him sometime before 1771. She had no children before coming to the Pen, and in June 1771 she had a miscarriage. By November of that year, for certain, she was clear of Egypt Harry.

'Wednesday, 20th November 1771:   My Damsel having been at the Bay last night to see her husband (Mrs North's George) got bit terribly on the leg with a dog. She concealed it, but I found it out, had it dressed, flogged her well & put her in the bilboes.

Tuesday, 3rd December 1771: Gave Damsel a Ward's ʜ
Pill, took her out of the bilboes till the evening, when put her in
again.
Friday, 11th September 1772: Between 5 and 6 o'clock in the
evening Damsel was brought to bed of a girl [Nelly] by Kirkpatrick
old grande Phibbah.
Saturday, 9th April 1774: Received for asparagus, 2 bitts ...
Note: 3 bitts worth brought back by Damsel who is a very
indifferent market woman.
Wednesday, 5th October 1774: This morning I found another
goose dead in the goosehouse ... Had Damsel well flogged for
not telling of it, her sullenness, &c. She never cleans the
goosehouse out.
Wednesday, 9th November 1774: *Cum* Damsel *(mea) Sup.
Terr* ....'

Damsel must have been someone special. Not that he took her
often, this was the first of only eight times in the seven years; but
she always got, perhaps demanded, 4 bitts instead of 2.

On Sunday, 16th April 1775 Damsel was again in childbirth.
This time, tended by Egypt grande Quasheba, she produced a son
[Quashe]. On the 20th May she got her tie-cloth money, 3 bitts.

In January, 1776 Damsel made her match with Solon who had
been abandoned by Maria. In April, she and Nelly caught the
chickenpox, and in September Quashe had the yaws. But they all
survived.

Bess — as we know, was not Thistlewood's property. At the age of
11 she had been given by Mrs Bennett to Phibbah for her lifetime
and then to Mulatto John. The transfer had been executed in John's
name simply because he was a free person. Legal responsibility for
her, therefore, rested with Mr Thistlewood. Not surprisingly, Bess,
who would have been about 16 years old in 1770, was a house slave.
At first apparently housed with Dick, she had by 1770 moved into
the Thistlewood cookroom with Damsel and Jimmy, and, temporarily, Sally. Abba had her own house.

At the beginning of 1770 Bess was being treated by Dr
Drummond for an unspecified illness. Her medicines included boluses
[large pills], and she was, it seems, for a long time after required to
wash with an ointment. The ailment later proved to be venereal.

'Wednesday, 21st November 1770: 'In the morning flogged
Bess for not bathing as ordered in a morning for her sickness.
Had words with Phibbah.'

Bess remained sickly at the start of 1771, and in late June suffered a miscarriage. In July, she was sent to Miss Bessy Murray 'to learn to darn, mark, &c.'

'Sunday, 3rd November 1771:   Heard a drumming last night at the Negro house. Got up and went to see. It proved Bess, beating upon a gourd. In the evening had words with Phib. about her ill-humours, &c. Also locked Jimmy, Bess and Damsel up in the cookroom.'

In August 1772 Bess was brought to bed of a boy [Bristol]. It was a painful labour, presided over by Kirkpatrick Old Phibbah.

'They were obliged to tie her, she was so unruly.'

At the beginning of November:

'Bess has got a running again, either fresh or the old one returned.'

At the end of 1774 Bess was said to have made a match with Mr White's Coffee. In 1775 she came also to the attention of Mr Thistlewood, 3 times. In January 1776 Bristol fell ill 'of a bad breaking out'. It was not his first disorder. In 1774 he had swallowed a fish bone (through Bess's 'usual careless manner' in feeding him, said Thistlewood) and Dr Samuel Bell, who attended him, gave him a vomit to bring it out. In December 1775 he had been ill and subjected to a bleeding, but all this he survived.

On 25th February 1776, with Egypt Quasheba in attendance, Bess was delivered of another boy. By March 10th, mother and grande had given him up. Thistlewood called them 'bad nurses indeed', for the child was not yet dead. But he lasted only another day. Bess seemed always to have a hard time at childbirth. She now continued ill through most of April and May; and in early May Bristol was also ill, 'swelled as if he had the dropsy'. He was given a mercury pill and rhubarb.

'Tuesday, 9th 1776:   My Bess & one of Mr Wilson's New Negroes, named Jimmy, have made a match.'

Fanny − This was Mr Say's slave who, with Strap, was bought by Thistlewood in 1773. She was probably a Creole, for on Thursday, 11 August 1774, she was given leave 'to go and see her cousin, the late Mr Mitchell's girl'.

In October, she and Phoebe had been sent to Mrs Edwards to have their babies. Fanny had a girl, Patty, who died on 1st April 1775.

'Sunday, 26th February 1775:   Received a note from Mr

Thompson [Overseer at Glen Islay Estate], by Dick; Fanny's pickanninny sick last Tuesday, &c. She did nothing.
Saturday, 25th March 1775: About noon, Fanny come home, her child ill of the flux.
Saturday, 1st April 1775: About noon, Fanny's child died. Had it buried.'

On Monday 3rd Fanny was at the Pen 'sulky and threatening to make away with herself, very obstimate, &c.' Next day, when put with Phoebe to weed she was '. . . very refractory' and Thistlewood threatened her 'very much'. She soon was sent back to the field gang. Through 1775 and 1776 she remained with them, sometimes ill (but not very seriously), sometimes said to be 'unwilling to go to work', and in February 1776 she was punished for that reason, in the bilboes and flogged. Thistlewood took her once.

Strap — was, to his misfortune, tried out as fisherman.

'Tuesday, 28th August 1774: . . . as he brings nothing at night, and only brought 3 bullheads today, for dinner, flogged him and sent him to work in the field.
Wednesday, 7th September 1774: . . . at home lame of a toe. Put him in the bilboes.
Sunday, 25th September 1774: Flogged Strap for losing part of yesterday.
Sunday, 9th October 1774: Am told Strap is exceedingly lazy and good for nothing. Steals cane, &c.'

Later in the month he was put under treatment for crab-yaws, and Phoebe was sent to Masemure in his place. And, much later, in August 1776, he got another flogging 'for mistreatment of a horse'.

Joe — a New Negro boy purchased in December 1775 from Mr James Wedderburn at 'an incredible price indeed' had, by the end of 1776, served as Thistlewood's attendant for a year, during which he seems to have avoided the whip. But he could not avoid all ills.

'Friday, 24th September 1776: Joe has got the yaws; at least it is greatly feared he has.'

Notes

1 Pot-hook, Patook, or Patoo. Nowadays a triangular wooden yoke put on the necks of animals to prevent them straying; earlier an iron collar locked around a person's neck. See Cassidy & Le Page, (1980) p.361.

2 Classed as the 'best quality' in a cargo of slaves.

3 'Broughta' or 'brawta' is the extra bit over the purchased amount. See Cassidy (1971) p.210.

4 Made of strips of manatee hide, this was thought to be 'too cruel, and therefore prohibited by the customs of the country', Cassidy and Le Page (1980) p.290. quoting Sloane. But Sloane seems to have been either wrong or out-dated. (Sir Hans Sloane, *A Voyage to the Islands* ... 2 Vols. Lond. 1707).

5 A later continuation of the death rituals in which, until a final 'play' about a year after death there were recognised periodic returns to celebration. The 'Coombie' or 'Gumbe', a handbeaten drum. (Cassidy & Le Page (1980) pp.202–3).

6 A thick ointment made of wax and oil with other ingredients.

7 Probably black sage. See Cassidy & Le Page (1980) p.48.

8 Probably 'Jalap', a purgative made from the roots of a vine, bindweed.

9 Commonly prescribed in attempts to cure gonorrhea, the 'bougi' was at the time described as '... a Catheter Probe, or rather a Wax Candle [or, other thin, flexible surgical instrument] made small on purpose, and dipped in oil, and passed gently into the Urethra ...' [James Handley, *Colloquia Chirugica; or the Art of Surgery* ... London, 1733, pp.196, 197.]. Thistlewood knew from bitter experience the torment of wearing one.

10 John Hartnole had left Egypt and was now overseer at Retrieve Estate.

CHAPTER 9

The establishment of Thomas Thistlewood, 1770–1776

Introduction

Here we have Thomas Thistlewood, Esqr., Justice of the Peace, and Lieutenant of the Fort at Savanna la Mar at the top of his fortune and, the usual illnesses apart, at his most comfortable. Within and beyond the parish his horticultural interests and expertise are recognised and his garden has become an attraction to visitors. Nonetheless, he is not resting on accomplishment. In these years he introduces new activities – hives of bees, an indigo patch, and a trial export of annatto.

With great satisfaction and an abundant hospitality he entertains, and is entertained by, some of the wealthiest and most influential members of the sugar-plantocracy; and they seem to regard him as a social equal – perhaps in acknowledgement of his wide interests and his outstanding horticultural achievement.

Perhaps his only real disappointment lies in the behaviour of his son, Mulatto John, who is not turning out to be the intellectually inclined reader of books his father seemingly hoped for; and whose veracity is occasionally questionable. He is spoiled, Thistlewood thinks, by his mother. But there is hope that he might yet prove himself in more practical pursuits.

But again, life in Westmoreland is disturbed by war (of American Independence, 1775–1783) and by the threat of slave revolt spreading south from the parish of Hanover.

In these years Thomas Thistlewood established himself as a member of the landed gentry. His property in land and slaves was relatively small and he was not among the sugar producing aristocracy, but his skills as a horticulturist gave him prestige, and his long and continuing association with the Cope family gave him social entrée. At the same time, his open and affectionate association with Phibbah and her relatives and friends apparently gave him a special consideration among some of the slaves, and, equally, tempered his behaviour towards them.

'Monday, 23rd January 1769:   a.m. rode into the Savanna. Called at Mr Stone's. He says as he expects to make but a short crop, shall not want to hire Negroes; thence rode to Mr Weech's and from thence, to Three Mile River where saw Mr Carr and spoke to him in respect of running the lines between me and Kirkpatrick, which he says shall be seen about when Mr Rankin, the surveyor, comes down this way. Then I rode to Bluecastle Estate & agreed with Dr James Wedderburn about my Negroes for the crop, at.3 bitts per diem ...

Sunday, 29th January 1769:   Wrote to James Wedderburn, Esqr., and about 4 p.m. sent my Negroes to his estate (Bluecastle) to work, Vizt. Lincoln, Dick, Solon, Cudjoe, Johnie, Caesar, Sukey, Franke, Sally, Maria, Nanny, Coobah, Mirtilla and Peggy = 14.

Sunday, 5th February 1769:   To Mr Little for 10 lbs of beef 8 bitts, and for bread a bit.

Many of my Negroes over from Bluecastle, praise it much, being easy worked.

Friday, 17th February 1769:   A little after noon, rode to Egypt and dine there, as did also Mr Cope, Robt Baker, Mr Samuel Lee, Dr Gorse, Capt. Binden, and Capt. John White. After dinner drank hard, I got away about 5 p.m. a good deal in liquor, but the rest sat longer, and were all in for it very much. Mr Hartnole, I hear, was quite drunk, insomuch that the boilers could get no lamp oil for the boiling house use, &c., Mr Cope stayed all night and sat up till midnight, &c., but went home before day. Capt. White and Capt. Binden fought, &c. I was much disordered, but got home very well and slept well at night. At dinner Mr Cope ordered Mr Hartnole to let me have 4 puncheons of rum, strong proof, a cask of 30 gallons ditto for my own use, and a flour barrel of sugar. It seems, last night Little Mimber came from the Bay to sleep with Mr Hartnole.

Saturday, 25th February 1769:   A play this evening, at Egypt, made by Daniel, to throw water for his Boy, Fortune, killed by Paradise mill wheel last crop.

Tuesday, 28th February 1769:   Rode into the Savanna to Mr Emetson's and stayed 2 to 3 hours with him. He gave me a ball of chocolate. Showed me his will, which I read over. He leaves Mary Emetson, his Negro wench, free at his death; £100 to the little girl of the late Mr Dickson's Mrs Emetson took; £500 to his niece at home; and the rest to Mrs Underwood! Surprising. I rode home to dinner. Mr Pommells, myself, and Mr Underwood, executors.

Wednesday, 22nd March 1769: Egypt Lucy acquainted P privately, that the Myal dance has been held twice in Phil Coobah's house, at Paradise Estate, as also Egypt Dago Job, who are both Myal-men attend these dancings.
Monday, 27th March 1769 [Easter Monday]: Nanny's child sick. Kept her at home and gave it a dose of physick. It is feverish. Last night John lay in my bed again and he p . . . . . d it.'

April brought a more disastrous wetting. Heavy rains on Saturday 1st swamped the garden and left parts of it under water for several days.

'Tuesday, 4th April 1769: Kirkpatrick Cudjoe at my house to draw Phibbah's teeth, but could not get at them, being stumps and so far back.
Sunday, 9th April 1769: For 10 lbs of fresh beef, 8 bitts: very bad indeed, near carrion.
Wednesday, 12th April 1769: Little Mimber at the Pen today.
Thursday, 13th April 1769: Hear Mr Jno. H- is building Little Mimber a house at Egypt.
Sunday, 16th April 1769: House Franke, and Phibbah's Coobah over here today. Reprimanded Coobah severely about the Myall affair.
Wednesday, 19th April 1769: About 10 a.m. Emetson's Mary sent me word privately, by a Negro man, that Mr Emetson is now very bad indeed.'

Mr Emetson died in the morning of Friday 21st and was buried on the 22nd in the Anglican churchyard.
And, as for himself and Phibbah:

'As a running which stains a yellowish brown still continues & also a continual headache, took a dose of physick this morning, which worked indifferently. Phibbah is still frequently troubled with the toothache and is restless at nights. Her menses are coming on, but not quite as they should.
Saturday, 29th April 1769: a.m. Rode to Savanna la Mar, and about 11 o'clock Dr Thomas King drew my aching tooth, it was in the upper jaw, the last but one on the right side, firmly fixed, he had 3 trials at it, and the operation was intolerably painful; however when drawn I was pretty easy. Phibbah also walked to the Bay and he pulled out two stumps for her which gave her a good deal of ease. In the evening Phibbah and Vine walked home in company, my Bess and Vine's Sally with them.
Monday, 15th May 1769: Whitsun Monday. This morning sent

John [home as usual for the week-end] to school again; gave him a bitt. Hear Port Royal, at Egypt, died today.
At night Egypt Lucy come over to acquaint us Mr Hartnole had put L. Mimber's chain about his neck.
Sunday, 21st May 1769: For 8 lbs of beef, 8 bitts.
Beef is raised to 7½d a pound again lately. For bread, a bitt. Served my Negroes 24 bitts.
This morning flogged every field Negro I could find at home for not getting to work till 8 o'clock Monday morning.
Monday, 29th May 1769: Borrowed of Phibbah £9 15s 0d. In the evening rode over to the Wilderness to see Mr Wm. Pommells. Drank tea, &c. and in the dusk rode home. Mr Pommells lent me: *Observations upon the Growth and Culture of Vines & Olives, &c.*; written at the request of the Earl of Shaftesbury, to whom it is inscribed, by Mr John Locke, Feby. 1st, 1679. Lond, 1766 ... Also *The Art of Preserving Health*, a poem; a new edition, price 1s 6d by John Armstrong, M.D. Lond. 1765 ...'

On Monday, 4th June 1769, all of Thistlewood's slaves, except Damsel, were back on the Pen, having finished working at Bluecastle. There they found him complaining that their hogs had once again 'made sad havoc' in the provision ground; and there were others:

'Monday, 26th June 1769: Kirkpatrick Quasheba cow in my provision ground this morning and had eat up a good deal of my corn, than which I never saw finer, &c. Shot at her legs with a ball, but missed them.
Tuesday, 27th June 1769: Planted all the low part of the garden with Rice, 4 in a hole, rows 4 feet apart and 3 feet in the rows.'

In mid-July 1769, the continuing depredations of his own and Kirkpatrick cattle notwithstanding, he went into another burst of planting in his garden, Indian Kale, sunflower, Indian Pinks, balsam, sage, rosemary, marjoram; and in the provision ground, callaloo and ochroes.

'Monday, 17th June 1769: Dr Wedderburn says, that of those who have been long in this island, he looks upon it 4/5ths die of the venereal disease, one way or other, occasioned by it.'

Hardly a comforting remark to Mr Thistlewood.
On the 2nd August 1769, Thistlewood began to take the Spanish Town newspaper [probably the *St Jago Intelligencer*]; and he listed the titles of sixteen books he had received from England since the beginning of the year. Most of them had arrived in February and

included works in history, agriculture and plantership, dictionar.
and other books of reference. He had also been acquiring, from M.
Hayward, a number of children's books which he would soon begin
to give Mulatto John.

'Monday, 7th August 1769: Mr Prynold, surveyor, lent me a
*Letter from a Farmer in Pennsylvania, to the Inhabitants of the
British Colonies*, Boston 1768, 8vo.
Sunday, 13th August 1769: Mr Say dined with me. He says he
will certainly leave Cabaritta Estate in all this month; and that
John Prince has left Petersfield Estate.
Mr Hartnole and Mimber have both the Itch badly.
Friday, 18th August 1769: Note: Last night I took a mercurial
pill & gave Phib. one; this morning a dose of salts, and gave
Phib. a dose of purging powders.
Finished picking all my annatto and cut the dead branch ends
off from which the annatto was picked; trimmed the trees, &c.
Sunday, 20th August 1769: Gave John the *History of Jack the
Giant Killer* in 2 parts.
Monday, 21st August 1769: Gave Egypt Lucy 2 bottles of
porter for Daniel who is very ill and longs for porter.
Thursday, 24th August 1769: Mr John Hartnole dined with
me, gave him 4 mercurial pills.
Sunday, 3rd September 1769: Returned to Phibbah £27 2*s* 6*d*,
money I borrowed of her in crop time, out of her own, House
Franke's and Egypt Lucy's money. House Franke at the Pen
today. a.m. her and Phibbah walked over to Egypt.
Sunday, 24th September 1769: Last night Quamina at Egypt
christening his house, a play, supper, &c.[1] Mr Hartnole leaving
his furniture in his piazza, through carelessness, his saddlecloth,
harness, bridle, &c. were all stolen out of it. Minos & Adam
watchmen, but little Doll watched in Adam's room. The play
continues today, a pay dinner, &c.
Monday, 2nd October 1769: Betimes this morning 14 of my
Negroes, Vizt. Lincoln, Dick, Cudjoe, Johnie, Caesar, Sukey,
Franke, Mirtilla, Phoebe, Maria, Nanny, Peggy, Coobah and
Sally, set out for Cabaritta Estate with 12 of Mr Hayward's . . .'

They had gone to construct a trench from Peters plain and to fence
off estate lines. The work would last for some weeks; and while it
did they stayed at Cabaritta.

'Saturday, 7th October 1769: Last night let Capt. Charles, and
some of his people, sleep in Lincoln's house. They called up to
sell tobacco. Mr Say and Vine disagree sadly. She is going to
Roaring River tonight.

Sunday, 8th October 1769: Gave John the *History of Tom Long the Courier*. He has already *Jack the Giant Killer*, and *Tom Hickathrift*. Gave him a paper of ink powder.
Monday, 9th October 1769: This afternoon broke in my corn in the corn piece, which fell far short of my expectation. Believe Solon has stolen great part of the best; broke in Abba's likewise, which has also suffered; he is exceeding sly. Hear Old Sharper, at Egypt, died this morning.
Thursday, 2nd November 1769: Gathered a good deal of my Rice today in the garden, ripe but parakeets, black-birds, &c. make sad havoc with it.
Saturday, 18th November 1769: About 4 p.m. our Negroes come home, having finished fencing Peters plain. Wrote to Mr Hayward by Dick, Negroes' labour as follows ...'

The bill included £98 5s for 68½ chains of a double ditch and bank planted with penguins, on Peters plain; and £4 12s 6d for 49½ days labour on Cabaritta Estate. The total amount, of which £60 had already been paid in cash, was due to S. Hayward and T. Thistlewood from J. Meyler.

'Note: our Negroes have just earned us 3 bitts 2 pence, or 2 shillings and a half-penny, per day each.'

Having been warned the day before, Thistlewood set off on the morning of the 5th to Salt River 'to exercise', the first time for many months. The exercises were now regularly resumed, once a week, sometimes at Salt River, sometimes in Savanna la Mar.

'Wednesday, 13th December 1769: Rode to Savanna la Mar, Lincoln Dick & Cudjoe met me in Paradise canoe lent me by Mr Hartnole. To Capt. James Lake for a barrel of herrings, £2; ditto of shads, £1; Keg of biscuit, 7s 6d ... Paid him and had his receipt. Open Keg of bread, barrel of herrings, & ditto of shads, and served my Negroes 4 shads & 2 herrings each.
Monday, 25th December 1769 (Christmas Day). Served my Negroes this morning 4 herrings and 4 mackerels each, gave Lincoln and Abba each a bottle of rum; Cudjoe and Johnie a bottle; Dick and Solon a bottle; girls a bottle; Pompey, Chub and Caesar each a dram, &c.
In the morning, *Cum* Phib.
Little Mimber's James over to see John.'

On the 26th, and again on the 27th the militia were exercised, on the second occasion 'by a soldier, Col Myrie', who kept them at it until almost noon.

By the year's end, his and Phibbah's infections had abat
Because of them it had been sexually a relatively quiet year. He had
kept close to Phibbah, but he had also found occasion with Maria
four times, Coobah three, Nanny twice, Bess and Mirtilla once
each, and with Sally twice – but on each occasion with her it had
still been *'sed non bene'*. There had also been a couple of entangle-
ments with strangers. All had been proudly recorded, and the year
ended on a note of another sort of satisfaction:

> 'Sunday 31st December 1769:   Mr John Hartnole breakfasted
> with me .... Rode to Savanna la Mar. Thence went to Mr
> Stone's and received from him a Commission of the 21st Instant
> date (which he procured for me) to be a Lieut of Sav la Mar
> Fort. Paid him Ten pistoles expenses, to the Secretary, &c.
> Rode to the Thatch Tree, and as Sav la Mar company, Salt
> River company, and the Rangers were already under Arms,
> called Capt Tomlinson aside, and showed him the Commission.'

Appointed by His Excellency Sir Williams Trelawny, Bart, Captain
General and Governor-in-chief, Thomas Thistlewood, Gentleman,
in whom was reposed 'confidence in your experience, courage, conduct, fidelity, and skill in military affairs', was now given the
responsibility and duty 'to exercise the inferior Officers, Gunners
and Soldiers thereof in arms' and to hold them 'in good order and
discipline'.

> 'Monday, 14th May 1770:   Put the following letters in Captain
> Richardson's bag, of the 12th Inst. date: one to my brother
> including a bill of lading & scheme of the comet orbit of 1769
> [which he had closely observed]; one to Mr Henry Hewitt Snr
> containing a bill of lading and list of things desired; and one to
> Mr Henry Hewitt Jnr enclosing list of things proper for the
> young man who intends coming out.'

He was, in a few months time, to receive and give hospitality to two
new arrivals in Jamaica until they found employment; as he had
once been favoured by William Dorrill. And, at about the same
time that Henry Hewitt Jnr was writing to solicit assistance for his
friends, Thistlewood was developing his local influence.

> 'Mr Morris, Mr Weech, Capt. Blake, Capt. Atkins, Mr Chambers,
> Mr Hartnole, Dr Wedderburn, dined with me. Had a fine roast
> goose and paw-paw sauce, stewed giblets, stewed land turtle,
> stewed fish, a roast coot & 2 roast plover, boiled pudding,
> cheese, &c. Grog, punch and porter .... Lent Dr Wedderburn,
> *Tull's Husbandry*, & *Cooper on Distillation*.'

A few months later, 'upon my asking it for him', John Hartnole was employed by Mr Weech as overseer on Retrieve Estate. He left Egypt at the end of October, 1770, with Mr Cope still owing him £107. At Retrieve he was to get £100 a year. Mr Cope, Mrs Cope, John Cunningham from Salt River, Mr Parker 'a Scotchman, late overseer at Salt River but now employed at Egypt', and Thistlewood all dined at Egypt on the day of Hartnole's departure. The two ex-overseers and the new replacement obviously discussed the Egypt slaves:

'Adam and Derby run away. Big Mimber, Big Doll, Old Sharper, London, Kinsale, Port Royal, Morris, Violet, Mountain Susanah, Deborah dead.'

Mountain Susanah had died on 22nd September at about noon. Other deaths noted by Thistlewood in 1770 included that of Dr John James Gorse who died on 15th May, at about 55 years of age, and whose burial 'in the new Church yard' at Savanna la Mar was attended by a large gathering, including Thistlewood; Salt River's 'Doctor Will' who had died on a night in early June; Andrew Seims (Simms), the sugar-baker at the end of September; Vineyard Phibbah, sometime in September or October; and in more detail:

'Friday, 5th October: Hear Old Quashie died at Kirkpatrick before day this morning. He was very sensible, and handy, also honest & trusty. He was a Coromante Negro, and brought into this Island when the Duke of Portland was governor, a man-boy; so consequently is between 60 and 70. Has for the most part been very healthy.
Saturday, 29th December 1770:   Theodore Stone, Esqr. one of the Representatives for this Parish, died at his house in Savanna la Mar, between ten and eleven o'clock this afternoon. A great loss to the parish in general, and Savanna la Mar in particular as he had their interests greatly at heart. He would have been 58 the 10th of June next.'

It had not been a healthy year for Phibbah, or indeed for Thistlewood himself and their son.

'Friday, 12th January 1770:   Last night I took a mercurial pill (Phib. also) as both have a running which stains, and symptoms, &c. rest excessive badly, &c.'

The venereal symptoms and treatments continued, off and on, through the entire year, and in the middle of the year their discomfort was increased by a violent itching which afflicted all three of them.

Thistlewood, nonetheless, was busy supervising the development of the Pen and looking for new enterprises. In January the slaves, under Cumberland's supervision, were gathering and preparing materials for a goat pen. In May, he sent 'a small cake of annatto, and a phial of annatto seeds' to England by Capt. Atkins whom he asked to 'enquire the price'. On Sunday, 2nd December, Mr Parker from Egypt, Mr Limburner from Paradise, and Mr Ellis from Sweet River dined with him. After dinner they walked in his garden and:

> '. . . perceived a swarm of bees upon a fig tree leaf, but where they should come from God knows.
>
> Friday, 7th December: Mr Hayward lent me, *An Essay on the Management of Bees*, by John Mills, FRS Lond. 1766.'

He soon began to capture swarms of bees and to market honey.

Early in 1771 there came the unchallengable evidence of his social acceptance by the large landed proprietors.

> 'Wednesday, 16th January: Vine lent me 2 tables, 4 chairs, some knives and forks, wash hand basins, tumblers, wine glasses, &c. . . . Sent 3 pails for drinking water, quite to Salt River.
>
> Thursday 17th: Last night had the fat goose killed, and this morning Coobah's barrow . . .
>
> Vine is so good as to assist Phibbah today. Mr and Mrs Cope, Mr and Mrs Weech, Mr John Hutt, Mr Wm. Blake, Mr Chambers, and Dr Panton dined, and drank tea &c. with me, and in the evening went home. Had goose and paw-paw sauce, roast pork & brocoli, roast whistling duck, stewed hog's head, shaddock, water melon, oranges, madeira wine, porter, punch, grog & brandy.'

And so, with evident self-satisfaction, he shortly afterwards recorded:

> 'Wednesday, 27th March 1771:   This day am 50 years of age, being born March 16th 1720/21, old style. So, return thanks to the Almighty for preserving my life so long, and for the many blessings I have received.'[2]

The 'many blessings' obviously excluded physical well-being. Although these years were to pass without serious and prolonged venereal recurrence there was hardly a month in which Thistlewood, or Phibbah, or John did not suffer some indisposition or another. Even as he wrote his birthday note they were down.

> 'Friday, 29th March: Yesterday evening Phibbah took with a violent shaking cold, followed by the headache, fever, pains in her belly, sides, shoulders, &c. and a bad cough withal. She got no rest all night. Neither had I scarcely any rest. About 4 this afternoon got Vine to take a little blood from Phib.'

She remained ill through the following week. On Sunday 31st, her daughter Coobah, and Prue, Charles, and Clara and her husband, all from Egypt, came to see her. Early in April Dr Panton prescribed:

'... a phial of mixture for Phibbah. Gave her 2 spoonfuls of it every 2 hours. Note: she got no sleep last night, nor I neither.'

In between the illnesses there had been the usual rounds of entertainment and amusement, such as the races:

'Wednesday, 30th January 1771:   About 3 o'clock this morning Phibbah, John and Damsel, with Vine, &c. set out for the Race. Phib. rode Nelly, and Jimmy carried John on Mackey as far as Cabaritta Estate. Gave Phib. and John 5 bitts to spend .... I set out from home at ½ past eight o'clock on Prince horse [he had in the meantime taken Abba, but with little success: "*Cum* Abba, *mea, Sup. Lect. meo in domo*, (Impotˢ)."] ... Jimmy rode Mackey, and got to New Market Course before 10, and in about an hour the horses started, Mr John Dawe's Presto beat Mr Samuel's Snap the 2 heats, so consequently won.'

At dinnertime, he and others went off to dine at Retrieve Estate, with Hartnole, then back to the races and, in the evening back home. But:

'Phibbah, Vine, John, &c. at the Retrieve also with Mimber; but they went to Venus's house at Cabaritta to sleep, only left John with James [L. Mimber's mulatto son] at the Retrieve. Vine rode her horse, Powder-tail .... A great number of people at the Race, and money plenty among the Sportsmen, however scarce at other times. Many young sparks wore Corsican hats, the first I have seen.'

Next morning, Phibbah & Vine 'weary of the race' came home; but not before Thistlewood himself had once again enmeshed with Abba, *Sup. Lect*: this time successfully, and then, at about 7.30 a.m. returned to the racecourse on his own.

'Sunday, 17th February: Mr Parker[3] says that Mr Drummond, book keeper at Friendship his shipmate, and about 10 days ago having received some wages at Sav la Mar, and meeting with him accidentally, would go along with him to see Egypt, and between 4 and 5 p.m. set out for home, somewhat, tho' very little in liquor. Going through the Savanna, he met with a Negro wench who said she belonged to Mr Stone, and agreed to go among the bushes together, where, when they had got, she desired payment first, upon which he pulled out his purse of knitted green silk, through which she easily saw his money (being about 20 pistoles in it), and holding it rather carelessly, she snatched it out of his hand starting immediately; and he has never since heard of it, nor does he think he should know the girl again'.

On Wednesday, 10th April 1771 Capt. Richardson brought the *Henry* into Savanna la Mar.

'. . . in the evening received a note from Mr Hayward acquainting me, that 2 young men were come passengers in Capt. Richardson, from Mr Hewitt to me.'

They were William Thompson and Francis Scott. Thistlewood made them welcome and noted 'they seem both sensible, well behaved men'.

Capt. Richardson had also brought goods for Mr Thistlewood. There were boxes containing cloths and clothing. Phibbah got 6 pairs of shoes and 'much cloth for herself', John got 12 pairs of stockings; and not long after, his father:

'Began to wear today, 7 new white shirts, 6 cravats, & 6 new night caps. White hat broad cloth coat every day.'

There were tubs of English trees, most of them dead. And there were books: *The Life and Opinions of Tristram Shandy, Gentleman.* Vol. 9th. Lond. 1767 (curious plates); *The Wanton Widow, or the Amours and Intrigues of John Stewart and the Widow Carleton.* Lond. 1769; Benjamin Franklin's *Experiments and Observations on Electricity*; and many other works of fiction, biography, philosophy, medical and dental care, law, travel, and agriculture. The arrivals of Capt. Richardson were red-letter days in the Thistlewood household.

The two new arrivals, Thompson and Scott, were gardeners. They spent a few days on Thistlewood's Pen helping in the garden and planting seeds Mr Scott had brought with him. They also had an early introduction to slave ceremony. On Saturday, 20th April, Rose, the Egypt 'doctress' died. Next day Thistlewood took them to her burial, where they 'saw the dancing, &c'. At the beginning of the next week they both went to Retrieve Estate as book-keepers, each at £35 a year. Early in 1772 Thompson went as overseer to Mr Weech's Spring Garden Estate in St Catherine. Francis Scott stayed longer at Retrieve and was a frequent visitor at Mr Thistlewood's where, with a common interest in horticulture, they worked in the gardens and became fast friends. In February 1774, Scott went as overseer on Ackendown Estate in Westmoreland.

For some time before 1771 there had been no mention of the Maroons, and in that year there was only one when, in late March, a party of them arrived on the Pen offering tobacco for sale. Thistlewood bought 2 rolls for 4 bitts, 'which I sold again'. Nor, until the later part of the year, was there any reference to punishment for prohibited behaviour or unrest among the slaves.

'Saturday, 2nd November: Hear Frazier's Beck, on Thursday last, was tried for having a Supper and a great number of Negroes at her house last Saturday night. Had her ear slit, 39 lashes under the gallows, and 39 again against the Long Stores. Tomlinson's Abbington (Vulgo, Hamilton), a bit cut out of his ear, and ditto lashes. Also several others flogged, &c. Several are run away.'

In April of 1770 Samuel Say had accepted an offer from Martin Williams of the overseership at Old Hope Estate and had gone to live there. His pen, which he visited from time to time, was left in the care of Vine, for whom a new house had been built by carpenter Cumberland. Thistlewood kept a supervisory eye on the property. Vine and Phibbah were old friends, and now each was in charge of a household, the former for her absent master, the latter in her own home. Thistlewood's notes on the two women and their friends and relations, some of whom he also knew very well, are illustrative of his attitude towards and relationships with individual slaves, not all of whom were of privileged domestic or skilled occupation.

'Monday, 22nd January 1770: Hear Jack (Paradise Franke's husband) has got the yaws. She has never had them.
Friday, 29th June 1770: Little Nancy, Paradise Coobah's [and thus Phibbah's grand-daughter], took with a vomiting last night. Phib. stayed in the cookroom to assist little Catalina with her all night.
Sunday, 19th August 1770: Old Pompey (Vine's father) belonging to Mr Meyler, come to see Phib.
Wednesday, 12th September 1770: Vine quarrelled with my Negroes for taking dry wood from off Mr Say's land. I discharged them from going there again as I have a great abundance. ... Luna [Mr Say's] here baking cakes.
Thursday, 20th September 1770: House Franke slept in John's bed tonight. She is going to Egypt.
Saturday, 3rd November 1770: p.m. Vine and Mrs Cowling's Ancilla over to see Phib. Gave them some grapes.
Saturday, 17th November 1770: A daughter of [the late] Mason Quashe, named Franke, belonging to Mr P. Gordon, and her

husband, a Negro fellow, a mason, belonging Middle Ground, named James Knight, came here to see Phibbah.

Thursday, 13th December 1770: This morning lent Vine Mackey horse, to ride to the Old Hope, Mr Say [who had been ill] being worse again.

Sunday, 31st March 1771: Phibbah's Coobah [who with others was visiting her sick mother] brought a mare, and asked me leave to let her go here.

Friday, 19th April 1771: Gave Phibbah's Coobah a pistole! She is going to England soon.

Thursday, 6th May 1771: Gave Vine a Ward's Red Pill, for her father, Old Pompey, who is not well. (Vine gave me a fine musk melon).

Monday, 19th August 1771: Little Mimber carried from Egypt to Paradise this morning in a canoe; said to be going to miscarry.

Sunday, 1st September 1771: Returned Franke's money to Phibbah, 5 doubloons and 2 pistoles = £26 2s 6d, the money I had of her December 7th and 31st, 1770.

Saturday, 7th September 1771: Coobah's husband here today, also Dianah from Paradise; I have not seen her of many years.

Saturday, 28th September 1771: Egypt Lucy slept upon the ironing table in the cookroom last night. She is in poor state of health yet. [She had been ill for months. On 23rd June Phibbah had gone to Egypt to visit her "very ill."]

Wednesday, 13th November 1771: Hear Phibbah's Coobah has got herself christened at home.

Sunday, 1st December 1771: Hear Mr Parker sent Little Mimber, very bad, in a canoe to Paradise this morning.

Thursday, 2nd January 1772: The *Cranbrook*, Capt. Suttie, come in this evening. Mr Cope 3 daughters & Coobah came ashore.

Sunday, 5th January 1772: Sent Mrs Cope 50 bunches of grapes, flowers, and a pr. wild ducks, per Jimmy. Jimmy also carried Little Nancy home; and John went with him likewise. Sent House Franke & Coobah, pr. teal.

Thursday, 9th January 1772: Early in the morning, Old Pompey died. Lent Vine Jimmy, to go acquaint her friends at Cabaritta Estate.

Saturday, 11th January 1772: In the middle of last night, Phibbah's Coobah come from Paradise to see her.

Monday, 13th January 1772: Jenny Young (Coobah) come here to see her mother today.

Monday, 6th April 1772: Paradise Little Mimber (or rather,

Egypt one) going this day, to live with Mr John Hartnole [at Retrieve Estate]. Suspect she is not yet clear from the clap, as she had it very bad when she went to Paradise 2 or 3 months ago sick. Mr C ... also had it soon after, and Mr J. Hart ...le certainly in for it now.

Saturday, 11th April 1772:   Paradise Coobah, alias Jenny Young here to see her mother. She, Vine, Sally, Sancho, Juba [from Say's Pen], Lewis, Neptune [from Egypt], Jimmy, my Coobah, Abba, Maria, &c. [Thistlewood's], fishing in the deep rock holes; but too much water for them yet. However, they got god-dammes, &c.

Thursday, 21st May 1772:   Mr Say's Vine has the fever very bad yet, and her master, &c. takes but little notice of her.

Friday, 5th June 1772:   As Vine's hogs makes sad work in the Rockhole provision ground, sent her word this morning, and she is greatly affronted.'

Three weeks later, on the 27th, after her long illness, Egypt Lucy died and was buried next day. Phibbah and John went to her burial.

'Tuesday, 21st July 1772:   p.m. Vine's hogs in Standing Limekiln provision ground. Showed them to her.

Friday, 24th July 1772:   In the morning Mr Hughes called at my house and I was witness to his paying Vine £17 for a horse he bought of her.

Sunday, 16th August 1772:   Bought of Coobah, alias Jenny Young, her heifer (Dianah cow's calf) for £5, which I paid her, before Phibbah.

Sunday, 6th September 1772:   Sent Mrs Cope some asparagus, by John, who rode to Paradise to see Jenny Young, and Franke, who are said to be both sick.'

Through all these events Thistlewood had not in any way neglected his gardens and provision grounds. There was a constant planting of seeds, seedlings, suckers, slips and young trees, often received from neighbours, regularly from England, and occasionally from North America.

'Wednesday, 9th May 1770:   Sent Mr Hayward some Indian Kale roots; he sent me some seeds, vizt. carrot, radish, turnip and parsley.

Thursday, 17th May 1770:   Sowed a bed of Battersea asparagus seeds .... This day flowered an English pink (of a beautiful red) in my garden, which is the first I have seen, or heard of, to have flowered in the island. The plant is flourishing and will have many flowers.'[4]

And, like all other gardeners, he knew the perils of floods, droughts, and insects.

'Tuesday, 17th July 1770: Never knew so many caterpillars. Cabbage, savoys, broccoli, &c. &c., turnips, peas, cucumbers pumpkins, &c. &c., all eat to pieces by them; even the grass and bushes in the pasture full of them.'

In September he had listed the things 'In my garden, September 1770, growing ...' The list included about 30 varieties of trees, flowering and timber; about 25 kinds of ornamental shrubs and flowering plants; 35 sorts of fruit trees; about 20 different herbs and spices and 20 varieties of vegetables and legumes. Of tubers he had several, including yams and potatoes, and he was experimenting with cereals, rice for himself and his slaves, and barbery for his horses.

'Monday, 1st April 1771: Cut my lucern, which is now in flower. Also cut my Barbery wheat which is now above 2 feet high, and was cut 5 or 6 weeks ago, for horse meat.'

Of the trees and seeds from England, the majority had failed. In the 3 years 1768–1770 he had imported over 200 different kinds, of which only about 20 were still growing in September 1770.

His produce was in demand on special occasions.

'Sunday, 29th March 1772: As the Governor [Sir William Trelawny, Bart] dines at Mr Cope's today, I sent them, by Bess, a teal, a whistling duck & 2 Spanish snipes, 10 large broccoli, about 3 quarts of English peas in the pods, and a large calabash full of asparagus; also 4 ripe figs, 3 sweet limes, and flowers.'

Then, on the 31st, he sent flowers to Mr Weech's house where the Governor and his party had stopped; and, on 5th April, as His Excellency dined with Mr Herring, Thistlewood was again the supplier of '12 heads of fine broccoli, English peas, asparagus, and flowers aplenty'.

'Saturday, 11th April 1772: Mr Weech says the Governor and his Lady several times expressed a great desire to come and see my garden, but were prevented by Mr Haughton's representing the road to be so very rocky and bad.'

Early in March, Thistlewood had supplied eight varieties of local seeds to be delivered to a Dr Lowther in England. They included Poinciana, Barbadoes Pride, Ringworm Bush, and Spanish carnation, with references to literary notices of them, for instance 'The Ringworm Bush, Vide *Brown's History of Jamaica*, p.224 ...', for some of the others, 'See Miller's *Gardener's Dictionary*, article Poinciana; & Grainger's *Sugar Cane*, p.36, notes'.

'Thursday, 19th March 1772: This is the day of choosing church-wardens and Vestrymen at Sav la Mar; but I did not go as it is all a farce, for at all Vestrys the Justices carry all as they please owing to their numbers.'

Thistlewood was not yet himself a magistrate, but he served as a juror, and he had complaint there too. In January, on the Grand Jury, they had, for dinner, consumed:

'... punch, cherry brandy, mixt white wine in great plenty, mutton chops, &c. &c. in a very extravagant manner. Came to 26 bitts each.'

And, when he paid John Collom, the foreman, he re-emphasised (in his diary if nowhere else) his disapproval of such 'a vile and shameful custom'.

'Wednesday, 15th April 1772: In the evening called at Mr Weech's, supped there. Miss Cook played us many tunes on the harpsichord and sang also. Capt. Richardson & Miss Polly Cope there. Stayed till past 10 o'clock, then went home.
Sunday, 5th May 1772: Moll Stout (Mulatto Davie's sister) and Lucy, kept by Mr Neil, the wheelwright, come to see Phibbah.'

In mid-May, he paid his taxes. Parish tax on slaves at 3s 9d each, and on stock at 1s 8d each cost him £5 11s 8d. Poll tax, at 2s per slave and 6d per head of stock, cost him £2 14s 6d more.

'Such enormous taxes were, I believe, never known in Jamaica before. Mr Thos. Tomlinson [the Collector] says his commissions, he expects, will be £500 this year.
Sunday, 17th May 1772: Phibbah sold her filly (Phillis mare's) to long Pond Melia for £5 13s 9d cash, and delivered her.'

In August, Mulatto John was in trouble. He had been given money to pay Mr Hughes for a quarter-year's schooling, and change was expected back. He brought home a note from Mr Hughes and 1 ½ pistoles instead of the 2 which his father expected. Thistlewood wrote to Mr Hughes and sent back the money.

'Friday, 21st August 1772: In the evening, Mr Hughes came home with John, and protests he sent a pistole and 2 half ditto by John, who altho' he stiffly denied to me, now confessed that he opened the paper on the road, against Mr Stone's, and dropped a half pistole. But, as he is given to lying, what confidence can be put in what he says? His mother promotes his ruin by excessive indulgence and humouring him beyond all bounds. Received the pistole & half of Mr Hughes and I won't sit down content, with the loss of the half pistole. So ends the affair.

Monday, 7th September 1772: Had some words with Phib this morning about Jimmy's behaviour yesterday when sent on an errand, and she bringing the handkerchief for him to screen him.'

In December, Mr Say, who had been ill, died at Old Hope and was buried in Mr William's burial ground. 'He was born in 1729, so was about 43 ½ yrs old.' He had named Thistlewood as one of the executors of his will, and this was to become enormously burdensome to Thistlewood. Mr Say's business affairs had been exceedingly complicated. On Say's death, Martin Williams offered Thistlewood the Overseership of Old Hope. Not surprisingly, the offer was refused. Thomas Thistlewood was now gentleman Pen-proprietor and horticulturist of note.

'Friday, 1st January 1773: a.m. I shot an alligator in Coromante Pond ... Mr Richard Crutcher, and John Ricketts, Esqr. of Ridgeland present. Mr Ricketts gave me an advertisement of Trees, &c. sold by Wm. Prince, near New York.
Saturday, 2nd January 1773: Phibbah made me a present of £10 18s 1½d, all in silver; money she has earned by sewing, baking cassava, musk melons & water melons out of her ground, &c. &c.'

On 3rd February, he visited Morelands Estate, and:

'... drank chocolate with Mr George Williams. Saw his Curacao birds, Mountain Witches, Bantam Fowls, &c. &c. Monkey, Fox, Squirrel, Racoon, Rabbits & Guinea Pigs, &c. &c. (Jimmy with me).'

In late April the annual clothing supplies arrived and Phibbah got her 'check, linen, handkerchiefs, needles, hat, cloak, &c.', and John, 'his hat, shoes, stocking, &c.' In May, John was encouraged in kite-making by the gift of a ball of twine for that purpose; and mid-month:

'John's quarter being up at school, he fetched his books &c. home. Paid Mr Hughes £5, full to this date, and had his receipt. Intend keeping John now at home to learn him the mensuration of superficies & solids, &c. &c.'

And, it would seem, John was not an entirely wayward student for in November he was given 'my prospect glass, which I have had ever since I was a boy . . . . Magnifies 4 times.'

'Thursday, 9th September 1773:   About 8 a.m. John Merrick Williams Esqr. and Mr Ferris come to see Mr Say's houses & pen, which I showed them, and asked £1,200 for them.'

They did not buy. Later in the same month Say's slaves were given a day off 'to clean themselves' then, next day, Tuesday 28th, they were taken to Savanna la Mar and sold. Thirty in number, they fetched £2,216. Thistlewood bought 2: Strap for £77 and Fanny for £85. The Pen remained unsold until November when it was purchased by Mr James White for £1,500 payable in three instalments.

'Friday, 17th September 1773: Received a letter from Wm. Henry Ricketts, Esqr. with 2 mango stones, covered with wax, and 12 Bengal peach stones. Received them by Mr John Hartnole's boy.

Monday, 20th September 1773:   Planted in new garden, eleven Bengal peach stones, and 2 mango stones. Note: one of the mango stones is about 4 inches long, 2 broad, and ⁸/₁₀ thick. Both furrowed length-ways. Enclosed in wax from 2 to 3 tenths thick, and this wrapped up in a waxed cloth. Seemed pretty fresh.⁵

Monday, 25th October 1773:   Received a letter from Mr Pommells with the loan of *The Natural History of Barbadoes*, in Ten Books, by the Revd Mr Griffith Hughes, Rector of St Lucy's Parish in the said Island, and FRS Lond. 1750. With a map of the Island. Figures of Plants, &c.

Tuesday, 16th November 1773: Heard today . . . that Dr Drummond has bought Mulatto Tommy Drummond from John Fitzgerald, at a vast price, & given him Free.

Friday, 26th November 1773:   Vine at my house in the evening. When she went home had good sport by pulling a line with a cloth tied to it, she is so exceeding timorous.'

On the Pen, he was involved in developing one of his more recent enterprises. Mulatto Davie had been hired for some weeks to carry out general repairs, and also to build a bee's house.

The year 1774 opened sadly for Egypt Primus who, on January 12th, lost his second wife. He had had more than one. Egypt Betty 'one of Primus's wives' had died in August 1772. Now it was Egypt Dido, once a great favourite of Mr Thistlewood. There were other notable deaths during the year. In June, Hugh Gunning, who had been Overseer at Long Pond Estate 'and the best Overseer I knew'; and, on the last day of the month, 'Hear old Mr Benjamin Banton [one of his neighbours at the Vineyard Pen] of St Elizabeth is dead. In August, on Saturday 6th, another past favourite, Egypt Susanah, died at Egypt of the smallpox, which was then epidemic; during July Mr White, recently come to live on his newly purchased Pen, had lost five slaves by it in three days. And in October, the body of one of the planter class who had died in England, Mr Williams Lewis, grandfather of Matthew Gregory (Monk) Lewis, 'is arrived at Sav la Mar, brought by Capt. Duthie, to be buried at Cornwall', at his request to be put beside his wife Jane Lewis in the family mausoleum on Cornwall Estate.

'Saturday, 22nd January 1774: Took a Boxing Stick,[6] today, from Paradise Sam. It is made of heavy hard wood, is about one inch square, & 20 7/10 inches long, rather tapering towards the end held in the hand, and rounded for better holding in the hand for near 10 inches, with a hole for string 3 8/10 inches from the end. This is a very unlawful weapon for Negroes to be permitted to have.'

On Sunday 23rd, as on most Sundays, the slaves went visiting. Paradise Franke visited Phibbah, as did Egypt Maria. The latter had come on business too. On more than one occasion Thistlewood, and presumably Phibbah also, advanced capital or credit to enable individual slaves to acquire goods for trade.

'Gave Egypt Maria an order, or letter, to Mr Abraham Tavarez, Snr to let her have what she wanted, as far as 40 shillings. (She took up £2 1s 3d.).'

Phibbah had recently been finding that weakening eyesight was hindering her performance with needles and thread. At the beginning of February, Thistlewood provided her with 'a pair of spectacles, as her eyes begin to be so bad, she cannot sew without them except very coarse indeed'.

Although Mr and Mrs White had moved into the neighbouring Pen, Vine was still there, and was still, it seems, in pursuit of companionship.

'Monday, 9th May 1774: Dugald Ferguson came a-courting this afternoon to Vine!
Monday, 23rd May 1774: Mr Dugald Ferguson, Vine's sweetheart, slept with her last night, and now at 8 o'clock in the morning is not yet up. He gave her a piece of base metal, which he called a pistole, that is worth nothing. The woman's a fool!

Thursday, 23rd June 1774: This morning Vine left her house in Mr White's land for good, being partly drove away, to make room for their mother, the widow Calom, who is disordered in her senses. Vine is gone to Cabaritta Estate, I believe'.

And there were others who were, from other causes, pushed to move. John Cope had long been in debt. Egypt Estate was heavily mortgaged and creditors were pressing. On 20th May 1774, Mr and Mrs Cope sold Paradise Estate (1,650 acres) with all its works, houses, Negroes (except 75 to be retained by them), cattle, &c., to Mr John Sommerville & Mr John Cunningham, as equal partners, for £10,500. Mr Chambers was the lawyer involved, and his son and Thistlewood were witnesses to the Copes's signatures. The Copes were to move later in the year to Egypt; but, meanwhile, the old Egypt great house was being torn down and re-built.

And at Salt River, also once the property, and the home, of William Dorrill, at the same time, the Deputy Marshall's men were:

'... making a levy upon some of the Salt River stock, the Negroes rescued them before they could get out of the pasture; upon which a scuffle ensued in which several were wounded on both sides, and one of the Salt River women shot, who is since dead. Affidavits making by Mr Broadie, and by Gilbert Senior, Senior's Overseer, so will be a deal to do about it.'

Five days after the sale of Paradise, John Cope's son, 'Master Haughton Cope' died. His body was taken to Egypt for burial. Phibbah, Damsel, Jenny Young, and Egypt Quasheba had sat up with the body on the night of 26th May. And sometime during 1774, a much older acquaintance, 'Mr Vassall's Mulatto Dick' formerly of Vineyard also died.

Phibbah herself was soon to go down again with one of her now fairly frequent illnesses. On 6th June she was 'sick at her stomach'; little Nelly, House Franke's child, apparently spending time with Phibbah, was also ill; and both Phibbah and Thistlewood had been having teeth pulled. Nonetheless, the work, and the gossip, and all the rest went on as usual.·

'Wednesday, 7th 1774: Planted in the garden, Rose-apple seeds [brought for him from Kingston by Mr Peter Richardson] and Abbay, or Macca-fat nuts [sent him by Mr Duncan].
Tuesday, 14th June 1774: Hear Mr Lopez's Mulatto sweetheart, in Mr Lopez's absence at the Estate, had Cumberland, Creek Venus's son, catched in her room with her in the night, &c. and that she has chains put on her neck & sent into the field.

Thursday, 16th June 1774:   Several vessels gone out this morning. Mr Thos. Audley gone off in Capt. Blake; George Robert Goodin, Esqr., William Woolery, Esqr., and his wife, John Ricketts of Ridgeland, &c. in Capt. Venhorne to N. America, &c. &c.

Wednesday, 22nd June 1774:   Wrote to John Cope, Esqr. by John, returned *Robinson Crusoe*, 2 Vols. and sent him a paper of distances on Cabaritta river . . . . Returned Dr Panton's Milne's *Botany*, also gave him some borage, celery, curled parsley & cardoon seeds.

Saturday, 20th August 1774:   The head of Gold, the Rebel, carried to Leeward this evening, to be put up as a terror. Warren is to be transported.

A White man hanged at Savanna la Mar also today, for killing a sailor at Lucea. It seems he made many bitter speeches against the Scotch, not all agreeable to them, being pretty near the truth.'

There was no further explanation of the activities or the apprehension of Gold, or of Warren. Nor had there been any note of recent slave uprisings. Even the Maroons were scarcely mentioned, once only in 1773 when one of them captured Egypt Dover in the Mountains and brought him home, and in mid-April, 1774, when Thistlewood barely noted 'A strange report of the Wild Negroes impudence and refactoriness'.

'Saturday, 13th August 1774:   Paid Mr Thos. Tomlinson, Collecting Constable 12*s* for Deficiency Tax, to 28 June last.'[7]

In mid-August, John Hartnole suffered the barbs of misfortune. At the 'earnest request' of Mr Parker, Little Mimber was taken away from him and sent back to Egypt to wash and sew. On that estate, work on the great house was in progress. The Copes still lived at Paradise, but John Cope spent days at Egypt seeing to the work and often spent the night at Thistlewood's house in the Blue room', and, it seems, alone. For a change, Thistlewood was in his debt. He owed Cope for rum, sugar, and two years of Phibbah's hire, totalling £54 4*s* 0*d*. from which he would deduct £25 for two steers he had sold to Cope.

'Monday, 19th September 1774:   Received a note from Mr Abraham Tavares, Snr by a Jew on foot, begging a few sprigs of myrtle to adorn their Tabernacle, but I had none. Received a note from Mr Moses Nunes, Jnr begging some myrtle. Sent a large bunch of flowers.'

On 16th October Jenny Young 'made a match' with Mr Limburner from Paradise. On the 17th Thistlewood visited the Copes at Paradise, then on to Mr Haughton's where he found Mr Cope 'trimming vines' in the garden, then he and Cope went on to Mr Blake's where again they walked in the garden. But for Thistlewood, the most memorable events of the end of 1774 came perhaps on the evening of 8th November. On that day, he visited Mr Pommells at his property, The Wilderness.

'Walked in his indigo plantation, &c. very pretty, about 4 acres very fine, and 4 acres more ready to plant as soon as he receives the seed from N. America. He has already made about 150 lbs weight, very good indeed.'

And then, on his return to Breadnut Island Pen, he found Mrs Cope & Miss Polly Cope there. Mr Cope had gone to Kingston on Assembly business, and they had been at Egypt to see the work going on. They stayed the night, sleeping in the Blue Room, with 'a candle burning all night in the hall'. They left next day, with gifts of sweet times, flowers, and forbidden fruit.[8]

'Wednesday, 18th January 1775:   Went to Dr King's to see Mr Matthew Bowen and he gave me a great variety of flower seeds, sent him from N. America by Mr Goodin. And Dr King lent me *The History of the Reign of the Emperor Charles 5th*, Vol. 1st, 2nd Ed. Lond. 1772.'

A week before he had borrowed from Mr Hayward 'a book called *The Fable of the Bees, or Private Vice, Public Benefits, with an Essay on Charity and Charity Schools*, &c. 9th Ed. Edinburgh 1754. 374 pages. Wrote by Bernard de Mandeville'.

'Sunday, 12th February 1775:   For 235 corn, 7 bitts. John bought them in the road.
Saturday, 18th February 1775:   Began to learn John to shoot, this day, & he shot 2 plover the first shot.'

On 10th January John Cope had been sworn in as Custos of Westmoreland[9] and now, at the end of February, he was entertaining the new Governor, Sir Basil Keith. Again, the supplies came from Thistlewood's Pen: plovers, a mess of cuckold increase peas, 14 carrots, 12 cucumbers, a large mess of broccoli, asparagus, 6 sweet limes, a water-melon, ripe prickly-pear fruit, and plenty of flowers.

'Wednesday, 15th March 1775:   John Cope, Richard Vassall, William Blake, Esqr. dined with me, and stayed till about 9 in the evening. Mr Cope stayed all night. Had mutton broth, roast mutton & broccoli, carrots & asparagus, stewed mudfish, roast goose and paw-paw, apple sauce, stewed giblets, some fine lettuce which Mr Vassall brought me, crabs, cheese, musk melon, &c. Punch, porter, ale, cyder, madeira wine & brandy, &c.'

Next day, he (and perhaps others too) was 'very unwell, with drinking too much wine yesterday'. But he had entertained some of the elite plantocracy. John Cope we know, short of money, shorter of land than he used to be, but, nonetheless, the Custos; the Blakes, whose family owned over 4,500 acres in Westmoreland, St Elizabeth, and St Ann; and Vassall, whose family owned land in Westmoreland, St James and St Elizabeth (even though the Vineyard had been sold) totalling about 6,500 acres. And five weeks later the Copes returned the invitation. On Tuesday, 21st March, he dined at Paradise in the company of Mr and Mrs Cope and their daughters Hannah and Polly, Judge Blake, Capt. Blake, Nicholas Blake, Mrs Blake and her sons, Mr and Mrs Vassall and their daughters, Capt. Towers, and after dinner the company was joined by Mr and Mrs Beckford (who had landed in state from the *Earl of Effingham*, Capt. Jesse Carling, two months before), and young Mr Bellamy. After tea, Thistlewood attended by Jimmy, rode home.

'Jimmy very drunk. I must enquire how he comes at the liquor &c.'

On Monday, 1st May 1775, Mulatto John, now 15 years old, born 29th April 1760, was apprenticed to Mr William Hornby, a carpenter. The indenture was for 6 years to begin that day, and Thistlewood paid down £8 in cash. Next morning, accompanied by Jimmy, who carried his bed and brought back his horse, John went to live at Hornby's to come home only as his master allowed.

In June, Thistlewood began experimenting with indigo, some of which he grew in his gardens. Mr Pommells was highly complimentary. He said that Thistlewood's indigo was '. . . the best he has ever seen made in the Island, and is equal to the Guatemala indigo'. In July, he, Cope, and William Henry Ricketts went back to Pommell's where they all viewed:

'. . . the house, indigo cistern, &c. Mr Sharpe of 3 Mile River was with us also . . . Rode into the indigo piece, &c. about 10 acres now planted &c. &c.'

At the end of April, the Cope's house Negroes, Mirtilla, Sukey, Big Nelly, Peggy, Nancy, and Jenny Young had been transferred from Paradise to Egypt. A month later, Mr Parker left the Egypt overseership. He was succeeded by James Limburner, which, in

Thistlewood's opinion, was a sure sign that 'Mr Cope resolved to ruin himself'. Very soon after, in late May and early June, Phibbah endured another of her sudden bouts of severe illness. On 30th May she, and Little Mulatto Bessie (daughter of Salt River Cooper Davis and his woman Deborah) who had come to stay with her, were both ill and Thistlewood had them bled.

> 'Thursday, 1st June 1775:   At 1 p.m. wrote to Mrs Cope, by Jimmy, for Jenny Young, who came directly, & stayed all night. In the evening Mr Limburner rode over & stayed awhile, & many of Egypt Negroes as Quasheba, Little Mimber, Sibbe, Julina, Little Nelly, &c. &c, came to see Phibbah.'

After medication, and with her daughter's care, Phibbah gradually recovered. Jenny Young went back to Egypt on Friday 2nd, and, on Tuesday 6th, 'At night, *Cum* Phib'.

> 'Wednesday, 7th June 1775:   a.m. Rode to Savanna la Mar, returned to dinner. Great expectation of news from North America, however very little in the paper.'

On 1st July Thistlewood again listed the plants growing in his gardens and provision grounds. There were over 300 items. But, it seems, the mangoes and the Bengal peaches had not grown. Many were plants of little use, for he named everything from uncultivated fungi in the fields 'John Joes, a Species of Mushroom so called', through to recently imported plants 'Rose-apple, lately introduced from East India'; flowers, trees, and vegetables of which he had imported the seeds, such as 'Virginian Stock' and 'Blue Lupines' from North America, and 'Asparagus', 'Purple and White broccoli', and 'Ash', 'Elm' and four varieties of 'Apples' from England.

Of particular interest is his list of food crops in the Negro provision grounds. They were: 'plantains (horse & maiden), bananas, maize or Indian corn, guinea corn, scratch toyer, coco roots, cassava bitter & sweet, pindas,[10] and sugar cane, &c. &c.' About 60 of his listed items had been sent by Henry Hewitt of Brompton, about 25 had been obtained from various sources in North America, and the rest were from local gardens, fields, and waysides. It was an impressive collection. Mr Thistlewood's half of the almost ruinate Paradise Pen which he and Mr Say had jointly acquired was now a show-piece.

Not so next door. In June, Mr White had sold his Pen to Mr Hugh Wilson, a surveyor, who moved in in August.

> 'Monday, 8th August 1775:   Mrs Wilson and 2 Mulatto women at his house. Slept there tonight, and I believe are come for good. This it seems, is his wedding night with Mr J. Townshend's Mulatto daughter, Sally.'

The other Mulatto woman was Sally's sister, Nancy Browne, and they soon became frequent visitors to Thistlewood's house where they gossiped with Phibbah and, from time to time, were entertained by Thistlewood himself who showed them his prints and put on the magic lantern show.

In mid-August Thistlewood rode to Egypt and had tea with Mrs Cope and her daughters, now in residence, and Miss Polly Clarke from the Valley Tavern.

'Mrs Cope says Messrs Haughton, Blake & Herring, have received letters from Town intimating that this island will shortly be invaded by the Spaniards.

Thursday, 31st August 1775: In the morning rode over to Egypt. Returned Mr Cope the evidence, &c. lent me [on the Petition presented by the West India Planters & Merchants to the Honble House of Commons], and lent him *The Present State of Great Britain & her North America Colonies* .... Rode with him to Top-hill, &c. He has just had all the ginep trees[11] cut down! Surprising notions he has. I returned home to dinner.

Saturday, 23rd September 1775: Mr Wilson having just got home from town this afternoon, come over and drank tea with us. Received my watch from him, cleaned, &c. by Mr John Urquhart watchmaker in Kingston, for which I paid £1. Mr Wilson has patented a piece of land in my name without acquainting me of it till now! Not the thing.

Sunday, 24th September 1775: Sent Mr Wilson a cuba teal & a bunch of asparagus.

Thursday, 28th September 1775: It seems Miss Sally says Mr W. ... has only (to use her own words) pleasured her 3 times since he had her, & they came August 7th.'

At the end of October Thistlewood sent his horse for John who was very ill at Mr Hornby's. Medicated, bled, and looked after by Phibbah, he remained at home until 20th November when he was well enough to go back 'to his master's to go to work. Gave him 2 bitts.'

'Friday, 20th October 1775: The Custos offered to day [he had dined with the Copes] to get me a Commission to be a Justice of the Peace, if I would act.

Saturday, 2nd December 1775: Mr Cope lent me (the first Vol.) of *The History of Jamaica* in 3 Vol. 4to. Illustrated with cuts. Lond. 1774. (Long's). These are Mr George Murray's.

Sunday, 17th December 1775: Received a letter from Mr Wardlow, acquainting me that the Governor has been pleased to appoint me one of His Majesty's Justices of the Peace for the Parish of Westmoreland. Dated 15th Inst.

Sunday, 31st December 1775:   About 11 p.m. Mr Wilson come down and called me, he hearing several guns fired towards Savanna la Mar suspected it to be an alarm. I got up & went to him, but take it only to be people drinking out the old year.'

And so it was, for January passed without much comment on war or rebellion.

'Sunday, 7th January 1776:   . . . met one of Nisbet's Negroes with 2 mahogany chairs, which bought of him at 4 bitts each, & ordered him to carry them to my house & wait till the evening that I should be back. But he told Phibbah I had bought them of him at 5 bitts apiece, and had ordered him to apply to her for the money, which she was weak enough to believe, then he immediately went away.

Saturday, 27th January 1776:   p.m. *Cum* Little Mulatto Bessie Hungerford, Cooper Davy's, *Sup.* Bench, under shed, in New Garden. *Sed non bene.*'

Undeterred by this dissatisfaction, he twice again took Bessie to the bench; but never to his pleasure.

On 18th February, he dined at Egypt where Mr Cope showed him letters from the governor who had been informed that a great force of 'a squadron of ships of the line' was assembled at Hispaniola. A meeting of the gentlemen of the Parish was to be called 'to consult what to do in case of an invasion'. The Parish Vestry had already had a meeting on that subject.

On 27th February, the *St Peter*, Capt. Towers, arrived. One of those arrived in her was Egypt Little Nelly 'just come from England'. Thistlewood was expecting the *Henry*, with his usual supplies of clothes, and clothing. She came in on March 1st.

Throughout March Jenny Young was ill. She was pregnant, and Mr Limburner was discussing plans and conditions.

'Monday, 8th April 1776:   Mr Limburner told me of their (his Jenny Young's, Franke's and Phib's) intention to giving Negroes for Nancy's freedom, & the child Jenny Young is now big of, if a Mulatto, &c.'

But, on 16th April, Jenny Young miscarried.

In mid-April, Egypt watchman Harry died and was there buried. On 17th May, Dr Richard Panton, aged 36, died at Mrs Bennett's in the Savanna. Buried:

'. . . in Church yard (the new one), 70 or 80 white people at his burial . . . [including Thistlewood]

I am very sorry for the loss of Dr Panton, as he was a very sensible man, of a surprising quick apprehension, a good scholar, and knew his business well. Besides a friendship between us, as having something of the same turn for botany, &c. &c.'

Indeed, he had made a copy for Dr Panton of his 'diary of the weather' in 3 books; and this was shortly returned to him from the doctor's effects. The original version and several other papers were put in the hands of Capt. Richardson of the *Henry* to be delivered to Edward Long, Esqr.,[12] London. The parcel, which Mr Long must have received with mixed feelings of interest and impatience, contained:

'A Journal of the weather from the beginning of 1770 to the 7th [June 1776] inclusive, & quantity of rain fallen, heights of the thermometer, &c. also a general account of rain fallen since the beginning of 1761, &c. A Table of carats fixed & specific gravity of gold, of alcohol & water, &c. Elegy on Dr Robinson's death, his man of consequence, conclusion of his epistle to Mr Long, &c. Also a catalogue of trees, &c. in my garden, with remarks. General remarks on the weather, &c. Bearing and position of London & Breadnut Island, their distances, differences of time, &c. &c. Also a letter of yesterday's date.
Wednesday, 17th April 1776: His Majesty's frigate *The Squirrel* . . . in at Sav la Mar & has seized a N. American ship.
Wednesday, 12th June 1776: Saw Capt. Van-Horn, who is lately come down from Town, having been took by *Lady Hewitt* scooner, going from the Cape in Hispaniola for Philadelphia, with 20 tons of gunpowder, 12 hundred stand of small arms, &c. &c. He walks about at liberty.
Thursday, 13th June 1776: A report that the N. Americans have took some of our vessels.
Friday, 14th June 1776: Dr King lent me, *The Rights of Great Britain asserted against the claims of America, being an Answer to the Declaration of the General Congress*, 7th Edition to which is now added a refutation of Dr Price's *State of the National Debt*. Lond, 1776.
Monday, 17th June 1776: This morning the ships (fleet) sailed, under the convoy of the Antelope man-of-war.
Mr Cope [who had been given a year's leave by the Governor] is gone off in the *St Peter*,[13] Capt. Towers; Mr & Mrs Witter & children, and Mr Foreman in Capt. Duthie; Dr Allwood, his son Bob, & Jackie Dobson, &c. in Capt. White: Mr Thos. Parkinson & Rob. Nicholls in Capt. Richardson; and Mr Wm

Pommells in the *Beckford*, Capt. Hayhurst. Mr Michael McLocklin is also gone in the same fleet.
Wednesday, 3rd July 1776:   It seems the North Americans have took the *Lady Juliana*, Capt. Stephenson; the *Reynolds*, Capt. Reesden; and the *Juno*, Capt. Marsam.
Friday, 5th July 1776:   [a note from Mr Hayward, and the loan of] *Observations on the Nature of Civil Liberty, the Principles of Government, and the Justice & Policy of the war with America*, to which is added an Appendix containing a State of the National Debt, &c. By Richard Price, DD, FRS Lond. 1776.
Sunday, 7th July 1776:   Great signs of an intended Rebellion of the Negroes in Hanover, Negril way, &c. A store at Lucea robbed of cutlasses (bills).'

On the 17th, Mr Wilson and other militia-men were ordered to muster immediately, and 'The Negro who brought the message said he heard of a French War and the Negroes rising at North Side.'

'Thursday, 18th July 1776:   Rode to Savanna la Mar to hear the news. It seems some disturbance had been on some estates at North Side, owing to a foolish indulgence of the Negroes. Returned to dinner. Killed a turkey cock. Mr Dobson & Mr Hartnole dined with me & stayed till evening.'

Nonetheless, he seems to have been apprehensive and jittery. That evening he set a body of troopers after a 'Negro well-mounted', who had turned into Egypt gateway apparently to avoid meeting the troopers. Thistlewood had questioned the man. He had no ticket, and he had ridden off leaving some of his belongings on the roadside. Thistlewood then shouted 'Gentlemen, that Negro's a rebel', and the troopers had set off in pursuit. They got his horse, but he had managed to escape. He was later identified as a slave from Mount Eagle estate.

There were other signs of nervousness. A New Hope distiller shot a 'Negro fellow . . . supposed innocent'; the overseer at Orange Grove had beaten 'the hothouse girl' to death. 'but the Jury brought it in a natural death'; and Mr Fisher of the Free School[14] had, under the influence of liquor, shot a white man while on guard duty at the Fort. For that, and other acts presumably, he was replaced as Master of the school by 'a Mr Dixon', who, said Thistlewood: 'bears an excellent character'. He had previously commented on Mr Fisher's fondness for the bottle, and his long delay in returning a borrowed book.

There was, however, more to it than alarming rumour. Ever since 1760 there had been occasional evidence of unrest among the slave population who now outnumbered the whites by about twelve to one. In 1765 there had been another planned rebellion in St Mary, again led by Coromantee slaves and again quickly localised and quelled by the whites. In October, 1766, Thistlewood and others had been sent out on hurriedly mustered expeditions against rebellious slaves in north-eastern Westmoreland. Three years later slaves plotted to burn the city of Kingston and take control. Now, in 1776, revolt was again centred in the western parishes; and led this time not by Coromantees but by Creole slaves.

Early in July of that year a regiment of regular troops was despatched from Lucea, in Hanover, to reinforce the British forces engaged against the North American revolutionaries. The plan was to seize this opportunity to attack the weakened whites; but in mid-month, before it had been brought fully into action, it was discovered. Again, regular troops and neighbouring militia were sent into Hanover to assist the local forces, but there was doubt of the support of the Maroons and they were indeed suspected of being involved with the rebel leaders.

By late July details of the uprising were known to the now much alarmed Westmoreland planters and Thistlewood had begun to record events.

On Monday 22nd, at the New Hope Estate mill house, where a guard was stationed, a trooper brought an account:

'... of about 70 Negroes being already took up in Hanover, and many more to be took up; that many already executed & many more going to be. That the head Negro Women about Lucea, even those kept by white men, were concerned; the Mulattoes on Haughton Tower Estate, deeply concerned. That there is a report of half the Negro men on Anchovy-bottom Estate, Martin Williams's in St James, being gone in the woods, &c. That a Negro named Prince, belonging to Peter Priest, was their King, or head man. That Mr Worrall first discovered oil in his pistols; that they were first to have begun last new moon, on Tuesday (some say Wednesday) night on the Spring Estate & Richmond Estate (James & Chambers) then collected near Lucea, burnt it down killed all white people, seized the arms, ammunition, &c, then proceeded & been joined by the estates as they went along, &c. The guns in Glasgow piazza rammed full of dirt &c. Billy Brown greatly blamed for stifling intelligence he received some time ago, to save some valuable Negroes of Mr Carr's, whereas if some examples had then been made, might have prevented this, &c.

Saturday, 27th July 1776:   This evening Mr Swinny received an express from His Excellency, laying an embargo on the shipping till further orders.'

On Tuesday, 30th July, martial law was declared in Savanna la Mar. Early August brought 'Strong suspicions of the French in Hispaniola', a 'report of two N. American privateurs cruising off the West end', and:

'It is strongly reported the Maroon Negroes are at the bottom of the Negro conspiracy, &c.

Thursday, 8th August 1776:   Many young men at Savanna la Mar have got a sort of uniform dress, and call themselves the Light Infantry. Mr Thos. Barker, it is said, is to be their Captain, Charles Pain, Ensign.

Wednesday, 11th September 1776:   Read in the Montego Bay paper, the North American declaration of themselves an Independent people, &c.

Monday, 17th November 1776:   A report of the Negroes at Montego Bay attempting to poison all the butcher's meat, &c.

Monday, 9th December 1776:   [At the Copes, they received news from Kingston] . . . an account of Captains Hore, Harvey, McDaniel and McCoy, from this port, Capt. James Foot, and many others of the August fleet being took by the N. Americans.'

Amidst all these concerns, however, other interests had not been entirely neglected. There had been exchanges of garden produce, seeds, and trees, with others in the parish; and in September he had noted a special acquisition:

'Received a letter from Mr Charles Graham, dated September 8th 1776 . . . with a box containing 5 double flowering myrtles.'

He had planted them next day, the 12th. Then, later:

'Sunday, 22nd September 1776:   The honeysuckle (trumpet), or woodbine, in my garden is now in flower, & is perhaps the first & only one ever in this island yet.'

And, war news apart, he had been reading.

'Dr Bell lent me *Emilius; or a Treatise of Education*, translated from the French of J.J. Rousseau., citizen of Geneva. 3 Vols. Edinburgh 1773.'

On the domestic front, Jenny Young had visited with her new husband, 'Jimmy Stewart, a Mulatto from the New Hope Estate'; and across the Cabaritta: 'A report Mr Cope has sold Egypt to Mr Peter Holmes', to whom the estate was mortgaged. Jenny Young's previous husband, Mr Limburner, had died at Egypt in late June. On 1st November, Egypt Titus went; and on 13th November, Thistlewood had news that Mr Pommells, who had gone to England in mid-June, had died there. This brought further business for Thistlewood who had accepted his power of Attorney.

Notes

1 Another form of 'play' intended to bestow protection on the house. Marina's 'House-warming' (as Thistlewood then described it) on Vineyard would have been of this sort.

2 Following the astronomical observations of Tycho Brahe (1546−1601) and others, Pope Gregory III in 1582 sponsored a reform of the calendar. To compensate for an over-accumulation of days measured when the calendar year had been reckoned a few minutes longer than the real year, ten days were dropped from the calendar. To prevent further such accumulations, every fourth year would be a leap year, except the century years, unless the century year was divisible by 400. Thus, whereas 1760, 1764, for example, would be leap years, 1800 would not, nor would 1900, but 2000, divisible by 400 would. The 'Gregorian Calendar' was not, however introduced in Protestant Britain until 1752. Thus Thistlewood's calculation.

3 Parker had succeeded Hartnole as Overseer on Egypt.

4 As we have seen, Thistlewood occasionally claimed to be the first to have brought a plant into flowering in Jamaica. The best known Jamaican gardener of the later eighteenth century was undoubtedly 'Hinton East. Esqr. in the Mountains of Liguanea', at Gordon Town. A catalogue of the plants in his garden lists the plants, giving the botanical name, the popular name, and place of origin and the name of the individual responsible for the first importation (or planting) or non-indigenous species. Mr Thistlewood's name does not appear; but he [and probably others, as Mr Ricketts] was certainly entitled to mention for there is clear evidence that he was up-to-date with, and in some instances ahead of, the listed innovators. Let us take two important examples: a very popular fruit, the mango; and what became, after emancipation, a very popular 'food', the breadfruit. According to Arthur Broughton, the compiler in 1794 of the Hortus Eastensis catalogue, the breadfruit first arrived in Jamaica in February, 1793, on *H.M.S. Providence* from Tahiti [Captain Bligh of earlier *Bounty* fame]. The plant was not listed among those in Mr East's

botanical garden. (There is however, an earlier reference suggesting that it was grown in Jamaica before 1790 (Cassidy [1971] p.342.) The 'mango tree' and the 'mangostein' according to Broughton were in the East garden and had been brought to Jamaica by Lord Rodney in 1782. (Rodney had captured a French vessel bringing mango seedlings from Mauritius to the French West Indies and had sent them to Jamaica). But Thistlewood records earlier plantings of both.

5 Here we have Thistlewood planting mango 'seeds' (not seedlings) in 1773. They did not grow, it is true; but in January 1786, on Friday 6th, he planted a mango seedling and a breadfruit sucker, and seven years before in 1779 almost to the day he had gone to see a young mango tree 'now about 2 ½ feet high' on Greenwich (Friendship) Estate. Even earlier, on Thursday, 5 October 1769, he had noted:

'Hear Drs Drummond and Ruecastle have purchased [Dr] Frazier's place at Negril; that Mr John Pulley Edwards has rented Basin-Spring [Beeston Spring]; and that Montague James, Esqr. is introducing the mango into this island.'

He gives no further mention of Mr James; but perhaps it was from this earlier introduction that he received his mango seeds in 1773. If so, there were bearing trees in Jamaica before that date.

6 Used in stick fighting. See Cassidy (1971) p.214 and Cassidy and Le Page (1980) p.424, 'stick licking'.

7 Landed proprietors were, by the Deficiency Laws required to employ one white person for every 30 slaves in their possession, or pay a tax. Thistlewood paid the tax.

8 A citrus fruit, so-called because of marks on the skin 'Supposed to be Eve's finger marks as she plucked the fruit'. (Cassidy, 1971, p.354.)

9 Succeeding James Barclay.

10 Ground-nuts, peanuts.

11 Bearing bunches of green, grape-shaped, brittle-skinned fruit, round-seeded with a sweet, pulpy overlay. Of no commercial value then, and not cultivated even today, but much favoured.

12 Edward Long, another wealthy Jamaica proprietor of the mid-eighteenth century, whose *History of Jamaica* had been read by Thistlewood. Thistlewood's 'Weather Books' are now with the Edward Long Mss in the British Museum.

13 Still suffering cash-flow problems, he was off to see whether he could be put on the 'half-pay list' for retired servicemen, and/or, raise money by other means.

14 Manning's Free School in the Savanna was one of five such in the island. Manning's, established in 1730, was named after its founder who provided money for the education of poor whites. Mulatto John, as we know did not go there.

CHAPTER 10   Acts of Men and of God, 1777–1780

Introduction

Thistlewood's prosperity continued into these years but, soon, misfortune was to strike first his family, and then his farm. Mulatto John, unhappily apprenticed, was apparently happily enrolled as a militia man in the Free Black Company, and was briefly involved in military exercises. Following in his father's style he became, with tragic result, involved with a slave woman on the Old Hope Estate.

As the American War progressed people in Jamaica, as in the other British Caribbean colonies increasingly suffered shortages of food and other essential supplies. The war, as we would expect, interfered with the usual arrivals and departures of vessels from Britain. More importantly, it brought to a close the very important trade with the English colonies on the North American mainland. Under the laws governing British colonial trade and commerce, British colonies were permitted to trade only within the imperial territories and, most importantly, with Britain. American mainland colonists had built up a large commerce in the Caribbean by which the sugar-producing island colonies of Britain were supplied with essential commodities such as lumber (scarce in colonies in which land was cleared for sugar planting), fish (especially the salted cod), flour, and grains. It was, said Bryan Edwards,

> '... not a traffic calculated to answer the fantastic calls of vanity, or to administer gratification to luxury or vice; but to furnish food for the hungry [referring especially to the slaves] and to furnish materials (scarcely less important than food) for supplying the planters in two capital objects, their buildings, and packages for their [sugar and rum].'

When the war ended with the independence of the United States of America, the British Caribbean colonists were legally required to cease all trade with the Americans, now foreigners. The planters protested, and eventually a limited trade with the mainland was re-introduced in the 1790s.

In the meantime, however, Jamaica suffered the lashings of five hurricanes, in 1780, 1781, 1784, 1785 and 1786. That of 1780, as Thistlewood tells us, was the most devastating. He suffered loss, but he and his slaves were better off than most others in Westmoreland. Throughout the island, thousands (most of whom were slaves) were said to have died as a consequence of shortages of food resulting from both the cutting of the American trade and the destruction of provision grounds by the hurricanes.

On the 1st of January, 1777, as was his annual practice, Thistlewood took stock of his possessions. He had £212 16*s* 4 ½*d* in ready money and Messrs William Beckford and George Lesley, and Bluecastle Estate together owed him about £60 for slave-labour. His debts were few: £18 due to Mr Cope for Phibbah's hire to November, and small sums to Mr Dobson, Dr Panton's estate, and to Dr Drummond whose bill for over £17 presented in June was 'monstrous extravagant'.

He had lent books to Messrs Wilson and Hayward, and borrowed from Hayward and Robertson.

He owned 29 slaves, of whom 15 were, on 1st January, working on the King's road. In 1776 he had given out 252 tickets to those going off his property, mostly, it would seem, to his gangs going out to labour away from home.

Of livestock he listed three horses, 28 cattle of his own and two he was pasturing for others, 45 sheep, two hogs, 13 geese, four muscovy ducks, 13 turkeys, 19 dunghill fowls, two guinea fowls, two dogs, three cats, and six whistling ducks supposedly tame but always in the morass.

The month passed quietly enough. Mr Meyler, who had recently purchased the house and 3 acres of land which he occupied in the Savanna for £600, contracted to employ Thistlewood's slaves.

Thistlewood himself was uncomplaining of his health, save for a large persistent sore on his jaw where he had shaved the head of a boil; and was attentive to Phibbah. Mulatto John was still with Mr Hornby, but:

'Friday, 31st January 1777: This evening John come home & skulked behind the cookroom that I might not see him — which however I did. He then told me that he had come with Egypt Davy in his canoe, which proved false, as Davy came (accidentally) the instant, riding from the Bay. He then pretended that his master had given him tomorrow, to work for himself, that he might feed himself, &c. &c.
Saturday, 1st February: Wrote to Mr Wm. Hornby, by Phoebe, about John.'

For the time being, John submitted to the routine of his apprenticeship, but he seems to have looked forward to approved absences such as when he went off to muster with the militia. As we shall see, John perhaps had good reason to be dissatisfied in the service of William Hornby.

Of Phibbah there was little important mention in 1777. Early in May on an evening when Egypt Lewie was at the Pen Thistlewood noted 'suspect him & Ph.'; but no more was said. Then, at the end of June, Phibbah was ill of a fever which was briefly alarming.

Early in May the ship *Henry* had arrived with the usual boxes and packages for Mr Thistlewood, and Phibbah, John, and the house women Abba, Damsel and Bess all got their pieces of cloth, &c. It was a quiet year, but nonetheless full of interest.

'Sunday 16th February 1777: Received a letter from Wm. Mure, Esqr. of Saxham Estate in Hanover, with 3 plants of the Bamboo-cane, & a cutting of the Coral tree. Wrote to him & sent him 6 young cypresses, 6 sarsaparilla plants, & 2 malabar nuts, 6 cuttings of the African rose & 6 ditto of the Cyprian fig, some melongina, changeable rose & musk, ochroe seeds, also a Red bean of a different sort from his.
Planted the bamboo-cane & coral tree in the old garden.'

On Monday, 3rd March, Thistlewood received books and sundry papers bequeathed to him by the late Mr William Pommells.

'Sunday, 16th March 1777: Strap wants much to throw away Franke, now she is with child by him. He is impudent, & wanted to drink grave-dirt[1] today that he would not make it up with her. He keeps a girl at Egypt it seems.'

(Franke's child, a daughter, was born on 2nd June and died on 3rd June.)

'Friday, 2nd May 1777: In the evening flogged Lincoln, for disobedience in not fishing for me as I ordered him when the Negroes went to work at Meylersfield. Put him in the bilboes, and then flogged Dick for not bringing him to me but permitting to stay [with the others at Meylersfield] although I had told him that Lincoln was not to go. Also flogged Strap for going with grass to the Bay to sell without coming for a ticket, several times flinging his old hoe into the penguin fence bottom, & other impudent tricks.'

Next day was given to the Negroes, but Lincoln remained in the bilboes until Sunday evening when Egypt House Franke begged for him. Monday morning he went fishing – and brought fish. Others were employed in the new garden planting yam seeds which Thistlewood was purchasing at 2 bitts for 80. He had calculated that yam-growing could be a profitable enterprise, but he was to be disappointed.

'Monday, 12th May 1777: Dr King lent me, *An Inquiry into the Nature & Causes of the Wealth of Nations*, by Adam Smith, LLD & FRS 2 Vols. Lond. 1776.
Monday, 19th May 1777: Mr Wilson walked over in the evening & slept in the Blue Room as Miss Sally is expected to be brought to bed tonight.'

But her labour was long. It was near 10 o'clock the following night that she was delivered of a girl, who died the next day. A month later:

'Wednesday, 11th June 1777: Mr Wilson was over last night till about 9 o'clock. Note: he is in for it, but conceals it; brought it down from Town with him.
Rode to Savanna la Mar, dined with Mrs Antrobus & son, &c. Sat the evening then rode home. Saw Dr Bellace's crocodile in Dr Pinkney's yard.'

Friday, 20th June was a horse-race day and Thistlewood gave his Negroes leave to go. He also went, as did Phibbah, Mulatto John, Phibbah's daughter Jenny Young and her husband Jimmy Stewart from the Old Hope.

'Rode to the Race Course & saw the race; 4 horses started, all English, Viz. Sir Simon Clark's & Mr Cozen's mares, Mr Samuel's & Mr Nathaniel Beckford's horses. Mr Cozen's mare won.'

But Thistlewood thought that Sir Simon Clark's mare, Macaroni Moll, had in fact won one race which had been declared a dead heat with Cozen's.

'Saturday, 28th June 1777: Mr Hornby says John has never been at work since the rains, &c. [which had begun about the end of May].
Wednesday, 2nd July 1777: Wrote to Mr Hornby about John. As John has not been at work with his master, neither on Monday nor Tuesday, though he affirmed he had, had him put in the bilboes when he came from muster & kept him in all night; also took up Mr Hornby's Jimmy who suspect to be run away also & put him in likewise & put a watchman over them. Thursday, 3rd July 1777: Wrote to Mr Wm. Hornby & sent down John & Jimmy tied, by Dick & Jimmy. Received an answer.

Monday, 4th August 1777: Returned Dr King, Smith on the *Wealth of Nations*, 2 Vols . . . . and lent him the *Pilgrim*, 2 Vols . . . . He lent me an *Essay on the History of Civil Society*, by Adam Ferguson, LLD, Professor of Moral Philosophy in the University of Edinburgh, 4th Ed., Lond. 1773 . . . . Also, the *History of the Decline & Fall of the Roman Empire*, by Edward Gibbon, Esqr. Vol. 1st. 2nd Ed. Lond. 1776.

Saturday, 9th August 1777: It is said that cayenne pepper sprinkled on the floor of a room where people are going to dance, as soon as they begin to warm, it rises and has such an effect upon the women's thighs, &c. that it almost sets them mad and easy to be debauched. A wicked trick if true.'

In late August Thistlewood rode to Savanna la Mar and having dined with Mr Hayward, went to see William Hornby and Hornby's son, James. It was agreed that John Thistlewood would leave William Hornby and go to work, learning his trade, with James Hornby:

'. . . as Mr Wm. Hornby, for this month past has employed him only in cutting & carrying bushes, digging trenches, &c. and now is gone to Town.'

September and October were months of childbirth, child death, and illness among the slaves. In mid-September, Thistlewood's Phoebe, Jimmy's wife, was to be with child; and a few days later Mr Wilson's Clarissa was 'brought to bed of a boy for Lincoln'. Thistlewood's girl slave Lucy became ill in October, with what Thistlewood described as 'rheumatic pains or a crick in her neck, &c. is frequently convulsed'. By mid-month she was seemingly past recovery, and on Wednesday 15th, she died at about half-past seven in the evening. Solon dug her grave, and Thistlewood was 'very sorry for her death indeed'. After all, she had survived infancy. Still, her place might be filled for Phoebe was with child, and so too, in November, was Fanny. Late November Abba's Little Phibbah had yaws, and so too did Joe. Earlier in the month Thistlewood had undertaken a journey into the hills above Savanna la Mar.

'Thursday, 13th November 1777: This morning after I had breakfasted, set out on Prince horse & Jimmy with me on Mackey. Called in the Savanna for Mr Robert Chambers & we set out from thence at 8 a.m. Went slowly & got to Witter's about ¼ before 10, & to Mr Hambersley's at Darliston, just at noon.

Mr Hambersely has got an excellent house, or rather fortification, being very strong; piazza 67 feet long and 14 wide. Mrs Dicke there very ill [she died on the 26th], and one of her daughters attending her. A Miss Cateness there, Mr and Mrs Hambersley and their son, Mr John Hambersley. A fine cool agreeable air. We diverted ourselves at billiards, cards, &c.'

It was a bird-shooting visit and they were out on the following days bringing in bags of birds, especially ring-tail doves which were a favoured dish. On the 16th, Thistlewood returned to his Pen. About a month later, Mr Hambersley paid a return visit. He stayed with Thistlewood, visited Hugh Wilson next door (recently reconciled with Miss Sally who had earlier left him after a quarrel) and was entertained with a magic lantern show. His visit lasted four days.

Among the slaves, it would seem that Strap might have had as much reason to complain as did Franke.

'Saturday, 6th December 1777: Flogged Franke & Strap for disturbing me last night between 10 and 11 o'clock, quarrelling about Caesar being catched by Strap in her room. They made a terrible uproar.

Also flogged Mirtilla & Nanny for almost killing themselves with eating cassava badly prepared, although they are well acquainted with it by which means I lost [their labour] all yesterday, beside purges & vomits, &c. and the risk of losing them.

Thursday, 29th January 1778: A Report of ten thousand Spanish troops being arrived in Hispaniola.'

The news was the more disturbing because an inspection of the fort at Savanna la Mar in the previous month had found it in a very sad state of disrepair, with unserviceable guns, no powder, and lacking most of the basic needs such as a guard room, a store house, a cistern, a hospital room, and barracks. For the time being, however, there seemed to be no fear of imminent attack.

On 9th January, Phoebe was delivered of her child, a girl. Early in February Mr Wilson's Clarissa died.

'She was greatly swelled about the stomach & is supposed by Dr Bell either to have eat dirt or swallowed the cane trash when chewing cane, which is spongy and indigestible. My Lincoln kept her. Miss Sally says Mr W . . . . . beat her very much just before she died.'

Mr Thistlewood's Negroes were employed felling, sawing and chipping logwood, and working in the gardens.

'Monday, 23rd February 1778: Mr Ballantine[2] rode over & made a complaint of Fanny, Sukey & Bess beating Egypt Flora

(Quasheba's daughter) at Savanna la Mar yesterday. Flogged Sukey & Bess, but Fanny's belly's too big at present, though she was chief in the fray.'

On the 25th, Thistlewood bought another slave, a woman named Mary, formerly belonging to Mr Samuel Burton and now sold by the Marshall for debt. He paid £39 10s.

'Mary is of the Chambah Country, about 20 years of age, pitted with the smallpox & has had the yaws, her ears are bored; tolerably black,with black mark under each eye, thus Brand marked ＼TT／ on each shoulder, but fairest on the left; and is 4 ft 11 ½ inches high.'

Meantime, the social rounds had been followed. On 14th February, a Saturday, Thistlewood rode over to Sweet River and spent the day in the company of his first employer, Florentius Vassall, now an old man full of shaky reminiscences, but very clear in his views of the current struggle:

'He wishes the North Americans might beat the English, else they will be enslaved and ruled with a rod of iron, & next, us, though the Americans will never bear it long, as what army we can keep there will never be able to keep in awe an extent of two thousand miles.'

Vassall was exceedingly friendly. They conversed long and widely, and he offered Thistlewood land, free of charge for life, to settle on, or for a provision mountain, or for a garden, on any of his properties.

'Thursday, 19th February 1778:   Rode to Mr Wicksted's, the painter's, at the house on Mr Foot's place near Smithfield. He showed me his portraits, very curious especially Mr & Mrs Beckford & Captn. Carling, Mr & Mrs Beckford in another, George Pointz Ricketts & his lady, Mr George Inglis, Parson Poole, Jimmy Tomlinson, &c, &c, a holing gang of Negroes, &c.

Wednesday, 19th March 1778:   Mr Cope's Cuffee (now John Davis) who arrived yesterday at Sav la Mar, played on the fiddle tonight at Egypt and the Misses Cope danced, &c.'

On Breadnut Island Pen there were the now familiar sorts of notices.

'Friday, 3rd April, 1778:   Flogged Lincoln well, new marked him on the right shoulder low, & put him in the bilboes, as he scarce brought any fish and threatened if I insisted on fish that he would run away, & a great deal more impudence.

Mr Gooden's Monday at the Pen. Wants to keep my Maria, I am told. Upon his application to me I gave my consent.
Sunday, 5th April 1778: In the evening Miss Sally & Bessie (Mr Burt's lady) down at my house. Pulled Lincoln out of the bilboes at Miss Sally's intercession.
Tuesday, 14th April 1778: Jenny Young brought to bed of a boy today.
Monday, 20th April 1778: Phoebe's Charity has got the gripes, &c.
Monday, 11th May 1778: Joe still lame [yaws], flogged for leaving the cookroom last night & going to Mr Wilson's.
Tuesday, 12th May 1778: About 4 o'clock this morning, Fanny brought to bed of a girl, had a hard time of it. (Egypt Quasheba grande).'

In mid-May Thistlewood began shipping his logwood on board the *Henry*, Captn. Richardson. On the 25th he sent down the seventh and last boat load, and he 'let John go in her this time'. John was still playing truant from work and was now, apparently, using his militia duties as opportunities for escape from apprenticeship.

'Friday, 22nd May, 1778: About 11 o'clock last night, was called up to Maria, found her in a fit, speechless, & her teeth set fast. Applied spirits of hartshorn to her nose, &c, but to no purpose although moved into the fine [fresh?] air. At last suspected she might have eat bitter cassava, poison crabs, or some such thing. Had her teeth forced open and got down 6 grains of emetic tartar, then a little warm water & oil, &c. At last it operated, and as soon as she got anything up, was perceptibly better, her teeth opened, she drank of herself, began to get her speech, &c. She complained wholly of her stomach. About 3 in the morning I went to bed again. (Monday with her). Had her forehead also, at first, rubbed with warm vinegar, her neck, breast, stomach, &c. with warm vegeto-mineral water &c.
Saturday, 23rd May 1778: About 7 this evening, Peggy brought to me very ill with her stomach & belly, having eat something unwholesome, as new crabs, &c. Gave her oil & water, which made her vomit, after which she was easier.'

And, a month later, Sukey, in a fit and speechless, was treated, successfully, as Maria had been.
From the beginning of June the war news increased and the war came closer.

'Monday, 8th June 1778: Mr Wilson came over in the evening, brings news from Savanna la Mar that a guard is going to be kept, and that the Assembly is to meet next Thursday, and it is supposed the sailing of the fleet [of merchant ships assembled for convoy] will be put off, &c. owing to our dangerous situation, preparations of the French, &c. &c.'

Florentius Vassall did not live to experience the excitements of the next few months. On Tuesday, 9th June he died at Sweet River. Thistlewood was to be the only invited person at his funeral, other than the bearers; but that did not take place until the 17th, and meantime there was business (mixed with pleasure) to be attended to.

'Thursday, 11th June 1778: Rode to Hertford (had Jimmy with me) carried Mr Beckford the rose-apples. Mr Beckford took up his protested Bill, which was for £219 1s 5d Stg, and replaced it with a fresh set for £249 6d, Sterling, drawn on Messrs Beckford & James in London. Breakfasted at Mr Beckfords ... [and later] ... he, Mr Wm. Woollery & myself walked into the guinea grass pasture upon the little hill, &c. Played at billards, &c. Looked over many Folio Volumes of excellent plates of the Ruins of Rome, &c. &c. Dined, & drank tea. Mr Beckford gave me some geranium slips, flower seeds, jonquil roots, &c. In the evening rode home, where got about ½ past 7. At dinner Mr and Mrs Beckford, Mr Wm Woollery and his wife, Mr John Lewis & his wife, Mr Alderson, Mr Riches, & myself. In the evening Mr Beckford & Mr John Lewis, &c. played at cricket.'

And at the end of July Mr Beckford sent him 'the six following views': 1. Part of the River Cobre near Spanish Town 2. Roaring River Estate 3. Fort William Estate 4. Bridge Crossing Cabaritta River on Mr Beckford's estate 5. Spring head of Roaring River 6. Bridge Crossing the Rio Cobre river near Spanish Town.

'Wednesday, 17th June 1778: At half past six o'clock this morning set out & rode to Sweet River, to attend Mr Vassall's remains to Paradise barcadier. His bowels, &c. were took out, he was enclosed in a wood coffin & then in lead soldered up. He was brought out and placed in the hall with the pall over him, & part of the funeral service read over him by Dr Bartholomew & the Clerk. Then carried on Negroes shoulders to the seaside, with great difficulty & very slowly, though often spelled with fresh hands, and was twice, or oftener, thrown down in the road. Mr Beckford was chief mourner. Mr Cope,

Mr Meyler, Mr Haughton, Mr White, Mr Antrobus & Mr James Williams bearers; myself, parson, clerk, & Dr Pinkney. All attended him to the water side, where got at 11 o'clock although we stopped in the road almost every minute. He was then put in another strong wooden coffin, immediately put in a boat which directly set off for the shipping. He was 70 or more years of age, & as many minute guns were fired. His smell was very offensive, some defect being in the lead coffin. I had a pair of black gloves & hatband given me, being the only person invited who was not a bearer; and that by his own desire while living. (Mr Vassall was sent in the *Fort William*, Captn Ayton).'

On Thursday, 25th June the fleet sailed from Bluefields Bay. Next day there was a general muster of troops and militia at Savanna la Mar.

'Wednesday, 1st July 1778: Received a note from Mr James Hornby acquainting me that John has not been at work since Thursday last.

Friday, 3rd July 1778: John at home this morning before sunrise & wanted to go to Carawina to muster & shoot at a mark, &c; but I had him secured, laid down, & flogged, then sent him in a rope, by Solon, home to his master at Sav la Mar. He is so sullen that he will not tell who harbours him.'

And, on the same day, in the evening, 'Nago Jenny died at Egypt'. That was all he said.

On Wednesday 8th, John again ran away and was caught in Cudjoe's watch-hut. Both were punished and next morning John was bound and sent back to James Hornby. Surprisingly enough, James Hornby shortly afterwards purchased John's indenture from his father, William Hornby, for £20. But the war and the weather were soon to bring relief to John's frustrations.

'Wednesday, 5th August 1778: A Review today. The Brown Infantry had guns given them: brass barrels.

Thursday, 13th August 1778: The Militia reviewed today by Chevalier Cook. John is made a pioneer.'

Meantime, on the Pen, in July, many of the slaves, and Thistlewood himself, had suffered bad colds: Abba, Sally and Solon had been ill; on the 17th, with Egypt Quasheba attending, Damsel had been brought to bed of a girl; and, on the 23rd, Driver Dick had been flogged 'for not making the Negroes work', and then Jimmy had been flogged 'for not exerting himself in flogging Dick'. Early in August:

'. . . a man showing sleight of hand tricks. eating fire, &c. &c. . to near 200 people of both sexes above stairs in Moses Mendez Monfante's house, now rented by Mr Kennedy, tavern keeper, in the height of the diversion the floor fell down with them, 8 or 9 feet, to the great surprise & terror of everybody. However, luckily no limbs broke, but some badly bruised, as young Mr Antrobus, Mr John Chambers, &c. &c. Many hats, shoes, &c, and some watches lost. (Jimmy Tomlinson lost his watch worth 6 pistoles, & some others). The show-man made his escape & fled for fear, though no ways his fault. He is said to be now at Black River. A Mulatto wench & a Free Negro wench died in a few days after, occasioned by it. Mr Donnet, being drunk, had drove the Negroes out of the hall underneath just before it fell.
Sunday, 9th August 1778: Bought a young horse of Egypt House Franke, for which I paid her £12 cash down. Salt River smith, Charles, present.
Advanced to smith Charles 10s to buy me a hog.
Friday, 14th August 1778: Last night about 10 o'clock Joe left the cookroom & went to the Negro houses. Had him flogged.'

And on that day another death. 'Mr John Hartnole died, about 4 p.m. at his house in Burnt Savanna of a putrid fever. Aged about 30.' Thistlewood attended the funeral and was a bearer.

Early in September Thistlewood spent another few days at Mr Ralph Hambersley's at Darliston. It was three and a half hours ride from his house, and three hours and twenty minutes from Mr Chambers' in the Savanna; but it was sometimes risky to be abroad on horseback, especially in the town.

'Wednesday, 9th September 1778: Rode to Savanna la Mar, but returned to dinner, lest my horse should be pressed for the soldiers who set off for Town [Kingston] tomorrow. Mr Dobson sent his horse to my pasture that he might be out of their way. Martial law proclaimed in Town last Friday, & an embargo laid on all ships and vessels, even to a plantain boat.
Saturday, 12th September 1778: . . . met at the Fort (Vizt. Lieuts & gunners) and agreed to keep guard, a Lieut & a gunner at a time, 2 days & 2 nights. Mr Wardloe & Mr Haldane take till Monday morning 9 o'clock, Mr Alexander & Mr Wickstead till Wednesday morning, Mr Hayward & Mr Fullerton till Friday morning, myself & Mr Stewart till Sunday morning, then Mr Dobson, &c. Mr Lock is first Lieut. No Captain now Captain Brown is gone.
A trooper (Mr Lyon) at my house in the evening, who showed

me an order from the Commander in Chief; to send an able Negro next Monday morning to Bull-head Pen, with a bill, hoe, ax, basket & seven day's provisions, to assist in putting up a building for the women and children, in case of necessity.'

He sent Strap. Of the others, in September, Cudjoe had the clap; Damsel, who had complained about her eyes at the end of August, was given 'eye-water' to bathe them 'as she has a film coming'; and Bess and her husband Jimmy, 'a Mocho Negro', quarrelled.

On the night of Tuesday 15th Savanna la Mar and its environs suffered from gales. On Thistlewood's Pen, the winds damaged his dwelling house, the cook room, the Negro houses, the sheds and animal pens; blew down his lightning rod, and uprooted trees and food crops. At sea, ships had been driven ashore. The damage was widespread and considerable.

'Friday, 18th September 1778: We shall nearly have a famine.'

And, indeed, at the end of the year Thistlewood noted an expenditure of 231 bitts on the purchase of corn. Even before the storm there had been a shortage of provisions on the Pen. At the end of August, John had come home with a fever: '. . . by being in the canoe all Saturday night fetching plantains from Parkers Bay.' Later in the year, engaged in guard duties, helping his father to repair the damaged buildings, and shooting wildfowl in the morass on weekends, John, for a time, found life less oppressive.

'Monday, 21st September 1778: For 30 plantains, 2 bitts. No bread to be had at Sav-la-Mar.

Wednesday, 30th September 1778: Hear 3 barrels of flour have lately been sold in Town at £150 each. A very false report. Mr Harrison, the Attorney General gave £20 for a barrel, and 3 barrels have been sold for £50, this is certain.

Sunday, 4th October 1778: Bought a filly of Egypt House Franke for £6. Paid her in cash.

Tuesday, 6th October 1778: Received a note from Mrs Cope about my Sally whom she suspects has stole a turkey pp [chicken] of hers from Derby's watchhut; but my Negroes think she is blamed wrongfully. Wrote to Mrs Cope.

Wednesday, 7th October 1778: Lent Mr Hayward, Abbe Raynal, *History of The Indies*, 5 Vols.'

On the 19th, Lincoln was again in trouble over fish. Thistlewood and Pompey escorted him to Egypt where, with Ballantine's permission, Egypt driver Quashe administered a flogging. He was given 2 bitts for a job well done. Later, back on the Pen:

'At night flogged Fanny & Nanny for fighting & scolding.'

War-scares, however serious, did not apparently preclude revelry, even among those on guard duty.

'Saturday, 7th November 1778: I was Captain of the Fort tonight. Guards came as follows: Wilson, Pinkney, Oldman, Steele, Robertson, Thistlewood, Lewis, Hornby, Lightfoot, Smith. Set the watch at 9 & took an hour each; but I took all night, upon the platform for the most part. Had a supper, 2 cold fowls, a tongue, cheese, &c. ale, porter, wine, brandy, anniseed water, &c. Those seemed to be found by Dr Lightfoot, Mr Smith, Mr Lewis & Dr Pinkney.'

And later others came to join in what seemed to be a roaring wet night.

On the Pen, Thislewood's recently acquired Burton's Mary had made a match with Egypt Robin; and Lincoln was again in trouble, but not, this time, with Thistlewood. The date should have led him to act with greater discretion.

'Friday, 13th November 1778: Monday being in bed with his wife Maria, about 3 o'clock this morning, Lincoln came home from the morass, & brought a load of cane with him, which he carried directly into Maria's house, & began to enquire for his countryman, but Monday not permitting her to speak, Lincoln proceeded to search for victuals & then to go into her room to sleep with her, but Monday laid hold of him first, &c.'

In the following week Lincoln got another beating, this time from Mr Ballantine for stealing canes on Egypt.

In late November and early December many of Thistlewood's slaves were being treated for various ills, or being innoculated against smallpox by Dr Bell. Sally, Mirtilla and Joe had yaws. Cudjoe, seemingly recovered from the clap, was 'bad of his Burstin' or rupture. Joe, Bristol, Nelly, Jenny, Tony, Quashe, and Phibbah (the children) were all given 'preparatory powers' in syrup, and little Mulatto Bessie, for whom no powders had been sent, was given 'a small mercurial pill' instead. Probably just as well, for by this time Thistlewood had taken her eleven times, though on seven occasions '*sed non bene*'. Following the 'preparatory powders' came doses of salts, and then, on Monday 7th December, Dr Bell innoculated them all. In the next couple of days, more powders and more salts. On the 24th, Christmas Eve, Dr Bell was paid for his treatments which seemd to have been successful. Thistlewood must have been relieved, for already he had heard of the deaths of two children —

one next door at Mr Wilson's had apparently succumbed to the innoculation. The able-bodied had been engaged in repair work following the September gales.

'Friday, 18th December 1778:   Thatching the sheep pen & horse stable, but they are making very bad work. Flogged Dick & all the thatchers; and as Dick is so excessive stupid & obstinate, put him to work & made Strap driver.'

Christmas Day, 1778:   'For 225 corn, 9 bitts.' On Christmas Eve Thistlewood had shot one of his cows, 'a trouble-maker'. Now he sent a fore-quarter, about 70 lb to his neighbour, Mr Wilson, 'for his Negroes'.; saved some for himself to corn 'as it was good meat'; sent Jenny Young and House Franke a piece each; and divided the remainder, about 3 ½ lb each, among his slaves. On Christmas Eve night he had given them the head, liver, lights and guts for their supper. With the meat there was the accustomed distribution of rum, and a special 12 bitts to Abba, 'to assist her'. Phibbah got seven bottles of rum, John got 'a pair of new shoes, the only remaining ones of the light sort', and friends around received gifts of fish, fruit, or flowers. But the war had been getting closer.

'Tuesday, 8th December 1778:   Hear the French, a few nights ago, catched two or three of Mr Dorward's Negroes at the sea near Negril.'

And domestic problems were not yet resolved:

'Tuesday, 29th December 1778:   Received a note from Mr James Hornby ... that John is not yet gone to work.
About 10 o'clock at night Egypt Jack, Little Pompey, & Prince brought John. I got up and put him in the bilboes.
Wednesday, 30th December 1778:   This morning flogged John pretty well, pulled off his shoes, and put them up. I wrote to Mr James Hornby and sent him home by Solon, with his hands tied behind him.'

On 1st January, 1779, Thistlewood listed ready money as £184. He had spent more than usual buying provisions; and because of the time spent in logwood cutting and chipping, and in repairs to buildings, his slaves had earned him only £70 for hired labour. Local sales of his Pen's produce had earned him 1352 bitts, or £42 5s. The greatest earnings had come from fruit and vegetables (520 bitts), wildfowl (315 bitts), domestic poultry and eggs (301 bitts), and honey 126 bitts from a much reduced number of hives. Six of his 16 'stocks' of bees had been lost by vermin, moths, maggots & desertions'.

Of slaves, there were now 32, as follows: Men – Lincoln, Dick, Solon, Cudjoe, Pompey, Caesar, Strap, Jimmy, and Joe (9); women – Sukey, Franke, Phoebe, Fanny, Maria, Nanny, Mirtilla, Sally, Peggy, Burton's Mary, Abba, Bess and Damsel (13); and his own slaves' children, boys – Quashe, Bristol, and Tony (3); and girls – Nelly, Vine, Charity, Mary, Betty, Jenny and Phibbah (7). In 1778 he had issued 145 tickets.

He now owned 5 horses, 25 head of cattle, 71 sheep, a couple of barrow hogs, and the usual variety of poultry.

He was owed about £150, and he owed about £50; and Dr Bell, Mr Hayward, Mr Robertson, and Miss Cope all had books from his library.

'Thursday, 7th January 1779: Billed my path through Mr Wilson's pasture to the Kings road (had 15 hands) . . .
Saturday, 16th January 1779: Bess was bid 14 bitts for the gander at Sav la Mar, but refused it & had it raffled off at Egypt for 16 bitts. Gave [her] 2 bitts to buy a bottle of rum out of it.'

One morning in the following week, with Jimmy in attendance, he set off to the Chambers' house in the Savanna. They were to go shooting on Friendship Estate with Mr Bodington, the late Florentius Vassall's overseer. John Chambers, unfortunately, could not go 'having unexpectedly received some deeds . . . to be done immediately'. Thistlewood and Robert Chambers set off in the latter's carriage:

'. . . by Hatfield, Cross Path, & over Barham's bridge to Friendship Estate, where got ½ an hour after 10 a.m. Mr Wm. Lewis of Sav la Mar also with us.'

In the evening, Mr Lewis went home, Mr Bodington went to sleep at Sweet River, Thistlewood and Robert Chambers remained at Friendship and slept there. Next morning, early, Bodington returned and all three:

'. . . rode about a mile & half to see the young mango tree. It is in a plantain walk considerably to the NE of Greenwich works, in a fine rich soil, at about 20 feet distance from Cabaritta River. This young tree is now about 2½ feet high.'

In March of the following year they went back to see it, 'about 8½ feet high; has branches out at 7 feet; seems thriving'.

'Sunday, 24th January 1779: p.m. Mirtilla had a fit, but recovered in a little time. To Waterford, for bleeding Mirtilla, 2 bitts. Waterford gave me two crab-catchers he shot, exceeding fine.'

Waterford was a slave from Egypt who was now often called on by Thistlewood when there was a bleeding to be performed. Mirtilla, as we know, suffered these occasional 'fits' which were sometimes, as in this case, followed by a short illness.

'Monday, 25th January 1779: Stopped my Negroes at home, & a.m. dug the yams in New Garden, 44 rows, 19 planted in each row, but as many died suppose only 12 grew in each row = 528 yams. All the yams weighed only 1,115 pounds, which is near 25⅓ lbs. per row, and somewhat better than 2 pounds per yam.

Gave the Negroes each a good meal of yams.

Made my Negroes fetch wood to the cookroom door, and gave them the afternoon to help themselves, then to set off for Meylersfield.

Flogged Fanny for fighting with Phoebe, & twice after for her great impudence.

Tuesday, 26th January 1779: Fanny laid up at Meylersfield.'

On the same day, Hannah, one of the Cope's daughters, '19 years old today', was married at Egypt to Dr Robert Pinkney. Parson Bartholomew performed the ceremony in the presence of twenty guests, including Thistlewood.

'Phibbah went to Egypt, to the wedding & stayed till the evening. In the evening Mr Hugh White [who had given her away] & the Bride danced a minuet, Dr Pinkney & Mrs Swinney, &c. Then Country dances, &c. I went home about 8 p.m.'

On Friday, 2nd February, and this was neither the first, nor the only expedition of its kind, Thistlewood set off with little Jenny to Poole's Rock where they spent about two hours gathering the seeds of the sensitive Mimosa. Thistlewood measured it at about 8 ounces, troy, of clean seed. It was for export to Mr Hewitt. Satisfied with the collection they rode home, past Mount Eagle where Thistlewood dined with Mr Samuel Delap, then Rickett's Savanna, Paul Island, and on to Breadnut Island. En route:

'Called at a neat white house, to leeward of Morgan's Bridge, to ask the way to Mount Eagle & Vine come out, being (it seems) kept by one Ortolan, a distiller, who lives there.'

A fortnight later, Thistlewood set off on another, much longer ride of visit and exploration.

'Tuesday, 16th February 1779: This afternoon Mr Nickolas Blake & his wife, & Mr and Mrs Swinney went in a chariot & Kitterine to my house to see me. Phibbah made them tea, gave them porter, &c. under the guinep tree in the garden.'

Thistlewood was not at home. At twenty minutes to nine that morning he had set off, through Savanna la Mar and Bluefields, to Ackendown where he arrived at 12.30 p.m. and dined with his friend Francis Scott and others.

Next day they walked and rode around Ackendown. Then, Thursday morning, Francis Scott took Thistlewood further afield. Through Mr Stewart's Robin's River, through 'Basinspring' [Beeston Spring] which was all in ruins and ruinate, to Bog Estate, 5 ¾ miles from Ackendown. From Bog (Mr Cameron), they could see Mr George Scott's Hopeton, and Lennox hills, but not any buildings. They rode on to Lennox. Mr Walter Scott, the overseer, showed them the view from the piazza. The night was spent at Bog. On the way back to Ackendown, near Bog, 'saw plenty of ringtail pigeons'; and then, more local riding around and up to Brotherton, where Thistlewood noted a good hardwood house with an extensive view.

On Saturday 20th Thistlewood set out for home. Through Cave, where Mr John Scott 'has plenty of potherbs, &c. &c., bees, &c. locks his gates. Has a very good house'. Through the Blue hole plantain walk to Paradise and the road west.

'Thursday, 4th March 1779:   Dined at Egypt. [He had spent the day there, riding around with Mr Cope] as did also Dr & Mrs Pinkney. In the evening rode home. Miss Polly [Cope] ill, seems to fret much for J.H.' [John Hartnole]

Perhaps it was his day's riding through Egypt with Mr Cope that led him to note a few days later that 'To be the owner of a sugar work is to have external dignity for inward or internal grief'. But it was not only sugar planters who were sometimes in grief. Mr Wilson, next door, had borrowed money from Thistlewood, and in April he had lost his white employee.

'Monday, 12th April 1779:   Today Mr Burt left Mr Wilson & went for Hanover where he intends to set up. Mr Wilson & him parted good friends. p.m. Suspect L. Mul. Bessie and Mr W . . . . . at his house.'

He must have wondered how it went, for he had already taken her six times that year, the last occasion a mere three days before, and each time had recorded 'sed non Bene.'

'Tuesday, 13th April 1779:   Phibbah gave me a calabash packey[3] curiously marked sent her by Driver Sam, Nanny's husband.

Monday, 10th May 1779: ... about ½ past, 10 heard firing
out at sea, went upstairs [he was at Mr Chambers's house in the
Savanna] saw an engagement, & three ships out at sea, in a line
with the ships in the harbour, the firing all over before 11. They
prove part of the Cork fleet, the *Nancy*, Captn Steele, took just
off the harbour by a French privateer. The other ships gave no
assistance to *Nancy*, but ran away. The whole Bay spectators of
the engagement.'

And even those who did not see were in other ways made aware of
the war.

'Scarce any person has now any butter. None to be bought
under 10s. per lb.'

During May, Thistlewood was busy with Mr Bodington and
others appraising Mr Vassall's properties at Friendship and Sweet
River. Mr Clement Cook Clarke, Mrs Vassall's brother, had arrived
from England on 10th May with Captain Watkins, one of those who
had failed to go to the help of the captured *Nancy*. Also arrived
with Captain Watkins was Mr Foster's Betty, who soon after paid
Phibbah a visit.

Mr Bodington had shown Thistlewood 'a sheet of patent paper,
4 feet 5 inches long & 2 feet 6 ½ inches wide', which Thistlewood
obviously admired.

'Friday, 21st May 1779: Mr Bodington gave me 2 black lead
pencils, & promises to send for 12 sheets of the large paper, he
having a relation living with Sir Joshua Reynolds.'

The arrival of the Cork fleet seems to have at least temporarily
allayed some of the food shortages. On Sunday, 6th June, House
Franke had sent Thistlewood some fresh butter, but during the next
few days he went shopping:

'Monday, 7th June 1779: Bought of Mr John Munro, 2 half
barrels mess pork for which I paid £6 10s. Bought of Messrs
Blake & Harrison, 9 lb bacon at ⅓ = 11s 3d; 2 pieces Scotch
oznabrig (257 yards) at 11 ½d = £12 6s 3 ½d; 1 barrell flour, 2
cwt 2 qrtrs 7 lb, £6 2s 5 ½d.
Bought of Mr George Inglis, 2 firkins of butter (65 lb & 64 lb)
= 129 lb at 2s = £2 18s 0d; 2 ½ barrels mess beef = £6 10s 0d;
3 loaves of Bristol single refined sugar, 26 ¾ lb at 20d = £2 4s
7d.'

And, from Samuel Webster, another 2 firkins of butter. On the
Saturday he bought from George Inglis a box (61 lb weight) of
tallow candles at 2s, and 2s 6d more for the box = £6 4s 6d.

'Wednesday, 16th June 1779:   Hear that Tabia, Miss Sally's mother belonging to Wm. Henry Ricketts Esqr. of Canaan, died about 4 o'clock this afternoon.

Sunday, 20th June 1779:   Delivered to Mulatto Jimmy Stewart, of the Old Hope, 3 pair of new shoes & 3 pr ditto pumps, which I sent for, for him in payment for cutting the young horse bought from House Franke & breaking another ...

Monday, 5th July 1779:   Received a note from Mrs Cope, by Waterford, and delivered up Little Mulatto Bessie, now 4 ft 6 $^{8}/_{10}$ ins high, Mrs Cope having gained her trial against Mrs Senior for her & her mother Deborah. Went away just 20 mins before 11 a.m.

It seems Lincoln was shooting pigeons 3 days last week in Egypt morass. On Tuesday, the Overseer Mr Whitehead, a Barbadian, [who had succeeded Mr Ballantine who had gone elsewhere at £100 p.a.] & Waterford catched him and brought him to Mr & Mrs Cope a little before noon. He had shot 6 pigeons & said I was going to have company & had sent him out to shoot me some. He had a soldier's musket, which he told them was John's gun; but Waterford says, is Mr Lesley's Coffee's. No wonder he scarce brought any fish last week.

Tuesday, 6th July 1779:   Flogged Lincoln.'

During the summer months of 1779 Thistlewood was, as usual, busy around his gardens. He exchanged seeds and plants with a number of other proprietors and overseers including John Cope at Egypt, William Lewis at Cornwall, Mr Meyler at Meylersfield, John Ricketts at Ridgeland, Mr Bodington at Sweet River and Friendship, Francis Scott at Ackendown, and others. And, also as usual, he experimented. In mid-July he went over to Egypt where he had two puncheons of rum in store for him. He put pineapples into one and cashews into the other, sealed them, and, a day or two later, had them sent on board the *Henry*, consigned to Mr Hewitt.

From mid-August until mid-September war nerves were taut. In Savanna la Mar there was a scare.

'Saturday, 14th August 1779:   Soon after 10 o'clock [a.m.] great guns, which suspect to be an alarm fired; and proved such .... Five vessels off, which caused the alarm, & frights many people. Many carts carring away goods, and the women hurrying off the Bay. Mr Wilson dined with me. p.m. we rode to the Bay in the evening, received intelligence that the vessels are Friends: one of them a Packet going home. Myself and Mr Wickstead took guard in the Fort tonight by our own consent.'

But invasion was expected and the troops had been ordered to move to Kingston. At the fort in Savanna la Mar, however, the duty guards again spent their watchful hours noisily spirited by supplies brought them by Mr Antrobus who sat drinking with them till nearly 3 a.m.

> 'Sunday, 15th August 1779:   About 2 p.m. John set out for Savanna la Mar, to be ready to set off for Town. I gave him 32 bitts, & Franke [gave him] a dollar. Gave him a Memorandum Book & black lead pencil. He had his red coat & 3 suits of clothes in his knapsack; also 3 bitts worth of bread.
>
> Monday, 16th August 1779:   Mr Cope slept at Smithfield last night & set out for Town today. The Brown Infantry set out in the forenoon, the Grenadiers & part of the Light Infantry at different times today. Hear John pressed a horse in the road near Kirkpatrick.'

On Friday 19th, the Free Negro Company set off for Town. At the beginning of the next week guards were posted at the Fort, at Smithfield wharf, and at Cross Path. At about 2 p.m. on Tuesday 24th, Mr Donnett, Salt River overseer, a trooper, arrived in a great fright announcing that:

> '... 5 French ships of the line had been battering Black River and had landed 400 men who were upon full march down into Westmoreland, this he had from Mr French ...'

An enormous confusion followed. Terror, 'especially amongst the few white women remaining and the Negroes, &c.' But, again, it was a false alarm. There had been two small French privateers; one of which had been taken by a packet coming from Pensacola, and fifteen prisoners were brought to the Savanna la Mar fort: ten French, four Spaniards, one Italian, and a Curaçao Negro. The other privateer had escaped along the coast.

> 'Wednesday, 25th August 1779:   It is said the expense at Head-quarters is now £3,000 per day. By letters from Town the French are expected before Sunday next.
>
> Friday, 27th August 1779:   In the morning received a note from John, dated Old Harbour August 23rd, by Mr Lesley's Billy.'

Next day, another note from John. Thistlewood replied on Monday 30th by the post.

> 'Saturday, 4th September 1779:   Received a letter from John of the 30th August date. Cut off and gave Phib 8 yrds of brown oznabrig to make John 2 pr, of breeches.
>
> Monday, 6th September 1779:   Wrote to John, by Salt River

Cumberland, and sent him ... twenty shillings in silver, a pr. of new shoes, 2 pr. stockings and 2 pr of oznabrig breeches unmade up, not having time. Gave Cumberland 4 bitts for himself.'

Meantime, at the Fort, the guards were still much occupied. There was a wager of half a dozen claret between Dr Gardiner and Mr Ramsay about the correct spelling for the number 14. Gardiner said 'forteen', Ramsay said 'fourteen'.

On Thursday 16th, the troops came back from Town. The expected invasion had not materialized. John, who had been encamped at Longville Park, east of Kingston, got home that evening. They had set out from Longville at 10 a.m. on Monday morning. On the 21st he went back to Mr Hornby's.

At the Fort, perhaps now in celebration of danger escaped, the Fusillers were on guard — Mr Joseph Williams (Carawina) Captain; Billy Williams, Lieut, John Graham and others. They supped.

> 'Tuesday, 22nd September 1779: At supper: Joe Williams, Billy Williams, John Graham, Little Billy Lewis, Mr Dobson, Dr Lightfoot, the two Captains & myself; very merry. A Mr Watson, a book-keeper, entertained us exceedingly, took off an overseer, book-keeper, Negro wench, &c. &c., and is exceeding active, &c. Many clever fellows among them.'

For Mr Thistlewood's slaves, the time of tension brought problems which had little to do with the war.

> 'Tuesday, 10th August 1779: Maria laid up of a swelled leg. Hear Monday is runaway.
> Sunday, 15th August 1779: Hear that both Mirtilla & Sally have now yaws about them.
> Tuesday, 31st August 1779: p.m. Strap come home and complained of Mr Whitehead beating him badly with his cowskin. He is indeed much abused, and a vein on his arm hurt greatly. I rode over with him to Egypt and reprimanded Mr Whitehead.'

Thistlewood's field slaves were at the time hired out to Mr Cope. By early October:

> 'My Negroes seem quite weary of Egypt. Complain very much of Mr Whitehead.'

But the work there did not end until 5th November.

> 'Sunday, 26th September 1779: Reprimanded Phib. for permitting John to sleep in the cookroom & Negro house.

Saturday, 16th October 1779: John at home, & 2 of Mr
Hornby's Negroes assisting him to make 2 gates – one for
Olive Tree ground, the other for enclosure west from home
garden. Gave Pump & Jack each 2 bitts.'

Also at work on Breadnut Island Pen in late October and early
November was Mulatto Sukey Crookshank, daughter of previous
Egypt employee Crookshank and Egypt Mirtilla. She was an Egypt
house slave employed sewing. Thistlewood paid Mrs Cope 7s 6d a
week for her services with the needle, and paid her in person at a
higher rate for other satisfaction:

'Thursday, 18th November 1779: *Cum* Mulatto Sukey Crookshank, *Sup. Terr*... Gave [her] a dollar.'

In the garden stood several alligator (avocado) pear trees. Some
were laden with fruit, and one tree was raided.

'Tuesday, 23rd November 1779: Flogged all my field Negroes,
except Dick, Sally, Peggy & Burtons's Mary, for stealing my
alligator pears last Friday night.
Monday, 29th November 1779: Hear a French picaroon carried
off 8 or 9 of Mr John Dorward's Negroes last week.
Monday, 6th December 1779: Between 10 and 11 a.m. Dick
& Strap brought home Sukey speechless & senseless, in a fit.
Put her in a cool, airy place, chaffed her temples & wrists with
warm vinegar & water, applied hartshorn, & spirit of Sal
Ammoniac with quicklime to her nose, &c. About ½ past 12
Mr Wilson bled her, but she would not bleed & had scarce any
perceptible pulse. Rubbed her legs well with a cloth dipped in
warm water, & gave her some burnt wine with a little cinnamon
in it, a little of which got down. About 2 p.m. she spoke, & her
pulse greatly improved. About half past 2 Mr Wilson tried
again & she bled pretty well. Soon after, gave her more burnt
wine & a mercury pill. Continued low and weak in the evening
& complained much of a pain in her head & neck, &c.'

But she recovered.

In Savanna la Mar, the year went out in a blaze which brought
an estimated loss of £40,000.

'Tuesday, 7th December 1779: Between 1 and 2 o'clock this
morning heard a shell blow at Egypt, and about half past 2 a
violent explosion, like a mighty cannon, but proved to be powder
in the Fort.'

Before midnight a fire had broken out in a shop rented by Mr Abraham Lopez to a white carpenter (named White) who, apparently, was at the time drunk. The one fire-engine could do little and the sea was at its lowest ebb. The Fort was, except for 'the necessary house & some sentry-boxes', completely burnt out though some cartridges were saved by throwing the boxes over the wall into the sea. The ruins, said Thistlewood, were 'a shocking scene'. Woodbine's shop, store, and all the houses thence to the sea were burnt, except Mr Antrobus's and Mr Mellish's houses, stores and wharves which miraculously escaped. The worst damaged were Dr Bell's and Dr Lightfoot's, Wilson & Benison's store, Mr Allwood's, and Mr Dickie's Tavern; but many others were badly burnt: Nunez's house and shop, McHogan's old house, Mr Antrobus's old house, Hylton's store and all the long stores, Mr Haldane's house and Mr Dobson's and Mr Thomas Tomlinson's, Mr Murray's office, Salter's Tavern, and others. Mr Meyler lost about 80 tons of logwood 'burnt to ashes'.

> 'Saw Negroes digging up flour, salt, &c. The morasses and environs of the Town full of pipes of wine, puncheons of rum, beds, chests, trunks, &c. &c. Bills, hoes, hinges, axes, iron pots, iron hoops, nails, glass bottles, &c. &c. all about. Gun barrels, &c. The sea remarkably low, & the Negroes so busy plundering & stealing that few could be got to fetch water.'

Thistlewood himself escaped lightly. He lost about '2 pistoles worth of sundries' in Mr Baker's store where he had left them for sale.

On Christmas Day he distributed rum and calf-meat among his slaves. On Boxing Day he noted:

> 'Old Sam exceeding jealous of Nanny with Egypt Cubbenna.'

On the 30th he had fifteen hands at work on the King's Road; Joe was sent to Mr Whitehead for a bleeding for an inflammation of his stomach, Abba and Damsel were ailing, and Mr Thistlewood took Sally (*mea*) in the evening in Mr Wilson's pasture.

On the last day of the year he set down the details of a proposal for tax reform which he had submitted to the Justices at a Vestry meeting in October. It was designed for the encouragement of small landowners, such as himself. Each landowner should be allowed, free of tax, six acres for each slave and three acres for each head of large stock in his possession. Beyond that acreage, he should pay one shilling per acre. More particularly, to encourage small settlers and new beginners, properties of less than 100 acres should be altogether exempt from tax, and those over 100 but under 300 should pay 3*d*. per annum rather than 1*s*. There should be large penalties for faulty 'giving-in' or delinquency in payments, and the land of those who did not pay should revert to the crown.

Disasters notwithstanding, it had been a good year for Mr Thistlewood. Local sales of Pen produce had yielded 1929 bitts, or £60 5s 7½d. To that total, sales of fruit and vegetables had contributed 636 bitts; veal, 548; wild-fowl, 377; honey and beeswax candles, 162; and small amounts from mutton, poultry and eggs, pork and starch. Hired slave labour had yielded about £150, with payment yet to come for work on the King's road.

On Saturday, 1st January 1780:   he listed £306 10s 10d in ready money: £32 10s owed him by Francis Scott; and about £70 Stg to his favour in account with Mr Hewitt in London. He owed Mr Bodington £1 7s 6d for brandy, and his neighbour, Mr Wilson, for 38 days Negro labour. He now had 32 slaves, 7 horses, 26 cattle, 72 sheep, and poultry. In 1779 he had issued 253 tickets to his slaves.

'Saturday, 1st January 1780:   Gave Solon my old brown cloth coat, & began to wear every day Blue Broad Cloth coat; Casimere waistcoats, India dimothy breeches, & 7 new shirts marked with red silk; also put on new green baize cover on study table.'

Early in the year the war came close once again.

'Thursday, 20th January 1780:   A report that about 40 people from an American privateer landed yesterday about 5 p.m. at Parker's Bay & took 2 of Mr Hoggs's best Negroes & plundered his house, a Jew's shop, &c.

Wednesday, 26th January 1780:   Hear the French, or Americans, took 5 Negroes from near the Hope, where Mr Thos. Parkinson's house [he had very recently died] was building, Little Bay, last Sunday night.

Thursday, 27th January 1780:   Our Fleet passed by Savanna la Mar today, going to Leeward, 54 sail (Capt. Leicester says) and the Admiral's flag flying, &c. It is supposed they could not get to Windward.

Dined at Egypt & stayed till past 8 at night. Dr Pinkney, Mr Wilson, Mr Cope & the ladies danced. Company: Mr and Mrs Cope, Miss Cope, Dr & Mrs Pinkney, Mr & Mrs Leicester & Miss Ann Leicester, Mr Wilson & myself. At last I left Mr Wilson dancing & went home by myself.'

Next day, he borrowed chairs, tables, and plates from Mr Wilson and entertained all the previous evening's company at dinner.

And although Lincoln had been ill − 'gave him a dose of Jalop, & he voided many worms' − and Mirtilla had endured another fit,

Abba was recovered, and Bess, on the 27th, had been delivered of a boy by Egypt grande Quasheba. And Bess's older son, Bristol, was to be taught carpentry:

> 'Sunday, 13th February 1780: Ordered Bristol to go with John, to learn to be a carpenter for me. He is just 4 ft 1 inch high, about 7 ½ years old. Marked him on the left shoulder TT
> Tuesday, 15th February 1780: Albany fishermen & 2 belonging Long Pond, took today by a privateer's people, supposed to be Spaniards.
> Thursday, 17th February 1780: Sold to a Negro wench, named Phibbah, belonging to George Robert Goodin Esqr., 5 turkey cocks at 20 bitts a piece, for which received a 55s piece & 12 bitts in silver.'

A month later she returned and bought 2 geese at the same price: '. . . but could not pay for them, there being a mistake in the gold they brought, so I trusted them.' Another month later he was paid in full.

On March 2nd, Abba was brought to bed of a boy. Next day he died – lock jaw.

> 'Sunday, 12th March 1780: Rode to Egypt, dined there, as did Mr Joseph Williams of Carawina. I stayed till night, then rode home. Egypt is not sold yet, but believe it must. Mrs Cope is exceedingly averse to it, & well she may. The marriage of Miss Cope and J.W. [Joseph Williams of Carawina] will be in about 10 days.'

And so it was. They were married, at Egypt, by parson Bartholomew on Thursday 23rd.

> 'Monday, 20th March 1780: John at home laid up of a bubo. Jimmy & Phoebe, having took mercury pills Saturday night & last night, gave them each a dose of Jalop with them to take this morning.
> Saturday, 25th March 1780: Reprimanded Phib. for sending [Miss] Sally, &c. dinner every day. She is now so used to it that she depends more upon Phib's dinner than anything she provides for herself. Sally takes care to send to see what we have got, & dinner is sent her, covered up secretly.'

Early in April, with the sale of Egypt pending, the Cope's sons, Dorrill, Jack, and Robert came home. In May Mr Whitehead left for a securer seat and young John (Jack) Cope was made overseer under his father's direction. But that was not what he had come for.

He was, noted Thistlewood, 'very uneasy; says his father declares he can do nothing for them.'

'Saturday, 20th May 1780: After breakfast, rode to Egypt, thence to Mr Chambers in the Savanna along with Mr Cope; made Dorrill Cope & John Cope Jnr a present of 20 dollars each.'

On news of the arrival of the Cope sons, Phibbah had immediately gone over to Egypt to see them. Earlier in the month she had herself had a visit from an old friend:

'Friday, 12th May 1780: Salt River Jude called to see Phib today. Have not seen him for several years past. Lives at Tripoli Estate, St Ann's.

Tuesday, 6th June 1780: Mr Wilson's Jimmy (Mocho Jimmy) Bess's husband, attempted to hang himself, &c, and was very refractory. He is of a very sullen disposition.'

Then, on Friday, Strap was severely flogged. On 28th May Thistlewood's horse Mackey, had run home from pasture with his belly slashed and his guts hanging out. Attempts to sew him up were unsuccessful and he died. Strap was suspected, and it would appear that Thistlewood took time to investigate. On Friday, 9th June:

'In the evening flogged Strap for stabbing Mackey horse, Sunday 28th Ultimo.

Wednesday, 28th June 1780: Strap in whipping Mary, it seems, almost cut one of Peggy's eyes out, her right eye.'

This had happened in the field where Strap was driver, and Peggy was laid up for some days.

'Saturday, 1st July 1780: Flogged Strap for lashing out Peggy's eye and ordered him to lopping logwood; made Dick driver again.

Flogged Mary about ditto, and Maria for going in the rain to Mr Wilson's Negro ground, camp Savanna, in the rain, & getting sick.'

On Monday, 10th July news was received in Savanna la Mar of the taking of Charlestown.

'Tuesday, 11th July 1780: It seems almost everybody drunk last night at the Bay upon the news . . . . Firing of great guns, muskets, &c. till midnight, strange quarrels & confusion, &c. Mr Hayward's house pelted with brick-bats & dirt, &c. because he did not put up candles.'

Whatever Mr Hayward's sympathies, he had recently been very ill; but clearly there were some in Savanna la Mar whose support of the British in America was at best lukewarm. Colonel, the Honourable Custos John Cope would not have been one of those but he had closer pressing concerns.

On the afternoon of 17th July, John Cope and Thistlewood had dined at Carawina in the compnay of Mr and Mrs Joseph Williams, Dr Pinkney (but not Mrs Pinkney), Mr Benjamin William Blake and Billy Hughes. Then, early next morning, Cope and Thistlewood had set out for Mr Hambersley's at Darliston. Mr Cope had a piece of land in that area, and they had gone to select a site for a great house, which Thistlewood laid out. The place was to be called 'Petherton' after Mr Cope's birthplace[4]. From the house site, Mr Hambersley's house lay SW 84° and Mr Lewis's Wales NW 75°. The land contained ten acres of provisions and about six and a quarter acres more of cleared land around the great house site. 'Fine springs of good water in his provision ground at the foot of the mountain.' But it would be a social come-down for the Copes to move from sugar-planting in the lowlands to farming in the mountains.

On Thursday, 8th August he received a present from Mr Nicholas – *The Detail and Conduct of the American War, under Generals Gage, Howe, Burgoyne, & Vice Admiral Lord Howe*. 3rd Edit. Lond. 1780.[5]

'Sunday, 13th August, 1780:   Rode into the Savanna, called at the Free School (Mr Dixon's) and saw his new set of maps, the World, & Quarters, exceeding good ones.'

These were maps of 1772 and subsequent date.

On Monday, 14th August: Cudjoe and Pompey were watchmen on the Pen; Lincoln was fisherman; Dick, Jimmy, Strap, Caesar, Fanny, Nanny, Sally, Peggy, Mirtilla, Phoebe, Mary (Burton's), Maria, Franke, and Sukey were all employed at Egypt. Solon, with a swollen testicle, was weeding asparagus beds in the garden, Abba, Bess, Damsel and Joe were about the house. The younger slaves were about various light tasks. Mulatto John Thistlewood, at work at Mr Hornby's, spent much of his free time at the Old Hope where he was friendly with Mr Samuel's Mimber. On most weekends he came home. On Sunday 20th his father 'gave John my old rasor and strop.'

'Wednesday, 30th August 1780:   Abba very ill, sent her on Prince horse to Miss Bessie Grant's, who bled her. Pompey led the horse.'

And Jimmy and Solon were also unwell, but the former was soon to
be up and about.

> 'Friday, 1st September 1780: Mr Samuels waiting man called
> and acquainted me of John's being very ill. Sent Jimmy to try if
> he can't ride home in the morning.'

Next morning, a letter came from one of the Hornbys:

> 'John is too bad to come home; sent Phib to attend him. She
> was obliged to walk, set out half past 8 a.m., gave her 10 bitts
> with her: received them back again. Note, Jimmy would not
> stay to bring John, but came to the New Hope last night.
> a.m. Rode to the Bay, went to see Mrs Little, who is very
> poorly yet.
> Dined at Mr Hayward's, in the evening rode home.'

Phibbah had walked westward to attend John while he had ridden
into Savanna la Mar to visit others. That night Phibbah remained
with her son and he, at Breadnut Island, took Sally (*mea*) to bed.

> 'Sunday, 3rd September 1780: This morning Phibbah brought
> John from Mr Samuels, as far as Egypt, Jenny Young's. In the
> evening I rode over to see him & when I returned sent by
> Pompey a wax candle & 7 grains of James's powders.
> Monday, 4th September 1780: This morning Phib brought John
> home from Egypt, got home about ½ past 7 a.m. He is very
> weak indeed & not in his right senses.'

Next morning the doctors were sent for. Dr Bell was not at home.
Dr Ruecastle who happened to be over at Mr Wilson's came. He
said that John was in great danger. In the afternoon Dr Bell came
and stayed till evening. He confirmed Dr Ruecastle's opinion that
John could not recover. He recommended doses of bark and rhubarb.
No sooner had he departed than Ruecastle returned:

> '... much in liquor, gave John 10 grains of James's powders, &
> in about ½ an hour more, also laid blisters inside each thigh;
> but he still continued light headed.'

On Thursday 7th, a little after midnight, he seemed to recover
slightly:

> 'But his belly puffed greatly. They gave him a glister which
> brought away a great quantity of putrid blood. A little before 5
> (8 or 10 minutes) in the morning, he died, burning with the
> fever. He was born 29th April 1760, between 8 and 9 a.m.'

He was buried on the same day, a little after sunset, 'in the old
garden, between the pimento tree and the bee houses'. The service

was read by Mr Thomas Mordiner. The casket-bearers were: Mr Daniel McDonald (carpenter), Dickie Perrin (carpenter), Billy Townshand (tailor), Dickie Watkins (carpenter), William Snow (carpenter), and Edmund More (boatman). Others present were: George Dorrant and John Oldmost (carpenters), Mrs Brown (who had attended him in the last two days), Miss Bessie Bowen, Jimmy Stewart and Jenny Young, House Franke, Egypt Sukey Crookshanks, Little Mimber, Lopez's Mimber, Jenny Graham, and Daphne and her daughter Jenny. Jenny Young stayed with her mother over the following two weeks.

There was much speculation about the cause of John's death, but it seems likely that he was poisoned.

'As John's nails turned black, Phib and several others suggest he has been poisoned down to Leeward, through jealousy or spite, with powdered grass or some other matter. Mr Samuel's Negro postilion or coachman, named Port Royal, suspected. His intestines were tore in pieces also.

Friday, 15th September 1780: Received a note from Messrs Wilson & Benison acquainting me that John is indebted £7 to them for a piece of fine printed linen & a woman's hat.

Saturday, 16th September 1780: The Jew Constable, Isaacs, told me John was about 40s in his debt for bread, cheese, saltfish & potatoes which he trusted him when about the cook-house.'

On Monday 25th, Thistlewood and Phibbah were visited by Mr Samuel's Mimber. She was kept by a Mulatto brother of Mr Samuels:

'. . . but John it seems got great with her [and gave her the hat and linen] as we are informed, but she stiffly denies it. However, she seems to think John was poisoned by Port Royal because he had left his house.'

John apparently, used to eat in Port Royal's house and share his food with him:

'. . . but as soon as he went to Mimber's house, Port Royal turned his horse out of the stable, rode him out o'nights, & showed his spite in everything he could.'

Dr Bell, however, thought otherwise. He said that John had died of a putrid fever.

'Sunday, 10th September 1780: p.m. Lincoln & Abba got to fighting in the cookroom & hurt Phib's arm in endeavouring to part them. Put Lincoln in the bilboes for a while, but at the entreaty of Jimmy Stewart, let him out.

Sunday, 1st October 1780: Mrs Blake says Mr John Rodon's mother lives at the Cross, is kept by a Negro man & has several Mulatto children.'

The evening of Monday 2nd was 'gloomy, dark & dismal in the south', the sea roared 'prodigiously', and the weather looked 'very wild'. On Tuesday morning it rained heavily. At about 1 p.m., as soon as he had finished his dinner, Thistlewood went up on the hill east of his house to see how it looked, but the strong wind drove him back and he then decided to rope round the south end of the horse stable, but 'the rope although strong, went like a cobweb'.

Soon, the garden fences went down, the hardwood posts snapped 'as nothing'. Then, the breadnut tree by Pompey's hut was blown over. Thistlewood ordered all fires to be extinguished and all his slaves into the hall of his house 'as the safest place I had'. The move was just in time. Negro houses and trees were blown apart, terrible flashes of lightning and roars of thunder:

'... the air being darkened with leaves & limbs of trees, &c. which flew with great violence.'

Pouring rain flooded his gardens with 'waves' of water. Between 4 and 5 p.m. the cookroom, store house, fowl house, horse stable, sheep house, bee houses, garden house, 'and even the Necessary house' were blown in bits and pieces 'quite away over the hill into the morass'.

'Then my dwelling house began to go and about sunset (a little before 6) the wind coming to the south, or rather westward of the south, being then I think at its height, & raging with the utmost violence & irresistible fury, tore in pieces the remainder of my house, dispersing it in different ways ...'.

The hurricane continued until midnight. Next morning he took stock. A small part of Nanny's house and one wall of John's room in the main house, where he and the slaves had 'stood all night in the rain which came like small shot ...', alone remained standing. Many of his sheep were dead or dying. he let the slaves eat them.

'The external face of the earth, so much altered, scarce know where I am. Not a blade of grass, nor leaf left, or tree, shrub or bush. The face of the earth looks as it does at home in winter, after a week's Black Frost. The morasses & beds of logwood, &c. appear as if fire had passed through them & those trees that are left standing, have all their limbs broke off.'

All of western Jamaica had suffered varying measures of destruction. 'Sad havoc all through the countryside.' The water was polluted, roads were impassable, and stench was in the air. In Savanna la Mar:

> 'After the hurricane, whites & blacks about the Bay, &c. pirates, thieves & plunderers, &c.
> Mr Woodbine says there perished in the hurricane at the Bay, about 70 whites, and at least as many people of colour and blacks as make up 500. He kept the best account of anybody. Dr Samuel John Lightfoot, Wm. Antrobus Jnr, Mr Hollister, Arthur Hornby ... Indian Sarah, Nelly Russell (Miss Say's mother) and her mother, old Nanny Henn, or Blue – all among the dead.'

And the Justices of the Peace had written to Vice-Admiral Sir Peter Parker asking for a sloop of war:

> '... to afford us protection from any evil designs of our slaves, who were at that time exceeding turbulent & daring, well-knowing a number of Inhabitants had perished in the storm, and almost all our arms & ammunition destroyed.'

From Egypt, Strap and Jimmy Stewart, who had been there, brought news that Egypt driver Johnie had drowned in the flood; and Egypt Peggy, badly bruised, limped in from Savanna la Mar with word that Little Mimber had perished at the Bay.

> 'Sunday, 8th October 1780:   Many people seem much afraid of the Negroes rising, they being very impudent.'

But there was no real evidence of any such upheaval, and, on the Pen, the work of rehabilitation was immediately begun. At first, there was need to provide basic living accommodation for the people and shelter for the animals; the debris had to be cleared up and the provision grounds and gardens repaired and, where necessary, re-planted. Thistlewood threw away ruined books, papers, maps, and documents, and gave over 100 books, presumably only slightly damaged, to Mr Wilson.[6]

> 'Saturday, 2nd December 1780:   Gave Lincoln, Burton's Mary & Peggy a ticket to go to Mr Hambersley's mountain to buy provisions.
> Tuesday, 5th December 1780:   Flogged Dick, Sukey & Franke for quarrelling last night, & disturbing me in the middle of the night.
> Saturday, 9th December 1780:   Tony exceedingly ill, said to be dead several times, but he's much the same.
> Betty struck with convulsions, all at once, in the afternoon.

Sunday, 10th December 1780: Phoebe's Tony died. He was a wonderful fine boy.

Monday, 18th December 1780: Last night Abba miscarried of a boy.

Wednesday, 27 December 1780: Sally wanting. Sent Solon to look for her, & he brought her at noon.

Friday, 29th December 1780: Flogged Joe for leaving the cookroom and going to Egypt last night.

Mr Wilson's Will (who is an Obiah, or Bush Man) catched in Abba's house, at work with his Obiah, about midnight last night, and made her believe Damsel is the occasion of her children being sick, & of her miscarriage, &c. A sad uproar. Took him home this morning, with his Obiah bag. Mr Wilson flogged him well.'

It had not been a good year.

On Christmas Day, Thistlewood distributed the usual holiday extras; this time, 2 ½ lb of saltfish each, and rum. He dined, as he had done before, at Mr Chambers'. His Pen produce had yielded less this year – only £47 from local sales; and perhaps, at Mr Chambers' table he rehearsed his ills as he was to list them at the end of the year. In March, Mr Wilson's dog had bitten him and the bite had taken six weeks to heal. In the same month Strap had stabbed Mackey, horse. In June he had lost a big steer, lately cut and died; and Strap had lashed out Peggy's right eye. In July he had found a hogshead of his rum all leaked out. In September John had died. In October the hurricane had smashed his Pen; and, in December, Tony had been lost.

He would enthusiastically carry out the re-building of his property; but the year 1780 was his watershed. Thereafter, occasional optimism notwithstanding, came the decline.

Notes

1 Thus sanctifying an irrevocable decision.

2 Now Egypt overseer, succeeding Parker.

3 A calabash gourd, hollowed out, with a lid made from the circular piece cut from the top when hollowing. See Cassidy & Le Page (1980) p.335.

4 Petherton, though shown on a survey map of 1890, is known today as Valetta.

5 A good example of the speed with which publications in Britain were acquired by readers in Jamaica.

6 Nonetheless, he left a large library after his death. A list of its contents, and all his other property (excluding his land) is to be found in the Jamaica Archives, Spanish Town, Inventories Liber 71, folio 200 ff.

CHAPTER 11   Towards the end, 1781–1786

Introduction

In this final chapter we find Mr Thistlewood battered by ill-fortune but resilient almost to the end. Successive floodings ruined his gardens and the weather brought more than the usual incidence of illness among his slaves.

Clearly he felt that he could not go on much longer on the Pen and he began to make arrangements for the purchase of a smaller property – but he did not live to complete the transaction; and, by losing him we lose also what contact we have had with Phibbah, Lincoln, Bess, blind Mary, and the rest.

In these six years Thomas Thistlewood was to decline in health and, occasional good business and accompanying optimism notwithstanding, in fortune. He began the year in bad health; his 1st of January accounts indicated little damage from the October hurricane, but he had lost his buildings, his crops and trees, and a few sheep.

'Monday, 29th January 1781:   Sukey wanting this morning, but soon came. At noon served my Negroes each a quart of English peas.

Monday, 12th February 1781:   Made watchmen, house Negroes, & field Negroes pay me a bitt a piece for stealing my water melons.

Flogged Lincoln today.

Wednesday, 14th February 1781:   Had Dick flogged for letting them plant potato slips the wrong end in the ground.

Wednesday, 21st February 1781:   Sent an advertisement of Breadnut Island Pen, &c. to be sold, to the publisher of the Montego Bay paper with 3 dollars, to insert it as long as he can afford. Also sent another to Mr Baker at Savanna la Mar to stick up in his office:

"To be sold in the parish of Westmoreland, a small settlement, known by the name of Breadnut Island Pen, situated about two miles to the westward of Savanna la Mar, containing 160 acres, between 60 and 70 of which are high-land, and are Negro grounds and pastures, very clean; most of the rest is a rich open morass, great part of which in the dry season is good pasturage; it affords fish of various sorts, more especially mudfish, also crabs, and in the season plenty of wild fowl. There is only the ruins of a dwelling-house at present, but the proprietor has already collected a sufficient quantity of stone upon a very eligible spot, for building a dwelling-house, &c, from which there is a prospect of the shipping in Savanna la Mar harbour, and the country all round. There is likewise a lime-kiln, built, & fit to set fire to. Also, along with the above, 26 or 28 Negroes, 15 of which are field Negroes, the rest fishermen, house Negroes, watchmen and children. Likewise 25 head of horned cattle & about 60 sheep. For particulars apply to the proprietor, Thos. Thistlewood, on the premises (spot), whose only motive for wanting to dispose of the above is his ill state of health requiring him to leave the island; so only cash, or good Bills of Exchange, can be took in payment. Whoever such place may suit, and can comply (agree) with the above terms may have it exceeding reasonable.''

But, as far as we know, there were no interested persons and Thistlewood remained in occupation until his death. There was, though, a later indication that even if he failed to sell the Pen, circumstances, particularly of health, would compel him to move to a smaller property.

'Tuesday, 6th March 1781:   Lincoln brought a few bullheads & god damme's about half past 12. Ordered him to work in the field, made Dick fisherman & Strap driver.

Wednesday, 7th March 1781:   It is said fine flour at Bristol in 1779 cost 12*s* per hundred, and 1780 16*s*, for which we give 50*s* & £3 per hundred here.

Thursday, 8th March 1781:   Laid out 20 bitts in bread (which made my Negroes pay me on the 12th February for stealing my water melons). Shared the bread amongst them, and gave them some saltfish also.

Tuesday, 13th March 1781:   A clamminess, and suspect I see a staining & feel symptoms.

Flogged Nanny & Mirtilla for scolding & disturbing Mr Wilson, & Strap for letting them.

Friday, 23rd March 1781:   This morning a Negro woman of Mr Meyler's, from Meylersfield, named Mary, came with a complaint that Sally had, last night, they being ship-mates, enticed her to sleep in her husband's house at Mr Hayward's, and this morning robbed her of her pocket, with 2 knives, &c. in it, & her

victuals. Found the pocket on Sally & the knives, which returned to the woman, but could learn nothing concerning the victuals. Gave Sally a good flogging. The woman was very impudent indeed, while I was endeavouring to right her.
Friday, 30th March 1781: Sally wanting this morning. Sent Pompey to look for her; but he can hear nothing of her.'

Next day, Solon was given a ticket and despatched to continue the search. Sally eluded capture until Friday, 4th April when Solon brought her home. Thistlewood 'Flogged and marked her & put on a pothook'. He also recorded that she was 'just 60 inches & ½ high'.

'Sunday, 1st April 1781: But few provisions today at market. My Negroes bought pumpkins for the most part. Toyer & Quacoo[1] have been the chief support of the Negroes in this parish since the last 4 months. Toyer heads require boiling 8 or 10 hours, and the water to be several times shifted else they will scratch & itch the throat abundantly. The fingers are better than the heads & don't take so long boiling. Quacoos are very good, especially the fingers. The quacoo leaves are very large, the toyer leaves less and rounder, and have a purplish cast – but there are several sorts of each.
Tuesday, 4th April 1781: Very unwell today, a pain about the heart. Also pains about the testicles, groins, &c., and as it were puffed up.'

His records of sexual activity reflect his poor state of health: in January 5 times (twice with Phibbah, twice with Bess, and once with Phoebe); in February not at all; in March twice (Phibbah and Peggy); now in April twice with Phoebe and Phibbah; and not until August when he took Phibbah twice, Bess twice, and Sally once, did he manage to equal his January performance. Phoebe, whom he had taken on 18th April, though she was then 'laid up with her big belly', produced a daughter on the 23rd of the same month.

'Saturday, 14th April 1781: Flogged Joe for leaving the cook-room and buttery, and going with grass to sell last night. Also had Pompey flogged for letting the cattle break into the Trumpet Tree Bottom [recently replanted with a variety of garden seeds], and for getting drunk in the night & making the most infernal noise I ever heard.
Made my Negroes work all day, for making a noise last night & disturbing me greatly. Jimmy bit Phoebe's lips, &c.'

Early in May, he suspected his slaves of having slaughtered one of his cattle whose horns and carcass he had found in his morass beside a much used path. But there was no proof and he seems not to have taken any action. The field Negroes, or most of them, were then busy removing all the blown-down timbers and hauling or carrying them up on to the hill where he intended to build. Others, Mirtilla, Sally, and Peggy were weeding pasture.

'Saturday, 19th May 1781:   Gave the Negroes today, but first made them pay me 16 bitts, vizt. the suspicious ones, a bitt-apiece, for stealing & selling my limes, as fast as they fall, so that am yet forced to buy, altho should have enough if they would let them alone.

Croomba, Jimmy Stewart's mother, come to see Phibbah.'

On 30th May, a long-standing and good friend, Mr Hayward, paid a visit. He was going to England. He left £200 in cash with Mr Thistlewood to feed his Negroes, spent a pleasant morning, went away, returned at about 7 p.m. and:

'. . . bid Phibbah goodbye, as he did not think he should come again before he went off. Sorry I am to lose such a friend.'

Mr Hayward's departure was to be more immediate and more absolute than anticipated. On Monday, 4th June, he became very ill, vomiting blood, and that evening he died. He was buried in the Savanna la Mar chapel yard, attended by 'about 30 whites & a great many of colour'. He left three children, Bessie, aged 21, and Jenny and George. Mr Thistlewood once more became deeply involved in the affairs of a deceased friend.

In mid-June, Joe was in trouble, having made 'a strange mistake' about a bag of cocoa he had been sent to bring from Mrs Meyler; but had apparently escaped punishment for:

'Phib. always excuses & hides Joe's faults & blunders, &c. Had words with her about it. She seems very fond of him.
Monday, 18th June 1781:   Burton's Mary wanting.'

She had been ill during the previous week 'of her belly'.

'Tuesday, 19th June 1781:   Lincoln ill yet. Gave Charity a dose of rhubarb. Burton's Mary come home this morning, complains ill of her belly. She has got the clap I believe.
Wednesday, 20th June 1781:   Flogged Strap for not minding the Negroes good.'

At the end of June, Egypt Estate was sold to Mr Robert Kenyon; but for a month or two more the Copes remained in residence. The house at Petherton was not ready.

'Saturday, 21st July 1781:   Damsel killed her hog & made me a

present of the head. Bought a leg of her, 4 ½ lb at 5 bitts. Now sold at 10d per 1b. The whole, 50 lb weight in 12 small pieces comes to 63 bitts, which she received.
Thursday, 26th July 1781: This evening my Negroes come in a body, to ask me for clothes.'

This request very probably followed losses in the 1780 hurricane; and now there was to be another one, though less devastating.

'Wednesday, 1st August 1781: Walked about all night as I every instant expected my house & other buildings all to go. My dwelling-house was soon so damaged that my bed, papers, books, &c. &c. were all as wet as if they had been dipped in the sea. Many things broke, & spoiled, &c.
Thursday, 2nd August 1781: So tempestuous, could do nothing.'

Once again trees were blown down, gardens swamped and destroyed, Negro houses and outbuildings all damaged, corn and plantain crops lost. Once again, the damage in Savanna la Mar and the west was severe. Stores and houses blown down, McHay's wharf carried away, vessels driven ashore, and food and cane crops flattened on many estates. On Egypt, the still house and the trash house were down; shingles blown off the boiling house and the great house; a mule killed; and, as elsewhere, another great flooding rain. Thistlewood ranked the hurricanes:

11th September 1751, Violence or Force, NOT Velocity, say 6
3rd October 1780, say 10
1st August 1781, say 4 ½.

And, 'The greatest I ever saw at home, about 3'.

On Breadnut Island Pen, Mr Thistlewood set about to build a house that would, he hoped, better withstand future weather. And, to make doubly sure, his plans included a separate 'stormhouse' to which they might all repair when next a hurricane struck. He ordered 800 feet of hardwoods, roughly 5 inches squared to be delivered to Cabaritta bridge at 57s 6d per 100 feet. He bought flagstones, window-frames, and bricks. He paid William Lewis, Esqr., £50 for 114 cedar boards, 12 feet long and 1 ½ feet wide.

In the midst of all this he did not neglect his reading:

'Wednesday, 15th August 1781: Mr Nickolas Blake lent me (a manuscript) oration, in praise of General Guise, wrote by Matt. Lewis, Billy Lewis of Cornwall's brother .... Think it is very ingenious & well wrote. He is said to be very clever.'[2]

At the end of August his slaves got their 'year cloth & thread' which they had come demanding a month before.

'Monday, 24th September 1781:   Mary wanting. It seems she went up on the mountain to see Robin & come away yesterday dinner time.'

She had, however, failed to turn up at the Pen and Solon was given a ticket to go in search. At night he returned, without Mary and nursing a bite from Mr Tomlinson's dog. The search was renewed, but Mary remained at large until early October.

'Thursday, 27th September 1781:   Abba miscarried.
Sunday, 30th September 1781:   p.m. Had Joe flogged for impudence to me, appears to be drunk; and had Bristol corrected for lying & impudence also.
Saturday, 6th October 1781:   This morning had Mary flogged, put her on a steel collar with a few links of chain to it, and marked her left cheek ＼TT／, then let her go. Hear she soon set off for the mountain again.'

Four days later she was brought in from the mountain by Strap, and given another flogging.

'Wednesday, 10th October 1781:   Flogged Dick for selling all the fish & bringing me none.'

On the 20th, Sukey hurt her neck while bringing timber up from the sea-side to Thistlewood's house site. He sent her to Miss Bessie Grant to be bled, and on her return gave her calabash juice and rum to drink, and 'Rubbed her with rum, & soap & antidote coccoon scraped'.[3] In the evening she suffered a bad fit, but recovered.

By the end of December Thistlewood was ready to start building his new house. On the last day of the year, at about 11.30 a.m. Mr Turner and three Negroes, and Mr Sanders and two Negroes, the hired construction teams, arrived and work commenced.

It had been an expensive year and a half for Mr Thistlewood and local sales of Pen produce in 1781 reflected the setbacks following the hurricanes. He sold only about £35 worth, and on 1st January 1782 his ready cash was NIL, but the flock of sheep had recovered. From 68 on 1st January 1781 they had increased to 83 by 31st December. His slaves, to whom he had issued only 30 tickets in 1781, though discomfited by shortages of food, were in no worse health than usual and their number had been increased by the birth of Phoebe's child.

Mr Thistlewood himself was still not strong. Added to rheumatic pains, a deafness in his right ear and a dimness of the eyes, he had at the end of November and early December suffered the additional discomfort of 'a small fishbone stuck a little way within the anus [causing] a painful swelling to arise, which is troublesome'. Nonetheless, he still dined out at Christmas, and left something for his slaves.

'Monday, 24th December 1781: p.m. Shot a heifer, to give among my Negroes. She was a little lame from the Negroes throwing her down & hurting her when a calf, having a sore navel, and has never throve as she ought.'

Earlier in December there had been celebrations over a piece of war-news.

'Wednesday, 5th December 1781:   The hulk of the ship Austin-hall burnt tonight, by way of a bonfire, upon account of hearing Clinton has joined Cornwallis, &c. &c.'

But by Christmas, the mood was dampened.

'Monday, 24th December 1781:   People terribly alarmed, for fear of an invasion.

Tuesday, 25th December 1781:   It is said Governor Dalling is returned to Town; could not get the Windward Passage for French men of war cruising in the way.'

And, on the Pen, Pompey, perhaps moved by the spirit of the time, demonstrated his own fire-power.

'Saturday, 29th December 1781:   Pompey frequently lets such loud farts that we hear him plain & loud to my house & cook-room, between 130 & 140 yards from his hut.'

By the end of May, 1782, the fears of invasion had been almost removed by the defeat of the French fleet under the Count de Grasse by Lord Rodney. Thistlewood, though much involved in the victory chatter and celebrations, was faced with considerable domestic problems. His first need was for ready money to pay for the full rehabilitation of his Pen, and, particularly, the building of his new house. Moreover, because of the general devastation of provision grounds, and shortages of imported foodstuff, the costs of feeding his slaves and his own household would, for a time, greatly increase. And, at the beginning of the year he was again more unwell than usual. Early February he noted 'I ride out o' mornings, but this morning could scarce sit my horse'.

Following the October 1780 hurricane appeals for assistance had resulted in a grant-in-aid from the British Government. In Westmoreland, individuals were proportionately recompensed and Thistlewood's share was estimated at £140 5*s*. But the money was a long time coming. On Wednesday, 9th January 1782, he sold his share to Mr Rankin, a book-keeper, for '51 half Joes and 5s' which equalled £127 15s.[4]

A week later he sold at Vendue some bits and pieces — a small drip-stone (£2), a rifle barrel (£5 5s), a fowling piece (£1 5s) — which, after paying 5% commission to the Vendor brought him £8 1s 6d. Later in the year there were to be more such goods disposed of. Other more important sources of income were his exports (mainly logwood and rum); sales locally of various imported goods, and with a good eye for business these, in 1782, included household furniture; and various fees and commissions paid for services as valuator or administrator of the property of deceased or absentee friends, and as a land surveyor.

On the Pen he was still dissatisfied with the performance of his slave driver, now Strap.

'Tuesday, 22nd January 1782:   Flogged Nanny & Franke for abusing Strap in the field; Fanny for her exceeding impudence; and Strap for carrying no authority.

Saturday, 9th February 1782:   Last night Damsel brought to bed of a boy, by Dr Lowther's old Quashebe. [The child died on the 13th].

Friday, 22nd February 1782:   a.m. Mr Dalby [now the Kenyons's overseer on Egypt] rode over. A miff between him & Mr Kenyon about flogging the Negroes. Mr K. can't bear to see them flogged.

Friday, 1st March 1782:   Flogged Caesar & Joe for lying, letting the cattle & horses get in the gardens, &c.

Saturday, 2nd March 1782:   a.m. Flogged Lincoln & Sukey for taking Joe's box, & harbouring him. Sukey fell in one of her fits. Wrote to Miss Bessie Hayward, and Dawney came over and bled her; she was pretty well in the evening. (Joe still in the field). When she was in the fit, Lincoln told Jimmy Stewart, that if she did not recover he would cut his own throat.'

On the next day Sukey was still not well, Abba had a bad crick in her neck, and Bess had a belly-ache. Thistlewood noted 'This unreasonable damp weather, is very unwholesome'; but with Bess it was more than the weather. That night she miscarried.

Early in the same month came news of the death of an old acquaintance, 'Dr John Freebairn, in St Elizabeth'. He had been the Vineyard's doctor in Thistlewood's time.

'Monday, 11th March 1782:   Martial law proclaimed at Sav la Mar today.

Saturday, 16th March 1782:   The French and the Spaniards are certainly expected about the full of the moon. Everybody terribly alarmed, and carrying their valuables up into the mountains, &c.

Wednesday, 27th March 1782: Intelligence is arrived that the Spaniards are embarking their men to invade this island; and part of the Milita is ordered to Town.

Friday, 29th March 1782: Gave Franke a ticket, and sent her with Phib's trunk, of her most valuable clothes, &c. to Jenny Young in the mountain, as a place of greater safety than here.'

Jenny Young, House Franke, and others of the Copes's slaves from Egypt were now, with the Copes, in occupation at Petherton.

'Sunday, 31st March 1782: The Grenadiers, Light Infantry, and Brown Infantry set out for Headquarters this morning. In all about 200 fine men. The 4 companies have 45 men each; and about 20 troopers go.

Thursday, 18th April 1782: Peggy being remarkably meagre, had her searched, & she is found "very bad with the venereal disease."

Sunday, 28th April 1782: In the morning Mr Mitchell come down & breakfasted with me. A report that Admiral Rodney has took 5 and sunk 1 French ships of the line; that the French Admiral is among those he has taken; and that the train of artillery intended to be made use of against this island is fallen into his hands; and that he still was in pursuit of them. They were to have rendezvoused off Port Royal on the 4th May.[5]

[In] the middle of the afternoon, Pompey's hut upon the hill by the little gate was burnt down; supposed to be set on fire purposely by Peggy belonging to Canaan Estate, an old wife of his. There was no fire near it, and she was seen to go out of it not 5 mins. before, and met by my Negroes, by Vine's old garden, with fire in her pipe .... Pompey was at the Bay.

Friday, 10th May 1782: Sally ill of a bad cold. She is said to be breeding.

Saturday, 11th May 1782: Wrote to Miss Bessie Hayward, by Sally, & sent her to have her collar took off and a little blood took from her. Soon received a note from Miss Bessie ... that Sally had miscarried in the path. Sent 4 bitts to provide for her.

Sunday, 12th May 1782: Received 4 bitts from Mirtilla for the day that Dick brought no fish. Last Wednesday. [He had come in at night with only a few drummers and had been well flogged].

For 140 plantains 14 bitts.'

On Wednesday 15th, Thistlewood rode to the Bay. There, he 'found Sally very bad' and sent for Dr Bell to come to her. She was bled and the doctor prescribed 4 grains of James's powders every 2 hours. (She returned to the Pen on the 23rd, 'somewhat better'.) Also, at Savanna la Mar on the 15th, Thistlewood signed the letter 'from this parish to Admiral Rodney. (Said to be wrote by Mr Beckford).' He thought it an 'excellent' composition.

On the 20th, Burton's Mary ran away, and this was to be a very long absence. Despite continual search and follow-up of rumours she was not brought back until January, 1784.

On Wednesday, 22nd May 1782, there was great excitement, and Thistlewood who had gone to Savanna la Mar to buy cedar shingles at £5 per thousand, rode on into the thick of it at Bluefields Tavern.

> 'The fleet at Bluefields, now 88 sail but continually increasing. The *Sandwich*, a 90 gun ship, there, on board whom is Sir Peter Parker, the Count de Grasse, &c. The Admiral's chaplain ashore buying yams, limes, fowls, sheep, hogs, &c.&c. and the house full of sea-faring people.
> Saturday, 25th May 1782:   The fleet sailed this morning from Bluefields; at 3 p.m. the main body of them a little to the west of the true south, a very pleasant sight, extending from far SW to near Bluefields. Could see them pretty well out of my new dwelling-house door.
> Sunday, 26th May 1782:   For 178 plantains, 14 bitts.'

Early in June there were other purchases for the slaves' use: 2 dozen bills and 2 dozen hoes at 45*s* a dozen; 6 felling axes at 5*s* each.

> 'Sunday, 16th June 1782:   (At Hatfield gate). For 168 plantains, 13 bitts. For 2 cabbages, a bitt.'

Late in July, there was to be an interesting change of drivership. Strap, driver, had on 23rd June been put to watch some beef, and at night the kidneys and fat had gone from both hind quarters. Strap said the dogs had gone with it while he was in bed. Thistlewood said 'False'. Three days later:

> 'Tuesday, 25th June 1782:   Flogged Strap for last Saturday night's work and put Jimmy driver in his stead.'

Jimmy remained driver until 22nd July when Joe, Thistlewood's attendant and house slave, had to be treated for crab-yaws, and Jimmy, his predecessor in that job, was taken back into service.

'Put Joe's feet in steep for the crab-yaws. Took Jimmy to wait in his room, till he come out again, & ordered Phoebe to take the whip.'

And, next day, he left her in charge while he went off on another day's visit, to Bluefields. The Fleet was in again with captured French ships of the line. Thistlewood and others visited several, including the *Ramilies*, a very fine 74 gun ship, and *La Ville de Paris* which had a 'most stupendous battery', and on which

'... the master ... (a sensible man, blind in one eye) ... says Admiral Rodney might have took as many more French ships if he had known what he was about.'

On board, and ashore, there was much eating and drinking. They sailed on the 25th.

'Sunday, 28th July 1782: For 144 plantains, 12 bitts.'

But prices were soon to become easier for a while as provision grounds were brought back into production.

'Tuesday, 6th August 1782: Phibbah gave me £5 6s 8d in cash. Sunday, 11th August 1782: Between 10 and 11 a.m. Mrs Hannah Pinkney hanged herself in her room, with 2 handkerchiefs tied together. It is said she drank a great quantity of laudanum yesterday & has not been right some time past. Some say a decanter of rum.

Mr Blake says Jack Cope has lately collared & struck his father, &c. And that Mr J.C. kicks Mrs C. out of bed & openly takes girls of 8 or 9 years old, &c. &c. Jenny Young says it is not true, but that Mr C. collared and struck Jack.

Wednesday, 21st August 1782: In the evening when I got home, found Mr Francis Scott there. He has left Ackendown. Mr Wildman discharges everyone.'

In the first fortnight of September there was more than the usual incidence of sickness among the slaves. Franke had a bout of fever, Little Nancy was ill, Sally had the clap, and Bristol, Quashie, Nelly, [Abba's] Phibbah, and Sam all had mumps. And there were to be other ills and outcries during the year.

'Saturday, 28th September 1782: About 3 o'clock in the morning was called up, being told that Fanny's Betty was in a fit & speechless. Found her bad, but brought her to herself by fresh air & hartshorn.

Friday, 4th October 1782: Bess still sick. Sally's mouth sore, &c. And last night, Maria going by the hothouse for water,

Lyn [dog] bit her leg very bad, so that she could scarcely stand.
Sunday, 20th October 1782:   Catched Fanny eating dirt.
Sunday, 27th October 1782:   Abba brought to bed about 3
p.m. of a boy.
Sunday, 3rd November 1782:   Before midnight last night a
great out cry at the Negro house. Lincoln having catched the
Retrieve Shamboy in bed with his wife Sukey.
Thursday, 7th November 1782:   Lincoln ill of the mumps.'

On 19th November, Fanny was delivered of a girl. Soon after she
became ill and on Friday, 6th December she died. Thistlewood had
a coffin made and she was buried on the night of the 7th, '. . . a
many Negroes & much noise'. On Monday 9th, Mr Hayward's Sally
came to try to suckle Fanny's baby, and Phoebe was put to help her
at the Negro house. Surprisingly, the child survived.

Thistlewood and Phibbah had also suffered during the year.
She, earlier, had been 'very ill' in April. He, more or less constantly
in complaint, made another specific note in September:

'Exceedingly unwell. Itch very much, have boils on my right
hip, very painful, and a swelling in my right groin, painful also.
Great inward heat, &c.'

But at about the same time he was able to record, with some
relief in another direction:

'Sunday, 15th September 1782:   The most provisions at the
Bay today that has been since the October hurricane. Good
plantains, 15 per bitt, good corn 20, ditto.'

Since his friend's death he had been finding provisions for Mr
Hayward's slaves as well as his own, and it had not been easy.

And, ill-health notwithstanding, he had continued his magisterial
duties. On 23rd September, at a Vestry Meeting, he had subscribed
to a unanimous resolution.

'Resolved that the Custos shall write to the Governor about the
insolence of the press gangs lately at Savanna la Mar, in the
Savanna, and all the neighbourhood.'

In December, on the 6th, he entertained. Mr Cope, Mr Joseph
Williams and Mrs Williams [of Carawina] and Mr Cruickshanks
'Dined in New Hall, the first time'. And on the 14th he was visited
by Captain John [Jack] Cope, now reconciled with his father, and
now with the Mulatto Company of the Militia.

More purchases in the month included 25 lb of salt fish for 13s

9*d*; 180 yd of oznabrig at 13*d* per yard (but he got a discount of 15 shillings); and 104 plantains for 6 bitts. At shell-blow on the 12th he served out oznabrig and thread to his slaves.

'Sunday, 22nd December 1782: Great news today, by Mr John Chambers from Town, of Lord Howe's beating the combined fleet, &c.'[6]

Among the Pen's slaves there was little domestic cause for celebration. On Christmas Eve Dick was flogged for 'villainy & neglect', and Lincoln, sent out 'to shoot a bulkin to give the Negroes', shot 4 times and missed, so, no beef distributed for their Christmas. And Jimmy, now for some time restored to the drivership was flogged on New Year's Eve 'for letting the Negroes quarrel last night'.

The year 1782 had been a little more rewarding in local sales from the Pen which totalled just over £41 (1,323 bitts). Veal, beef, mutton and wildfowl had yielded over 1,000 bitts, showing quite clearly the effects on the gardens of the two hurricanes. But yields from other sources had over-compensated. On 1st January 1783, Thistlewood's ready money totalled £1,059 14*s* 9½*d* (and an additional £65 11*s* 10½*d* 'in purse at the Bay – presumably the remainder of Mr Hayward's £200 to feed his Negroes)

There were now 34 slaves: 9 men, 12 women, and 13 youngsters and babies. In 1782 he had issued 62 tickets in all.

Livestock included five horses, 29 head of cattle, 98 sheep (up from 83), 35 various poultry, a hog, two dogs, and a cat.

In the household, the new year began with Phibbah very ill with fever and headache and being visited by her daughter Jenny Young, and by House Franke who herself was not bright and had been sent down from Petherton to stay at Salt River 'for a change of air'. Also at the Pen, and staying there off and on while he looked for another job was Thistlewood's horticultural friend Francis Scott.

'Monday, 3rd March 1783: Mr Francis Scott engraved upon a piece of copper: This house founded by Thomas Thistlewood, 1781; and I placed it secure under the south door threshold where it may lie many years.
Monday, 10th March 1783: Flogged Joe & Pompey for drumming last night.
Saturday, 15th March 1788: p.m. Mr James Hornby, carpenter, at Sav la Mar, died.'

On Tuesday 25th he recorded the particular employments of his slaves as follows:

'Joe & Bristol, waiting boys
Abba, washerwoman
Bess, sempstress
Damsel, cook & stock girl, assisted by her daughter Nelly
Dick, fisherman
Lincoln, fowler sometimes. Him and Jimmy cleaning brass door-
locks today
Nanny, making mortar
Sally, fetching water for Nanny
Phoebe, carrying stone & mortar
Caesar, sifting lime
Peggy, fetching lime
Solon, picking up wire grass ⎫
Sukey, Maria, Mirtilla picking ⎬ to be mixed in the mortar
up horse dung ⎭
Franke, selling garden stuff at the Bay
Cudjoe, Pompey, watchmen
Burton's Mary still runaway.'

The children, unnamed, were presumably employed tending livestock, and carrying out other 'small gang' labours. For Dick, the
fisherman, it was not a happy day.

'Dick catched a blue shark about 3 feet long, & it bit his
hand terribly.'

For the next two weeks or so he had to rest, and Lincoln was put as
fisherman.

'Thursday, 27th March 1783:   This day I am 62 years of age.
Thursday, 29th May 1783:   Old Sam at Meylersfield is very ill.
Let Nanny go this evening to see him.'

Sam was Nanny's husband. She remained with him at Meylersfield
for a couple of days.

At the end of June two other people well-known to Thistlewood
died. John Merrick Williams died on the 28th at Retreat Estate,
and, on the next day: 'Egypt Dido died at Petherton'. July was the
infants' turn. On the night of the 10th, Damsel gave birth to a girl
who died on the 17th. And, on the 21st:

'Hired Strap to himself for 3 bitts today to go bury his child at
Mrs Blake's.
Saturday, 16th August 1783:   Joe very ill. Dawne came & bled
him & laid on a blister.'

Phibbah also had been ill again, visited by Jenny Young and Jimmy Stewart.

'Sunday, 17th August 1783: About one o'clock last night, Mr H^d [?] Roger come here from Glen-Islay, and catched Strap in bed with his wife Sally, & tore Strap's frock from off him, &c. Monday, 18th August 1783: Joe very bad this morning. Wrote to Dr Bell & he come to see him, took a little blood from him, but found it good. He is ordered to drink cornwater, with a dram of nitre dissolved in each pint, and to take every hour a tablespoonful of water, in which 10 grains of emetic tartar is dissolved in each half-pint, so as just to make him sickish, in hopes it may cause a perspiration.'

Next day Dr Bell was back to see Joe who had not been able to urinate since the Sunday. The doctor now:

'... put a bougi up his urethra, ordered him glysters and a warm bath, also to take a pill every hour & half made as follows: 20 grains of James's powder & 12 of calomel, made into 6 pills, with a little bread crumb. He took of these; about 9 o'clock at night they worked him well downwards & he made water. His stools are bloody & black matter. He also parted with 4 worms.'

Wednesday 20th, with Joe 'scarce any better, if at all' and Franke and Nanny also ill, but far less seriously, Dr Bell was back. He left, and was recalled.

'About 7 o'clock in the evening Joe was so bad that I expected he would die every minute. Wrote to Dr Bell, received an answer, and gave him some brandy toddy, with 30 drops of laudanum in it, which was of infinite service to him and made him easier.'

Or so it seemed; for Dr Bell was called, or came in daily and Joe remained exceedingly weak. At about 10 a.m. on Sunday, 24th August, he died. Thistlewood provided his coffin and a bottle of rum for those at his burial next day.

The misfortunes, though less fatal ones, continued. On the day that Joe was buried, Little Phibbah was found to have measles. On Tuesday 26th, Franke was stung by a scorpion '... or I rather imagine a tarantula, on the inside of her right thigh'. She was laid up for a few days in great pain. On 4th September she was still incapacitated, but now it was her belly. She 'could neither go in the bush nor make water'. Thistlewood treated her as best he could in accordance with Dr Bell's instructions. She recovered.

'Monday, 13th September 1783:   At night flogged Lincoln about his 3 Mile River, [Estate] wife.

Tuesday, 11th November 1783:   Cudjoe's bowels are come down, by neglecting to wear his truss.

Tuesday, 25th November 1783:   Cudjoe has made it up with an old woman named Chloe, belonging to Mr Beckford.

Thursday, 11th December 1783:   At Dinner time Bess was brought to bed of a boy for Joe Dorrent . . .'

Dorrent was a carpenter working on Thistlewood's house. The boy died a week later.

'Wednesday, 31st December 1783:   Phoebe brought to bed this morning of a girl.'

Meantime, there had been other noteworthy events. Francis Scott had found a position as Overseer at Mount Pleasant; Phibbah's ground had been prepared, fenced in, and a gate put up; Mr Simpson, now Egypt's overseer, had been sent to a sale of slaves in Montego Bay on the first Thursday of December and bought two men (privilege Negroes) at £70 and duty = £71 each, and two women of the cargo at £64, including duty, each.

'Note: 63 & duty, and 68 & duty cargo price for women and men.'

It had not, financially, been too bad a year. Local sales had increased to 2,045 bitts or £63 18s 1½d, and the garden produce was once again substantial: Veal, 743 bitts; French peas, 318 bitts; Mutton, 254 bitts; Kidney beans, 234 bitts; Wildfowl, 191 bitts; Turnips, 183 bitts, and other items, 122. Even with slaughterings and deaths, his flock of sheep now numbered 121; but he had not kept his cattle. On 4th October he had sold his remaining 26 head at £8 10s a head to be paid for in bills in July 1784.

So, no beef for the slaves at Christmas. He served them about 2 lb of saltfish each, and the usual rum, and went off himself to dine at Mr Clement Cook Clarke's in the Savanna. 'An excellent dinner, plenty of claret, &c.'

On 1st January, 1784 he had £732 8s 6½d in ready money 'besides crowns, dollars, &c. laid up', and his small debts were outmatched by sums due to him. Livestock was now reduced to four horses, his sheep, the various poultry, and his dog and cats.

In 1783 he had issued only 28 tickets to his slaves: 8 men now, with Joe gone; 12 women, but with one, Burton's Mary, still runaway; and 14 children, though one, Abba's Mary, blind, born December

1761, was now listed among the women. The others were: Abba's Jenny, born August 1772, Phibbah, born April 1776, and Ben, born October 1782; Phoebe's Charity, born January 1778, Nancy, born April 1781, and Franke just arrived on 31st December 1783; Fanny, who had died, had left two now living with her husband Cudjoe, Betty, born May 1778, and baby Fanny, born November 1782; Bess's Bristol, born August 1772, and Sam born January 1780; and Damsel's Nelly, born September 1772, Quashe, born April 1775, and Vine(y) born July 1778.

At the beginning of the year, and periodically throughout, his slaves (and Mr Hayward's) were employed cutting and chipping logwood. In mid-January, hearing that Burton's Mary was in the Lucea gaol, he sent Mr Hayward's Coffee for her. A few days later, she arrived:

'Thursday, 22nd January 1784:   About 3 p.m. Coffee brought Burton's Mary from out of Lucea gaol, for whom paid £2 18*s* 1½*d*. Had a receipt. Also gave Coffee 4 bitts to bear his expenses. Received a note from Mr Edwin Lewis. Handcuffed Mary & secured her in the bilboes.

Friday, 23rd January 1784:   Took Mary out of the bilboes and had Sally's collar with two prongs put on her secure. Marked her on each cheek, gave her a new bill & sent her into the field to work. Cudjoe took her for his wife.'

Thistlewood himself was again complaining of his health.

'Friday, 2nd January 1784:   Am very unwell.

In the morning rode into the Savanna, called at Mr Chambers's and paid the Honble John Cope £18 for Phib's hire to the 16th November last. Had his receipt.

At night *cum* Phib.

Sunday, 4th January 1784:   My hand shakes so today that I can scarce write, and is sometimes seized with such a sudden twitch, or numbness, that I am obliged to drop the pen.'

On Sunday 11th, he recorded a local sale of slaves. John Tharp, Esq. of Good Hope Estate in Trelawny:[7]

'... has bought 430 Negroes from a gentleman in Carpenter's Mountain at £50 per head; all Creoles, many children, invalids, &c. and some fine Negroes; to pay in 10 years, by 10 annual Bonds. No sores on any of them.'

A week later, the *Earl of Effingham* arrived at Savanna la Mar bringing his usual crates and boxes of clothing, books, foodstuffs, trees, &c. He spent the next weeks bringing in and unpacking his goods, planting his English trees, watching another comet in late January and early February, and looking for Burton's Mary who had again run off.

'Monday, 9th February 1784: Bought of Mr John Thompson, 2 barrels of flour at 40s. per barrel ... and a keg of brandy for 40s. p.m. Received by Mr Robertson's cart, my 2 barrels of porter, barrel containing 4 hams & 8 smoked tongues, & 2 barrels of flour. They only brought them to Mr Wilson's little garden in the valley as the cattle would not draw up the hill. Gave the cartman & boy 4 bitts. Rolled them home afterwards. Tuesday, 10th February 1784: Flogged Dick & made him pay me 3 bitts for bringing such bad fish.'

And Dick was to be flogged twice more in the month for the same reason; and Pompey, once, for letting Mr Wilson's livestock stray into Thistlewood's gardens. Mr Wilson's pastures, he noted, were in very poor condition.

On Monday 23rd, Burton's Mary went off again, news was had that she was somewhere about Batchelor's Hall Estate near Lucea. Coffee was sent in search, and a letter with her description despatched to the overseer there. Eventually, on the 27th March she was brought in and put in irons until 6th April when she was released and sent into the field 'under charge'.

In March, Thistlewood was again complaining, this time of rheumatic pains in his right wrist and left hip − 'Can scarcely walk' − and, perhaps, it was his continuing ill-health that led him to a previously unrecorded (since his arrival in Jamaica) activity:

'Sunday, 7th March 1784: a.m. Rode to the Bay, served Mr Hayward's Negroes, &c. Attended divine service in the Court house. Mr Stanford preached a very good sermon. Text 2nd Chap. Job 10th verse. A good congregation, at least 150 of all colours.'

Next .day, he recorded another much more practised occupation, though, in a sense, it too was a first time for him.

'Monday, 8th March 1784: *Cum* Abba's Mary, *mea. Sup Illa lect in illa dom.* Gave d° 4 bitts.'

Mary was, at the time, six months pregnant. In June she bore a daughter for Three Mile River Quacoo, but the baby died when only a week old.

'Friday, 9th April 1784: Let Strap (at Phib's request) go to Petherton, to acquaint Jenny Young of her husband Jimmy Stewart being dangerously ill.'

Jimmy Stewart recovered, but later in the month another acquaintance died, carpenter Cumberland.

May, 1784, was dry and provisions scarce. On the 24th, Solon was sent 'into the country to look provisions'. Sally, sent to the Bay with grass to sell on the 2nd, failed to return. Two days later, Pompey's hut caught fire. 'He left fire in it carelessly', and he was, at month's end, again flogged for letting cattle, this time from Kirkpatrick, stray into the gardens. During the month Lincoln, Abba's Ben, Damsel Maria, and Bess's Sam all suffered ailments; and Thistlewood himself perceived the signs of another venereal infection. In early June, Abba was temporarily very ill. So too was Phibbah who had 'violent looseness, sickness at the stomach &c. on the night of the 7th.

> 'Friday, 25th June 1784:   A Spaniard in at the Bay. Took down Mary [Burton's], but they would not buy her. Say they are going to Town, and want to buy a thousand New Negroes for the King of Spain. It is said they have got a prodigious quantity of dollars on board. Only one of them speaks English.
> Monday, 28th June 1784:   Nanny at home ill. Flogged her for standing in the rain on Saturday.'

Next day, the weather went from one extreme to the other. Flood rains drowned his gardens.

> 'Saturday, 3rd July 1784:   In the evening Mr Wilson, his elder brother the surveyor, and Sir James Richardson come over & eat some bread & cheese and stayed till about 11 o'clock. Sir James is a sensible man. Mr John Richardson is a younger brother of his, who wrote the noted dictionary, English, Arabic, Persian &c. &c. He says out of 190 Negroes he has bought in 14 years, he has lost 141 of them, such bad luck has he had. He allows that prudence & industry are highly necessary, but thinks that most succeed from a lucky combination of circumstances.'

But Sir James clearly was not disheartened. In November, he would buy Paradise Estate and its provision mountains for £5,000.

Meantime, on 6th July, Egypt again changed hands, sold to Thomas Hill for £2,800. The slaves, about 100, were bought by Hill and three others for a total of £5,000, the livestock to two others for £950 at an average of about £15 a head. Even the furniture was sold at auction a few days later.

Sally, who had returned from her absence in the Bay, went away again.

> 'Monday, 26th July 1784:   My Sally wanting. It seems

Mr Robertson's George's wife [i.e. the slave wife of a slave at Kirkpatrick] sent her out yesterday, with bread &c. to sell. Saturday, 31st July 1784: Sally brought home. Caught in the Dean's Valley plantain walk by one of the Paradise men. Had her flogged.'

In the last days of July and the first of August the rains came again with strong winds which drove boats ashore, flattened plantain trees, and damaged other trees, crops, and buildings. The heavy weather caused anxiety if not alarm. It caused damage to Nanny who in running into the storm house fell and hurt her hip so badly that she was laid up for weeks after. It was kinder to Sally, helping the night to give her cover:

'Monday, 2nd August 1784: Yesterday evening, Franke having picked peas in my New Garden for market today, in the night Sally stole the peas & basket also & is gone.'

Solon, as usual, went out in search, but did not find her. On the following Sunday, she was brought home. A Maroon who said his name was Jonas Williams had captured her on the Barracks road. Thistlewood paid him £1 3s; and put a chain round Sally's neck 'and locked her to Mary's [Burton's] chains'. So harnessed, they were made to work in the days.

'Wednesday, 4th August 1784: This forenoon Damsel brought to bed of a boy ...' [he died on the 11th]

Abba, now the mother of four living and several who had not survived, and soon to become a grandmother, had acted grande; and subsequently was called upon to act in that capacity on the Pen and neighbouring estates.

At mid-month, Nanny was still laid up, Strap's feet were in steep for the yaws, Peggy was ill 'of the foul disease', Maria had severe toothache and Bess had fever.

'Saturday, 14th August 1784: Lent Jimmy Stewart Strap horse to Petherton. Returned on Monday morning.'

On the 29th Thistlewood, with much relief, recorded that he had at last succeeded in selling Mr Hayward's slaves, fifty two of them and one young child, to Julines Herring, Esqr. for £5,200 to be paid off in three years with security given on Paul Island Estate. The people were to be 'delivered' at Paul Island on 1st October. At first, some of them 'declare they will not go & are quite refractory', but by the end of August they were said to be 'now reconciled to going'. Thistlewood gave no suggestion that any threats had been used.

'Sunday, 5th September 1784: Captain Arthur is arrived from Philadelphia. Came in yesterday. He asks £5 per barrel for his flour.

Thursday, 16th September 1784: Yesterday & today perceive like hairs floating in the air before my eyes, sometimes like larger watery bodies, which commonly seem to descend. Am greatly alarmed at this. They are inflamed somewhat.

Jimmy has got a sore foot. Made him lie up. He has also got some ugly red spots about him; suspect he is going to be distempered.'

But Jimmy was nevertheless sent early in October on Strap horse 'to Mr Roger's to buy provisions'. Thistlewood gave him 4 bitts for expenses on the journey.

'Monday, 4th October 1784: Jimmy lies up lame yet.

Tuesday, 12th October 1784: In the morning had Damsel flogged for not keeping the cookroom clean.'

And during that month, Lincoln was exceedingly active and successful in his forays into the morass shooting wildfowl. But, also in that month, roaming cattle had ruined Phibbah's ground (fence and gate notwithstanding) and had then turned their attention to the Negro ground. Jimmy had twice fired on them without effect.

'Friday, 5th November 1784: Had Mary & Sally carried to the Bay, by Strap, but McNish only bid £50 for both, so sent them back.

Tuesday, 9th November 1784: In the morning Lincoln[shot] Taurus, near Phib's ground, which is destroyed. Shared among the Negroes.'

On Tuesday 11th, perhaps feeling that if cattle were to ruin his gardens they might as well be his, Thistlewood bought four cows, a calf, and a heifer from Miss Eleanor James, Mr Layton Smith's housekeeper at Chantilly, for £36.

On Sunday he returned to church. After service, he, Mr Stanford the clergyman, and others had dined. According to Mr Stanford:

'. . . to fright a dog, open your arms & seem earnest to catch him & he will almost surely run away, however fierce. And if a mad bull, ox, or cow, make at you, ever so furiously, turn your back & stoop with your head down between your legs, your face towards them, they will certainly make away instantly.'

Mr Thistlewood, who was more widely experienced in such matters, commented: 'Dangerous experiments'.

'Sunday, 21st November 1784:   Mr Lewis Robertson, Mr James Robertson, Mr Charles Lewis Robertson, Dr Robert Ruecastle, Mr John Thompson, Mr Hugh Wilson, and his cousin the cooper, dined with me. Had soup, boiled mutton, a leg of boiled mutton & caper sauce, fish, roast mutton, savoys, boiled crabs, baked rice pudding, 2 roast ducks & a teal, cheese, shaddock, sweet-limes, forbidden fruit punch, grog, brandy, Madeira wine, and porter, &c.

Monday, 29th November 1784:   a.m. Rode to the Bay. Signed a Petition to the King's Most Excellent Majesty, another to the Honble the House of Commons of Great Britain in Parliament assembled − praying that some of the duty may be took off from our produce, & that we may have supplies from America, &c.

Tuesday, 30th November 1784:   a.m. Mr Thos. Hill & Mr Ralph Hylton called, and I sold Mr Hylton Burton's Mary & Sally for £40 apiece, and immediately sent them down to Mr Lyon's store, by Strap, who delivered them on board the vessel. Had Phoebe flogged for refusing to look after the cattle, and impudent speeches.'

At the beginning of December the slaves were employed in building − a new cattle pen, a new sheep pen, an arbor for the granadilla vine, and other sheds and props. On the 4th, Phibbah's granddaughter, Mulatto Nancy, paid a visit and Thistlewood gave her a dollar 'against Christmas'.

'Monday, 13th December 1784:   Damsel's Vine is full of little spots, suspect is the yaws. Caccaw, as the Negroes call it'.

On the 23rd, he paid Mr George Woodbine in Savanna la Mar £31 2s 6d for weighing and wharfage of 83 tons of logwood. The price in England would be £9 − £10 per ton. The local price was about £5 per ton. On Christmas Day, he served out beef and rum to the slaves, gifts to friends, and he dined at home with Mr Wilson and others.

'Thursday, 4th January 1785:   Noticed Strap in the cookroom with Ph. early in the morning.'

The possible twinge of jealousy perhaps reflected his awareness of his own declining sexual activity. Not that he was inactive − in 1784 he had taken Phibbah 33 times, and Bess 14, and there had been 21 other occasions with eleven others of whom all but one belonging to Mr Wilson were his own. But that was a far cry from the days when in a year handicapped by long ill health he had proudly recorded 87 times with Phibbah alone.

Early in January the ships came in and he unloaded his boxes: books; clothing; six barrels of porter, of which he sold three at £3 5s each; foodstuffs; plants, &c. He gave Jenny Young a present – a silk handkerchief.

Dick, fisherman, was frequently in trouble. Early in March he was flogged and chained to three 56 lb weights for having brought 'little or no fish'. Two days later he was set free and sent back to fish, and, next day, the 7th, Thistlewood noted, perhaps with some chagrin:

> 'My house Negroes now get great quantities of stone basses, tarpons, some snooks, & fine mudfish, in the morass SW from large caves. Also some sorts of sea-fish.'

In mid- and late March Thistlewood complained less and entertained more and again involved himself in supervising the planting of seeds, seedlings and saplings, oranges, shaddocks, forbidden fruit, &c.

> 'Monday, 4th July 1785: Gave Sukey today, as she had been confined, attending Lincoln – who had been ill since 24th June.
> Sunday, 17th July 1785: Rode to Cabaritta Bridge early this morning, but no corn come; plantains seemed plenty but sold only 15 for a bitt.
> Saturday, 23rd July 1785: Last night, blind Mary brought to bed of a girl, by Abba. Three Mile Quacoo is her husband.
> Wednesday, 27th July 1785: Solon has got the clap. Gave him a mercurial pill.'

Again, on 1st August another spell of very heavy weather, almost a hurricane, damaged his newly planted trees and gardens. The reverses were now frequent, but he gave no indication of despair.

> 'Tuesday, 2nd August 1785: Dick brought a snook weighing upwards of 13 lbs.'

A few days later, Mr Wilson's fisherman, George, doubled the standard by bringing in one weighing 25 lb.

> 'Friday, 12th August 1785: A flood today.
> Saturday, 13th August 1785: In the evening went to see Senor Cortez, &c. perform, in Mr MacIntosh's yard. He performed on the tight rope very well, as did also his Buffoon, 2 girls, & a little boy. Also on the slack wire; danced, tumbled, &c.&c. Paid a dollar entrance. Mr. Nickolas A. Blake, Mr John Stewart, Mr Cruickshank, Mr John Thompson, Mr Cameron, &c.&c. there; also many Mulattoes &c. (Negroes pay half a dollar).

Imagine they would receive between £15 & £20. Got home before 10 o'clock at night.'

On Thursday 18th, in the morning, both Lincoln and Nanny were missing. Lincoln arrived at about 9 a.m. from Retreat Estate, Nanny came in the evening. She had been away looking after her husband 'Old Sam' who was 'very bad'. Thistlewood 'received 3 bitts for her per day'.

In the second half of the month the rains set in again and continued into September. The logwood cutting and chipping slowed down and stopped altogether later in the month.

'Sunday, 18th September 1785:   To Franke for a hog's head, 6 bitts. Her hog came to 60 bitts at 10d per lb.

Thursday, 22nd September 1785:   Disturbed last night & the night before & indeed almost every night by Negro plays at Egypt.

Sunday, 25th September 1785:   Gave poor old Egypt Plato 2 bitts to buy fish. He come to see Phib, from the Delve [Estate].'

Perhaps because of the unsettled weather, September had been an unhealthy month for Phibbah and Thistlewood, and at the beginning of October he was once again complaining of his stomach, his kidneys, and general discomfiture. He began wearing a flannel waistcoat under his shirt to see if it would help; and on the 7th, he sent to Dr Drummond for medicines. Next day the doctor visited.

On the 13th Maria was laid up with a headache and the doctor came back.

'Friday, 14th October 1785:   At night *cum* Phib very poorly.

Saturday, 15th October 1785:   Maria still lies up, & Nanny gone home with old Sam.

Saturday, 22nd October 1785:   At night *cum* Phib badly.'

But the garden work went on. He planted broccoli, savoys, cabbages, cauliflower, lettuces, &c. So did the heavy weather. 'Tuesday, 25th October 1785:   These frequent storms will entirely ruin this island.' Once more the corn was beaten down, all the European trees bent and broken. On the 27th he entertained guests at dinner, but he was unwell, the weather was still bad, provisions were scarce, and Lincoln should have shot '3 times as many as he did'. The judgement seems a little harsh, for with 72 loads of shot he had brought down 87 birds.

'Friday, 28th October 1785:   At night *Cum* Phib.'

In early November there was another planting – lettuce, turnips, radishes, melongena, endives, broccoli, parsley, sage. Lincoln, Abba, Nanny, and Thistlewood himself all suffered some ailment or another and it was time for the children to be innoculated against smallpox. Dr Drummond was attending to Mr Wilson's people and Thistlewood took Sam, Nancy, Franke, Ben, Fanny, Prue, and Jenny Young's Jimmy to be done. The usual pre- and post innoculation treatment was given. At the end of the month they all seemed to be well, except Jenny Young's little Jimmy. His father visited, and Thistlewood lent him a horse to ride back to the New [Old?] Hope Estate.

'Wednesday, 6th December 1785: Dick has let his machete fall upon his foot & cut it, suspect wilfully. Had him flogged & chained to a 56 lb. (Gave him a dose of Jalop). Put Lincoln [to fish] for the present.
Gave the smallpox [innoculated] Negroes physic.'

On Monday 12th Damsel went in to Mrs Mary Pinkney's Savanna to have a baby. Mrs Pinkney operated what was then one of the more popular taverns in Savanna la Mar, the 'Free and Easy'. On the 13th, Damsel gave birth to a girl. Two days later:

'Jenny Young's Jimmy has cold sweats, a purging & some ugly symptoms. Wrote to Dr Smith, by Franke, & received an answer.'

On the 17th, 'Jenny Young come' and the doctor returned. Bess was put to tend the boy. He survived the Christmas, but on 5th January he died.

On 1st January 1786, Thistlewood's slave force was back to 34. Sally and Burton's Mary had been sold; but blind Mary's Prue and Damsel's Juno had arrived. His ready money was down to £136 and a few pieces laid by but he was owed over £200 and his only debts were his doctor's bills and £18 to Mr Cope for Phibbah. He now had nine head of cattle, 136 sheep, and his various poultry.

Local sales from the Pen had brought in 1,964 bitts or £61 7s 6d. Despite the bad weather, sales of garden produce had brought £28 10s of that total, and mutton, grass and all remaining items together, had each brought in about £11.

On 29th December the shipping had arrived with Thistlewood's packages. He was able to open 1786 with sartorial style.

'Sunday, 1st January 1786: Began to wear new silk purse, and Black Hat every day .... New long walking stick .... Gave Jimmy my old white hat.'

For the first half of the year, indeed, he seemed to be in comparatively good health and very active on the Pen; though, obviously, war and successive natural disasters had brought severe losses to many and tiredness to him.

'Thursday, 5th January 1786:   In the morning received a note from Mr Rose by a Negro with a box of plants. Gave him 2 bitts. Wrote to Mr Rose & sent Sukey, Franke & Maria for the remaining ones. Plants received: Breadfruit, Mango, Camphor, Maderia Peach or Clingstone of Americ, Lichee or Persian Plum ... and a variety of cotton and flower seeds.'

He planted them out next day. On the 5th, little Jimmy Stewart was buried, attended by his parents, his grandmother Croombah, Free Daphne, Mr Hayward's Betty and others.

'Friday, 7th January 1786:   The mango tree planted yesterday is 15 inches high, the lichee 11, Madeira Peach 6 ½ ... and the breadfruit 18 ins and has but 4 leaves.

Monday, 9th January 1786:   p.m. Received a note from Mrs Mary Pinkney.

Wrote an answer and sent her some paw-paws. Received for a turkey cock from her 26 bitts.

Had Mulatto Jimmy [Stewart] reprimanded for idling his time away so much here. Phib not pleased at all, but it is necessary, as he wants to make this his home, & takes a great deal of waiting on and attendance.

Thursday, 17th January 1786:   Mr Joseph Williams died at Petherton today, 4 p.m. Aged 35 years.'

On Sunday, he went to church. There were '... between 30 & 40 people there, above half Free Negroes & Mulattoes'.

'Monday, 23rd January 1786:   The Marango trees in my garden in full flower, very handsome.'

Next day he sent some fish to Mrs Pinkney. He was a fairly regular supplier of foodstuffs and of grass to her inn.

On Wednesday, 1st February he brought up from the Bay 'the case of trees brought by Messrs Clarke & Blake from North America', and on the 2nd he planted them, although the weather on the Pen was 'excessively dry'.

'Wednesday, 15th February 1786:   Received a puncheon of Norward corn, by Andrew Black's canoe, said to contain 13 bushels at 10 bits per bushel & 20s the cask, which has only wood hoops. The corn just fills my corn chest, which ... holds about 12 ½ bushels.

Our Lieut Governor, Brigadier General Alured Clarke dined this day with Mr George Scott, last Thursday with Mr Cope at Petherton, on Friday with Blake and Clarke, Saturday at the Free and Easie – Mary Pinkney's – Sunday with Mr Murray, Monday in the Court house, dinner by subscription, Tuesday with Mr John Lewis, and today with Mr John Campbell at the New Hope. Tomorrow, it is said, with Mr Hylton.
Tuesday, 28th February 1786: Bought of Capt. Jimmy Foot, 4 barrels of superfine English flour, 280 lb each, at £3 5s each, & he is to send them.'

At the beginning of March, Peggy's hand was badly injured and she was incapacitated for over four months with, at the start, frequent attendance by the doctor. Among the others there had been, and continued to be, the usual round of complaints – lameness, bellyache, headache, fever, etc.

'Saturday, 11th March 1786: Jenny Young came today, and brought a fine half head of wild hog, dried & smoked; also some balm. Gave her a keg of biscuit. Note, made 27 bitts of the other 5, which is within one bitt of what they cost.'

He had bought seven kegs at Vendue at the end of February at 4 bitts per keg and had given one keg to Mr Hayward's Mary who was, he said, having a hard time of it.

Mid-month, he kept Strap with him in the New Garden 'assisting me to trim the fruit trees'. Phoebe was also there, weeding and he assailed her on the 20th, and again on the 23rd by the granadilla arbor.

'Tuesday, 9th May 1786: Bought of Capt. Robinson, one of the Norward horses lately seized by Mr Swinney, &c. for £25.'

The horse was six or seven years old and 13 ½ hands or 4 ½ feet high.

Late April and early May brought another period of drought which lasted until the beginning of June when it was broken by flood rains. This was most unseasonal for May was a month in which rain was normally expected. Trees and plants again dried up, provisions became scarce, and 'most of the exotics in my garden are dead or dying.'

'Friday, 12th May 1786: At 1 p.m. rode to Mr Davis's at Stone's great house in the Savanna. Gave [i.e. offered – and his offer was apparently accepted] £1800 for the house & 35 acres of land surrounding it, payable in 6 years equal payments. Mr Davis calls it Stonehenge. At dinner, Mrs Davis, Mr Davis, Mr Cruickshank, Mr Clarke, Capt. Duthie & myself.

Wednesday, 28th June 1786:   Barrel of flour done, opened the 13th Inst., received 104 bitts made of it = £12 12s 6d (404 bitts) made of the 4 barrels which is only 7s 6d less than they cost, for which have used flour since 2nd March.'

At the end of June the Three Mile River slaves were advertised for sale at Craig's Tavern. 'Capt Duthie bought 2 families, 18 in number, I think' In the following week Thistlewood attended the sale.

'. . . thinking to buy Quacoo, Mary's husband, but he was not put up.
Scarce any bidders, so the Negroes ordered home.
Saturday, 8th July 1786:   Gave my Negroes today to seek provisions, which are the scarcest ever known.'

He was now frequently giving them money to buy food.

'Sunday, 16th July 1786:   The estates likely to change masters in the parish are: (Egypt, Paradise already have), Shaftsden, Bluefields, Paradise again, Salt River, Smithfield Pen, Three Mile River, Camp Savanna, Mountain Spring, Ridgeland, Midgeham, Albany, Canaan, Retreat, Old Hope, New Hope, Williams's Moreland, Jones's Moreland, Springfield, Mint, Lincoln, Petersfield, Mount Pleasant, Dean's Valley Dry Works, Dean's Valley Water Works, &c.'

Whether or not he was exaggerating it is clear that estates were in difficulty. So too, but not obviously for either financial or labour problems, was he. But he still kept on planting on the Pen.

'Wednesday, 19th July 1786:   Received a note from Wm. Hylton, Esqr., with the following seeds from North America . . .'

The list included beet, spinach, onion, squash, lettuce, saffron, parsnip, carrot, turnip, canteloupe, cabbage, moldavian balm, sage, rue, summer savoury, sweet basil, celery, radish, mustard, and about 30 sorts of flowers.

'Thursday, 20th July 1786:   Abba's Mary complains of hunger much. Gave Abba a dollar to assist them. I never saw such a scarce time before, that is certain. Nothing to be had for money.
Friday, 21st July, 1786:   Sukey, formerly Mr Lewis Robertson's housekeeper come over to see Phib. She brought me a little indigo. Gave her kidney beans to plant.
Monday, 31st July 1786:   Abba is sick. She is starving. Gave her a dollar.
Wednesday, 2nd August 1786:   Great corn is now sold a bitt a

quart (wine quart), flour & rice a bitt a pint, 4 plantains a bitt, 6 or 7 corn ditto. Butter by the firkin 3 bitts per lb. Fine flour £5 per barrel. Beef £6 and pork £7 per barrel at Savanna la Mar.'

And on that day the rains came. A little after noon there was a bolt of lightning that destroyed trees on the Pen, a frightening clap of thunder, and a deluge.

'Wednesday, 9th August 1786: Two bunches of plantains & some cassava gone out of the old garden, as supposed by Strap on Monday night, being his watch.

Thursday, 17th August 1786: Dined at Mr Davis's, Stonehenge, & in the evening rode home.

Sunday, 20th August 1786: My sempstress Bess, brought to bed of a boy, about 1 p.m. by Abba. [Died, 29th August].

Tuesday, 22nd August 1786: About 10 a.m. Wm. Beckford Esqr. and Mr James Hay came, dined with me, & stayed till the evening. Mr Beckford is very affable & free. Says he thinks the views from my house exceed any in Cook's Voyages [which both he and Thistlewood had read]. Mr Hay returned Brown's *Vulgar Errors*. Lent him Byron's Narrative, and lent Mr Beckford *Swinburn's Travels*, 8 Vols. At dinner, stewed & fried mudfish, stewed crabs & boiled crabs, a plate of shrimps, a leg of boiled mutton & caper sauce, turnips, broccoli, asparagus, a roast whistling duck, a semolina pudding, cheese, water melon, pine, shaddock, punch, brandy, gin, Madeira wine, porter, Taunton ale.

Thursday, 24th August 1786: Had Mirtilla flogged for impudence when she purposely threw herself into a fit, & was in it above 2 hours.

Friday, 25th August 1786: Mirtilla still lays up.

Sunday, 27th August 1786: Today my Negroes bought 15 tolerable corn for a bitt.'

During that week Thistlewood and his neighbour Hugh Wilson went out. They rode to Paul Island Estate to visit Julines Herring and walked through his garden. They spent the night there, then on to Mr and Mrs Anderson at Belle Isle, visited Mr Anderson's garden and Pen, then rode home by Frome Estate.

On 1st September Thistlewood sowed his North American seeds. He had begun the year actively enough and he now continued planting, visiting, reading and exchanging books, corresponding with his brother and Mr Hewitt, performing his magisteral duties, sitting on a committee planning the new gaol to be built in Savanna la Mar, and of course, maintaining his journals. But once more he had begun regularly to complain of ill health with pains all over, and his stomach inflamed and puffed up.

'Tuesday, 12th September 1786:   At night *Cum* Phib.'

It was to be his last time with her or anyone else.

'Monday, 18th September 1786:   Bought of Capt. Arthur a barrel of superfine flour at £4 10s.
Bought of Mr Wm. Moore, a barrel of mess beef at £6.'

He opened both and began to use them. On the 25th he killed a wedder sheep with a sore belly for the children. 'He was good meat'.

On the 26th he received a package, sent to him from Wm. John Glenville, Esqr., barrister at law in Kingston, with two mango seeds which he planted. On 3rd October he sent marango and other seeds to Mr Glenville. Meanwhile, on the Pen, in addition to the usual gardening some of his slaves were helping Joe Dorrent the hired carpenter to re-shingle the stables, repair the storm house, and carry out other building maintenance.

In October he was very weak, aching all over and taking medicines sent him by Dr Drummond; but for the first three weeks he still moved around.

'Friday, 6th October 1786:   Lincoln shot 3 times this morning, at large flocks & brought a pair of teal only. He is a great villain without doubt.
Friday, 20th October 1786:   No work could be done .... Very ill, often fit to faint as I walked about ...'

And, again, a violent storm:

'tore off the piazza roof and some shingles from the body of the house, so the rain beat in. *Vide* weather diary. At night took a specific pill.
Saturday, 21st October 1786:   Must defer giving account of the damage done till I have better health & can look about me.
Used the warm bath in the evening & took a specific pill.
Sunday, 22nd October 1786:   A great deal of damage done in the country, it seems, among the buildings.
Monday, 23rd October 1786:   Last night Phoebe brought to bed of a girl.
Put Sukey to attend her. Gave her 4 bitts to buy candles.' [The baby died on the 29th].

Following the storm on the 20th there were more flood rains. Solon's house was damaged, and:

'As the young corn I took so much pains with is all destroyed made them plant it over again, Negro fashion.'[8]

He was now, clearly, very ill and friends and neighbours were coming in to see him. On the 27th and 28th he was in so much pain that he could not describe his condition, could scarcely notice his visitors, and 'Cannot enumerate what I take, or how I rest'. His handwriting had become very weak, and his journal entries very sketchy.

'Tuesday, 31st October 1786:   Am quite confused, don't know how things go on.
Wednesday, 1st November 1786:   Putting up a house for Abba's family'.

But this seems not to have been completed, for in December/January she, her children and her granddaughter were housed with Lincoln and Sukey.

'After 6 in the evening, bathed in the warm bath, then was rubbed, & took laudanum & hartshorn. Surprising reveries in the night, not to be described, but have had worse nights than this.
Thursday, 2nd November 1786:   Negroes putting up Maria's house.'

And now he rallied. His handwriting became stronger, his language clearer, and he complained less of acute pain. Dr Bell visited him almost daily.

'Monday, 6th November 1786:   Negroes about Nanny's house. Pompey and Cudjoe watchman. Dick fishing. Phoebe & Jimmy lie up. Lincoln shot 4 squab whistling ducks, sent Mr Wilson 2 of them.
Cannot describe how I am, yet think feel [?] & stronger. Wrote to Dr Bell, by Bristol, received a purge, which took & operated poorly. Did not bath at night. A terrible night.'

And he relapsed. Through the next week, attended by Dr Bell, and visited by Mr Wilson and others, he worsened. The final entry in his diary was for Friday, 14th November. His Negroes were employed as before:

'Negroes d°. Lincoln shot 9 teal. Sent Mr Wilson a pr. Sold 2 pr. for them rec'd 6 bitts = 1,785 bitts.'

On the 25th he made his last Will and Testament. On the 30th, he died, Thomas Thistlewood, Esquire, was buried in the Church of England churchyard, Savanna la Mar, on 1st December 1786.

Notes

1 Both root crops. Cassidy and Le Page make no reference to Quacoo as a root crop. Toyer (Taya) was, and is, a commonly used name for one of the many varieties of the coco root, which they list.

2 Another reference to Matthew G. (Monk) Lewis, well-known author of novels in the Gothic style, and of *Journal of A West India Proprietor*, published posthumously in 1834. (John Murray, London).

3 A bean which when scraped is used to treat bites, stings and other pains. See Cassidy (1971) p.373.

4 The Joanna, or Joe, a Portuguese gold coin equal to £5 10s, equal to four Pistoles

5 In February, 1782, the French fleet under Admiral de Grasse had sailed from Martinique to combine with a Spanish fleet for a joint attack on Jamaica. The French move had, however, been observed by the British Admiral Lord Rodney who intercepted them and defeated them in the Battle of the Saints — so called because it took place near a group of tiny islands of that name off the coast of Dominica. In recognition of his victory which saved Jamaica from attack and possible capture he was welcomed with wild rejoicing and the Assembly ordered the erection of a statue to his memory in the square at Spanish Town.

6 This was on the other side of the Atlantic, the British relief of Gibraltar.

7 John Tharp had purchased Good Hope from Williams of Westmoreland in 1767 for £74,000. It was a large property, 3,000 acres, and John Tharp was at this time rapidly extending the family's wealth and landed property.

8 Probably a reference to the way in which he had been shown by the Vineyard slaves in August 1751: 'Plant corn thus: ∴ 9 inches from corner to corner in squares, rows 5 feet apart, and 3 feet in the step.'

Appendix One

Aftermath

Mr Thistlewood's last will and testament was made on 25th November 1786, and proved on 31st January 1787. His Executors were Thos. Anderson, Esqr. and Charles Payne, Merchant. He bequeathed – to 'William Henry Hewitt of Brompton, near Kensington, London, by way of remembrance', £50, sterling, and – to 'Francis Scott, lately of this parish, planter' £50, sterling, and:

> 'I order and direct that my Executors hereinafter named do as soon as is convenient may be after my decease purchase the freedom of a certain Negroe woman slave named Phibba the property of the Honourable John Cope and who has been living with me a considerable time past provided nevertheless that no more is required for such freedom than the sum of Eighty Pounds current money of Jamaica.
>
> In the event of such Manumission being procured (but not otherwise) I give devise and bequeath unto the said Phibba my Negroe woman slave named Bess and her child named Sam together with the future issue and increase of the said Bess to hold the said slave named Bess and her Child Sam together with her future issue and increase unto the use of the said Phibba her heirs and assigns forever.'

[And also, provided the manumission was secured]

> 'I order and direct that my Executors do lay out the sum of One Hundred Pounds current money aforesaid in the purchase of a Lot or piece of land for the said Phibba wherever she shall chuse and that they do build thereon a dwelling-house for the said Phibba suitable to her station so that land and house do not exceed the said sum of One Hundred pounds.'

---

* Bess, it will be recalled, had been a gift from Mrs Bennett to Phibbah and Mulatto John. As a slave, Phibbah could not lawfully *own* a slave, and Bess had therefore always been 'given in' as one of Thistlewood's. There is no indication why Bristol, her son, aged 14 in 1786, was not also left to Phibbah.

[But, if the manumission should NOT be secured, all the above should be Void]

'And then and in such case I give unto the said Phibba the sum of Fifteen pounds per annum during her life.'

To enable this to be done he authorised the sale of his estate 'for the best monies obtainable' to provide for all the above, and then, the balance should go three-fifths to 'William Thistlewood son of my brother John Thistlewood of the County of Lincoln' and two-fifths to 'my niece Mary Annet daughter of my said brother John Thistlewood'.

The will was signed by Thistlewood in the presence of Samuel Bell, Wm. Hay Davis, and James Robertson Jnr, witnesses.

Manumissions (Jamaica Archives. Vol. 7, f. 119)

John Cope and Mary Cope manumit John Thistlewood, a mulatto boy slave, son of their Negro woman slave Phoeba. Entry dated 3rd May, 1762. No payment was recorded. [I am grateful to Mr Clinton Black, Jamaican Government Archivist for this entry in a volume which, due to its fragile condition, is not available for search.]

Phibbah's manumission was secured on 26th November 1792. On payment by William Tomlinson (on behalf of Thistlewood's estate) of £80 currency to John, Mary, and Dorrill Cope, they did:

'Manumise, Enfranchise and from every tie of Slavery or Servitude set free a certain Negro Woman Slave named Phibba to hold the said Manumission Liberty and Enfranchisement so thereby granted unto the said Phibba and her future issue and increase ...'

I have been unable to trace the purchase of land for Phibbah in the official records; but, all things considered, it is a fairly safe assumption that she got her inheritance. With the sale of the land and slaves of Breadnut Island Pen, it is a plausible supposition that she chose a piece of land in the Darliston hills, by Petherton, where she would be near her daughter and grand-daughter, House Franke, and many other old friends from Egypt days.

Jamaica Records Office: Deeds. Vol. 374 f. 75

19th August 1789
Chas Payne as sole Executor (Thos. Anderson having gone to reside in Britain) sells to George Robert Goodin for £600 currency 'all that settlement or Penn commonly called and known by the name of Bread Nut Island containing 160 acres'.

Appendix Two

Mr Thistlewood's slaves, 1786—7

In *households* as listed in an *inventory* after his death, with additional information from his diaries.

*{
Solon	Purchased 1761, about 42 years old in 1787, then valued at	£60	
Damsel	Chamboy, purchased 1765, about 35 yrs old in 1787, valued at	£60	
Nelly	Damsel's child, b. Sept. 1772, valued 1787 at	£65	
Quashe	Damsel's child, b. Apr. 1775, valued 1787 at	£50	
Viney	Damsel's child, b. July 1778, valued 1787 at	£30	
Juno	Damsel's child, b. Dec. 1785, valued 1787 at	£10	£275

Lincoln	Ebo, purchased 1756, about 47 yrs old in 1787, then valued at	£50	
Abba	Purchased 1758, age unknown, 'old' in 1786, then valued at	£40	
Sukey	Purchased 1761, about 40 yrs old in 1787, then valued at	£70	
Jenny	Abba's child, b. Aug. 1772, valued 1787 at	£65	
Phibbah	Abba's child, b. Apr. 1776, valued 1787 at	£40	
Ben	Abba's child, b. Oct 1782, valued 1787 at	£20	
Prue	Abba's Mary's child, b. July 1785, valued 1787 at	£15	
Mary	Abba's child, blind, b. Dec. 1761, valued 1787 at	£1	£301

*{
Jimmy	Coromante or Shanti, purchased 1765, about 32 yrs old in 1787 valued	£130	
Phoebe	Coromante, purchased 1765, about 34 yrs old in 1787 valued	£80	
Charity	Phoebe's daughter, b. Jan. 1778, valued 1787 at	£40	

*{
Nancy	Phoebe's daughter, b. Apr. 1781, valued 1787 at	£25	
Franke	Phoebe's daughter, b. Dec. 1783, valued 1787 at	£15	£290

Cudjoe	Coromante, purchased 1765, about 42 yrs old in 1787, ruptured, valued	£10
Betty	Fanny's daughter, b. May 1778, valued 1787 at	£25
Fanny	Fanny's daughter, b. Nov. 1782, valued 1787 at	£15 £50
[*Fanny*	Purchased 1773 died Dec. 1782. Cudjoe's 'wife' and mother of the 2 girls]	

Bess	A gift from Mrs Bennett to Phibbah in 1765, about 33 yrs old in 1787 valued	£70
Bristol	Bess's son, b. Aug. 1772, valued 1787 at	£85
Sam	Bess's son, b. Jan. 1780, valued 1787 at	£25 £180

Dick	Purchased 1761, about 52 yrs old in 1787 when valued at	£30
Mirtilla	Soco, purchased 1765, about 42 yrs old in 1787, valued	£50 £80

Nanny	a 'new Negro' purchased 1761, about 47 yrs old in 1787 valued	£60
Maria	Purchased 1761, about 40 yrs old in 1787, then valued at	£50
Franke	Purchased 1765, about 35 yrs old in 1787, then valued at	£80
* *Peggy*	Purchased 1765, about 39 yrs old in 1787, blind in one eye, distempered	£10
* *Caesar*	Purchased 1761, about 40 yrs old in 1787, valued at	£40
Strap	Purchased 1773, age unknown, valued in 1787 at	£80
Pompey	Coromante, purchased 1761, about 42 yrs old in 1787 when described as old, distempered with elephantiasis	£5 £325
		£1,501

*On 24th January 1792, the HOUSEHOLDS and the indivuals thus marked were sold to Mr Isaac Allen. I have not traced the others. But Bess and her son Sam would have remained with Phibbah.

Index

CPSIA information can be obtained
at www.ICGtesting.com
Printed in the USA
LVOW04s1612141016
508828LV00022B/305/P